Richelieu

The face of authority. Richelieu. By Philippe de Champagne. The sensitive eyes were fixed lynx-like upon the unruly.

Richelieu

D. P. O'Connell

Europe, il faut périr plutost qu'être sujette
Il faut qu'au prix du sang la liberté s'achette
Richelieu – Demaretz, *Mirame*, III, 2

The World Publishing Company
Cleveland and New York

Ad Amaryllidem consiliorum adjutricem

Published by The World Publishing Company
2231 West 110th Street, Cleveland, Ohio 44102
Published simultaneously in Canada by Nelson, Foster & Scott Ltd.
First World Printing 1968

Library of Congress Catalog Card Number: 68 – 27612

First published in Great Britain by Weidenfeld & Nicolson Limited

Printed in Great Britain by The Garden City Press Limited,
Letchworth, Hertfordshire

Contents

Illustrations

The author and publishers are grateful to the owners for permission to reproduce the photographs.

Map by Surrey Art Designs.

Preface

Politics and diplomacy are arts calling for professionalism, and the professional is confronted with a terrible dilemma; what is morally right may be politically erroneous. Is the politician or the diplomat to evaluate his actions solely from the point of view of expediency and success; or should he pursue the paths of personal honour and righteousness though the end may be failure? Not since the Thirty Years' War has the conscience of mankind been so distressed as it is today by the problem of the deployment and use of power both within the State and in the community of nations; and no statesman's career better illustrates the tension between professionalism and moral values than that of Cardinal Richelieu, who resolved it by formulating a double standard of moral conduct – a strict one in the perfunctory administration of justice – a relaxed one where the security of the State is imperilled. Thereby he quietened a conscience that was forever oppressed by a sense of Divine purpose, and achieved professionalism in government without losing sight of the relevance of moral standards. His efforts to defend the integrity of France against internal subversion and external constriction, with all the interplay of internal and external policies that this involved, are strikingly paralleled by the events of our own day: for we too are familiar with the diplomatic artifice of the use of force short of war and by the tendency of States to be drawn into a vortex of increasing violence by the logic of commitment.

Richelieu has been misunderstood by previous generations not confronted with his dilemma, or at least not disturbed by the moral problem of the pursuit of national integrity in face of divisive conspiracies and fundamental differences of opinion on the nature of political society. Many of his actions as a statesman can be criticised in respect of their moral quality and their political expediency, but his role in formulating the concept of the modern state as a necessary moral end, and in delineating the boundary between the craft of politics and the philosophy of the State was highly significant in the seventeenth century, and remains significant to-day.

He was a religious man, an important church reformer, and a distinguished theologian who confronted problems of doctrine that are once again important issues in our time – liberty of conscience, toleration, reunion, grace and the sacraments, curial dominance and papal authority. In the ecclesiastical as in the secular sphere he is an enigma only to those who fail to understand that he was at one and the same time the supreme theorist and the supreme pragmatist – a proclaimer of goals, but an adroit practitioner who forever tried to take the middle way, an autocrat imperious by instinct who was often moderate in his methods and liberal in his achievements. His successes as a political reformer have been exaggerated, and his diplomatic views have been largely misunderstood. In religion, government and diplomacy he was only more or less successful, and his greatness lies in the personal influence he wielded in all these spheres, rather than in the actual changes he brought about. His defects of character are those of his generation; his virtues are those of Counter-Reformation Europe; and his life is worthy of study by all who would understand the problem of regulating human affairs.

D. P. O'CONNELL

1

The Grandson of Lawyer La Porte

1585-1608

South of Tours the Atlantic air softens the shadows of the poplars on the waters of the Vienne as it flows to join the Loire near Chinon. This mat-green country is Poitou. Two main routes traverse it, one from Tours and the other from Saumur, and they converge in the provincial capital, Poitiers. Between them on a tributary of the Vienne called the Mable is the little town of Richelieu. A regular quadrilateral with houses and two little squares of uniform style and elevation, it is the embodiment in stone of the spirit of Poitou, the province that almost simultaneously produced the master rationalist in philosophy, Descartes, and the master rationalist in politics, Armand-Jean du Plessis de Richelieu. It is, in fact, a village called into being by the Age of Reason, proclaiming its sense of order and authority. This essay in town-planning is the Cardinal's own, intended by him as a suitable appendage to the great château of Richelieu, which his architect, Jacques Le Mercier, constructed nearby. Of the château itself nothing remains. It was confiscated at the time of the Revolution and sold early in the nineteenth century on condition that it would be demolished, and its only relics are a pavilion and the moats of its medieval ancestor in the midst of a great park. The Cardinal, ill and overworked at a time of war and national crisis, did not see his creation completed, or even more than half-finished, but he gave no indication of any regret: for the château and the village existed, not to accommodate him, but to symbolize the entry of the family of Richelieu into the ranks of the great houses of France; they were a gesture, a proclamation of success, an expression of the satisfaction of having arrived.

To build the château the fortified manor house of Richelieu's youth was demolished, but the gothic chapel and the salon in which the Cardinal's mother had taught him the importance of being an aristocrat were incorporated in the new mansion: it was a sentimental act which betrayed the Cardinal's self-consciousness of his own restricted and rather humble childhood. It is by no means certain that Armand-Jean was born at Richelieu. During his own lifetime Mlle de Montpensier visited the new château, and wrote, after the Cardinal's niece had shown her around, that one would have expected that the room in which he had been born would have been preserved. Contemporaries of Richelieu, however, mention that he was born in Paris on 9 September 1585, and there are allusions in his own writings which support this. Certainly he was baptized in the Paris church of St Eustache on 1 May 1586, and the baptismal register shows the parents as resident in the rue de Bouloy. Whatever his birthplace, Armand-Jean, the sickly child with the lively, impatient, unforgetting and unforgiving temperament, grew up with a widowed mother and a domineering old grandmother at Richelieu before going to school at the Collège de Navarre in Paris. To say that the family of Plessis de Richelieu was poverty-stricken would be to exaggerate, for they were still able to provide the children with education and careers, but that there was a persistent problem of money and that it influenced Armand-Jean's character is beyond doubt.

Men are not born to greatness, nor do they have it thrust upon them; they achieve it. Greatness in fact exists rarely and its compounds are difficult to isolate, but at least it may be said that two things are requisite for it; the first is intelligence of a high order, without which no one can achieve more than mediocrity; and the second is tenacity, an inflexibility of purpose sufficient to triumph over every obstacle and eliminate the opposition of those who have neither the inclination nor the energy to resist indefinitely.

The awareness of young Armand-Jean that the family fortunes were sinking, that the whole middle and lower nobility were on the brink of economic and social disaster which would condemn them to be quarrelsome and indigent partisans of the great ducal magnates, provoked in him, at first subconsciously, but later with complete self-awareness, a determination to restore the honour of his house, and not only to restore it but to dignify it. From this response to a challenge which was intensely personal developed the sense of grandeur which the Cardinal was to attribute vicariously to France. At the end of his life he was to write in his *Testament politique* that the gentry who, like his own father, had been entrusted with public office and invested with honours, had paid for these by the ruination of their economic position: if the fidelity of such people was to be assured in the future it would be necessary to create conditions whereby they and their creditors would be relieved of financial anxiety, and thus from the necessity to intrigue and create factions.[1]

The House of Plessis de Richelieu typified the evils which afflicted the French gentry and against which the Cardinal was to struggle with limited success. The name Plessis comes from an old French word signifying a palisaded bailey – the earliest form of castle. There were plenty of places of this name in medieval France, and plenty of families whose names derived from them. The genealogists of Richelieu's own time were to provide him with a grandiose family-tree, in which they managed to incorporate every Plessis who had ever distinguished himself, though most of them belonged to families quite unconnected with Richelieu's ancestors. But if the genealogy was fictitious – as the genealogies constructed at this time for all but the most noble and historic of families generally were – the gentility of the family, which derived from the *plessis* in the parish of Néon near Blanc, on the border of Brenne and Poitou, is indisputable. They were petty vassals of the Bishop of Poitiers, who served the Kings of France or of England, depending on which of them had effective control of the province. The earliest recorded ancestor is Guillaume du Plessis in 1201, and his designation as varlet indicates his rather low place in the feudal hierarchy. He possessed, besides Plessis, two seigneuries, those of Breux and Vervolière. The latter passed by inheritance to a cadet branch of the family which broke off in the fourteenth century, and eventually took the name Plessis de Richelieu.

While the senior line of the Plessis sank into, or perhaps never rose beyond, the position of petty gentry to whom the hayfork and the scythe were more familiar than the sword and the cross-bow, the cadet branch began to rise in the world. They married well. In the reign of Charles VII Geoffroy du Plessis married Perrine Clérembault. Her brother Louis, who was *maître d'hôtel* to the Queen, had inherited the seigneury of Richelieu, acquired by marriage from the family of Mausson. In 1429, the Clérembault of the period had received permission to build a *manoir* at Richelieu and fortify it. It was the age of Joan of Arc, and the rude structure, which the Cardinal was to demolish, bore its imprint. The house was built on an island one hundred yards square in the Mable, whose waters constituted the moat. Woods surrounded it for miles and the only sign of the hand of man visible from the turrets of the château was the tower of the parish church at Braye, which still stands guardian over the tombs of the Clérembaults and Richelieus.

Louis de Clérembault died in 1490 without issue and left his estates, including the seigneury of Richelieu, to his nephew François du Plessis. A succession of distinguished marriages brought the Plessis de Richelieu to the fringe of the higher nobility, and even of the court. Several of them entered the Church to become prelates and abbots. When the Wars of Religion broke out in the 1560s the family was affluent and well-connected, but it was quickly brutalized by service in the armies of the local magnates of Poitou and Touraine, the Trémouilles, Montpensiers and Rocheouarts. The Cardinal's great uncle, known as Antoine the Monk, became notorious even among his peers for his savagery and plundering. Destined at the age of ten to be Abbot of St Florent de Saumur, Antoine obstinately refused to study, and after violent strife with his parents, in the course of which he was even imprisoned by them, he threw off his habit and ran away to fight in Italy, where Cardinal Caraffa relieved

4

him of his vows. Later, as a captain in the Catholic army of the
Duc de Guise, he was the author of celebrated massacres of the
Huguenots, and his name was mentioned with horror by both
parties to the civil war. In 1576 this debauchee, blasphemer and
ruffian met his end appropriately in a street brawl in Paris. His
brother François, only slightly less of a bandit, was killed by an
arquebus shot from Queen Elizabeth's army besieged in Le Havre.

The elder brother of these two adventurers was Louis, who
inherited the estates and devoted himself to producing five
children. He made a splendid match in marrying Françoise de
Rocheouart, whose family counted among the great in the realm.
She was a vulgar, tempestuous woman, who in her old age was to
become a harridan and to make life miserable for the Cardinal's
mother. Louis died young, leaving her to cope with her five
infants. The subsequent story illustrates the immoderate passions
which consumed the nobility of France, and the violent conditions in which their lives were led. Only a few miles from Richelieu, and sharing the village church of Braye, was the manor of the
Mausson family, out of whose hands the seigneury of Richelieu
had passed to the Clérembaults. The Mausson House and the
Maussons themselves were even more primitive than the Plessis;
and like all people of elementary feelings, the Maussons nursed a
grudge against those who had outstripped them in favour and
fortune. The ruffianly head of the clan seized the opportunity of
Louis' death to assert his precedence over the Plessis in the church
at Braye. The eldest of Louis' sons, though a boy, had the courage
of his House; he resisted, and when the Plessis-Mausson feud
became chronic he was ambushed and murdered.

Mme de Richelieu was not the woman to wail over her son's
body and then forgive his enemies. With sullen fury she plotted
her revenge. The next son, François, the Cardinal's father, was
summoned home from the court where he was a page boy and
was inflamed by his mother to assassinate Mausson. This he contrived to do by stealth at night, leaving Mausson's bleeding body
in the heavy waters of the Mable. For the morals of the Plessis
it was not a happy incident; for the future of the family it was.
François was forced to flee from France, and apparently he

attached himself to the King's brother, the Duc d'Anjou, when he was unsuccessfully courting Elizabeth of England. Later, when Anjou was elected King of Poland, François appeared in his retinue at Warsaw, and apparently became a favoured courtier. On the death of Charles IX, Anjou became King of France as Henri III, and with him, then thirty years of age, returned François du Plessis de Richelieu, to become Grand Provost of France and a Knight of the Holy Ghost. A sombre, pale man, nick-named Tristan the Hermit, he concealed beneath his withdrawn appearance the nervous energy and the consuming ambition which he was to transmit to his son. Following the famous day when the Catholic champion, the Duc de Guise, was assassinated in the royal apartments at Blois, the Grand Provost, at the head of a troop of men in armour, burst into the States General with drawn sword, shouting with every indication of the madness that in various forms affected many of his family: 'Kill, kill, fire, fire!' At this tempestuous invasion some deputies fled; others, who could not reach the doors, scrambled under the benches; some stood in shocked and bewildered silence. It was one way of putting an end to whatever element of popular consultation the French constitution afforded.

François was with Henri III when the friar Jacques Clémont, who had been reading too many pamphlets on tyrannicide issued by the Catholic party in the civil war, ended the royal life and the House of Valois with a knife thrust in the ribs. And it was François who with his own hand arrested the assassin. The event threw the Catholic cause into confusion, for now the heir to the throne was the champion of the Huguenots, Henri, the King of Navarre, whose white plume, like William III's white horse to the Orange-men, has remained a symbol of Protestant virtue. For a time the Catholic party found a candidate in the Cardinal de Bourbon, but when he died it became necessary to look for another further afield. The Duc de Mayenne and the Parlement of the Catholic League convoked the States General at Paris for this purpose. But hardly any of the second estate, the nobility, and not more than half the third estate, the commons, appeared. Only the clergy, the first estate, was there in strength. The ambassadors of Philip II of

6

Spain, with cabin trunks full of coin, advanced the candidature of the Spanish Infante, but in face of Henri de Navarre's conversion to Catholicism – the fourth change of religion he had made – the tumultuous assembly collapsed and vanished, and the Catholic League was gradually strangled for want of means and support. The Grand Provost had early divined which way the wind was blowing, and had joined the increasing throng that scrambled to the side of Henri de Navarre shortly after the death of Henri III, thereby retaining his royal office. He was with the erstwhile Protestant champion at the final battles of the Wars of Religion, but did not live to see him crowned as Henri IV. He died of typhoid in the camp at the siege of Paris in 1590 at the age of forty-two.

A second generation of Plessis de Richelieu had left a widowed wife and five children. François, in the intervals of his adventurings, had found time to marry, probably in 1566, when he was eighteen and she fifteen, Suzanne de La Porte. For the son of a Rocheouart this was distinctly a marriage beneath his caste: Suzanne was not noble; her grandfather had been an apothecary in a small town of Poitou; his son, her father, had become a successful lawyer in Paris and a councillor of the Parlement of Paris and thus a bourgeois of the robe, a patrician, but with some aristocratic connections and considerable pretensions. It has been suggested that François married her in the anticipation that she would inherit her father's money, and stave off the financial disaster that was threatening the seigneury of Richelieu. In this expectation he was sadly disappointed. But in terms of culture and intelligence the marriage was the salvation of the family, for Suzanne was a well-educated and sensible girl, as unlike her crude, high-born mother-in-law as it was possible to be. The future ruler of France owed much more to his middle-class ancestry than to his aristocratic forebears, and the consciousness of it in his early youth was a stimulus to his self-assertion.

The landed feudal nobility and the patriciate of the cities, conscious of being in certain respects inferior, each affected scorn of the other. The nobility, badly educated for the most part, and perennially short of money, attributed a superior virtue to the one

7

thing in which they excelled, fighting, so that they transformed what in the high Middle Ages was a necessity and a duty into a cult which became ever more irrational. The patriciate, aware that they were excluded from certain roles which the mystique of monarchy was endowing with great importance, became self-conscious, and compensated for their awareness of their generally inferior social position by asserting their superior good manners and wealth, and by creating their own cult of behaviour. They became stilted and pedantic in speech and writing, and they moved quietly with a rustle of velvet gowns and fur capes, while the nobles lost their tempers, slammed doors and trailed their long rapiers aggressively on the parquet. The aristocratic virtues of self-control and silent acceptance of fate are, in fact, bourgeois creations.

There is a story about Cardinal Richelieu's uncle, Amador de La Porte, which illustrates the intrinsically bourgeois reaction to the ritual of noblesse. This worthy man managed to break into the ranks of the Knights of Malta, and was for a time in the garrison on that island; his father had won an important lawsuit for the Order and Amador was admitted without the usual proof of genealogy. Thereby he acquired a sort of spurious nobility and shed his patriciate background. But in his soul he preserved the wonderment of the bourgeois for the trappings of aristocracy. During diplomatic negotiations with Savoy he saw his nephew assert precedence, as a prince of the Church, over the Duke of Savoy, who was by no means an inconsiderable sovereign. Clasping his hands in ecstasy, de La Porte was heard to exclaim: 'Look at that! Whoever would have thought that a grandson of lawyer La Porte would walk through a door ahead of the grandson of Charles v!'

The five children whom the Grand Provost left were Françoise, who was aged twelve, Henri, Alphonse, Armand-Jean and Nicole. The widow of forty, whose life was made miserable by her ferocious mother-in-law, set herself to educate the children and conserve the family's economic resources. The inheritance on paper sounded grandiose. There were the ancestral lands of Vervolière and Richelieu, several other seigneuries, three manor

houses of varying size and various other houses. But the seigneuries were little more than nominal. They gave privileges but
produced little revenue. The farms had been heavily encumbered
and drained of resources by the Grand Provost to support his life
at court. Speculation and devastation by war had aggravated the
decline. The situation of the family of Richelieu was the same as
that of most families of the French nobility. Revenues were to
some extent fixed, and the serious inflation that occurred in
Europe following the influx of American gold into Spain, and
which grew worse as the sixteenth century drew to its close,
meant that fewer goods and services could be purchased. The
relationship between gold and silver varied according to the
respective quantities of each in circulation; coins of lower
denomination were constantly losing their value in terms of those
of higher denomination, so that, whereas in 1550 there were three
livres to a crown in France, by 1600 there were eight; and as rents
and services were normally expressed in *livres*, the extent to which
incomes had depreciated in terms of real value can be estimated.
Then, the absence of the proprietor at the wars and at court meant
not only neglect of capital resources but extravagantly increased
expenditure; a courtier might well spend in one week the annual
income of his estate. Money was raised on the security of future
revenues at usurious rates. A sixteenth-century proverb summed
it up: too many châteaux and too many poor.

The financial dilemma that confronted most French noble
families could be avoided only by the pursuit of fortune at court,
or with one of the factions led by the great ducal houses. The
king bought loyalty, and incidentally made the survival of the
caste possible, by the grant of a variety of pensions and emolu-
ments and the multiplication of petty offices that carried with
them a stipend. But the court was in much the same economic
predicament as the nobles, and was under constant pressure to
produce the means of satisfying the latter's insatiable demands.
It so happened that the easiest means was by the granting of
ecclesiastical benefices. The concordat made between François I
and the Pope in 1516 had given the Crown the right of nomination to bishoprics, and this right, by a process of slow accretion,

had been extended to abbacies as well, so that by the time of Henri IV all the more important benefices of the realm were at the royal disposal. The needy nobles were granted these as part of a favour that cost the monarch nothing; and by the end of the sixteenth century church revenues were generally in the hands of local gentry, whose younger sons became bishops and abbots, without necessarily entering holy orders, and appointed poorly educated and miserably paid clerics to do their work for them. Sometimes heretics held ecclesiastical benefices. It was a scandal even in the France of the time.

Another cheap way of paying for services to the Crown was the grant of privilege – exemptions from tax, the rights of chase and keeping pigeons. But even these did not suffice, and the proportion of pension payments in the national budget was for ever on the increase, particularly in the reign of Henri IV, who considered that the repose of the realm could not be bought too dearly. At his death the annual budget, at least as disclosed in the audited accounts, was just over fifteen million *livres*, and of this, pensions and gifts consumed three and one half million *livres*, the court and the *comptant du Roi* four millions, and defence another four millions.[2] This left for public expenditure about one quarter of the revenue raised.

Eldest sons inherited the family estates, but the charges attaching to a seigneury were often as heavy as the benefits. The seigneur had the right to constitute a court and hold an assize, but since his jurisdiction was absurdly limited, and the royal magistrates had a parallel but more complete jurisdiction, this right had become a burden and an embarrassment. The Wars of Religion had seen the dispersal of income and capital on the raising of men-at-arms and the purchase of armour and weapons which were needed as much for security as for aggression. At the time of Richelieu's birth there were seventy thousand fiefs in France, all more or less in a state of defence, fortified and guarded by a handful of armed men. But if this was the condition of the eldest sons, that of their brothers was worse. They had no outlet for ambition except in intrigue and factions. It is not surprising that the Wars of Religion produced a generation of troublemakers who did not stop at assassination of elder brothers, brigandage and counterfeiting. They were insolent, turbulent and vindictive. Richelieu himself wrote: 'The nobles recognized liberty only in the licence to commit with impunity all sorts of evil deeds, for they felt they would be unduly hindered if one tried to keep them within the equitable bounds of justice.'[3] And later, summing up the whole caste in one of his typically pithy expressions, he said that 'each values his merit by his audacity'.[4]

When François du Plessis de Richelieu died the family was in such reduced circumstances that his collar of the Order of the Holy Ghost had to be sold to pay for his funeral. Armand-Jean was then five years old. In the next few years he came to realize that he had no advantage, as a third son, save a superior intellect, and that the exploitation of this was his sole road to success. Vanity and ambition were inflamed by the determination of the thin, delicate schoolboy at the Collège de Navarre always to be ahead of his fellows, and he emerged not only well-educated in the formal sense but with a conviction of destiny. A family council followed at which his future was decided. He was, inevitably, to be a soldier, not one of those vagrant ruffians who attached themselves to any marauding army, but soldier-courtier who could become a marshal of France. There was a cadet school of sorts in Paris called the Academy, which was run by a distinguished Gascon aristocrat, Antoine de Pluvinel, with whom Richelieu's father had travelled to Poland. Here Armand-Jean learned the military and courtly arts, how to smile and dissemble, how to joke and flatter, how to bow, how long a feather to wear in his hat, how to trail his cloak over his sword scabbard. The Academy did nothing to discourage Richelieu from becoming the *poseur* whose portrait by Philippe de Champagne is almost more an abstraction of the aristocrat than a picture of the man.

Richelieu was to spend much of his life playing at soldiers, but was never to be one. He entered the Church instead, without exhibiting any signs of what would nowadays be called a vocation. Henri III had granted Richelieu's father the right of appointment to the see of Luçon, a little town in the flat fenland where

Brittany ends and Poitou begins whose cathedral spire is observable for many miles around. After her husband's death Mme de Richelieu continued to enjoy the income of the see, appointing bishops who acted as revenue collectors and who delegated their own ecclesiastical functions to clerics of lower grade. The second of these middlemen bishops was uncle Jacques du Plessis de Richelieu, who went so far as to take holy orders but no further. He never resided in his see, but did history a service by taking an interest in young Armand-Jean, for whom he acted almost as a father. The revenues from Luçon were Mme de Richelieu's main income, and after the death of Bishop Jacques they were imperilled by a revolt of the cathedral chapter there. The canons decided they had had enough of absentee bishops and were tired of being for ever passed over for ecclesiastical preferment. It was important, before they managed to get the royal grant to the Richelieus revoked, to retrieve the situation by having a Richelieu consecrated bishop. The second son, Alphonse, was therefore nominated with the royal consent at the age of twelve. But on the day he was to take his first orders seven years later, Alphonse refused to accept the responsibility and left to become a Carthusian monk at La Grande Chartreuse. In due course he was to be torn from the silence of his cell by his younger brother to live a harassed existence as Cardinal Archbishop of Lyons and Primate of Gaul.

Alphonse's defection threw Mme de Richelieu into a panic. There was only one solution to the problem: Armand-Jean must take the see. The suggestion was not displeasing to the pallid young Marquis de Chillou, as he was now calling himself. Armand-Jean had doubts about his health, which might have interfered with a military career; and he had a strong inclination towards book-learning, debate and argument which a military career would not have satisfied. He also felt moderately religious and was not averse to the prospect of an early government of the lives of others. So in 1602 Armand-Jean left the Academy, ceased to be a marquis, and began to study theology at the Collège de Calvi. He threw himself into his new task with his usual compulsion, and his self-assertion was early demonstrated when he pestered the Sorbonne for permission to deliver a public lecture expounding his philosophical views. The rector and professors considered this a premature ambition, and thought to put the immodest young seminarian in his place. But his persistence prevailed to the extent that he had his forum in the Collège de Navarre and forced an unwilling scholarly world to acknowledge, if not his philosophical insight, then at least his analytical ability.

Trouble in the diocese of Luçon brought about Richelieu's early consecration. The provincial Parlement ordered that one third of the revenues of the see be devoted to repairing the long-neglected cathedral. The administrator of the diocese proved quite inadequate in the financial and legal crisis that followed and Mme de Richelieu petitioned the King to have Armand-Jean installed. Since he was five years younger than the canonical age for consecration a dispensation would have to be obtained from Rome. Henri IV made the necessary approaches, but the Vatican chancellery proceeded in the matter at its usual frustrating pace. Armand-Jean was not the person to leave his destinies in the hands of others beyond his influence. His ordinary reaction to a situation was to seize the initiative himself, assert his claims and negotiate directly. He was restless and impatient, consumed with anxiety when his interests were in issue. It was not usual for an applicant for a dispensation to appear in Rome and force himself on the Pope's attention, but this is just what Richelieu decided to do.

It was his one and only visit to Rome. The experience, though brief, was important. He conceived a dislike for the methods of the Roman curia that has been shared by many another French prelate, and for the rest of his life held himself aloof from Roman involvements. The pudding-faced Borghese Pope, Paul V, was at first cold towards the young man who claimed his attention, but wily and experienced though he was, fell victim – the first victim – to Richelieu's skill as a professional charmer. The seminarian knew that his application depended on the wooing of the pontiff; and he wooed him so successfully that before long Paul was committing the indiscretion of expressing his doubts about the religious sincerity of Henri IV. Richelieu defended his king so persuasively that the Pope, who prided himself on his Latin

witticisms, exclaimed '*Henricus Magnus armandus Armando*'.[5] Richelieu drained himself of all energy, as he was wont to do when
confronted by a major challenge, in demonstrating to all Rome
his learning and intelligence. The necessary dispensation was
obtained and he was ordained a priest and consecrated a bishop on
the same day, 17 April 1607, at the age of twenty-two. He
returned to Paris and threw himself into his theological studies
with renewed vigour, passing his final examinations with universal applause. Then, the challenge over and the tension relaxed, his
nervous system reacted. For months he was ill, and not until
Christmas 1608 did he arrive in his see.

2

His Kingdom is of This World

1608-14

The boy bishop, who cherished the pageantry of the world and the dignity of his own person, must have been mortified by his pathetic entry into his diocese. He had had to borrow an old carriage from an acquaintance and the money with which to buy his purple robes; he had no entourage, no pages and no cavalcade of armoured and befeathered nobles, only a dismal procession of seedy and hostile clerics and the functionaries of this very minor town. He found that since the Wars of Religion nothing had been done to repair the moral and physical damage of the years of turmoil and neglect. The subordinate clergy were in a miserable condition, their revenues insufficient to maintain them, and their discipline lax. The bishop's palace, parts of which, attached to the cathedral, still remain, was a medieval relic; the chimneys smoked, there was no garden, and there were no proper furnishings or plate. The vestments of Richelieu's predecessors had to be cut down to fit his slender form, for there was no money in the diocesan treasury with which to replace them. By dint of careful and extended savings he was able to place an order through a Mme de Bourges in Paris for twenty-four silver plates, costing five hundred crowns, and some tapestries.[1]

With his usual nervous energy Richelieu set himself the task, not only of accommodating himself in suitable dignity and of assisting his clergy to better their conditions, but also of reforming the diocese. For the first time in generations a bishop of Luçon took a strong grip on the see, and the clergy and people had not long to wait before their curiosity as to the character of their new bishop was satisfied. They saw a thin young man, who looked taller than he actually was, and whose narrow features, prominent cheekbones, sharp nose and pointed beard constituted a triangle framed by lank black hair. His hands were small-boned, with long, tapering fingers. They did not recognize that behind the haughty exterior and the cold-fire eyes was a soul for ever in turmoil. Like many other highly intelligent men he hid his nervousness and shyness only by a tremendous effort of self-control, and in the process emotionally exhausted himself. The result was recurrent periods of collapse and depression, persistent migraine and various stomach troubles. Later in life he was to suffer acutely from piles. But if the people of Luçon found him aloof and unfathomable they quickly came to respect him, for from the bishop's palace radiated an unaccustomed authoritarianism which penetrated the secular no less than the ecclesiastical sphere, and which quickly transformed Luçon into a petty theocracy foreshadowing the France of Richelieu's heyday.

On his arrival Richelieu faced the challenge of the local authorities to the Richelieu financial control of the diocese and the challenge of the demoralized clergy and the undisciplined local gentry. This time he did not depend upon anyone else to achieve what he wanted, and he did not need to make any great effort to please and persuade. Everyone at Luçon was his subordinate, and he made it clear from the outset that he would stand no nonsense from the cathedral chapter. Having thus immobilized the canons he commenced to negotiate a termination of the protracted legal proceedings concerning the diocesan revenues; a compromise was reached under which the ruined cathedral of Notre Dame, with its three thirteenth-century naves and its early flamboyant choir, was to be restored. Beyond this there would be no further interference with the flow of income to the House of Richelieu.

Luçon lies close to La Rochelle, at that time the citadel of

Protestantism in France, and since La Rochelle had no Catholic bishop Richelieu was its nearest episcopal authority. In his own diocese he had a huge Protestant minority, and thus in his first administrative years he was forced to confront squarely the problem of reconciling Catholicism and Protestantism in the period after the Wars of Religion. With the Huguenot pastors he engaged in constant intellectual struggle but he was never intolerant of anything concerning them save their opinions. A rationalist, he had an absolute conviction in the possibility of conversion by persuasion. Thirty years later he was to write a treatise on the methods of conversion in which he was to state that, while at Luçon, he had:

... often thought in the profound peace there, of the various means for bringing La Rochelle into obedience to the King. These thoughts used to pass through my mind like dreams or vain imaginations; but as God had since willed that what had formerly seemed to me to be nothing but fanciful schemes should be undertaken, so that this city should be attacked to reduce it to obedience, I thought during this siege of delivering from heresy by reason those whom the King was withdrawing from rebellion by force.[2]

Sceptics have suggested that Richelieu was interested in demonstrating to the world, in the only situation open to him at the age of twenty-four, his superior administrative ability; and that it was ambition alone that drove him to work on reconstructing his diocese until his health collapsed. The explanation betrays no comprehension of the man's character. He had an unquenchable urge to bring order out of disorder, which was later to drive him to the administrative reform of France at vast peril to his liberty and even his life, and he was consumed with a passion for thoroughness, symmetry and creativeness. He was, it is true, a bookman; but he was also a man of action who could not bear to be without an immediate goal or without creative work to do. When he was not running a diocese or the realm he took to writing books, simply because inactivity, even reflective inactivity, was irksome. He was, unlike his brother Alphonse, no contemplative. The see of Luçon provided him with an opportunity for administrative professionalism just as theology satisfied his sense of order and authority and challenged the subtlety of his mind. The local aristocracy found him an implacable enemy of duelling, who cajoled the civil authorities into stamping out this vice by every means available to the law. Incapable or inadequate priests were ousted. He may have regarded Luçon as a stepping stone, but he was sufficiently a product of the Counter-Reformation to desire reform for religion's sake as well as for its own sake: he was a moralist; he believed intensely in God; he was one of the first bishops in France to carry into effect the reforming decrees of the Council of Trent, and one of the first to found a seminary governed by them.

Richelieu's convictions as to the course French Catholicism should pursue were so firm during his period of power that one is apt to lose sight of the process whereby he acquired them. In 1608 the religious situation was highly fluid; ideas and policies were fomenting but parties and schools had not yet formed. The Wars of Religion had covered, by a temporary alignment of Catholics versus Huguenots, the deep cleavages between those who believed in a revived papal authority in church administration, the ultramontanists – those who looked beyond the Alps to Rome – and those who believed in a French Catholicism with the minimum papal connection, the gallicanists; between those whose approach to religion was mystical and those whose approach was rational; and between those who prayed with the imagination and those whose devotion was pious.

With the ending of the Wars of Religion controversy on these issues exploded, and Richelieu, entering into possession of his see within ten years of this event, found himself in a France seething with religious enthusiasm. From the first fifty years of the century more saints figure in the Church's calendar than from any other epoch in French history, and France has, it must be remembered, justified her claim to be the Eldest Daughter of the Church by producing a quite disproportionate number of them at all times. St Francis de Sales recovered Upper Savoy and Dauphiné from Calvinism; St Vincent de Paul organized his missions to the poor; St Louise de Marillac provided him with his nursing sisters; St

Jeanne de Chantal founded a new order of nuns; St Jeanne Les-
tonnac founded schools for girls; and Richelieu's friend, St Jean
Eudes, engaged in works of charity. At the height of his power
Richelieu was to encourage all of these by his personal interest and
his financial assistance. But these were only the outstanding
figures. Hundreds of people flocked to join the religious orders,
especially the new ones like the Oratorians, or the newly reformed ones like the Capuchins. The latter, in their patched and
dirty grey habits, plodded from town to town incessantly active.
They fasted, prayed, preached to the great and lowly, and converted the Huguenots in great numbers. Wherever there was
human suffering they were to be found, carrying stretchers, even
digging graves, and for ever bringing guidance and consolation to
souls in misery. The moral force exerted by the orders brought
about an incalculable transformation of society. Daughters of the
great Houses entered convents, lived lives of the most rigid discipline and inspired their sisters in Christ. Their brothers went off to
devote themselves to perpetual silence among the Carthusians, as
Alphonse de Richelieu did, or became missionaries at home and
abroad whose zeal was a rebuke to those who lived for the world
alone, and a challenge to heroic virtue in those whose spiritual
development was incomplete. St Francis de Sales, visiting Paris
for the first time since the Wars of Religion, was astonished.
He found 'Saints. Veritable saints, in great number and everywhere!'[3]

The bishop of Luçon was, in his own way, devout, but as the
Abbé Bremond was to say of him: 'He fears hell; he loves theology; he does not entirely lack interest in the things of God; but in
the final analysis his kingdom is of this world.'[4] The critical problem in Richelieu's life was the uneasy interaction of public
activity and religious and moral standards. Politics and administration, like any other human exercises, affect men's moral environment and their relationships with God; therefore the Church
is not indifferent to the actions of human authorities. But judgement is fallible; and the judgement of one man respecting a complex course of political conduct may differ radically from that of
another. Both may prescind from the same moral premise and yet

reach different conclusions, and each may regard the other's actions as damnable. The political actor himself is not only confronted with this problem of moral judgement; he is also in danger of losing something of his spirituality because of his almost total immersion in practical things, and because the very complexity of the moral judgement, leading to easy self-justification and facile solutions, has a deadening impact on the soul.

In the last five years of his life Richelieu was to experience a spiritual conversion, which was to lead him into devotional, even mystical, religion. But at Luçon his love of God was of the mind, not of the heart, a matter not of experience but of conviction. When he wrote on religion it was not devotional but apologetic writing; he did not instruct so much as debate, and he did not seek to raise men's eyes to God in baroque ecstasies of love so much as to combat falsehood.

The intellectual and the emotional each have a place in the culture of Catholicism, and at varying times and in varying traditions the one or the other predominates. In sixteenth-century France the intellectual, mystical, pietistic and devotional trends had been allowed to develop without any effort at assimilation, and once the Wars of Religion were over they stood out in marked contrast with one another. The Counter-Reformation in France thus assumed an aspect very different from that in Italy, and especially Germany. There the movement was controlled by the Jesuits, whose special relationship with the papacy supplied the critical element of hierarchy and authority which was lacking in France. The Jesuits were intellectuals, but they were not anti-mystical. On the contrary, they sought to embody the visionary approach of St Theresa of Avila in the instructional method, to produce a devotional, but rigidly dogmatic, religion. The result was an amalgam of metaphysics and imagination which the Jesuit baroque church typifies. All imaginative devices for demonstrating theological truth, whether it be perspective ceiling painting, windswept Fathers of the Church grouped around sunburst altars, clouds of angels symbolizing the abolition of the boundaries between this world and the next, or Margaret Mary Alacoque's cult of the Sacred Heart, were employed in a synthetic exposition of Catholicism. The senses as well as the mind were captivated and held in thrall. The result was the uniform religion-culture of baroque.

France avoided this integrating experience; and partly because its Catholicism remained diversified for the whole of the seventeenth century its culture embodied a compromise between the pietistic and the imaginative. That this is largely due to Richelieu cannot be doubted, for it was his deliberate policy to maintain a balance between the competitive tendencies in French religion; and his natural inclination to resist excess was reinforced by his anti-Habsburg policies, which went so far as to oppose the baroque as the religion-culture of the pretenders to European domination. Since the French suffered acutely from indiscipline, from what he time and again called their 'levity', he sought to impose a constraint upon them which had the effect of inhibiting the baroque imagination; and since he was himself the rationalist, the pure intellectual, he emphasized in his own writing, in his patronage of the arts, and in his domination of the world of the theatre and literature, the pure Renaissance strain, and thus helped to project a mannerist classicism far into the baroque age.

This mannerism is most obvious in his sermons, which were rhetorical, eclectic and pedantic, and relied for illustration on the importation of historical and mythological examples. In a Christmas sermon, for example, Jupiter and the Colossus of Rhodes figure, however irrelevantly, in an argument on the Incarnation. His systematized authoritative writing, even though it abandoned this literary apparatus, was equally mannerist in its involved construction and its striving for epigram. His first literary exercise was his *Ordonnances Synodales*, which he produced in 1613. These were instructions to the clergy and people about Christian conduct, public discipline and private morality. They are negative in character, full of prohibitions and injunctions; the people should go to communion at least four times a year; the priests should not neglect the divine office, or their vows of chastity, and they should not drink to excess.

It would be wrong to assume from his theological and catechetical works that Richelieu's approach to religion was exclusively intellectual, for there is abundant evidence that he recognized the importance of mysticism as a method of religious development. Almost his first action upon his arrival in Luçon was to found a seminary and to invite the leader of the French mystical movement, Pierre de Bérulle, to staff it from his newly founded order, the French Oratorians. This decision involved the rejection of the royal policy of Jesuit control of the seminaries, but it is not to be interpreted as the emphasizing of a native strain of spirituality at the expense of Jesuit cosmopolitanism. Richelieu never indicated any animosity to the Jesuits, who in his later years were to be his firmest supporters, but he did not himself seek spiritual direction from them or recommend it to others. His own soul, as well as his career, he placed in the hands of the leading mystic among the Capuchins, Père Joseph. The latter was to become his closest friend, a collaborator and companion whose superior religious insight became for him an assurance that his political decisions were morally justified; and as their moral quality became ever more controversial, and his own conscience ever more exercised, his reliance on his 'Grey Eminence' for spiritual nourishment as well as political guile tended to increase.

Père Joseph, the weatherbeaten friar who prayed as he plodded the roads of France, was then a man of thirty-two. Born François Le Clerc du Tremblay, he was also a product of Pluvinel's military academy, and, like his master, he had an instinct for the military as well as the spiritual, which he sublimated in a passion to preach a crusade against the Turkish infidels who held the holy places. Whenever he found a soul sympathetic to this fantasy Père Joseph's ordinary good sense immediately deserted him. For much of his life, though with ever-weakening voice and ever-diminishing hope, he pressed his schemes of a crusade on kings and princes, the Pope and any magnate who had armour and money. People who wanted to use him humoured him in this eccentric notion, so that he, who was to be regarded as the most guileful of diplomatists, was quite often himself the victim of the guile of others. He was preaching a substitute for a crusade against the Protestants of Poitou when Richelieu approached him to ask for some Capuchins to preach the Forty Hours Devotion in Luçon.

At that time Père Joseph was engaged in spiritually advising the fashionable convent of Fontevrault not far away, where a fanatical girl of the highest nobility, Antoinette d'Orléans, was convulsing the aristocratic nuns with her schemes of reform. Widowed at twenty-eight, she did what St Jeanne de Chantal did at about the same time, left her infant children for a life of prayer. Eventually Fontevrault as she reformed it proved insufficiently strict and she struck off on her own to found, with Père Joseph's backing, the Calvarian order. This was to remain Père Joseph's particular interest for the rest of his life, and in between his diplomatic wanderings and his drafting of innumerable state papers he was always to find time for tutoring his nuns in the mystical path to perfection.

In Bérulle and Père Joseph Richelieu discovered the two men who were to be most instrumental in assisting him to fulfil his ambitions, but, because he failed to recognize in them at this stage anything more than pastoral aids, he maintained only spiritual and intellectual relations with them. He relied for his advancement upon his brother, Henri, the Marquis de Richelieu, then on the fringes of the court, and on local ecclesiastical and civil officials, but they were mostly to prove feeble and unreliable. He was himself too young and inexperienced to recognize that the urge to power must be tempered by discretion, and channelled along covert ways. When he reflected how men of mediocre talents had risen to high office in Church and state, and grown rich in the process, it seemed inevitable to the clever and industrious prelate that he should become something more than the bishop of a small and miserable see in the west of France. But like many young men who assert their claims to preferment too soon he was doomed to a series of disappointments and frustrations that brought on depression and despair. The first was when he pushed himself forward for election as representative of the ecclesiastical province of Bordeaux at a conference of the clergy in Paris in 1610: the other bishops were astonished at this impertinence, and they elected the Archbishop of Bordeaux and the Bishop of Aure. The next was when he sought to force himself on the Queen, Marie de Médicis, following the assassination of Henri IV in the same year. Richelieu heard the news from his dean who happened at the time to be in Paris. He knew that the court would be in a state of anxiety concerning the intentions of the Protestants, and he calculated that an assurance of loyalty from the bishop of a city which was substantially Protestant would be reassuring – and that his own name and good services would be remembered. So he wrote, direct to the Queen, a letter which he took much trouble to compose, and in which he included an allusion to the will of God that France should have a Queen Regent of such wisdom and virtue.

Richelieu's problem was how to ensure that the Queen herself read the letter. His solution was to send it to his brother and have him pass it on from one gallant to another until it reached its destination. But Henri recognized the letter for what it was, an attempt at self-advancement, and was sufficiently worldly-wise not to have it delivered for fear the court would think that M. de Luçon had overreached himself. When the bishop heard of this he was seized by one of his abrupt urges to action. He would go to Paris and make his declaration to the Queen in person. It happened that his archbishop was still there after the ecclesiastical conference, so he wrote to him that he was coming, saying that in this moment of danger to the realm the Queen was in need of all the advice she could get. The archbishop no doubt recognized the hint, but, like most experienced administrators, knew how to react without overtly offending. He wrote a reply in a most friendly tone, but without saying that he would mention the bishop to the Queen. And that was the end of the matter. None the less, Richelieu came to Paris, selling his recently acquired tapestries to pay for lodging.

Partly as a result of overwork, but also no doubt partly as a reaction to this curbing of his ambition, Richelieu fell ill again. He blamed it on the damp sea-air of Luçon and resolved not to return for some time. His chapter had been getting obstreperous, and very likely he could not face the nervous exhaustion of dealing with it in person. Although cold and ironical he was rarely discourteous to his subordinates, and the letter that he wrote from Paris to his two *grands vicaires* indicates that he had lost control of himself. It discloses, not only petulance, but an arrogance that he was usually under great pains to suppress. 'Thanks be to God

I know how to rule myself, but I also know how those under me should be ruled,' he wrote. Then, telling them how to deal with the canons, he added that 'heat will only provoke others of warm blood, such as me'.[5] Having uttered this admonition he left Paris to spend some time at the priory of Coussay near Poitiers, where he lived a rustic life meditating on the things of God, and even more upon himself, and writing letters incessantly to all and sundry, in which he complained of his poverty and ill-health. It was a time better spent than, perhaps, he realized, for through his friend the bishop of Poitiers, La Rochepousay, whom he saw often, he was extending his range of contacts.

Three years passed. Richelieu was often at Coussay, but even from afar he ruled his diocese firmly. It was an experience in administration by paper that was to prove invaluable in later years when he was to become the most complete bureaucrat. Being a man of nervous disposition he preferred to negotiate in writing, when a case could be rationally and persuasively argued without the distractions of personal confrontation. Only when personal negotiation was absolutely necessary did he indulge in it, and then he put his whole emotional energy into the effort of persuasion. The older he grew the more he disliked the strain of argument and disputation, and the more he withdrew into his cabinet, pleading ill-health as the reason. Not surprisingly his anonymity was not recognized for what it was. People came to regard him as a sinister figure, all-seeing, all-knowing, a spider in the centre of a web that enmeshed everyone in France. And they came to hate what they could not understand.

This, however, was twenty years away. In the years between 1610 and 1614 the kingdom was showing every symptom of falling once again into the debility of the period of the Wars of Religion. Louis XIII was eight when his father was stabbed by Ravaillac, and the Queen, Marie de Médicis, as the Regent, was nominal ruler of the country. In fact the real rulers were her child-hood companion Leonora Galigai, the deformed daughter of her old Italian nurse, and Leonora's husband the Florentine adventurer Concini. Coming from Machiavelli's city where political advancement was an old-established art, the Concini had nothing to learn from the French in this matter. Compared with them the French nobles and statesmen who embezzled, took bribes and sold public offices, were the merest amateurs.

Not surprisingly, the great territorial magnates became restless. Had the Concini combined efficiency with corruption they might have kept the unruly in thrall, but they proved incapable of conserving the royal power, and poured money out of the royal coffers in bribes to members of the royal family in the false expectation that the support of the latter for the Regency could be bought. Sully, the only capable minister, was discarded within eight months of Henri IV's death, and within three years the treasury funds which had accumulated, amounting to nearly twenty million *livres*, were totally exhausted; during the same period expenditure rose by four millions and revenues declined by five. The country was bankrupt.

The collapse was disguised by exhibitions of pomp and circumstance which mesmerized contemporaries. One such display was organized to celebrate the engagement of Louis XIII to the Infanta Anne and of Louis' sister Elizabeth to the Infante Philip in 1612. The Place Royale, now the Place des Vosges, was just completed and its noble residents were able to sit at their windows and for three days at Easter enjoy the celebrations in honour of the Spanish ambassadors who concluded the arrangements. The Duc de Nevers, who had gained for himself a reputation in Rome for the splendour of his arrangements, was commissioned to organize a great carousel in conjunction with the Duc de Guise and the most elegant and handsome cavalier of his age, François de Bassompierre, Marquis d'Harouel. The court, the nobility and fifty thousand people sat on scaffolds in the square to watch the gyrations of the nobly caparisoned horses, the fantastic floats drawn by reindeer and lions, the illuminations, fireworks, and volleys of musketry, and their ears were stunned by the salvoes overhead of one hundred cannon from the Bastille. The upper nobility rivalled each other in the splendour and pomp of their equipages and in the expenditure of money. The Prince de Condé's equestrian quadrille cost him twenty thousand crowns. From viewing one another's grandiose exhibits at the carousel

the princes and the dukes turned their smouldering eyes on the court
in its lilied pavilion. Marie de Médicis, as an Italian, could never
have been popular, but now that this irrevocably stupid woman
had identified herself in the minds of the jealous and furious
magnates with a novel political gangsterism her claims to govern
were seriously weakened. Opulent and florid in figure, bedizened
in dress, she had no policy, was the willing captive of any
flatterer and in her ideas the victim of the last conversation. It
was only a question of time before the Regency would come to
grief; and the old ministers of Henri IV, identified in the popular
mind with Sully's unpalatable financial measures, and known as
the 'Old Fogeys', were individually and collectively too feeble
to prevent a crisis.

In February 1614 it occurred. The young First Prince of the
Blood, Condé, grasping, unprincipled, without talent or dignity,
an ardent Catholic and a man consumed with detestation of the
upstart Médicis who sought to rule France over the heads of its
royal sons, abruptly left the court and retired to Mézières, where he
was joined by four of the most powerful dukes, Nevers, Bouillon,
Mayenne and Longueville. They issued a manifesto, accusing the
Regent of squandering the national income and demanding the
summoning of the States General. The government was powerless
to do anything about the matter, and after three months of negotiations agreement was reached. Richelieu was later to comment
cynically upon it, and with justice, for these magnates who
threatened rebellion in protest against the prodigality of the
Regent submitted on receipt of enormous bribes to themselves,
adding nearly another million to the year's deficit of nine millions.
They also forced Marie de Médicis to issue writs for the summoning of the States General at the end of the year, hoping that thereby
they could organize a universal protest at the misconduct of the
Regency.

The States General was not a Parliament in the English sense,
but a consultation of the whole realm. The three estates, the first
the clergy, the second the nobility and the third the commons,
deliberated separately, meeting together only for the opening and
closing sessions. The States General had not met for sixty-six

years before it was convoked at Orleans in 1560 following the death of Henri II at a tournament. The three estates at that meeting squabbled furiously, the second and third combining to demand the distribution to them of the property of the first, and the second opposing the social advancement of the third. During the Wars of Religion both Catholic and Huguenot theorists argued that the States General was the depository of national sovereignty, and that the king was merely a delegate in the functions of sovereignty. Both religious parties therefore found in the existence of the States General a constitutional justification for their attempts to capture the Crown and make it the instrument of expression of their policies. During the reign of Henri III the States General was vehemently Catholic, and even Bodin, the most famous theorist of the royal sovereignty, led the third estate in its opposition to the king, who, according to Catholic theory as it was evolving, derived his powers from God, not directly, but mediately through the people. Richelieu's father had put a stop to all that nonsense, and, apart from the pathetic gathering at Paris to try to find a Catholic successor to Henri III, the States General had not met since.

Now in 1614 it was to meet again. People expected more of it than its history justified. The very name, with its suggestion of a general consultation of all classes, prompted notions of grandeur. It was believed that the country would immediately take on a new aspect – which really meant that privileges would be restored and caste divisions reinforced. Richelieu's cultivation of his ecclesiastical friends was bearing fruit. Largely through the efforts of La Rochepousay, the bishop of Poitiers, he was elected as one of the representatives of the clergy from Poitou – not in itself an astonishing achievement since one delegate had to be a bishop and there was only a handful of sees in the province. It was the most decisive event of his career, for it is difficult to see how he could have gained a dominant influence over the Queen had he not been presented with this opportunity to exhibit his talents. Even then he suspected, and after the States General he was convinced, that there was no one else capable of governing France effectively; and the fact of the matter is that he was right. The essence of greatness is a sound appreciation of one's own capabilities and limitations.

3

Negotiate Without Ceasing

1614-7

The solemn opening of the States General took place on 26 October 1614. At eight o'clock in the morning Louis XIII assumed the throne on a dais under a portal of the gothic cloister of the Augustinians, near the Pont Neuf. Beside him was the fleshy mass of his mother, and around him were the coterie of princes of the blood who sat glowering at her and the Concini with open animosity. The King was all in white. He had inherited Marie de Médicis' sallow complexion and soft, almost flabby features. His mouth was always half open as if the strangling lace collar made breathing difficult, and his cheeks bulged at the bottom so as to overflow his jaw. His hair was long, dark and curly in the new cavalier style and later he was to wear a thin moustache, and later still a Van Dyke beard. He had had a miserable childhood, alternately neglected and beaten by his selfish, bad-tempered mother, and not surprisingly the twelve-year-old was morose.

After the usual disputes about precedence a procession of the deputies got under way and filed past the royal dais, before which each person bowed, the clergy gravely, the nobility with exaggerated flourish of feathered hats, the third estate with heads lowered below their stomachs. The head of the procession passed out of the convent, along the Quai des Augustins, crossed the Seine by the Pont Notre Dame and so reached the cathedral. The

29

route was lined with the royal guards, each man's beard parted in the dashing fashion of Henri IV. Their costumes were half violet and half orange, with baggy breeches, and green and black slouch hats, and they carried their muskets at the shoulder.

A horde of beggars shuffled at the head of the procession, gathering the alms that were distributed. Following them came the religious orders in their various habits, and the corporations of the city with their banners. On both sides marched the Archers of the Grand Provost, holding candles in one hand and halberds in the other, and outside them were the Hundred Swiss in velvet, satin and taffeta of white, red and blue, with velvet plumed caps. There were also one hundred gentlemen of the Maison du Roi with torches and demi-halberds. Then followed the chapters of Notre Dame and Sainte Chapelle with capes and batons, the rector, professors and bachelors of the university in their gowns, and finally the people whose business occasioned the display, the three estates. First walked the two hundred deputies of the third estate; the judges were in long robes and square bonnets, and the officers of finance in short robes with cloaks open at the sides through which the arms could pass. Robert Miron, their president, had sought to wear his red robes as head of the Paris guilds, but this had been regarded as monstrous ambition, and he appeared with his colleagues, many of whom were, in fact, nobles elected from the provincial administrations, in sombre black. They progressed in ranks of four, and each carried a candle given him by the master of ceremonies. Then came the nobles in Spanish hats and court cloaks, richly dressed and wearing swords. Finally came the Church, first the representatives of the simple clergy, also in ranks of four, wearing soutanes and carrying their birettas to expose their tonsures to the chill autumn air, then the bishops and archbishops, in ranks of two, in violet with rochets and birettas. At the rear, in scarlet capes and Roman hats, were Cardinals Sourdis, La Rochefoucauld and Bonzy.

Just before the court marched the archbishop of Paris carrying the Blessed Sacrament beneath a canopy of cloth of gold supported by the Duc de Guise, the Prince de Joinville, the Prince de Condé, and the King's eight-year-old brother Gaston, the Duc d'Anjou. Beneath a second canopy walked the King, and near him in flamboyant widow's weeds, and veiled in black, was Marie de Médicis accompanied by the ladies of the court. Some distance behind followed the Parlement and officers of Paris, the governor of Paris, and various court officials in coloured robes. The streets were hung with tapestries and every window was crammed with sightseers. As the procession entered Notre Dame each took a seat allotted to him, and the King and his mother halted at prie-dieus before the high altar. There followed a boring sermon by Cardinal de Sourdis, and mass was celebrated by the archbishop of Paris. The Holy Ghost was invoked in the pious hope that this time the States General might not degenerate into the bear garden that the older people present no doubt remembered.

Next day, Monday, the opening plenary session was held in the Hôtel Bourbon, just in front of the Louvre, in a salon whose walls and ceiling were appropriately seeded with fleurs-de-lys. The court gatecrashed, and when the deputies tried to enter they found their seats nearly all occupied by gallants and ladies. After much sorting out, places were found for all and the speeches began. They lasted all day. The leader of the Old Fogeys, the long-bearded chancellor Sillery, began. The learned archbishop of Lyons gave what everyone agreed was the best speech. The Baron de Pont St Pierre, for the nobility, delivered a feeble discourse, and Miron the president of the third estate was too long-winded. Everyone knew that concealed beneath this grave rhetoric an explosive situation existed. Would Condé seek to use the meeting as a vehicle for launching an assault on the Court? In the event he was to prove too weak. He hoped his party might generate sufficient momentum to bring down the Concini, but he was not himself the man to fire the opening shots. In fact the situation was taken right out of his hands by Cardinal Duperron, who passed for something of an oracle both in France and in Rome. Charmer and controversialist, his ecclesiastical politics were ultramontane, and he was thought to be a supporter of the Jesuits. When the estates separated to begin their deliberations, this man with the great beard and the biretta tilted on one ear became the focus of the first estate. A group of younger bishops gravitated to him, and Duperron used them like members of an orchestra, selecting the right moment for a dulcet or a thunderous intervention. Richelieu became one of his group.

The meeting of the States General was a tremendous challenge to Richelieu. If he failed to impress his colleagues and the Court now the path of ambition would be closed to him. Therefore every ounce of energy had to be devoted to the effort to exhibit himself, persuade and dominate. One false move and he would be lost. The outcome was a triumph. As one of Duperron's orchestra he intervened early on a procedural point, and was chosen to head a delegation to the third estate to persuade them to follow the method of the first, including the administration of an oath of secrecy. This mission involved addressing the whole third estate, and it was well discharged. Later, when the clergy provoked both the Court and the third estate, Richelieu kept a silent tongue in his head. He was learning prudence. He saw no point in making enemies over a squabble about excessive pensions.

He also played a cautious and conciliatory role in the violent dispute that developed on the subject of ultramontanism versus gallicanism. The French bourgeoisie was frantically anti-Roman; it had seen two kings killed by tyrannicide, as a result, it was believed, of the propagation of the thesis that the Pope had direct, or even indirect, power over kings. The class which forty years previously had been vigorously arguing exactly the contrary now went much further than the Court in advocating the divine right of kings. Early in its deliberations it was presented with a motion from the City of Paris that there be adopted as the Fundamental Law of the State the proposition that:

... the King is sovereign in France; he holds his throne from God alone, and there is no power on earth, whatever it be, spiritual or temporal, which has any right in respect of his realm, which can deprive the King's sacred person of it, or dispense or absolve his subjects from their loyalty and obedience which they owe him, for any cause or on any pretext whatever.[1]

The motion was carried by the third estate without consultation with the other two. The nobility, awed by the passion demonstrated by the commons, and divided between patriotism and the ultramontane notions it had inherited as a class from the Catholic League, was nonplussed. The clergy, for the most part ultramontanist, was shocked.

Duperron was urged to deal with this threat to the autonomy of the Church. First he needed to gain the support of the nobility, so he appeared before the second estate and argued that the question raised by the commons, being theological, belonged to the first estate alone. The nobility accepted this, and next day sent sixty of its members to support Duperron when he harangued the third estate for three hours on the topic. His effort was of no avail. Duperron thereupon resolved to complain to the King, but before doing so needed once more the support of the second estate. Richelieu was dispatched to obtain it, and acquitted himself ably. The King ordered the withdrawal of the resolution of the third estate, but quietened the commons with a promise to reply to it none the less. Although the resolution never became the fundamental law it remained engraved on every heart; and if France became an absolute monarchy the commons were largely responsible for it. Richelieu knew that a campaign for centralized authority and national unity would not be lacking supporters.

So far Richelieu had done well, but he had not found himself in a position to attract the Court's attention. His opportunity came when a group of bishops, encouraged by the power and energy demonstrated by their estate, decided that a vigorous effort would break the scandalous reign of the Concini and the Old Fogeys, and launched an attack on Marie de Médicis. They behaved so intemperately, however, that they provoked the opposition of other prelates, who decided to protest vehemently and reassure the Queen that it would be an evil to separate the King's authority from her own – in other words, she should continue to rule France and be ruled by the Concini. Richelieu was given the task of developing their opinion before the second estate, and in doing so he became the Queen's champion. His flattery of the florid lady is only outrageous by the standards of another age; no one was disgusted by it; and it earned Marie de Médicis' approval to the extent that she intervened behind the scenes to have Richelieu chosen to present the memorials of the first estate at the plenary closing session on 23 February 1615.

Again all the seats were occupied by the cavaliers of the Court before the deputies arrived, and again there was vast confusion before the session could begin; even cardinals were pushed around in the crush. Richelieu had sought to be excused from the task entrusted to him. Perhaps he was a little terrified at the prospect of having to shine before the whole of France as the one spokesman of his order; or perhaps he thought that a little becoming modesty would not go amiss. The estate insisted on his undertaking the commission, and he expressed his willingness to obey. Having genuflected to the King he stood, and, bareheaded, spoke or an hour. It was a polished speech and it made a good impression. Deploring the situation of the realm, it proceeded, in the obsequious language expected of the petitioner, to approve of the policies of the Regent, and especially of her proposal to effect an alliance with Spain by marrying Louis to the Infanta Anne of Austria, the daughter of Philip III, and Louis' sister Elizabeth to the Infante Philip, Anne's brother. Richelieu also championed the resolution of the clergy that France should accept the decrees of the Council of Trent, which other Catholic countries had already implemented, and without which the reform of the Church could not be completed. He urged that priests should occupy first place in the royal councils. Concluding with an expression of confidence that the king, guided by the wise counsels of his august mother, would render his subjects happy and prosperous, he laid the memorials of the clergy before the throne.[2]

Court and Church were both pleased, and when Richelieu took his seat there was prolonged expression of approval. He was followed on behalf of the nobility by the Baron de Senecey, who, as he began his genuflection, was peremptorily ordered by a gesture of Louis to assume a standing position; he spoke briefly. The merchant guildsman Miron then advanced to present the memorials of the third estate. No royal gesture dispensed him from kneeling while he addressed the throne for three hours. Perhaps his discomfort reinforced the anguish of his words:

The poor people work ceaselessly, sparing neither body nor soul, that is to say sparing not their own life, to nourish the whole kingdom; they plough the land, improve it, strip it bare; they put to use what it produces; there is neither a season, month, week, day nor hour, which does not demand unremitting labour. And from their labour there is nothing remaining for them but sweat and misery. The sustenance of Your Majesty, of all the clergy, the nobility and the third estate, has their limbs for security.[3]

It was a social comment wrung unexpectedly from a rich middle-man by the very magnitude of the national problem.

M. de Luçon was entitled to return to his lodgings in the north-west corner of the new Place Royale satisfied with himself and confident that he was destined for advancement. He was now an outstanding and well-regarded bishop, and he had won the Regent's favour. But nothing happened. The deputies returned to their homes, the memorials were filed away, the Concini and the old fogeys continued to govern, and Richelieu was apparently forgotten. The tension within himself suddenly relaxed like a spring released and again he fell ill. He returned to the priory of Coussay and for six months tried to satisfy his restless energies with theological studies. Among other things he was reading refutations of the thesis of the Jesuit contemporary, St Robert Bellarmine, who had challenged the notion of the divine right of kings with the argument that ultimate sovereignty under God resides in the people.

The marriage arrangements between Louis and Anne of Austria (and reciprocally between Philip of Spain and Louis' sister Elizabeth) were satisfactorily concluded between the French and Spanish governments, and in due course in September 1615 the Court moved towards Bordeaux where the brides were to be exchanged. When it arrived at Poitiers Richelieu presented himself and had an audience with the Regent. The new Queen would require a chaplain. It had been proposed that the Bishop of Orleans should be given this office, but Henri de Richelieu had organized a little court intrigue in favour of his brother. It may be that at Poitiers Marie de Médicis spoke to Richelieu of this appointment, but he had to wait another two months before he had news from Bordeaux confirming it. With the prospect of activity in high places, his health improved.

Before Richelieu could join the Court Condé threw the realm into turmoil by a second rebellion, in which this time the leader of the Huguenots in the south, Henri the Duc de Rohan, as well as Mayenne, Longueville and Bouillon, participated. Richelieu was now to experience for the first time what his parents had endured in the Wars of Religion, and he was never to forget the lesson. Condé's troops rampaged through Poitou, pillaged the château of Richelieu, burned his papers in Luçon and carried off his possessions. His mother wrote to him that not in the forty years she had lived at Richelieu had she seen such men or destruction. It was, as Richelieu clearly saw, an aimless rebellion of little political purpose and unrelated to any national protest, and he was not surprised when a dreadful winter, followed by plague, took away the enthusiasm of the presumptuous but not very courageous Condé.

At Loudun, close to Coussay where Richelieu was fretting with inactivity while he awaited his summons to the Court, Condé halted. Richelieu was not to know it, but the decisive moment in his life had come – Père Joseph was to make his political début. The Capuchin friar was at the moment preaching in Loudun, and his brother, Charles du Tremblay, was a gallant in Condé's train. To bring peace is one of the duties of a priest, and Père Joseph took his duties seriously. He determined to adjure Condé to return to his obedience and end the civil war, and, when Condé indicated a willingness to negotiate with Concini he quickly found himself an intermediary with the Queen Mother. The task of peacemaking was made easier when Condé fell ill of influenza and was susceptible to Père Joseph's solemn hints of hell-fire. A peace treaty was drafted which settled nothing, but did remove for the moment the threat to Marie de Médicis and Concini. The other great nobles made their submission, and it was as if nothing had ever happened. During these negotiations Père Joseph frequently met Richelieu, who came to the Court, ostensibly to claim royal protection for his plundered property, but perhaps too in the hope that by hovering around he might find himself consulted in the complicated comings and goings that led to the settlement. The two had the opportunity to talk long and seriously about the state of the realm, the immoral nature of rebellion and the necessity for national unity as a moral good, and they found that their ideas were harmonious and that they themselves were congenial in ambition and talent.

Richelieu had, though he did not know it, made the best of all possible contacts. Instead of waiting, however, until Père Joseph was in a position to hoist him into power, he devoted himself to cultivating the new minister of finance, Claude Barbin, who was one of Concini's men, and was favoured by Marie de Médicis. Richelieu had met Barbin when the latter was merely *procureur* at Melun, and they had become friendly. Now Barbin was able to take Richelieu by the hand and present him to Leonora Concini. Later in his *Mémoires* Richelieu was to admit unashamedly that he won her husband's heart, and it is certain that she, like Marie de Médicis, became a captive of his penetrating, guarded and melancholy eyes and a victim of his flattery. The road to power is necessarily paved with the stones of insincerity and intrigue, and the taint of baseness remains a reproach on the consciences of all politicians who pass that way. It is the measure of Richelieu's greatness that once he reached his destination he did not permit this encumbrance to deflect him from his goals, and that he courted in full consciousness the dreadful charge of ingratitude and unworthiness.

As it happened, Richelieu's involvement with the Concini régime, which every day became more discredited, proved to be a fatal move which was to postpone the day of his arrival to power until he was in his fortieth year. There seemed to be no end to Concini's ambitions, and no end to Marie de Médicis' toleration of them. Having acquired a string of seigneuries from her, this Italian *arriviste* outraged the princes by becoming a marshal of France. They were even more outraged when he demanded the governorship of Picardy, which would not only enable him to gatecrash the select group of the great ducal houses, to whom governorships were principal perquisites, but would also place him in a position of political power in a territory adjacent to the

Spanish Netherlands, and within striking distance of Paris. Was he planning, with Spanish support, to carve out an independent principality for himself which would for ever have France at its mercy? So long as the Maréchal d'Ancre, as Concini was now calling himself, continued to dominate the Regency, Condé refused to return to Paris and resume his seat on the royal council. And so long as Condé held himself aloof the danger of his leading yet a third rebellion remained.

At Père Joseph's suggestion Richelieu was asked to go to Bourges and talk to Condé. It was his first political commission. He had prepared the way for a favourable reception by writing a fawning letter to Condé at the time of the Loudun negotiations. just as a reinsurance in case Condé might emerge the victor in the proceedings. No longer was he up in arms about the pillaging of his property by Condé's hoodlums; Condé had replied, and a correspondence had developed which Richelieu had not kept confidential, but which he had passed on to the Regent. Richelieu thus had a foot in both camps when he went to Bourges. His discussions with Condé were fruitful: Condé was promised that if he took his seat in the royal council all affairs of state would be disclosed to him; in return he promised to keep secrecy. He was also assured that neither the Regent nor Ancre was harbouring designs against him. In July 1616 Condé reappeared at court, but it quickly became evident that he was not to be managed by people as infirm of purpose as Ancre and Marie de Médicis. He found himself the centre of attraction and the focus of dissension, his house was for ever crowded with lobbyists, and his passions and ambitions were inflamed by a tempestuous throng who spoke openly of Ancre's assassination. In a spasm of determination Ancre decided to risk all on a coup, and Condé was arrested when entering the council chamber and lodged in the Bastille. His mother, hearing the news, sallied forth to bring fire and brimstone down on the court. Screaming 'to arms!' she went raving from her hôtel to the Pont Notre Dame, but the best she could achieve was to gather a mob which pillaged Ancre's house near the Luxembourg and carried the loot off to auction. The princes, Bouillon, Guise and Vendôme, vanished from Paris intent on raising rebellion in the provinces, and found a figurehead in Charles, Duc de Nevers, a French sprig of the great house of Mantua.

This man was a cosmopolitan and almost royal. His father was a Gonzaga, his mother a princess of Cleves in Germany, his wife a princess of Lorraine, and his paternal grandmother was a Palaeologus, one of the imperial family of destroyed Byzantium. As a representative of the Byzantine empire he had recently been approached by a delegation of Greeks from the Morea, led by one John Fantin Minotto, who proposed that he place himself at the head of a movement of political freedom against the Turks. It was an appeal that this Byronic man could not resist, but it was obvious that an uprising of Greek mountain peasants would not achieve much unless the Christian princes supported them with moral and military power on a considerable scale. Nevers was pondering this problem when, as a rebel leader in Condé's camp at Loudun, he encountered Père Joseph and found in him a kindred spirit who fostered his illusion that a gigantic movement of all Christendom would not only recover Jerusalem but would oust the Turk from the Bosphorus and in the person of Nevers himself restore the Byzantine dynasty. The two romantics mesmerized themselves with visions of the cross once more planted on the citadels of the East, conjured up Godfrey and Richard in spirit, and deceived themselves into believing that the cry of the Greeks for help was providential. Père Joseph would go off to Rome to talk Paul v into approving a crusade, and Nevers would go to Germany to collect the *landsknechts* who would be the hard core of the new crusading army.

Nevers was on the way to Germany when he heard of Condé's arrest. He wrote an insolent letter to the King, gathered his new crusader recruits, raised a rebellion in Champagne, of which he was the governor, and entered into relations with Bouillon, who had locked himself up in his stronghold at Sedan. Marie de Médicis and Ancre turned in their anxiety to Richelieu, who had come to know Nevers through Père Joseph. Would he go to Champagne and cajole Nevers into returning to his allegiance? If Nevers had listened to a friar, he must, as a man enjoying the reputation of great piety, listen to a bishop; he was to be told that, if he submitted, the King would take up the idea of a crusade with the Pope and the King of Spain. Richelieu returned from his mission convinced that he had succeeded, but Nevers proved more slippery than anyone had imagined, and maintained his posture of armed defiance.

This time the revolt of the princes was more serious for it was caught up with European events. In Germany Bouillon was raising troops, selling the timber from the forests round Sedan to pay for them. In Venice his agents were active, raising the spectre of a family compact between the Bourbons and the Spanish and Austrian Habsburgs to strangle the independent principalities of Italy in the name of the Counter-Reformation; and to the English he was hinting that the compact was the basis of a design to carry papal supremacy across the Channel. If Bouillon managed to give the dissident movement an anti-Spanish, and in consequence an anti-Catholic, bias, the Huguenots might rise and the whole miserable tragedy of the Wars of Religion be re-enacted. Richelieu's advice on returning from his abortive conference with Nevers was that the rebellion must be crushed forthwith and with resolution. The papal nuncio reported of him that he was 'ardent for war against the rebels; he judges it necessary if the King wishes to be King'.[4] For once the government acted without vacillation, and three of Nevers' towns, Soissons, Nevers and Rethel, were beleaguered. Nevers himself opened negotiations through his sister the Duchesse de Longueville, and it is significant of the position Richelieu had attained that she came first to him with Nevers' overtures.

A palace revolt created a vacancy on the royal council and there was no more obvious candidate for the post of secretary of state than the bishop of Luçon, who had demonstrated an unusual skill and firmness in these negotiations. At the end of 1616, a few days after his mother's death, Richelieu entered the ministry, and for the first time was confronted with the problems of foreign policy. The ambassadors who came to deal with him found him nervous, worried and confused by the magnitude of the diplomatic problems that confronted him. Since the death of Henri IV France had had no foreign policy, unless it was that of alliance with Spain. It was obvious to anyone who cared to think about it that unless France established an independent position in the affairs of Europe the time was near when internal dissension would be stimulated by external crisis. For in 1621 the truce between Spain and the Netherlands would expire, and everyone expected the Spaniards to attempt the reconquest of the Dutch provinces. Also, the Emperor Matthias was nearing his end, and with his death the vigorously Catholic Archduke Ferdinand of the Tyrol would make a bid for the imperial crown and it was obvious that some of the German Protestants would attempt to prevent him. An alignment of Catholics versus Protestants would mean an alliance of the Spanish Habsburgs and the Austrian Habsburgs against the Dutch and the German Protestant princes.

During the Wars of Religion Spain had intervened in the French squabble several times. Spanish armies had threatened Paris; Philip II had supported the candidature of his own son for the throne of France; and, as late as 1590, 2,500 Spanish troops had occupied Brittany and created a base there. Wherever the eyes of Frenchmen turned Spanish troops were poised on the borders of France. In the north they were in Belgium, in Arras and St Quentin and the whole province of Artois, with no serious geographical obstacle between them and Paris. To the east they were in Franche-Comté, looking down from the hills of the Jura on to the valley of the Saône. In the south they were across the Pyrenees on the lowlands of Roussillon, and the great fortress of Perpignan was their base for an easy advance to Marseilles or Toulouse. The Mediterranean was a Spanish sea; and in the Atlantic, despite all the adventurings of the English, the Spaniards were the dominant power. France was surrounded by them, unprotected by any natural barriers, and its vulnerability induced in many minds a dreadful sense of insecurity. This was particularly the case with the bourgeoisie, whose trade routes along the great river valleys of France from the Mediterranean to Belgium and the Rhineland were at the mercy of Spanish politics. If the riches of the East that flowed across the Mediterranean from Alexandretta or the isthmus of Suez to the port of Marseilles, and so throughout Europe, were to be intercepted, either at sea or by a closing of the Belgian frontier, the economic effects could be disastrous. The merchants felt they had more to lose from Spain than had the territorial magnates, to whom Spain was a protector and guarantor.

But there was an added dimension to the anti-Spanish complex of the French people. Spain was orthodox in religion in a quite old-fashioned and uncompromising way. It regarded itself as the saviour of Catholicism and considered Protestantism in all its forms as diabolical. The French bourgeoisie was to a great extent Huguenot, and having won a perilous equality with the Catholics in the Edict of Nantes the Huguenots had no wish to see Spain carry her version of the Counter-Reformation into France, by either fire and sword or more subtle influences at court. Anxiety was enhanced by the apparent greatness of Spain, which appeared to contemporaries as a political colossus. For a century no Spanish army had been defeated in the field; every year the plate fleet brought a new accretion of wealth, which seemingly would enable Spain to cast more cannon, build more ships, buy more military supplies, and bribe more people in the French government. Spain seemed to be at her greatest, and her cultural domination in this, the age of Cervantes, Lope de Vega, and Calderon, inspired awe in a France that had not yet produced Descartes, Pascal or Corneille. That already the Spanish economy was eaten up by the corrosion of Peruvian gold was unrecognized and only became evident a generation later when the Spanish cultural and military collapse was far advanced.

When Richelieu became secretary of state he had had no diplomatic experience, and had indicated no extraordinary interest in or understanding of international affairs. His five months in office taught him certain lessons, and prompted conclusions which were to dominate his thinking for the remainder of his career. It became evident to him that rebellion in France, which promised to be chronic, could not be confined, for the great French magnates had connections in neighbouring lands which implied that dissension in France would have European ramifications. Conversely, disturbances of the equilibrium of power in those lands would inevitably, because of these same connections, have repercussions inside France. The stability of France thus depended, not only upon the quieting of revolution inside the realm, but equally upon the stability of other countries. The very existence of Spain as a great European power implied the eclipse, and hence the instability, of those other countries. France, therefore, could not be disinterested in events in northern Italy or on the Rhine or the Moselle, for certainly violence there would spill over into French territory; and as Spain, even in the negative sense of attempting to hold on to what she already possessed in Europe, appeared as a provocation to France's neighbours, and hence as a threat to France's own internal cohesion, French diplomacy would tend to assume an anti-Spanish character.

It is traditional to assume that Richelieu deliberately deceived the world with respect to his attitude towards the Habsburgs, and that only when he was firmly in power in 1624 did he disclose his hand; and on the basis of the tradition it is still asserted that he betrayed whatever cause he fostered. This is to ignore the pragmatic element in his thinking. There is no reason to assume that before 1617 he was not a sincere supporter of the Bourbon-Habsburg compact, to which at the States General he had given his blessing. In 1616 the Venetian ambassador, reporting to the Grand Seigneury his appointment as secretary of state, wrote that Richelieu was not friendly to Venice because he was of the Spanish party, and even, it was rumoured, took payment from the Spanish Embassy. If in fact the ambassador was deceived so were others, for the papal nuncio wrote that Richelieu was one of the most eminent men in France because of his zeal for religion, his knowledge, eloquence and virtue, and that the Church could wish for no one better qualified to advance the Catholic cause of which Spain was the acknowledged patron; and the Spanish ambassador did not disguise his pleasure at the news of Richelieu's nomination, saying that there was no one in France who better served God, the Spanish crown and the public good.[5] It is consistent with Richelieu's mind and character to assume that his anti-Habsburg principles were provoked by the insight which he gained into Spanish policies during his months as secretary of state in 1617, and by his reflections on the mounting European crisis. His change of attitude followed a growing conviction of France's need to play an independent role in Europe, and there is reason to contend that the conviction was not absolute until the disclosure of Spanish designs during the French preoccupation with the siege of La Rochelle ten years later.

Bouillon's intrigues in Venice in support of Nevers' rebellion demonstrated the intimate connection between European and French politics. Venice was fearful of Spain, as were all the Italian principalities, for Spain dominated the peninsula from two centres of power, Milan and Naples. The Milanais was a bridge between Spain and Austria, and because it tended to draw the Spanish and the Austrian Habsburgs together it constituted the political centre of gravity of all Europe. While Nevers was in rebellion in France, Venice, almost by accident, was involved in war with the Habsburgs. It so happened that a nest of pirates in the lagoons at Segna was attacked by the Venetian fleet; Segna was territory of the Archduke Ferdinand, who retaliated and provoked the Spanish viceroys of Milan and Naples into engaging Venice in hostilities. Threatened by the awesome might of Spain, Venice turned to the little, dark, ambitious and restless Duke of Savoy, Charles Emmanuel I, Europe's principal troublemaker, and to Holland. The Dutch went so far as to send four thousand troops to the aid of the Serene Republic, these redoubtable Calvinists shocking the Italians by their Protestant practices.

It so happened that France and Venice had a treaty of mutual defence. If France honoured this the pro-Spanish faction in the government would be driven into the hands of Spain; and if it did not honour it the anti-Spanish faction would be driven into the camp of the rebels. In either event civil and international war would reduce France once more to ruin, and very likely to Spanish domination. To Richelieu it was an agonizing dilemma, and his method of escaping from it was by launching a diplomatic offensive in all the courts of Europe to bring about a quick settlement between Venice and the Habsburgs. He reckoned without Charles Emmanuel, who was energetically entangling the governor of Dauphiné, Lesdiguières, in his fine conspiratorial mesh. Lesdiguières was one of the great Protestant dukes, a man who maintained his own army and treated Dauphiné as his own principality. When reminded that governors held office for only a fixed term he merely laughed. At Vizille, a great château near Grenoble, which today is a presidential residence, he kept almost royal state and Henri IV nicknamed him *le roi dauphin*. That the King's writ ran in Dauphiné at all was due to his toleration and not to the government's power. The Spanish orientation of the Regency was anathema to Lesdiguières, as it was to all the Huguenot magnates, and the wily old warrior was not averse to any suggestion that might frustrate the Court's policy. He listened to Charles Emmanuel's schemes of a military demonstration to impress the Spaniards in the Milanais. Without telling Paris he raised seven thousand troops and marched them over the Alps in the dead of winter, dramatically appearing in Piedmont at Christmas 1616, a month after Richelieu took office, and just in time, so he claimed, to save Savoy from a Spanish invasion. Even Louis XIII applauded the coup which so compromised his government, expressing himself in an untranslatable idiom: '*Tant mieux,*' he said, '*cela fera baisser le nez aux Espagnols!*'[6]

Richelieu, faced with a *fait accompli*, decided to make capital out of it. The French demonstration could be explained to the Venetians and the Dutch as a gesture of aid. To the Spaniards it could be presented as a lesson that it did not pay to provoke the unruly Protestant magnates in France by political adventures in Italy. It accorded France an unexpected position of strength from which to negotiate, and enabled her to claim the role of arbitrator in the Italian dispute. France would preserve her liberty of action; the Spaniards and imperialists would court her in the expectation of French support when the imperial election took place; Spain, Venice, the Pope, Savoy and the Empire, would all come to Paris to present their cases to Louis as the arbitrator. Thereby France would be glorified and peace would be preserved. It had been proposed to send Lesdiguières a stinging reprimand, but Richelieu, enthusing over his new idea, toned it down until it read like a mild approbation.[7] There was in fact not the slightest chance that any of the parties involved would accept the role which Richelieu was proposing for France or that any of the contestants would be prepared to clarify the issues beyond the point where it wanted them clarified; all were engaged in a power struggle, in which issues were only excuses. Richelieu failed to persuade them to agree to a general settlement but he learned one lesson from the experience – to suppress crisis by keeping the negotiations going. 'Negotiate without ceasing, openly or secretly in all places.'[8] In fact the negotiations went on so long that they were eventually caught up in a succession of new disputes in northern Italy which ten years later led to Richelieu himself heading an army into Savoy.

4

Pompe Quasi-Funèbre

1617-20

In window seats and dark corners of the Louvre men could be seen whispering. A new royal favourite was in the making and Ancre's position was crumbling as the forces of opposition in the rebel camps and in the court coalesced. He was Charles d'Albert de Luynes, the King's falconer. A Provençal, whose father had a smallholding near Marseilles, Luynes was of the lowest gentry, and for this reason his quiet insinuation of himself into the favour of the deep, dissimulating monarch passed for a time unnoticed. The world dismissed Louis as entirely submissive to his mother and her régime, and as interested only in the hunt and making marzipan.

All those about her [wrote the Venetian ambassador] are entirely dependent on the Queen Mother, who chooses them as far as possible because of their indifferent ability and lack of intelligence, for fear that someone might put some virile thoughts in the King's head. Thus he remains in a state of obedience and respect; the authority of the Queen is complete and tending to increase. Her son never speaks, acts or commands save through her. In other respects the King is not without merit; he reacts quickly and is lively. He would be quite promising if his education had been better, and if he had a mind more inclined to serious things.[1]

Only gradually did the court become aware that the brawny

47

and manly Luynes was adored by the sullen and brooding Louis, and not until he was suddenly granted the castle and town of Amboise did they perceive in Luynes a rival to the despised Ancre, who continued to exhibit arrogance and feebleness in quick rotation.

Richelieu's preoccupation with his diplomatic problems did not prevent him from perceiving the danger to Ancre's position, and hence to his own, from Luynes' increasing influence upon the King. As a minister he could hardly expect to keep office if he did not retain Ancre's goodwill; at the same time he could not risk becoming too closely identified with the Ancre faction if he hoped to retain office in the event of Ancre's downfall. While he wrote affectionate letters to Ancre he offered his resignation to the Queen Mother, and when this was not accepted went to the papal nuncio and confided in him. A high office in the Church, perhaps the archbishopric of Reims, even a cardinal's hat, he let it be known, would satisfy him should he be forced to retire from the government.

Violent men sought to push the King into ordering Ancre's assassination, and Montpouillan, the sixth son of the Protestant Duc de la Force, was chosen to do the deed. The pious Louis, however, shrank from murder and would agree to nothing more than Ancre's arrest. Nicolas de l'Hôpital, Marquis de Vitry, the captain of the royal bodyguard, was given instructions, but the conspirators embroidered these with the admonition that if Ancre should show any resistance he should be shot. On Monday 24 April 1617 at ten in the morning Ancre, accompanied by a large entourage of followers, appeared on the drawbridge of the Louvre in front of the church of St Germain l'Auxerrois. A large number of petitioners crowded around him seeking to thrust papers into his hands. Vitry shouldered his way through the crush, and as the maréchal was glancing at one of the written petitions, he found Vitry's hand on his shoulder. 'The King has ordered me to seize your person!' Vitry cried. Ancre's reaction was to take a step back and make to draw his sword. Before the blade could leave the scabbard several of Vitry's men, who had been holding loaded pistols to their chests beneath their cloaks, presented them, and,

as the crowd heaved to both sides, they fired three balls into the
maréchal's body. Ancre fell on his knees, swayed for a moment
and then collapsed on his face. Vitry kicked the body and shouted
'*Vive le roi!*'

One of the Queen Mother's ladies-in-waiting, hearing the shots,
opened a window of the palace overlooking the drawbridge and
asked what had happened. Vitry, flushed with triumph, shouted
back that he had killed the maréchal. Slamming the window she
rushed to Marie de Médicis, who began wailing. 'They should
have escaped. I told them so. I have reigned for seven years and
now await only a crown in heaven!'[2] The Maréchale d'Ancre
was informed, and demonstrated a good deal more control than
the Queen Mother. The poor woman took to her bed to weep
silently. Hardly had she done so when Vitry's guards burst into
her room, overturned the furniture, carried off her jewels, rings
and money, and forcing her out of bed bundled her off to the
Bastille.

Richelieu was at the Sorbonne with the rector when the news
was brought by one of the professors who had been near the
Louvre. He hastened back across the Pont Neuf, and as his carriage
entered the stable courtyard he found a group of the ministers,
including Barbin, cowering there. They persuaded Richelieu that
since he was the least compromised with Ancre and his ecclesiastical position gave him a certain immunity, he should go to the
King and divine his attitude towards the ministry. Entering the
gallery of the Louvre Richelieu found the King standing on a
billiard table in a state of great excitement. A multitude of courtiers was rushing in from every door to throng around the table,
everyone protesting loyalty. Most of the contemporary historians
describe how, from his vantage point in the midst of the swelling
throng, the sixteen-year-old Louis caught sight of Richelieu
entering the gallery. 'How now, Luçon!' he is supposed to have
shouted, 'I have escaped your tyranny! Go on, remove yourself!'[3]
This is probably no more than the gossip of the faction which
created the legend that Louis was the cowed creature of the cardinal, and it need not be taken seriously. However, it can be believed
that Luynes, who was standing beside the King, intervened and said

that M. de Luçon had always given good advice to the Regent, and that the King then ordered Richelieu to attend at the council, which was forthwith summoned. When, however, Richelieu presented himself at the door, Villeroy, one of the Old Fogeys who had opposed Ancre and had been ousted by Marie de Médicis asked him what right he had to be there; and finding that no one spoke to him, Richelieu went out. He knew that Ancre's crash had brought him down too.

The maréchal's body was secretly buried in St Germain l'Auxerrois, but the Paris mob discovered and disinterred it next day. They hung it on the Pont Neuf, and behaving like a horde of Red Indians in contemporary America proceeded to hack it to pieces. Richelieu was setting out to see the papal nuncio, and as his coach turned to cross the bridge it was stopped by the butchery. Seeing the gutted and castrated corpse and the howling savages Richelieu knew instantly that he was in dire peril. It needed only someone to shout that he was an Ancre man for his bleeding carcass to be hanging on the bridge, and his entrails drifting down the Seine. Leaning out of his coach window he cried out: 'Look at the people who would die for the King! Let's all cry *"vive le roi!"* ' And so, he tells us, they allowed him to pass.[4] It was a scene that haunted his waking and sleeping hours for the rest of his life, and that came to mind whenever he reflected on the evils of public disobedience. Several times during his career he had good reason to expect that he would pass the way of Ancre.

Marie de Médicis' position was untenable, for the coup had destroyed the Regency and the King would now rule directly. She would have to be removed from all positions of power but it had to be done so as to preserve the royal dignity. Of all the former ministers only Richelieu was not behind bars, and she turned to him as a bishop and as someone who had often pestered her with exclamations of devotion to represent her in the nego-tiations concerning her future. Richelieu later complimented himself on the sacrifice he made in his chivalrous response to her request, saying that if he had been prepared to abandon her he could have retained his seat on the council, and that Luynes had offered as much.[5] The result of the negotiations was that the

Queen Mother should retire to the Loire. Richelieu also managed to save Barbin's life as part of the bargain. On 3 May 1617 Louis came to say good-bye to his mother, It was a painful meeting and both behaved in a very cold fashion. In the last carriage of her cortège as it left Paris were Richelieu and the bishop of Chartres, a cortège which was wryly described as '*pompe quasi-funèbre*'.

Marie de Médicis stopped at Blois, assembled round herself a court of flatterers and intriguers, bewailed her fate incessantly, and accused the world of ingratitude. As for the King, relieved of her presence, he was another character. The Venetian ambassador reported that during an audience Louis was giggling to himself. The new ruler of France was Luynes, and with him Richelieu, as Marie's personal adviser, continued to negotiate. Luynes, who was then forty, showed himself to be a well-mannered, agreeable and calm man, but neither he nor Richelieu trusted each other in the slightest, and each played a double game with the other. Luynes, showered with letters from Richelieu in which the bishop expressed the warmth of his devotion to the King, was not deceived, and he hinted that M. de Luçon would be well advised to leave the Queen Mother, and retire to his diocese. To Marie de Médicis' consternation Richelieu took the hint.

It was not alone to Luynes that Richelieu was writing, but to everyone who might influence the King on his behalf. He even wrote to Père Joseph, who was in Rome presenting his chimeric notion of a crusade. The letter was frank. It described Richelieu's misery, recalled their common struggle against heresy, and asked outright for Père Joseph's help in advancing his interests. But it seemed to the bishop of Luçon that he might as well have launched his letters into the blue spaces of heaven for all the result they brought. The papal nuncio, reporting his plight to Rome, wrote: 'The poor man has completely lost his reputation and his authority as a result of these events.'[6] Paul v, who remembered their engaging conversations, was touched, but could not think it a disaster that a bishop should be doing his duty in his diocese.

The control of great events is one way to satisfy the creative urge, and this explains the compulsion that some men feel to exhaust themselves in public office. When events cannot be controlled, then the control of ideas becomes a substitute. Richelieu took to writing books. Two treatises date from this period of political exile when Richelieu drowned himself in furious literary activity. The first was the *Principal Points of the Faith of the Catholic Church*, published in 1618, and the second the *Instruction of a Christian*, published the following year. The first is, in its way, a brilliant work, one of the most penetrating contributions to the analysis of Protestantism to appear from a French Catholic pen during the period of the Counter-Reformation, and it is specially remarkable that only Cardinal Duperron had preceded Richelieu in writing on religious topics in the vernacular, so that the bishop of Luçon had to establish his own conventions of polemical style. It was a time when the Wars of Religion had turned into a tournament of words, and theological debates were public spectacles. It so happened that the King's Jesuit confessor was dismissed because, it was alleged, he had asked Louis embarrassing questions in the confessional about Ancre's death, and he was replaced by another Jesuit, Père Arnoux, who had scarcely taken up his new office when he startled the world by seeking to demonstrate that the Protestants misused the Bible. To suggest that the exponents of literal intrepretation did not know, or falsified, the teachings of scripture was regarded as an unfair blow, and four Huguenot ministers of Charenton produced a written reply, *Defence of the Confession of the Reformed Churches*. A great literary debate was launched which convulsed all educated France, and in this Richelieu decided to intervene.

His *Faith of the Catholic Church* is a tactful, detached, tolerant and conciliatory work. In a preliminary address to the King, who would no doubt be reminded of Richelieu's existence and his talents, the bishop wrote: 'I shall tell him that the ways of gentleness are those which I consider best suited to deliver souls from error.'[7] This leads him to a discussion on the limits of religious toleration. He rejects the idea that heresy should be totally extirpated by force; equally he rejects the German solution that the religion of the prince should also be that of the people. There must be a limit to toleration, and it is to be found at the point where religious liberty leads to political action. As for the ideas of

Protestantism, the freedom of biblical interpretation is inadmissible. Since most people cannot read, they must be guided. The interpretation of the Bible by a minister thus substitutes for the interpretation of the Church. But how can the interpretation of one man be a better guide than the accumulated tradition of the Church? The people are merely being deceived when the ministers claim that all their doctrine is clearly stated in the Bible. Where in the scriptures is predestination to be found, clearly enunciated? Where is it said that anyone is assured of salvation? And if it is not there how, on the word of individuals interpreting the Bible, can it be an article of faith?

The deception does not stop there. On the basis of free interpretation the Protestants claim powers greater than those they deny to the Pope. In a passage crisp and devastating he comes to the point:

Neither the Pope, a bishop nor any man, Luther says, has any power to oblige a Christian by one syllable without his consent. So it seems that you teach subtly that human laws in no fashion oblige in conscience, which is a doctrine detestable to the Catholic Church.[8]

This was regarded by the Protestants as a blow even more unfair than that of Père Arnoux, and it provoked a torrent of protesting replies. Why, Luther had over and over again upheld civil authority, and to accuse the Protestants of contemning the law was to accuses them of political disloyalty. Their objection was well made but it did not blunt the point of Richelieu's comment, which was a far more subtle one than a mere insulting accusation of disloyalty. Richelieu was taking sides in the debate which was just beginning on the question of the ultimate nature of law. Is law a product of the will, or of the intellect? If it is a product of the will then it has no other support than the power of the prince who wills. If, on the other hand, it is a product of the intellect, it obliges the subject in conscience, because it has the backing of a moral criterion. The existence of this criterion depended upon the existence of a metaphysics of human society. Protestantism, with its roots in the nominalism of the late Middle Ages, had no philosophy to support such a metaphysics, and Luther's injunction to respect the will of the princes was one lacking any standards for judging the morality of expressions of the princely will. Quite logically, then, Protestantism conceived of law as externally binding the subject, but not internally encumbering his conscience. Coupled with a thesis that the sovereignty of the people precedes that of the prince, the Protestant argument contains the seeds of political anarchy. Richelieu saw more clearly than most of his contemporaries where a voluntarist theory of law must lead. Not for nothing had he been reading his Bellarmine.

The work was an enormous success among the Catholics, who applauded Richelieu as the champion in the tournament, and it made a marked impact on the Huguenots. Fifty years later even, the well-known Protestant pastor of Tonneins, Jacques de Coras, was converted by reading it.

While Richelieu was busy with his pen Marie de Médicis was busy intriguing against Luynes. The favourite could not but believe that Richelieu, who was receiving too many visitors, was the brains behind her dissension, and he decided that Luçon was too close to Blois for his comfort. On 7 April 1618, Richelieu, his brother Henri, and his brother-in-law Pontcourlay, Françoise's husband, received a royal order to go immediately into exile in the papal city of Avignon. Luçon saw its bishop depart on Good Friday without waiting to celebrate mass on Easter Sunday in his own cathedral. The roads between Luçon and Avignon crossed the northern end of the Massif Central, the uplands of Auvergne and the Limousin, which were regarded with horror by all civilized Frenchmen. After one passed Montluçon, there were no *grandes routes* with *pavé* surfaces until one reached the Rhône, and even there, after the neglect of the Wars of Religion, the *pavé* was often destroyed. Where there were inns they were primitive in the extreme, with wooden boards instead of glass in the windows. There were no changes of horses, which meant that the coach had to proceed slowly and with frequent halts. It took the party a month to reach Avignon. What they found there is very much what one sees today in Meknes or Fez. The narrow streets were crammed with itinerant hawkers and guides, mostly Jewish in outlandish oriental costumes. Craftsmen worked in the open or in little cubbyholes, and everyone seemed to cook in the streets. The common language was Italian, the senior officials who worked in the vice-legate's administration were Italian, and there was a society of sorts of petty French noblesse who had settled in the city and spoke a mixture of Italian and French.

It was a papal colonial outpost, and like all colonial outposts it was a ferment of personality difficulties, petty intrigues and absurd jealousies. Everything the Richelieus did and said was reported to the vice-legate and ultimately to Paris by the busy-bodies and professional spies who swarmed around them. They rented a house in an isolated quarter close to the convent of the Minimes. Richelieu dined occasionally with the pontifical officials, and with Bagno, the vice-legate, who was ten years later to be papal nuncio in Paris. But apart from this he was only seen walking on the promenade beside the Rhône in the evenings, watching the haze above Châteauneuf-du-Pape turn to vermilion and then to turquoise. He was fretful and nervous. Again and again he recapitulated the events leading to his fall, justifying himself a thousand times in all his actions. With the compulsion to discharge his energies on paper he penned apologiae for his relationships with Ancre. If writing to the favourite had been a crime, who was exempt? Why should he be criticized when a thousand others were free? It was a sad life, and his religious exercises, which he took seriously, were his only, but an insufficient, consolation. Paul v, when told of his situation, commented: 'What will become of the residence which he should have in his bishopric? And what will the world say at seeing him prevented from being where his duty requires him to be?'[9]

When his mind was a little more composed Richelieu took up his pen to write something more serious than recrimination. The result was his *Instruction of a Christian*, in which he returned to his first love, pastoral theology, with its pleasing structure of authority. The book, which betrays Ballarmine's influence on Richelieu in theology if not in political philosophy, was a simple catechism with special emphasis on the commandments. But political

55

philosophy enters, when a significant comparison is drawn between the power of God and that of the King:

A King, sovereign in France, testifies that there is no other person equal to him, and that all others are his inferiors: so God, sovereign King of the world, testifies that there is no one equal to Him, and He is unique.

It was the concept of the divine right of kings, drawn out of Bodin's abstraction of sovereignty, and rammed down the throats of the faithful of Luçon as a theological proposition. It was not, however, the notion of James I of England, for his theory of divine right had its roots in nominalism, the essence of it being that the subject must obey the prince, no matter what the prince might order: the prince might burn in hell for it, but that was his affair. Richelieu's theory was that the subject must obey the king so long as the king's will conformed with the divine will, but that disobedience would be permissible when the king willed evil. It differed from the Jesuit theory as expounded by Bellarmine mainly in that it denied the proposition that the king who wills evil might be deposed. Again the author enjoyed a great success and the *Instruction* was translated into several languages and for over a century was read in part from the pulpit of every parish church in France at Sunday mass. Its influence in propagating the notion of monarchy during the age of Louis XIV is incalculable.

To compound Richelieu's sadness bad news reached the Marquis his brother. Henri's newly wedded wife had had to be left at Richelieu because she was pregnant, and she died in childbirth without seeing her husband again, leaving a son. The Marquis sought the Court's permission to return to Richelieu on compassionate grounds to care for the baby, but seven months elapsed before the Court replied and the baby was dead when Henri reached Richelieu. The bishop of Luçon was left with Pontcourlay in Avignon, his heart full at the thought that the heir was dead who might one day have inherited the name, the glory and the riches that he had hoped to acquire, and now believed he would never acquire. Ill, and perhaps fearing the end, he wrote his will, leaving his silver to the cathedral of Luçon and his library and 1,000 *livres* to the seminary.

Of all the letters that Richelieu had fired into space, one had hit the target and penetrated the heart of Père Joseph in Rome. The Capuchin was back in Paris, gliding about in high places, and he remembered Richelieu's plea to keep his interests in mind. For months Père Joseph saw no opportunity to aid his colleague, but then events began to move into a conjunction favourable to his ends. Marie de Médicis had fled from Blois. It was an escape sufficiently dramatic in itself, but it had even more dramatic consequences, for now the Queen Mother of France was heading a new rebellion of the princes. This time it was the Duc d'Épernon who rose. He was governor of Angoumois and also of Metz. One of the Queen Mother's Italians, Ruccellai, was the instigator of the plot to put her at the head of an opposition party which would overthrow Luynes, and he turned naturally to the sixty-five-year-old favourite of Henri III who had his grudges against the new favourite. Leaving Metz in February 1619, d'Épernon reached his capital at Angoulême, and raising a band of cavaliers advanced to the château of Loches, not far from Blois. One of his valets entered the town of Blois in the middle of the night, mounted to the château, placed a ladder alongside the wall facing the street and climbed to the rampart. Here he placed a second ladder leading to Marie's chamber, the window of which was one hundred and twenty feet from the ground.

For a lady of her dimension and age it was quite an undertaking to heave herself through the window and descend the ladder to the rampart. Here she lost her nerve and refused to put a foot on the second ladder. So a slide was made, and she was launched to the ground on a cloak attached to cords. Supported by two conspirators she walked through the town to the bridge over the Loire. On the way they passed a group of soldiers who took her for a woman of easy virtue. She said, referring to her escort ironically, 'they take me for a good lady'. And with laughter all around she passed on to a rendezvous with Ruccellai. Near Loches she met d'Épernon with one hundred and fifty cavaliers and his son La Valette, the archbishop of Toulouse.

The news reached Louis XIII at St Germain and threw the Court into a panic. Now, it seemed, there could be a gigantic coalition of Bouillon, Condé, Guise, Lesdiguières and d'Épernon. Without examining the contradiction involved in the two notions, the council expected the Huguenots to rise and the Spaniards to come to the Queen Mother's aid. Louis' first instinct was to don his armour and go forth to combat, but such an intemperate action might provoke the magnates to flock together for mutual protection. Better, Luynes argued, to try by more subtle methods to detach Marie de Médicis, who was now sheltering under d'Épernon's government at Angoulême. And, who, Père Joseph hinted to Père Bérulle as he hovered at the fringe of the debate, was more likely to counsel wisdom and prudence than the bishop of Luçon? Getting rid of him had been the worst of all possible errors. Père Bérulle was in the counsels of Luynes, but he did not directly propose Richelieu's name. Rather, he suggested that Richelieu's dean of the chapter at Luçon, Sebastian Bouthillier, would be a sound and conciliatory man to have attached to Marie de Médicis, and the dean, when summoned and asked to undertake the task, requested also that his bishop be associated with him. Luynes wavered, and Bérulle and Père Joseph threw all their weight into persuading him that the hints that he had received from Marie de Médicis' entourage, and particularly from Ruccellai, to the effect that Richelieu had fomented disobedience were in fact poison designed to eliminate the bishop's moderate influence with the Queen Mother, and thrust that inconstant creature into the hands of more sinister schemers.

While Richelieu was in a state of emotional exhaustion a cavalier clattered over the bridge at Avignon. It was Père Joseph's brother, Charles du Tremblay, and he bore a royal command that Richelieu should forthwith resume his duty with the Queen Mother at Angoulême. It was March 1619, the Auvergne was still under snow and the journey was appalling. One year after Richelieu had left Luçon for exile, and on Wednesday in Holy Week, he reached Angoulême. First he called on d'Épernon, who received him politely and took him to Marie de Médicis. He told her that he had no intention of meddling in affairs already begun, and this attitude, so contrary to what was expected, nonplussed d'Épernon's cabal. It was too dangerous, they decided, to have him around and not know what he was up to. Would he not join the Queen Mother's council and give his advice? When asked his opinion he merely said that he would not have given the advice that others had given, because the means to oppose the King were lacking. At this Ruccellai walked out of the council and d'Épernon, who was weary of the cunning Italian, assisted his exit with a shove.

It was obvious to Richelieu that he was dealing with amateur conspirators, and when he added his arguments to those of Bérulle, who was in Angoulême to negotiate with the Queen on the King's behalf, it was not difficult to bring the lady to an accommodation. On 4 May 1619 she accepted the King's conditions, announced peace and had all the bells in Angoulême ring the *Te Deum*. The terms of settlement were in her favour, and owed much to Richelieu's adroit negotiation on her behalf, which, while it wheedled her away from the cabal, yet gained for her the appearance of having won a substantial concession from the King. Richelieu had insisted that Marie de Médicis have her own place of security and refuge so that she would not be an easy victim of those who made use of her restlessness. She was granted the governorship of Anjou and the town of Angers. Richelieu would have preferred Nantes, as a more secure place with access to the sea, and he spun the negotiations out interminably to this end.[10] He failed, but had good reason to be satisfied with what he had achieved. He had become a necessary man, and many saw his star again in the ascendant. Even the soured old first minister of Henri IV, the Duc de Sully, hovering always jealously in the background of public affairs, thought it would be splendid if a marriage were to be arranged between his family and the Plessis de Richelieus.

Richelieu was now in a position to control the government of Anjou through the Queen Mother. Uncle Amador de La Porte was made governor of Angers, and Richelieu's other brother-in-law, the Marquis de Brézé, Nicole's husband, was made captain of the guards, a position which was to lead him later to become captain of the royal guards, and eventually a marshal of France. Unhappily Henri de Richelieu was no longer available to become a recipient of Marie de Médicis' favours. Quarrelsome after the death of his wife and child, he clashed in the streets of Angers with the previous governor, the Marquis de Thémines. Blades flashed. Richelieu wounded his adversary, but the latter, having a short sword, came under Richelieu's guard and ran him through the chest. Richelieu had only time to gasp 'My God forgive me!' before he fell dead. Père Bérulle, who happened to be passing, gave him absolution. The hope of the House of Richelieu was now gone, and the bishop was in despair. His passionate efforts to suppress duelling henceforth derived, not only from a determination to uphold the law, but also from a knowledge of the pain that duelling could bring to innocent hearts. Nor did his worries cease when he became reconciled to his brother's death, for he had now to take over the property of Richelieu and try to do something about its encumbrances.

Once Marie de Médicis had been gratified with a province sufficiently removed from the court to ensure her independence, and also prevent her from meddling in the government, it became desirable that she should be publicly reconciled with her son. The meeting took place at the château of Couzières near Tours. Both shed tears, but neither knew what to say, and they separated feeling as cold towards each other as they had ever been. When Luynes released Condé from the Bastille and issued a statement concerning his imprisonment which read very much like an indictment of the whole Regency, she lent her authority to yet another rebellion. Richelieu would have us believe that he did his utmost to counsel prudence, and yielded only to the tempest in order to retain his good influence over the Queen Mother,[11] but he may have yielded more readily than he admitted, for he was exasperated by Luynes' deception of him in the matter of a cardinal's hat. He thought that, after his recent services, and considering his responsible position with the Queen Mother, this was his due. Luynes was for ever agreeing with him that indeed it was, and promising that something would be done about it. In fact he was able to prove his sincerity by producing evidence that the King had asked for the hat from the Pope. What he did not disclose was that the letter to Rome was accompanied by a strong hint that Luçon was not the man for it, a hint reinforced by a letter from the papal nuncio, Corsini, who had been thoroughly poisoned against Richelieu. The hat went instead to La Valette, the archbishop of Toulouse, the son of d'Épernon, and one of the recent rebels.

The court of the Queen Mother at Angers grew daily in numbers and brilliance. The buxom lady was in high spirits, enjoying the flattery and revelling in her morbid contemplation of the evil Luynes. The latter, who was no more of a politician than Ancre, did not realize that by releasing Condé at this moment he would stampede into Marie de Médicis' camp the other princes who were jealous of Condé's seniority, and wont to express doubt concerning his ancestry. The Duc de Maine suddenly left Paris for his province of Guyenne, and this was taken as an indication of a rupture. A dangerous situation was brewing at Angers, and Luynes became alarmed. Continuing to hold out to Richelieu the bait of the hat, he tried to convince him that the Queen Mother should come to Paris, where, of course, she would be under more strict supervision. It was a difficult issue for Richelieu. Quite apart from his interest in the hat, he had to avoid the appearance of provoking disobedience and treason. At the same time he could not counsel Marie de Médicis to abandon her independence. The fencing went on, while both in Paris and in Anjou tedious and sordid intrigues caused the tension slowly to mount until it seemed it would become unbearable. Eventually Luynes lost control of himself and resorted to direct assault. By letter he accused Richelieu of deliberately keeping the Queen Mother away from the King, saying that the latter was convinced of his mother's good intentions, and concluding with the ominous comment, 'We have until now believed of you what one ought to believe of an honourable man.'[12] Each finished up by regarding the other as the world's worst deceiver.

All the magnates had bands of armed men who were available to apply a little pressure here and there to reinforce political manoeuvres, and it was difficult to say when armed action ceased to be legitimate politics and became war. Either Marie de Médicis or Louis could take the decision to cross this nebulous Rubicon.

Gradually the accretion of military force turned the western part of France into a mobilization area in the form of a great crescent with one horn at Rouen and the other at Poitiers, with a string of fortified towns and castles lying in between in the hands of Marie de Médicis' supporters. This crescent was balanced in eastern France by a similar one stretching between Metz, where d'Épernon's son was for the Queen Mother, to Liège where Barbin was busy recruiting mercenaries. The German Protestant princes were being drawn into the intrigue, and more significantly, the emissaries of the King of Spain were active. Richelieu, as their confidant, was given an insight into Spanish policy that determined his convictions concerning that country's designs.

Luynes, irresolute as ever, did not know what to do. When another batch of near-royal relatives suddenly disappeared from Paris and made for the Queen Mother he did not dare to stop them. The contagion was spreading and Luynes had no policy. At a council meeting on 4 July 1620 Condé was all for war. Luynes still hesitated. The council looked from one to the other in uncertainty. Suddenly the King, who had never spoken his mind publicly before, electrified the meeting by saying: 'In face of so many dangers we must march against the greatest and the nearest; and that is Normandy! Let us go!' [13] Not a dissenting voice was raised; Louis was beginning to demonstrate that tough fibre in his being which hunting and melancholy had hitherto disguised.

The outcome was ludicrous. When the conspirators in Rouen found they were being confronted with the King in person and would have to yield or commit overt treason they lost heart and fled: Rouen fell to Louis and one hundred cavaliers. At Caen much the same happened. Having suppressed sedition in Normandy the King turned without drawing breath to Anjou. Within a month he had 12,000 infantry and 1,200 cavalry at La Flèche. At nearby Angers the vast collection of nobility was in a state of great excitement. Everyone counselled the Queen Mother to do something different; everyone gave orders that no one else obeyed. According to a pamphlet published just after the event Richelieu, when he could still all this flutter, addressed the assembled multitude. He asked Marie de Médicis' pardon for what he was about to say, and then said that arms would never triumph against a King who had the angels of God to guard him. 'There will not be one of your faithful subjects who will advise you to revolt against your son or support the views of the discontented. The complaints they can present to you are of little weight.' [14]

Delivered or not, this speech was of little avail. The disorder increased until it became indescribable, and Richelieu retired into a cold and withdrawn silence while a few miles away the King won the absurd little battle of Ponts-de-Cé against the Queen Mother's forces in a stifling heat-wave. As the noise of the cannon shots reverberated through the haze of the Loire Valley Marie de Médicis was wringing her hands in anguish, whimpering and refusing even to follow Richelieu's admonition that she should flee to Angoulême if she did not want to be at Luynes' mercy in the peace negotiations that would inevitably occur in a matter of hours. When they opened, with Richelieu and Cardinal de Sourdis representing the Queen Mother, Luynes demonstrated an unexpected eagerness for a settlement. So the *status quo* was restored, everyone was forgiven, and Marie de Médicis was merely required to promise that she would henceforth live in good relations with the Court and with Luynes. The King, delighted at discovering his aptitude for war, was willing to have a second reconciliation with his mother, and again there were tears. And at the meeting of the royal pair it was observed that Richelieu was smiling to himself. Luynes had proposed his own personal settlement with the bishop; his nephew, the Sieur de Combalet, would marry Richelieu's niece, Marie-Madeleine, the daughter of Pontcourlay, and the King would renew his petition for the cardinal's hat for Richelieu.

5

To Bend the Gods

1619-24

In the turbulence of the Queen Mother's two rebellions the great territorial magnates had demonstrated the fragmented nature of France and the ineffectiveness of the royal power. Not only were the princes and dukes powerful as the owners of lands and castles; they were, as provincial governors, almost petty kings, who could whenever they wished close their borders to the royal authority, and in the king's name utilize the national resources for their own acquisitive ends. But there was a deeper cleavage still in France, that of religion. The Huguenots constituted not merely a dissenting faith; they were, as Richelieu himself put it, a state within the state.[1] It was no epigram. In enclaves throughout the southern half of France they exerted an authority and independence which no other state in Europe tolerated, and the divisive consequences of which were a perpetual threat to the national survival. At Milhaud in 1573 they had set up their own political organization, with a States General of the Cause meeting every three months, a commander who carried the title Protector of the Churches and in the king's name appropriated the royal revenues, and an administration distinct from that of the Crown and duplicating the Crown's functions. Every officer took a solemn oath to remain a brother of his colleagues and a servant in the house of the Lord. It was freemasonry carried into politics.

The Edict of Nantes which ended the Wars of Religion in 1598 was a treaty designed less to settle discords than to give this group a privileged position. It had ninety-five public articles, fifty-six secret articles, and twenty-three additional secret articles. The public articles guaranteed liberty of conscience and practice of religion under precise conditions, and regulated cemeteries, wills, the constitution of the Protestant churches, and the payment of their clergy. The secret articles, which were extorted from Henri IV, granted the Protestants the right for eight years to retain all the fortified towns and castles which were occupied by them at that date, and the King undertook to pay 180,000 crowns for their garrisons. This left the Huguenots in possession of one hundred and fifty strongholds scattered over half of France, each of which was in a position to defy the royal authority. In 1608 the Venetian ambassador calculated that there were 3,500 Protestant nobles who could raise 25,000 troops although not two hundred of them would suffer martyrdom for their faith. Altogether there were about one million Huguenots in the realm – or about one in fifteen of the population – and they worshipped in seven hundred churches.

The patrimonial land of Henri de Navarre, the Pyrenean province of Béarn, was destined to provoke trouble because the local leaders refused to apply in reverse to the Catholics the benefits of the Edict of Nantes. The country's recent history was ambiguous. In 1512 Ferdinand, the Catholic King of Aragon, wrenched away the four-fifths of Navarre that lie south of the Pyrenees, leaving a rump on the northern side of the range which was violently anti-Spanish and, as a result, violently pro-French. The ruler of this seething relic was Henri d'Albret who married Marguerite d'Angoulême, the sister of François I. Their daughter, Jeanne d'Albret, a fiery neophyte of Calvin, married a distant sprig of the French royal house, Antoine de Bourbon, and became the mother of Henri de Navarre. Because Navarre was an independent state there was nothing to restrain the assault that took place on the Catholic Church. Catholicism was banned and all Church property was seized, and, as in England, appropriated by the gentry.

When the crowns of France and Navarre were united in the person of Henri IV the anti-Catholic laws remained in force in the province, now known as Béarn. Henri's conversion to Catholicism had won for him a relatively easy accession to the throne of France, but the price he had to pay for the papal absolution was a solemn and conditional promise to restore the property of the Church in his ancestral lands, or grant the Church the equivalent out of Crown property. It was a promise easily given but very difficult to keep, and Henri postponed the grasping of the nettle for the remainder of his life. The nearest he came to relieving his conscience was the appointment of two bishops for the province, who, however, did not leave the Court and made nuisances of themselves by pestering the King for a full execution of his undertaking. The issue provoked a lively and interminable legal debate. Was Béarn now part of France, and hence subject to French laws, including the Edict of Nantes; or was it still an independent state associated with France by the accident that the same person happened to have inherited two crowns? In other words, had there occurred a succession of states, or was there merely a personal union of the two crowns? In favour of the latter interpretation was the consideration that the Salic law did not apply in Navarre, and that therefore a daughter could succeed to the throne of Navarre although not to that of France. It was possible, therefore, for the two crowns to devolve in the future on different heads.

The legal debate became passionate when the States General in 1614 claimed Béarn as French. Catholicism and French patriotism combined to subvert the cherished autonomy of the territory, and when in February 1617 it was rumoured that the resolution of the States General was to be given effect by royal proclamation the Estates of Béarn assembled and declared that the constitution of their kingdom was a fundamental law which no king of Navarre could touch without their consent. This was not an idle gesture, for Navarre had inherited from the Spaniards very definite notions on the subordinacy of the king to the fundamental law. An appeal by the Béarnais for solidarity resulted in a declaration by the Huguenot Assembly of La Rochelle the following month that the cause of Béarn was that of all Protestant France. Instead of frightening the royal council as was intended, however, this trumpeting only provoked the Catholic party to increase the pressure on the King to act. In June 1617 it was decreed that all ecclesiastical property in Béarn should be restored to the Church and that compensation to the dispossessed proprietors should be paid by the Crown.

The reaction was violent. A Protestant leader cried, 'If I cannot bend the gods, I shall raise the demons of hell!' [2] And that is what the Béarnais sought to do. A royal commission sent to Pau to execute the Decree of Restitution was chased out, and the Estates of Béarn howled defiance, and declared their willingness to fight Spain, the French Catholics, Austria and any other enemy of their faith. In May 1619 they managed to persuade the whole Huguenot Church to issue an ultimatum that the Decree of Restitution be annulled.

Père Joseph was hovering about the royal court in Touraine. Béarn, where Christ was held captive by the heretic, was to him a substitute for Jerusalem, and he saw in the pacification of the Queen Mother's rebels and the concentration of military forces in the west of France circumstances favourable to drawing the King into the province to meet the Huguenot challenge. Père Bérulle and Père Arnoux joined him in bringing pressure to bear on Louis who, elated after his victory at Ponts-de-Cé, was easily prodded into going south on a flag-showing visit to his other kingdom. At Pau he was watched by sullen crowds too stupefied by the speed of his progress and the vigour of his actions to do more than indicate their resentment. The Catholic clergy took possession of the church of St Martin, a Jesuit college was founded and the decree of restitution was executed. The King, having done all that he could by his presence, departed for Paris on 7 November 1619, leaving the Huguenots dangerously excited. In December La Rochelle resolved to support the Béarnais, and a Huguenot faction seized the town of Privas in the hills just west of the Rhône midway between Lyons and Avignon, and the governor of Languedoc failed to retake it. Everywhere the Huguenots were for breaking off negotiations with the Court and holding out against it. They began raising troops, issuing commissions and purchasing supplies. It was civil war, exactly the fate which the Habsburgs might have wished for France so that they could be sure of a free hand in the Netherlands and Germany.

Richelieu was following the events in the south with a passionate but critical interest. There was, he argued, a clear distinction between the disobedience of the dukes and the restlessness of the Huguenots. The day had gone when the former could play the kingmakers, for the power they exercised was not their own but the King's and most of them had not dared to use it in the face of the King himself. Rebellion and conspiracy was a political game, not to be played too seriously for fear the actors might be hurt, but a game hardly ever lost because it usually resulted in the rebels being bought off with offices and dignities. The Huguenots he believed to be loyal to the Crown, and anxiety, not the game of power, had provoked them to revolt. The civil war in France and that already raging since 1618 between the Catholics and Protestants in Germany had become limbs of the same cancer, and this could have only one result, to make France the victim of the 'unbridled ambition of the Spaniard, which, prompting him to aspire to the monarchy of Europe, drives him to encroach on the states of our neighbours. The conquests of the House of Austria effected at the expense of all the neighbours of France will finally give it the means of mastery.'[3] Peace with the Huguenots and not their destruction was essential if Habsburg armies were not once more to tramp the roads of France. 'The most powerful state in the world cannot boast of enjoying an assured repose unless it is in a position to protect itself at all times against a surprise attack.'[4]

The royal council and the vacillating Luynes were, however, dominated by Condé, whose zeal for Catholicism was not matched by political foresight, and they opted for war against the Huguenots. The royal army advanced on Saumur, which surrendered, and then on St Jean d'Angély, which was held by Rohan's brother Soubise. When this fell by siege the question arose whether La Rochelle, the seedbed of sedition, should be assaulted. It was decided to bypass it and march again for the south, where the Huguenot nobility, into whose hands much

Church property had passed during the Wars of Religion, had been frightened into open defiance. Redoubtable old soldiers had joined Rohan's swelling army, among them the long-bearded, sixty-two-year-old Duc de La Force and his six fighting sons, and the hot bloods of Languedoc were being made drunk with overheated denunciation of the Jesuit-dominated King from the Huguenot pulpits. La Force, with three of his ten children, a formidable collection of Protestant gentry and a bevy of pastors, locked himself in the fortified town of Montauban, and presented what contemporaries called a 'brazen front' to the King.

In high spirits Luynes laid siege to the place, but he was quickly to demonstrate that his grand title of Constable of France was no guarantee of military genius. The assaults were conducted with vast enthusiasm and display of gallantry, and many fine cavaliers, including one of the commanders, the Duc de Mayenne, died splendidly. But it was not war, and these amateurs were no match for the professionals within the walls. The King, who had had a lackey killed at his side, lost interest and hunted hares instead of Huguenots. The royal encampment seethed with intrigue against Luynes, whose rapid consolidation of the great offices of state in his own hands had in no way extended his popularity with a jealous nobility. Even the King's Jesuit chaplain, Arnoux, was involved in the intrigue, only to find himself promptly discharged. The days dragged on, and typhoid invaded the army. Sixteen thousand cannon balls had been fired at the walls of Montauban without appreciable result and the guns were running out of ammunition. Finally, as winter set in with interminable rain to make everyone miserable, Rohan managed to pass reinforcements in to the besieged, and there was nothing to do but abandon the enterprise. Luynes was beside himself, blaming all the world for his own failures. Then suddenly the typhoid took him too, and on 15 December 1621 he was dead.

The news reached Richelieu in a letter written the same day. There was now no obstacle to a real reconciliation between Marie de Médicis and Louis, and a reassertion of the Queen Mother's influence in governmental affairs would mean that Richelieu would be near the centre of events once more. Marie de Médicis wrote a consoling letter to the King, and dispatched one of her most trusted advisers, Michel de Marillac, to talk to him. Marillac was able to report that Louis had decided to act henceforth for himself in the affairs of state, and that he had every confidence in his mother's affection. Richelieu sought to have her reinstated as a member of the council, and, though the ministers would have none of this and pushed Condé into violently opposing the idea, the King yielded, and the Queen Mother again took her seat.

Her interests and those of Richelieu coincided, so that for the next three years she was to speak with his voice, and he was to exercise through her a growing influence upon events. Physically he was at this time a miserable figure. 'My headaches,' he wrote 'are killing me,'[5] and as usual when he found that human frailty could not be overcome by temporal means he turned to God, writing a note to himself which lay for three hundred years untouched:

If it pleases divine mercy, by the intercession of the blessed apostle and beloved St John, to restore my health and deliver me in eight days from the dreadful headache which torments me, I shall inaugurate a mass which will be celebrated every Sunday of the year, and to this end, I shall provide the chaplain with an annual revenue of thirty-six livres for the masses which will be celebrated in thanksgiving.[6]

This is only one of the pieces of evidence which have survived of Richelieu's personal faith and sense of dependence on prayer and intercession.

The spring was coming and some decision had to be taken about the Huguenot rebellion. Richelieu was very much opposed to a renewal of the attack, and at his instance Marie de Médicis argued against it in the council. Condé, however, was as pugnacious and as religiously zealous as ever, and the decision was taken to march once more into Languedoc. While another royal prince, the Comte de Soissons, blockaded La Rochelle the King moved on La Force, who was forced near Bergerac to come to terms. He then brought fire and sword to the domains of the old Duc de Sully, who had for years been brooding over his loss of

office, and St Antonin was taken after a violent struggle. Montauban was still defiant and in a better state of defence than ever, so it
was decided to bypass it and move along the Garonne to the
Mediterranean. Carcassonne, Narbonne and Béziers fell in quick
succession, and the siege was opened of Montpellier, the Huguenot citadel on the Mediterranean.

It so happened that the new Constable of France was the great
magnate of Dauphiné, the Duc de Lesdiguières. This eighty-year-
old athelete of the Huguenot cause had recently been converted to
Catholicism, but had not lost his influence with his former brethren. He undertook to negotiate a general settlement, and the way
to this was made easier by Condé's departure. Disgusted at the idea
of an accommodation with the rebels, the First Prince of the Blood
went off to console himself on a pilgrimage to Loretto. The
Peace of Montpellier, signed in October 1622, was intended to
stabilize the situation as it then existed. The Huguenots had lost
eighty, or about half, of their fortified places. They were now
promised that their surviving political and municipal independence would be respected by the Crown, and on this basis the
Huguenots of Provence yielded. In Montauban and a host of
towns in the southern massif, however, they maintained their
defiance, and where they yielded they did so sullenly and in no
spirit of reconciliation. The Peace of Montpellier was no more than
a truce.

On the way back from Montpellier the King met Richelieu
at Tarascon. The bishop had come personally to thank him for his
efforts in the matter of the cardinal's hat. It was traditional to
have four cardinals in France, and the death of Cardinal de Retz
at this juncture had left a vacancy. With Luynes not there to
object, it was difficult any longer to resist Richelieu's claims, and
in September 1622 he was advised that the hat was his. In due
course he received it, as was customary, from the King's hands in
the chapel of the archbishop of Paris. Richelieu, with the gesture
of a graduate from M. de Pluvinel's academy for gentlemen, laid
it at the feet of Marie de Médicis and said: 'Madame, the purple,
for which I am indebted to the goodness of Your Majesty, will
always be a reminder of the solemn vow I have taken to shed my

blood in your service.'[7] That evening the new cardinal gave a splendid reception which the Queen Mother and the princes attended. Still young at thirty-seven and with a long apprenticeship in politics behind him, he believed himself to possess the power to influence the course of events decisively, and, although intermittently sick, could expect to exercise it for many years. His first move was to give up his see at Luçon, which he would now be unable to administer, but he could not altogether give up its revenues. So, pursuant to his ownership of the benefice, he retained an annual pension of 5,000 *livres*. He also bought the fine château of Rueil, near Paris. His last official action at Luçon was to approve the acts of his cathedral chapter adopting 'the holy and sacred Council of Trent'.[8]

If Richelieu thought the cardinalate would bring him nearer to his ambition of regaining the royal council he was disappointed. Although the Keeper of the Seals, Sillery, fell as the result of an intrigue in which Marie de Médicis played an important role, the King would have nothing to do with Richelieu, who, he said, was a knave. Richelieu, however, bided his time. Through Marie de Médicis, who was no more than his mouthpiece, his opinion was always available to the council, and was seen to be ever more sound and persuasive. The chief of the council, the rich but mediocre Marquis de la Vieuville, recognizing his administrative ability and wanting to keep him out of the council where he could become a dangerous competitor, kept offering him jobs, first in the administration at home, then in the French embassies in Madrid and Rome, but Richelieu kept shrugging his shoulders and saying he wanted to lead a private life. He was not going to be bought off, and he was determined to remain with Marie de Médicis over whom his influence was paramount. She kept pressing for his inclusion in the council, and Vieuville, driven to the point of indiscretion by her importunities, is alleged to have said: 'Madame, you want something which will infallibly bring about my ruin. And I am not sure that Your Majesty will not one day repent at having advanced a man whom you do not yet really know.'[9] If he said it, she had good reason to remember the admonition. In fact Vieuville yielded, and it was he who asked the

King to appoint Richelieu in an 'advisory capacity'. This was not good enough, and Richelieu stood upon his dignity. He asked the King straight out how long he proposed to keep him in the shadow. Louis yielded, and on 29 April 1624 Richelieu took his seat.

Any association of human beings is fraught with struggles for power, but the struggle is worst where authority depends entirely upon persuasion, and persuasion upon the exertion of personality. The clever manipulator of committees prevails for a time but then becomes despised as devious and untrustworthy. To this extent the pursuit of power tends often to be self-cancelling, and power based upon only personality contains within itself the seeds of its own corruption. Richelieu knew this, for he was by now very well experienced in the ways of the world, and he brought no naïve notions of integrity and goodwill with him to the council table. He could, with his brains and determination, prevail for a time, but only for a time. The permanence of his power would depend on the King alone. In this respect the royal council was unlike modern governmental cabinets or conferences of heads of departments; it was not an oligarchy of equally ranking competitors, but an authoritarian institution. A strong king could override any dissent by a mere indication of his will; a king's minister, provided he had the king's absolute support, could always prevail. In this way, the royal council could become an instrument of dictatorship; and Richelieu, who despised the sordid personality struggles which consume so much of the intellectual and emotional energy that should be expended on the substantive tasks of government, and distrusted the compromise solutions that committees usually reach, was determined to transform it into one.

His first move in the campaign was made the day after he took his seat. It was the move of the expert manipulator, depending for its effect on surprise, preparation and a careful assessment of the likely reaction. He laid on the table a long and minutely argued document in which he claimed, with the supporting apparatus of an elaborate citation of precedent, the privileges due in the council to a cardinal.[10] The effect was as expected. Vieuville, recognizing the mounting pressure, began lobbying, but he did it maladroitly, and only managed to anger the King who was weary of the personality conflicts in the council.

Louis XIII was now twenty-two, a tortured young man who had already contracted the tuberculosis that was to kill him, and whose neurasthenic condition made him his own executioner. A paradox to his contemporaries, he has baffled the historians. Capable of great kindness, he was none the less driven by a fiendish jealousy to suspect the motives of everyone; a passionate moralist, his acid soul corroded those who shared his life; an athlete who loved the chase and was never so happy as when acting the common soldier in the trenches, he was none the less the chronic hypochondriac who in one year was bled forty-seven times, took two hundred and twelve medicines and two hundred and fifteen purges; a man of simple tastes who was devoted to candy-making and blacksmithing, he was a vindictive nomad intent on diversion. Though brutal in his relationships with others, he was a sensitive musician who composed ably and danced in ballets for which he acted as choreographer. Obstinate, taciturn, smouldering with resentment of the charm, beauty and achievements of others, he was destined to destroy those to whom, in a clumsy and strangulated fashion, he gave the love that forced its way out of his disturbed heart. A withdrawn and thunderous majesty concealed his awkwardness of spirit; an implacable enforcement of the law substituted in his mind for justice; pride, effacement, timidity, anguish, superstition, secretiveness, a terrible fear of God, a mystic concept of kingship and an acute sense of his own human inferiority made this rigorist, this despot, an incomprehensible contradiction. But two qualities he possessed which he was to pass on to his son, and which were to be the salvation of France – an acute sense of the royal destiny, and an ability to recognize those with the talent to govern. Incapable himself of the application necessary to direct affairs, he looked for persons who could act on his behalf without ever causing him to feel that his royal will was in question or his royal functions alienated.

It was the particular merit of Louis that he did not allow his personal and intense dislike of the cardinal, whose sense of irony and intolerable air of superiority infuriated him as they did so many others, to obscure his recognition of the fact that he, and he alone, was the man for whom he was looking. For eighteen years they were to work closely together in a relationship that at times each was to find personally highly uncomfortable, and only one thing made it possible, and that was Richelieu's extraordinary tact, subtlety, quickness of wit and adroitness of expression. Time and again Louis was to turn on Richelieu, as he turned on everyone, and give vent to his petulance; time and again Richelieu was to save the situation by brilliant and sophisticated improvisation. On one occasion, Louis scowled at him: 'You go first, since you are the real King.' 'Then, Sire,' replied Richelieu, all charm, 'only to light the way!' And seizing a torch he adopted the role of a lackey. The royal dignity was accommodated, the government of France went on.

It was ten years since the States General had met. The memorials of the three estates had been filed away and no one gave them a moment's thought; the financial situation was as bad as ever; pensions, bribes and privileges continued to mount. In 1623 there were revolts of the populace, arising out of protests against taxation, in Rouen, Marseilles and Poitiers, followed in 1624 by others in Niort, Lyons, Figeac and Cahors. The government in 1624 was as inefficient as in the worst days of the Regency. The important thing was that the King recognized this to be the case. He called Richelieu before him and asked him what should be done about the council. Richelieu displayed no intemperate haste to see his opponents dismissed. He dissembled. It would not be wise, he advised, to make another change of ministers at this moment. The King pressed him, and with every indication of reluctance Richelieu yielded, nominating four of Marie de Médicis' following, Schomberg, Marillac, Champigny and Molé, who were known to be able and respected. The King agreed. Richelieu, encouraged, went on to deliver a quietly reasoned analysis of what was wrong with France and what remedies were required.[11] From that moment he was the King's man.

Poor Vieuville knew he had been outwitted, and confessed to the King that he was well aware that the Crown no longer wanted his services. Louis did not reply. Vieuville then asked for leave to present himself to Louis the next morning at St Germain. When he entered the King told him he was dismissed, and would be conducted with an escort to Amboise. The council was summoned, and the King called on Richelieu to speak. The Cardinal delivered himself of a carefully prepared and documented governmental programme:[12] it examined the situation within France, and the foreign policy of France; it exposed the fallacies, defects and inadequacies in the theories and policies hitherto pursued; it contained the proposition that 'the King should act in such a way that everyone would know that the King himself conducts his own affairs'. Louis was impressed. He replied briefly, freely acknowledging the errors of the Luynes administration. Henceforth he wished the affairs of state to be conducted efficiently, and he asked the Cardinal de Richelieu to undertake the task. It was 13 August 1624, and Richelieu was to conduct the affairs of France for the next eighteen years with an efficiency quite unexampled. For the time being he had only the title of Secretary of State for Commerce and Marine, and the position of chief of the council; it was with the former portfolio that he began his reform of the realm. Four years later he persuaded the King that a new post was needed, that of First Minister, and this title he assumed while retaining his old portfolio.

There were three questions before the council which called for immediate and vigorous action; the first was the Valtelline affair, the second the English marriage, and the third the implementation of the proposals for administrative reform made at the meeting of the States General in 1614. Richelieu had already made up his mind what course should be pursued with respect to each of them.

6

He Uses Pious Persons
1625-6

The Valtelline is the defile which carries the river Adda from its source near the Stelvio to the eastern shores of Lake Como. Between mountains of seven thousand to eleven thousand feet it runs, never more than three miles wide, some sixty miles due east to the Tonale, one of Europe's loveliest and least known passes. Some two-thirds of the way up, a side road over the passage of the Bernina climbs steeply through a remote landscape of silver rock and dark larch to reach the Engadine uplands at St Moritz, and another through Bormio crosses the nine thousand foot Stelvio and the lower Resia to the Tyrol. From the Tonale the direct road continues through splendid scenery until it tumbles over a vast escarpment in front of the city of Bolzano. There it joins the road over the Brenner. The busy and densely populated western end of the Valtelline, where the trapped sun is kind to the vineyards that scale the sharp slopes to the faded yellow campanili of mountain churches, is completely Italian; on the other side of the Tonale lie the German lands; and beyond the Bernina, where the Etruscans, and even the Saracen mercenaries of Frederick II, have left their influence upon village nomenclature, is the curious race of the Swiss Grisons who speak Romansh. The Valtelline has been destined by geography to be both a passage, and a cultural and linguistic watershed.

In the early seventeenth century the Valtelline politically included the eastern shore of Lake Como, the town of Chiavenna at the head of the lake, and the short plain at the foot of the Splügen and Maloja passes; its authorities thus controlled the traffic over the five passes which constituted the most direct, and almost the only strategically acceptable, link between the Habsburgs of Spain and the Habsburgs of Austria. From Genoa, which was a Spanish ally, troops, supplies and money could reach Austria from Spain only through the Milanais, which thus became the cockpit of Europe, the centre of all political gravity. From Milan, which was a Spanish vice-royalty, access to Austria was geographically possible along the shores of Lake Garda, but since this involved crossing the territories of Venice, which was perpetually hostile, it was an axiom of Spanish policy to keep the Valtelline proper open at any cost, so as to link the Milanais and the Tyrol. It was equally axiomatic that the route from Chiavenna over the Splügen and down the fantastic gorge on its northern side be kept open, for this was the most convenient land-route by which communications could be maintained with the Spanish Netherlands. In the event of the Dutch or the English closing the Channel to Spanish shipping passing to and from Antwerp, Gravelines or Dunkirk, dispatches, gold and reinforcements could reach Belgium only by the Rhine; and the most direct access to the Rhine was over the Splügen to Chur, down the valley of the Upper Rhine to Lake Constance, along the northern bank of the lake and so through Schaffhausen to Basle, or through the southern Black Forest to Breisach. Should the people of the Grisons close the Chur route, the alternative access would be over either the Tonale or the Stelvio and the Resia to the Habsburg hereditary lands, thence down the Arlberg to the Rhine.

When a nation decides that an interest is vital, then that interest ceases to be negotiable: the Valtelline to the Spaniards was not negotiable. It so happened, however, that the Valtelline was equally non-negotiable to the Swiss mountaineers in the Grisons, whose whole economy depended on their access to the riches of Italy through the Bernina and the Maloja valleys. The Valtelline had belonged to Milan before the Duchy fell to Spain. In 1513

Maximilian Sforza had ceded suzerainty over it to the Grisons, and it had thereupon, at the very moment in history when its strategic importance became paramount, fallen into an ambiguous juridical situation. It was still Milanais; it was at the same time a vassal of the Swiss canton. The Spanish sovereigns and the Swiss suzerains each claimed concurrent and incompatible rights. This was sufficient reason for trouble, but the difficulty was compounded by the fact that, while the Valtelline remained Catholic, the Grisons became Protestant. It was a Protestantism of an expanding and proselytizing kind, only too apt to provoke bitter resentment from the Italian valley-dwellers, who despised their uncouth mountaineer overlords.

Nor did the complication end there. Venice, for ever agitated at the spectre of Spanish hegemony in Italy, for ever fearful that Spanish enterprise in the Mediterranean would sever the commercial links between the island city and the Middle East, had struggled for a half a century to prevent the valley from falling into Spanish hands, and had connived at every assertion of supremacy by the Grisons. Should Venice find herself in trouble with Spain, it was through the Valtelline alone that aid could come – from France, from Holland or from the Protestant princes in Germany. As for France, the Grisons was a traditional recruiting ground for mercenary soldiers, and in return for a guarantee of protection the Grisons had given Henri IV a monopoly in this respect. France, then, also had an interest in this strange corner of the Alpine complex, and the real nature of this had been obscured and moralized by the invention of the concept of Swiss neutrality.

In 1602 the Spanish governor of the Milanese, Don Pedro Henriquez d'Azevedo, Duque de Fuentes, constructed a fort on Lake Como, called after himself, which blocked, or was capable of blocking, all access to any of the passes into the Grisons. It was the imprudence of Venice that caused the Spaniards to employ this obstruction offensively against the Swiss. For thirty miles the Venetian frontier ran along the mountain ridges on the southern side of the Valtelline. It was only a matter of a few miles across to the northern side, and in 1616, when, as they believed, they had been deserted by France following Lesdiguières' foray into Italy, the Venetians resolved to secure these few miles and make themselves independent of French whims. To this end they formed an alliance with their neighbours of the Grisons, the effect of which was to give them equal rights of passage through the Valtelline with either the Spaniards or the French.

If the alleged French monopoly in the area, created by treaty between Henri IV and the Grisons, could be so cavalierly waived, there was no reason why Spain should bother to respect it. The fort of Fuentes was used to cut all communication between the Grisons and Italy, and in 1617, when the people of the Grisons were threatened with not merely economic strangulation but even downright starvation, they were forced to sign a treaty which guaranteed Spain the right of passage over the passes to the Tyrol and the Upper Rhine, and also the right to recruit in the area – a right already pre-empted by France. The mountaineers had to ratify the treaty in democratic assembly, but they refused to do so, resolving instead, in an indiscreet excess of passion, to carry the fight into the enemy camp by a missionary campaign in the Valtelline. At Sondrio they opened a Protestant church, and that produced an explosion. Armed by the new Spanish governor of Milan, Don Gomez de Figueroa y Cordova, Duque de Figueroa, or Feria as the French called him, and as he is known to history, a band of Italian refugees from the Valtelline swept through the valley from end to end on 19 July 1620, murdering the Protestants to the number of four hundred. Down the steep, sunless cleft of the Bernina poured the Swiss heavily reinforced from Bern and Zürich. As they reached the valley floor at Tirano the Spaniards entered from the Como end to support their Catholic brethren. The wild men of the Grisons and their allies were thoroughly thrashed, and scattered up the mountainside. By October Spain was mistress of the whole valley and forts were being erected at Morbegnio, Sondrio, Nova and Riva.

The Valtelline dispute had meanwhile become merely an aspect of the great upheaval north of the Alps, which, as had been expected, accompanied the death of the Emperor Matthias. Before his departure from this world Matthias had sought to obtain the election of Ferdinand of Habsburg, Count of Styria, as

King of the Romans, which would guarantee his accession to the throne of the Holy Roman Empire. This long, serious man was a true product of the Counter-Reformation, one of the first generation of princes educated by the Jesuits, and no one expected that he would compromise on the religious issues, particularly the issue of the ecclesiastical domains in Germany, which the Peace of Augsburg in 1555 had left ambiguous. Of the seven electors, three were Catholic, the archbishops of Cologne, Mainz and Trier, and three were Protestant, Frederick V the Count Palatine of the Rhine, John George, the Duke of Saxony; and George William the Margrave of Brandenburg. The balance was held by the seventh, the King of Bohemia, who was none other than the candidate Ferdinand himself, as heir to Matthias. The Bohemian Protestants refused to recognize Ferdinand's succession, and on 23 May 1618 they bundled Ferdinand's agents out of a window of the Hradčany and offered the throne of Bohemia to the Count Palatine of the Rhine.

This added a European dimension to the problem, for Frederick's father-in-law was James I of England and his uncle and guardian was Henri de la Tour d'Auvergne, Comte de Turenne and Duc de Bouillon, the same Bouillon who was the acknowledged leader of the Huguenots in France. Bouillon was a convert to Protestantism. He had acquired the virtually independent principality of Sedan by legacy from his first wife, the heiress of the House of Bouillon, and then had married Elizabeth of Nassau, the daughter of William of Orange. He was thus the pivot, geographically well placed, on which the whole Protestant movement in Europe turned, and the link whereby events in Prague had their ramifications in Amsterdam and La Rochelle. His influence over Frederick was considerable, and through him he sought to extend it to the affairs of the Empire. Abetted by Frederick's ambitious wife Elizabeth of England, Bouillon and his relative Maurice of Nassau pushed the Count Palatine into accepting the Bohemian crown. The Bohemians under a great soldier, Mansfeld, made common cause with Bethlen Gabor, the Prince of Transylvania, and Protestant troops were thudding on the gates of Vienna when in August 1618 the election was held at

Frankfurt. The three Protestant electors had as their candidate Maximilian the Duke of Bavaria, who, as an ardent Catholic, might, they hoped, attract one of the ecclesiastical votes. Maximilian was head of the German Catholic League, a man of action, simple and pious. Brother-in-law of Ferdinand, he was also one of the first Jesuit products; and from their headquarters at St Michael's in the Neuhauserstrasse in Munich the Jesuits kept close watch on the Duke in the Residenz close by. Maximilian stepped down in favour of Ferdinand, who, voting for himself as King of Bohemia, was assured of the imperial crown. The Thirty Years War had begun.

His own territories overrun, Ferdinand turned to Maximilian for help. This spendid warrior, in return for an oral promise that Bavaria should be given the electoral vote of the Palatinate, undertook to throw the armies of the Catholic League into the struggle in Bohemia. At the same time a great diplomatic movement was initiated to draw into the quarrel the Spaniards, the Danes, the Poles and the French. At the end of 1619, just when the Valtelline difficulty was becoming acute, Count Wratislas Fürstenberg arrived in Paris to secure the support of Louis XIII for the Emperor. He based his appeal on the principle of legitimacy and the need for Catholic solidarity. Whoever defends rebels or lends ears to strangers who calumniate their prince, he argued, opens the door to internal sedition. It was an argument well calculated to impress Louis who was in the midst of his own internal struggles.

In his turn Bouillon raised the Habsburg bogy. Writing to Louis he argued that the House of Austria merely wanted to turn into a doctrinal issue what was really a fundamental conflict of political interests. Louis' ancestors back to François I had recognized that the interests of the Bourbons and the Habsburgs were incompatible; Austria invoked principles only when it lacked might; when it was mighty, principles counted for nothing. Finally, he protested, what an impertinence to identify the cause of Catholicism with the ambitions of Austria! Austria is the mortal enemy. However, Bouillon was too clever to suggest that Louis should reject outright the Fürstenberg overtures, for to present the King with a dilemma might bring him firmly down on the Catholic side. Rather should Louis seek to arbitrate the German dispute and thereby gain glory for France. It was Richelieu's policy with respect to the north Italian dispute, and although it had no chance of succeeding it at least had the merit of postponing commitment.

Luynes was at this time a worried man, for the Angoulême settlement with Marie de Médicis was breaking down, everywhere his enemies were working for his downfall, and he was dismayed at his expanding responsibilities. Two years previously the papal nuncio had handed him evidence, supplied by the Elector of Cologne, of Bouillon's intrigues in Germany and of his intention to involve France in the struggle against the Habsburgs, so that he was not unaware of Bouillon's motives in writing the letter. But to throw himself on the side of the Habsburgs was to abandon France's traditional allies in the Grisons and Venice. Luynes vacillated and sought to compromise between the cause of Catholicism and that of French independence – and promoted neither. The Duc d'Angoulême, a natural son of Charles IX, was sent as ambassador to Ferdinand to assure him that Louis would not recognize Frederick as the King of Bohemia, but also to try to mediate. It so happened that the princes of the Protestant Union were meeting at Ulm to decide on action to succour their brethren in Bohemia, and there d'Angoulême betook himself, arriving in June 1620. He talked both the Protestant and Catholic leaders into agreeing on an armistice: Ferdinand and Frederick should be left to fight out their quarrel; the rest of the Empire would remain neutral. In some haste this agreement was committed to paper.

It seemed to be a great diplomatic success for France: Ferdinand with his hands free would certainly destroy Frederick, and France could claim to have saved him and the Catholic cause. At the same time France could represent herself as the guarantor of the integrity of the other Protestant states of Germany, and the preserver of peace. There was a fatal flaw in this reasoning, reflected in the document. The parties to the Treaty of Ulm had merely undertaken not to fight each other; they had not undertaken to withhold assistance from either Ferdinand or Frederick.

It was therefore with astonishment and dismay that the French observed Maximilian, having secured his front door on the Danube, march out of his back door into the Bohemian Forest to deal a blow at Frederick. At the same moment Spinola, the Spanish general in Belgium, invaded Frederick's ancestral lands in the Palatinate with 25,000 troops. The effect of the French diplomatic foray at Ulm had been to disarm the Protestants at the very moment that their enemies were about to strike. The only thing to do was to try to disarm the imperialists as well, but no one would listen. Only Madrid, so the French envoys reported, had the ears of Vienna, and not once did they manage even to have a private audience with the Emperor. The French had been outwitted. In November 1620, four months later, Frederick's army was destroyed at the White Mountain outside Prague. Now the great empire of Charles v was on the point of being reconstituted; the Spaniards were on the Rhine and shadowing Alsace; the Austrians were supreme in Germany; and France, disintegrating once again into the chaos of the Wars of Religion, was at their mercy.

It was at this point that the Grisons invoked their treaty with France. The pressure to help them mounted as French public opinion reacted to the spectacle of Spain once more on the march in the lands of France's neighbours. But Luynes, faced with the alternatives of crushing the Huguenots or of risking war with Spain by a relief expedition to the Valtelline – for the Crown could undertake only one of the operations – continued to hesitate at the very moment when an energetic policy was demanded by events. Before opting he sent Marshal Bassompierre to Spain to seek reparation for the violation of French rights. To everyone's surprise Madrid proved reasonable, and on 25 April 1621 a treaty was signed which restored these rights, but at the same time guaranteed the position of the Catholics in the Valtelline. The Grisons, ever exasperating to their friends as well as to their enemies, once more refused ratification, while both the people of the Valtelline and the Pope raised an outcry at Catholics being placed once more under Protestant jurisdiction. The Grisons again took up arms, but they were crushed by a pincer movement of Feria, who marched from Chiavenna into the Upper Engadine, and the Archduke Leopold who marched from Landeck in the Tyrol into the Lower Engadine. Totally overwhelmed, the Grisons had to renounce their suzerainty over the Valtelline, once more open the passes to Spain, admit the free exercise of Catholicism in their valleys, and cede the Lower Engadine to Austria. At the very moment, then, when Luynes, thinking he had solved the Valtelline problem, began his march on the Huguenots, the whole question was once more opened up. Not until the peace of Montpellier in October 1622 could France again turn its attention to the Alpine passages. Within four months a treaty was negotiated between France, Venice and Savoy with the object of ousting the Spaniards from the Valtelline by force.

Spain, desperately anxious to avoid a confrontation with France at this moment when the Catholic cause in Germany was being successfully prosecuted, sought to forestall the French by proposing that the Valtelline be put into neutral hands, and when the Pope was suggested for the role the inept government that had taken over from Luynes' administration could think of no countermove other than to require that the Pope hold the Valtelline forts for three months only, and mediate a settlement on the basis of Bassompierre's treaty of Madrid. The troops of the Pope were the nearest thing in the seventeenth century to a United Nations force, but the prospect of a successful mediation which would enable them to be withdrawn quickly was no brighter in the Valtelline than in Kashmir or Cyprus in the twentieth century. In May 1623 the forts were handed over by the Spaniards to the papal troops, but it was not until November that the Pope formulated his proposals, which, since they did not refer to a Spanish right of passage through the Valtelline, were rejected by Madrid. When the Pope then incorporated this right the project was in turn rejected by Vieuville. By the time Richelieu took office an impasse had been reached, and Vieuville had already one month previously ordered the army of the Marquis du Coeuvres to mobilize on the Alpine frontier.

It is part of the poetry of history that the great actors in the drama of the Bourbon-Habsburg struggle were to make their appearance on the scene and to depart from it at very much the same time, so that the span of events in the twenty years that followed the papal occupation of the Valtelline forts appears to constitute some vast tapestry of personality conflicts. The Emperor Ferdinand II, Maximilian of Bavaria, and Philip IV of Spain more or less coincide with Louis XIII; Richelieu and his Spanish rival Olivares acceded to power and disappeared almost simultaneously; and in Rome there was a new Pope who was to survive them both and to dominate the diplomatic situation for most of the Thirty Years War. Maffeo Barberini was elected as Pope Urban VIII in 1623. He was then fifty-six, and the Venetian ambassador, reporting on the election, described him as a man of 'venerable aspect, tall, of olive complexion and noble characteristics, with black hair beginning to grey, an alert movement and lordly aspect. He speaks with gestures and with pleasing bodily motion.' He was interested in poetry, like most of his recent predecessors, and he united to 'a candour of intelligence a profound faith. In the affair of the Valtelline, which he has inherited from Pope Gregory,' the ambassador predicted, 'he will weigh with an entire equanimity the interests of France and those of Spain.'[1] Venetian ambassadors were ordinarily remarkably perceptive in their evaluations of character, but there can hardly have been many more accurate than this one.

Richelieu had watched with growing exasperation the vacillation of Vieuville, who could not make up his mind whether to accommodate the Pope and appear to be on the side of the angels, or to keep faith with France's Swiss protégés and betray the Church. He had let the papal garrisons into the forts; he had also appointed Coeuvres ambassador extraordinary to the Grisons with a commission to raise an army with a view to their expulsion. Coeuvres had, in fact, recruited nine thousand Swiss with the help of Zürich, and unless these were to be used France would be quite discredited in the eyes of its Swiss and Italian allies. Immediately upon taking Vieuville's place Richelieu sent Père Joseph to Spada, the papal nuncio, to discuss the feasibility of the French proposal that the Spaniards would only be denied the passage through the Valtelline for 'grave reasons'. Clearly the Spaniards would not be content with so vague an assurance, and it seems that the approach was a stratagem to distract attention from the military preparations for a seizure of the forts. The baffled nuncio wrote to Rome that:

... this Capuchin is certainly a clever negotiator, but his manner of negotiating is full of reticence and shifty moves. He never does anything without Richelieu, and even if their friendship is equal on both sides, their influence is not, the friar being subject more to the cardinal than the latter is to him.[2]

When Père Joseph reported that there was no possibility of the Pope's yielding in favour of the Grisons, Richelieu decided that there was no alternative but to present Urban and Spain with a *fait accompli*. In November Coeuvres was given orders to fall on the Valtelline, and within three months, and with the help of Venetian siege artillery, all of the forts, save those of Riva and Chiavenna, were in his hands. At the same time the aged Lesdi-guières crossed the Alps and lent his aid to Charles Emmanuel of Savoy, who as a diversion proceeded to besiege Genoa. The impression made on Europe by this decisive and energetic action was enormous, and it was obvious that in Richelieu a formidable statesman had emerged who would not be mesmerized by either the might or the virtue of Spain; nor even be awed, when French interests were at stake, by the moral authority of Rome.

The Holy See reacted to the capture of its garrisons with unusual promptitude, demanding immediate restoration of the forts of which it was stakeholder, and the punishment of Coeuvres; and Spada accused Richelieu of immorality. He brought pressures to bear on Père Joseph, who spent an hour with him deploring what had happened but found that the nuncio's terms for a settlement would involve a French betrayal of Venice, and were thus unacceptable. In the midst of the negotiations came news that the Huguenots had again risen. Rohan was in arms in the south, and his brother Soubise had seized the French fleet. The event could not have been less opportune, for Richelieu could no longer negotiate with Urban and with the Spaniards from a position of strength. He had to concentrate on Soubise's destruction, and had to seek the aid of Holland and England to this end. To protract the negotiations with the Pope until he had recovered his freedom of action became for him an object in itself, and the French ambassador in Rome, the Baron de Béthune, was instructed to propose as a basis of further discussions that the Pope should, with French consent, accord the Spaniards the right of passage when needed, provided that the Valtelline forts should be demolished. Then it was decided to take advantage of the visit of Père Joseph to Rome to attend the general chapter of the Capuchins. He was to create goodwill by the announcement that for two months military operations against the remaining forts would be suspended, and he was to reassure the Pope that in the overall struggle with Protestantism in Europe, France was on the side of the Church. When Père Joseph reached Bologna he found that matters had been taken out of his hands: the Holy See had decided on the extreme step of sending a papal legate to Paris, ostensibly to carry the dispensation for the marriage of Henriette Marie to the Prince of Wales, but in reality to overawe the French government in the matter of the Valtelline. The legate was Urban VIII's nephew, Cardinal Francesco Barberini.

Richelieu received with displeasure the news of Barberini's coming, for the presence in France of a legate could only be an incitement to political opposition. If Urban VIII had been shocked by the spectacle of a cardinal of the Church making war on the Pope, he was no more shocked than the devout Catholics of France, who, failing to understand the complexities of the problem, were now turning against Richelieu in indignation. Not even the prompt release of the papal prisoners-of-war and the return of their standards did much to alleviate the scandal. Failing to prevent Barberini's nomination as legate, Richelieu decided that the only course of action would be to appear to yield to moral sentiment while spinning out the negotiations. Francesco Barberini entered Paris on 21 May 1625. He was twenty-seven. Louis' brother Gaston, ten years younger, was delegated to receive him, and, booted and spurred and dressed in sea-green with gold embroidery, he rode on a horse covered in cloth of gold to the church of St Jacques du Haut Pas, on the left bank.

Here he presented the King's compliments to the legate, and they moved off together towards Notre Dame where the liturgical reception was to be held. Barberini, as tradition prescribed, would enter Paris on a white mule, reminding the faithful of Christ's entry into Jerusalem. He was in full scarlet wearing his tasselled hat, and he was accompanied by the princes and dukes, the orders of chivalry, the Hundred Swiss and thirty-eight prelates. Gaston rode at his left side, and pages carried a canopy over the legate's head. In the Rue St Jacques crowds of women tried to kiss Barberini's scarlet slippers, and at the entrance of Notre Dame a band of boisterous students from the university broke through the guards, and flocked around the legate. The startled cavaliers saw the canopy waver above the sea of heads, totter and fall to be torn into shreds. Next they saw the crowd open and a group of students abscond with the mule, leaving the legate a mass of bundled red on the pavement. Gaston's horse reared and would have thrown him had not one of his servants grabbed him around the waist and eased him out of the saddle. When he recovered, Gaston saw Barberini beating a terrified retreat into the cathedral.

Barberini's reception by the King at Fontainebleu was more dignified, and he was lodged in apartments, reserved for the princes of the blood, which lie between the staircase and one of the pavilions, next to the King's own chambers. Here, with suitable circumstance, the legate handed over the dispensation for Henriette Marie's marriage, and the official business was concluded. Behind the scenes discussions began on the Valtelline situation. Richelieu was not anxious to become too involved in them until he could hear how Père Joseph had fared with the Pope himself. By this time the Capuchin with the snub nose and straggly beard was a European celebrity, and Urban VIII was curious to meet him. On the way to Rome Père Joseph had completed a poetical endeavour, the theme of which was the crusade, and this he presented to His Holiness, as one poet to another. Urban was impressed by the poetry and took a liking to the poet, and the two got on splendidly. In due course Richelieu was to learn that the Pope's position was much less rigid than Barberini was representing it to be, and Barberini's impossible demands were rejected, without the legate being aware that Père Joseph had exposed them to be hollow.

When the Capuchin returned to France in August 1625 the Barberini discussions were deadlocked. At the same time Père Joseph, affected by the geniality of Urban VIII, was in a compromising mood, and he tried to talk Richelieu into a new basis for negotiation: France should have a monopoly of the passes, but the Valtelline should be autonomous, the Grisons preserving only nominal suzerainty, and France should accept certain other stipulations upon which the curia insisted. Richelieu, who knew that the Grisons would never agree to these terms, was inflexible, and Barberini, referring bitterly to 'eels which slipped all the more quickly through the hand the more firmly they were grasped',[3] broke off the negotiations and left Paris. He blamed Père Joseph whom he suspected, and not without reason, of having diplomatically outwitted him, and a Capuchin on the legate's staff wrote to the Emperor saying that 'when Richelieu is up to tricks, he always uses pious persons'.[4]

Barberini's decision to terminate the discussions caused Richelieu the greatest personal anguish, and he later wrote 'never in the midst of the great enterprises which it has been necessary to undertake for the state have I felt so near death as when the legate was here'.[5] The Huguenots were still in revolt, and even then, and much against their consciences, the Dutch, in return for French subsidies, were supplying the ships that France lacked in order to deal with Soubise, and they were doing so only in the belief that France was a link in the anti-Spanish fetter. The English, too, had to be persuaded that the assault on their co-religionists in France was not part of a general crusade against Protestantism, for these unpredictable people were quite capable, in a mood of anti-papist fervour, of turning their ships over to succour the French rebels. To abandon the Grisons as Barberini in effect demanded, and to accord the Spaniards the right of passage through the Valtelline so as to reinforce their armies in the Netherlands, would leave France friendless in Europe and bereft of diplomatic goals. A breach with Rome, on the other hand, would be a provocation to the zealous Catholics who, like Père Bérulle, had sided with Barberini. Overpowered by anxiety as he was, Richelieu did not relax his position, for, as he told the King, 'to make a bad peace is to prepare a new war',[6] but his own position was so insecure that he felt the need for reinforcement. To this end he persuaded the King to summon a Council of Notables – leading men in government and administration whose advice would be sought and whose support would be an insurance against the clamour of the papal party. The Notables were probably carefully selected, for they manifested a frightening anti-Roman and anti-Spanish sentiment, and demanded war with Spain.

Too little attention has been paid to the grave sense of disquiet engendered in French minds by events which occurred in Spain at the time of the Valtelline affair, and which were initially un-connected with it. Following his appointment as Philip IV's minister, Olivares on 25 December 1624 prepared a memorandum in which he argued that the most effective way for Castile to assert its authority over the other kingdoms of Spain would be 'to bring about some great popular tumult there' under the pretext of which troops could intervene, the laws could be reorganized, and the unity of the Spanish empire could be achieved.[7] The contents of this memorandum must have leaked out, for there are contemporary references to Olivares' policy of instigating Cata-lonia to revolt so as to have an excuse to deprive it of its privileges, and the unscrupulousness of it filled Frenchmen, and probably Richelieu, with disquiet. It was an Englishman who expressed the disquiet in an epigram. The French, he said, were given to com-paring the Spanish monarchy 'to a beggar's cloak made up of patches'. But if those patches were in one piece, what would become of the French king's 'cloak embroider'd with flower-de-luces'?[8]

The policy of unifying Spain by force seemed to carry overtones of unifying Europe by force. One aspect of it was Olivares' scheme of a Union of Arms by which all the kingdoms and provinces of Spain, together with Flanders, Naples and the Milanais, should contribute to a common reserve of troops which could be drawn upon to defend any one of them. Catalan troops could thus be drafted to the Valtelline to assist the Milanais – or worse, invade France under the pretext of assisting it. Hitherto certain of the principalities, particularly Catalonia, had been immune from compulsory service abroad; if this immunity could be lifted Spain's military position would be immensely improved. The significance of this plan of Olivares was enhanced by a crisis provoked by the Duc de Guise, which happened to involve Catalonia. While Lesdiguières was laying siege to Genoa and French troops were entering the Valtelline, Guise, who was governor of Provence, intercepted a large convoy of silver being shipped from Barcelona to Genoa to pay the Spanish troops in the Milanais, and followed this coup by seizing three Genoese ships off Marseilles carrying 160,000 ducats. The Genoese bankers offered the Spaniards half this sum should they recover the money. Olivares on 2 April 1625 issued orders for the seizure of French property in Spanish ports to the value of the lost silver, and Richelieu retaliated four weeks later by closing the Spanish frontier to all trade, whereupon Olivares decreed the sequestration of all French property in Spain, Flanders and other Spanish territories. The French government was bombarded with the angry complaints of French merchants whose businesses were threatened with ruin; Catalonia's trade was seriously affected, and the principality was in a dangerously excited state preparing for a French invasion as well as to resist Olivares' schemes. Tension between France and Spain mounted as Barberini's peace mission failed.

Richelieu can be defended in all his actions during the Valtelline crisis, and his courage at a moment when he was isolated and misunderstood, even by Père Joseph, and ill and worried to distraction, is impressive. Had he abandoned the Grisons none of France's traditional allies would have respected her honour or supported her cause. There would have been no alternative but to make France a pensioner of Spain – of a Spain that clearly intended to intensify its authority in France's borderlands, and ultimately to make France an instrument of Castilian policies. The price that Richelieu had to pay for France's independence was confrontation with the Pope, who found himself unwillingly in the same predicament as Richelieu, and searched as energetically for a way out of it. Each was the victim of circumstances beyond his control, and the captive of policies formulated by his predecessor, and each, with his gift for seeing both sides of a question, was conscious of the other's dilemma. Perhaps the only felicitous aspect of the crisis is that Richelieu and Urban VIII gained respect for each other's integrity, and it was this mutual respect which enabled the papacy to hold the balance between France and Spain for another decade.

Although Richelieu was throughout the Valtelline affair convinced of Spain's aggressive propensities, he does not seem to have shared the prevailing belief that France was incapable of standing militarily against Madrid. In May 1625, when the controversy over the pillaged silver was at its height, he prepared a memorandum for the King in which he argued that Spain – which he took for granted to be an 'enemy' – was so short of cash, and its people so restless, that it could not long sustain a war in the event of its being attacked simultaneously on several fronts with 'French fury'.[9] Without such a conflict he doubted the possibility of a sure and honourable peace with Spain, which would guarantee the position of France's allies. One obstacle to such a peace, he told Père Joseph, was the 'appetite' of Charles Emmanuel of Savoy.[10]

There was a violent outburst of pamphlets debating the position France had taken, and Richelieu decided that it was necessary to expound the morality of independent political action to a wide public. Accordingly he arranged for the publication of a work, called *The Catholic of the State*, which is of some importance in the history of Catholic political doctrine. It may even have been written by Richelieu, though it is generally attributed to one of his hired pamphleteers. It argued that casuistry might be acceptable in theology, but not in politics; laws, of their nature, are not casuistic, but are to be literally interpreted; kings fight wars to establish the peace of their subjects and the security of their states, and the decision that wars for this purpose are necessary, and therefore just, is not one susceptible of evaluation according to the principles of private morality. A state which is not prepared to fight for its security is necessarily feeble; thereby it earns the contempt of neighbours and invites their aggression. From this the conclusion was drawn that those who cry against war in fact cry against peace – a typical Richelieu epigram.

It was now proposed that, since the Holy See and France were at issue only on the question of the degree of political autonomy necessary to guarantee Catholicism in the Valtelline, and France and Spain were at issue on the question of the right of passage, an attempt should be made to separate the two issues and to negotiate them independently with Rome and Madrid. Richelieu sought to bring the Huguenots to terms with the hint that agreement was near with Spain so as to release French energy to suppress the revolt, and the Spaniards to terms with the hint that an accommodation was being reached with the Huguenots so as to release it in support of the Grisons. In this Richelieu was the victim of his own diplomacy. The French ambassador in Madrid, Charles d'Angennes de Rochepot, Comte de Fargis, received a letter from his wife, Madeleine de Silly, one of the court ladies in Paris, saying that Père Bérulle, backed by Marie de Médicis, had told her that, as a matter of conscience, her husband should make peace at any price. Fargis, on 1 January 1626, signed a treaty with Olivares without communicating the text in advance to Paris, and without having full powers to do so, and it contained the impossible condition that the Grisons should forfeit their title to the Valtelline in the event of their not observing the other provisions. The negotiations were already sufficiently complicated by allegations of bad faith to make it undesirable to repudiate Fargis outright, and so Richelieu decided to seek a settlement with Spain on the basis of this document, with suitable modifications. Fargis was given new instructions which reached him while he was accompanying the court on the first official visit of the reign to Aragon and Catalonia, and he was told that if Olivares refused to modify the treaty, he, Fargis, was to break off relations and return home.[11] At Monzon Philip IV, wearily engaged in tense negotiations for money with the Cortes of Valencia, on 5 March 1626 accepted a new text of the French treaty. It was believed that Fargis, in his anxiety to reach agreement, had offered French troops to help subdue the restless Catalans, against whose wrath he had to be protected. Be this as it may, he and Olivares were prepared to compromise to the point of self-deception. Urban VIII and Barberini were ignored, and the former at least was taken by surprise when the news of a settlement reached him. To Richelieu, the treaty was distinctly unsatisfactory, but, in an unguarded moment, and under pressure to appear to be a moral and Catholic statesman, he agreed to ratify it.

Since the loose drafting permitted either party to interpret it in its own interest, the treaty in fact settled nothing; on the contrary, as each party in the diplomatic entanglements of the next decade accused the other of being in breach of its engagements it became an obstacle to mutual comprehension and goodwill. Too many of Richelieu's treaties were ambiguous and enshrined a naïve hope that the French interpretation would prevail, but the Treaty of Monzon is the worst example. It did not specify that the Spaniards should not use the mountain passes – if it had they would not have signed it; hence it did not on the face of it interrupt Spanish traffic with the Rhine and the Tyrol, which was, of course, the crux of the matter. Richelieu hoped it might have this effect obliquely by virtue of the provision that the Valtelline should be restored to its legal condition before the troubles began in 1617; this implied acknowledgment of the superior authority of the Grisons over the passes, and their right to close them to Spanish armies. But the same provision stipulated that the Catholic religion should alone be practised in the Valtelline, and that the people of the Valtelline should elect their own officers of government, leaving the Grisons a nominal right of suzerainty and veto. As interpreted by Madrid, this meant that the Catholics of the Valtelline were free to make the decision to permit Spanish passage through the area, and the Grisons had no superior authority to prevent this; if France backed the Grisons in closing the passes, therefore, she would be in breach of the treaty.

This was not the end of the ambiguity. The treaty did not mention French rights of passage and recruitment in the Grisons or the French protection of Swiss neutrality. Therefore, in Spanish eyes, the treaty excluded France from all rights in the Valtelline, for she could enjoy rights only as derived from the government of the Grisons, and these rights would be restricted to the canton itself. The undertaking that France gave to hand back the forts to the Pope was on the face of it compensated for by the provision that within a specified time they should be demolished. This gave the treaty the appearance of a French diplomatic coup, for it undid the Spanish action which had provoked the crisis. But since the French withdrawal would inevitably be followed by permission from the authorities in the Valtelline for Spanish passage it was exactly the contrary. Furthermore, should Spain in the future force the passage of the Splügen so as to open the shortest route to the Rhine, France would have no status under the treaty to object. This is, in fact, precisely what the Spaniards did, and they scoffed whenever Richelieu denounced their breach of the treaty. Wishful thinking, he was to find, is no substitute for black and white commitments. Four years later, when faced once more with a treaty signed at Regensburg without prior agreement as to its text, he remembered the fiasco of the Treaty of Monzon and resolved not to repeat his error. The ambiguous settlement of the Valtelline dispute was to prove, in fact, no settlement at all, but the first of a series of diplomatic glosses which were to lead France deeper and deeper into commitment.

Unrestrained in His Passions

1625-7

English foreign policy at the moment when Richelieu came to power was the creature of one of the most unstable and self-deluding minds in Europe, that of the royal favourite, George Villiers, Duke of Buckingham. Richelieu, the intellectual and the theorist, expected other nations to act and react according to logical patterns, and he quite failed to grasp the pragmatism of English politics, or the fact that English policy-making was a crudely amateur business compared with his own professionalism. It seemed to him that James I should be as violently anti-Habsburg as were his boisterous subjects, for the Habsburgs had ousted his son-in-law Frederick and his daughter Elizabeth from the Palatinate. In fact, James' reaction to this event was the most unlikely possible; it was to seek a Spanish alliance against Austria with a view to Frederick's restoration. If Charles the Prince of Wales were to marry the Infanta Maria, sister of the King of Spain and of Anne of Austria the Queen of France, Spain would surely not refuse to help Charles' own sister Elizabeth. The fact that Spain was the devil incarnate to most Englishmen did not deter James from opening negotiations to this end. The Spaniards received the marriage proposal with pleasure, but for reasons that James quite misunderstood. They hoped that, at best, the heir to the throne of England would become a Catholic, at worst, the presence of a Catholic Spanish Queen would relieve the pressure on the English Catholics and curb the pugnacity of the English people towards Spain. Their real feelings towards Frederick they demonstrated by marching an army from the Spanish Netherlands to occupy Frederick's capital, Heidelberg. James was almost pushed by this event to a breach with Spain, but persisting in his illusion he decided to send a special envoy, one Endymion Porter, to Madrid to make another bid to conclude a marriage contract. As Porter left London in October 1622 his departure was accompanied by the cry of the whole nation: 'Bring us war!'

When Porter arrived in Madrid he found a court as unlike that of St James, and a monarch and a favourite as unlike James I and Buckingham, as could be imagined. Philip III had died on 31 March 1621 at the age of forty-three. Of his two sons, the younger, Ferdinand the Cardinal-Infante, had drained out all the residual energy of the Spanish Habsburgs, and was the true heir to the character of Charles V. His brother, Philip IV, was a shell, emptied of the capacity to rule, yet the embodiment of a national and a personal pretension to recreate the Spain of Philip II. The portraits that Velasquez painted of him show a wistful pretender, a counterfeit, a striker of attitudes, a man whose life was a stately yet purposeless pavane. The paradox is that it was the impassive, hypnotic gaze of Philip's lizard eyes that conjured up a cultural greatness to replace the political greatness of Spain: he was intelligent, sensitive, the enemy of cruelty, dishonesty and fraud, the lover of art, in which he perceived the distillation of truth, a man in whom, as in his whole nation, excessive religious devotion substituted for worldly action and prudence, and an abject faith in the providential role of Spain inhibited all awareness of the country's rapid decline into bankruptcy and disaster. That this fatigued Don Juan should have embodied the ambitions of the House of Austria, which so awed Richelieu, is a matter for delicate reflection.

To compensate for the listlessness of the monarch, in whom the will to act was paralysed, Spain possessed a favourite to whom power was a passion. He was Don Gaspar de Guzmán, Conde de Olivares; in two years he was to be created Duque de San Lucar, and because he retained the name Olivares was to become known by the incongruous title of the Count-Duke. He was tending already to obesity, and his balloon-like black clothes and cloak made him an enormous figure, though he was not as tall as he seemed. His lank black hair, his puffed jowls, his thick, prominent nose, his aggressive tuft of beard and great, flourishing moustaches and his strange, repelling eyes, haunt Spanish history and art. For Spain he was a disaster, a dictator who aroused universal hostility, but whose personal instability of temperament and lack of prudence condemned to failure and frustration much of his authoritarianism.

He was two years younger than Richelieu and there is a similarity in their careers. But Olivares, although an intellectual, an avid reader of books and the collector of a great library, lacked Richelieu's tenacity, power of concentration and deliberate and persistent pursuit of ends. He oscillated between an hysterical exaltation and a languid depression. At good news he would be fired to passionate enthusiasm and violent action, and vast plans would be made; at bad news he would slump into melancholy, the plans would be unfulfilled and the great designs halted. He was at times extravagant in thought, gesture and expression, making him seem from afar more dangerous than he was. He talked incessantly when aroused, and had vast powers of persuasion when in one of his oratorical moods. He was an ascetic in many respects, yet he felt the greatness of Spain in his soul as a passion, and his irresistible tendency to command was the result of a frustrated ambition to be a warrior. He was astute, saw through the intentions of others, and loved to avoid the point in a negotiation; yet he was capable of insensate rage which would undo all his subtlety. Whereas Olivares' name scarcely ever appears in Richelieu's detached writings, Richelieu's was an obsession with Olivares; and to the Spaniard the Franco-Spanish struggle was almost a personal duel. Olivares' Spanish biographer, a famous medical man, has traced the disintegration of his personality and has not hesitated to describe him in his later career as mad; and the instability of the minister, accompanying the languor of the King, led to a fatal equivocation in Spanish politics.

The English marriage proposal was a tragedy for Anglo-Spanish relations, for Olivares alternated between grandiloquent gestures of amiability and explosive hostility, which bewildered and offended the English. When Endymion Porter disclosed James' devious scheme of enlisting Spanish aid to help Frederick, Olivares lost his temper. It was absurd, he cried, to ask the King of Spain to take up arms against his uncle the Emperor, and against the Catholic League. And he went on to say that if that was what was intended from the marriage match he would have nothing to do with it. The matter would have ended there, and James I would have felt himself provoked by Spanish insolence to the point of war, but for the fact that, in a desperate bid to retrieve the situation, the English ambassador, the Earl of Bristol, took the matter to the King. Philip IV, who was hardly ever aroused, graciously made some gesture of sympathy for the Palatine's cause, which was taken in England to be a promise of support, and this kept the negotiations going and England neutral. Early in 1623 James I received the Spanish marriage terms, which included a demand for private freedom of Catholic worship in England, complete freedom of worship for the Infanta's household, and an undertaking that the children of the marriage should be brought up as Catholics to the age of nine. As for the Palatinate, it would be impossible to deliver an ultimatum to the Emperor.

There now occurred one of history's most ridiculous diplomatic forays. Buckingham, the pretentious and irresponsible gallant, conceived the idea of himself and Charles going incognito to Madrid, and in the fashion of cavaliers, with dash, poetry and charm, winning the Infanta. Charles at this time was far removed from the graven image of the period of the Civil War, and was fired by Buckingham's romanticism. Catching James off guard, they talked him, foolishly indulgent as he was wherever Buckingham was concerned, into consenting to the fantastic scheme. James was bitterly to regret his weakness when, after the discovery that the Prince of Wales and the favourite had disappeared, the country was in an uproar. Meanwhile, behind false beards and other theatrical apparatus, Buckingham and Charles were in Paris en route to Spain, and were peeping at the royal court and catching a glimpse of Louis XIII's youngest sister, Henriette Marie, whom it had once been suggested Charles might marry. In due course, grinning with delight at their exploit, they disclosed themselves to the Earl of Bristol in Madrid.

When he was told of the arrival of the Prince of Wales, Olivares was elevated to one of his moods of optimism, and in this respect he was matched by Buckingham. For a time there was a dreamy air of harmony as the Spaniards went out of their way to be agreeable and courteous; but, as anyone could have predicted, the outcome was disaster. No one would believe that the two had come merely on a skylarking adventure; there must be more to it; Charles must be intending to become a Catholic. Suddenly the visitors became aware that they were being subjected to a campaign of religious instruction with a view to their conversion. Charles was offended and retired behind the mask of remote dignity which he had already manufactured for himself. Buckingham disgusted the Spanish clergy by his flippant attitude towards religion and his lack of attention to serious theological discourse. His English sense of humour quite mystified Olivares; seeing the languid, elegant young King for the first time, Buckingham commented to Olivares: 'What, you have a King who can walk!'[1] Olivares was not to know that Buckingham's concept of a King was gouty James I, who hobbled like a spavined horse. The sedate Spanish court was dismayed by the undergraduate behaviour of the two knights-errant, and was deeply shocked when Charles climbed a garden wall and pursued the shrieking Infanta who had been gathering may-dew.

The negotiations for the marriage were complicated by the Pope's conditions for a dispensation for the Infanta's espousal to a Protestant, and on both sides patience shortened. Charles resolved to return to England. The farewells at the Escorial were conducted with the usual Spanish politeness, and were marred only by Buckingham's unpardonable discourtesy in boycotting them. A proposal begot in a moment of hallucination, and pursued in an atmosphere of misunderstanding and incomprehension, was now recognized to have been a major diplomatic error, and the negotiations for a marriage petered out some four months after the two wanderers returned to England in October 1623. Each side believed itself to have been deceived; and Buckingham, his vanity hurt, was smouldering with indignation against Spain. Publicly in the House of Lords he said he had been impressed by two things, Spain's inherent weakness and the duplicity of her rulers. Olivares, he alleged, had admitted to him that the marriage negotiations had been no more than an elaborate comedy. It was a speech well calculated to stir the rancour of the English nation.

It was in this mood that Buckingham turned to France, another Catholic country, for a substitute bride and an ally in a war of revenge against Spain. Early in 1624, even before the formal breaking-off of the marriage negotiations with Spain, secret missions were exchanged between him and Marie de Médicis to revive the idea of a marriage between Charles and Henriette Marie.[2] Richelieu, as the Queen Mother's confidant, must have been a party to the discussions, and it may be that the encouraging reply which Buckingham received was drafted by him. When Buckingham disclosed his new plan to James I the King was horrified. Once more there would have to be elaborate negotiations with the Pope for a dispensation for the marriage; there would be further demands for toleration of Catholicism in England; and Parliament in its current anti-papist mood was unlikely to welcome the match. James' instinct was correct, but the impetuous Buckingham opened the subject in Parliament in March, and taking no account of the reservations which his peers had about the proposal, was not to be diverted.

The negotiations between England and France would inevitably be difficult and delicate. Buckingham does not seem to have realized that he could not secure French support for the restoration of the Palatinate to Frederick V unless he was prepared to make concessions in return, particularly concessions in religion and about French policy in the Valtelline. In his turn Vieuville was so intent on getting England's support against Spain in the Valtelline matter that he glossed over the difficulties of obtaining a papal dispensation, and misled Buckingham into believing that this could be secured on no more than a vague undertaking about religious freedom instead of a strict engagement. As with the

Spanish, so with the French negotiations a basic misunderstanding of each party's position promised failure and mutual allegations of duplicity.

Richelieu early recognized that Vieuville was mishandling the matter, but he does not seem to have been aware at any stage of the negotiations that in Buckingham France was dealing with a man of limited political astuteness or with one who had no real political backing at home. It would not be correct to suggest that Richelieu rushed into the English marriage, for he had his misgivings, but it is arguable that he was not as sceptical as he should have been in the light of the stories that reached him of the extraordinary adventures of Charles and Buckingham in Spain. France and England, he reasoned, needed each other, the former because her claims to be an alternative continental power required the linking of England in anti-Spanish, anti-Habsburg bonds, the latter because France alone was in a position to secure by negotiation with the Catholic princes in Germany the restoration of Frederick's rights in the Palatinate. Failing to recognize that the anti-Spanish uproar in England was at bottom an expression of anti-papist feelings, and deceived as to the stability of Buckingham, he was unjustifiably optimistic about the fruits of an Anglo-French alliance.

Lord Kensington, shortly to become Earl of Holland, arrived in Paris to open the negotiations and was there when Richelieu first entered the council. Marie de Médicis received him and his overtures effusively; and this enthusiasm, which tended to suppress the political element in the affair, contributed to the deception of Kensington, who reported to England in the terms, not of a marriage broker, but of a romantic matchmaker. Buckingham may have expected that France would support Frederick's claims to the Palatinate, and join in an anti-Spanish crusade, but no such undertakings were given, or even seriously discussed; Vieuville may have hoped that English troops would create a diversion to reinforce the French operation in the Valtelline, but nothing was further from the mind of James I. In May 1624, when Richelieu had been a member of the council for a month, the Earl of Carlisle arrived in Paris to conclude the negotiations. Now for the first time the religious issue was clearly confronted. Carlisle's instructions were that it would be impossible to relax the penal laws against the Catholics in England; the most that could be promised was religious toleration for the Queen and her household. Louis XIII expressed himself totally dissatisfied on this point, and it became clear that further concessions would have to be made by James I if the discussions were to make any progress. Had either Vieuville or Richelieu had any real comprehension of the mood of England they would have recognized the futility of insisting on religious toleration. Both were anxious for an English alliance, and Richelieu supported Vieuville's proposal to send to James a diplomat whose persuasive powers were legend, Antoine Coiffier-Ruzé, the Marquis d'Effiat. Upon his arrival in London d'Effiat found an eager abettor in Buckingham, and the two proceeded to work in unison to persuade James, while Englishmen looked on in growing apprehension and hostility.

It was partly Richelieu's allegation to Louis that Vieuville was mishandling the negotiations that brought about the latter's dismissal. In fact it is doubtful if Richelieu, when he took the matter under his control, exhibited much more perspicacity or adroitness. True, he was aware that the Pope would require that England's religious undertakings should be in treaty form and under seal before granting the dispensation, and that Vieuville was presuming too much in letting d'Effiat negotiate on the basis of promises only, but he failed to realize any more than Vieuville that the only alternative to deceiving the Pope was to deceive the English Parliament; and that Parliament deceived was not likely to permit England to become the instrument of French policies. Immediately upon taking Vieuville's seat Richelieu instructed d'Effiat that nothing less than a treaty embodying concessions to the Catholics would be acceptable. When d'Effiat laid this requirement on the table, James, in Buckingham's absence, broke off the negotiations. In dismay d'Effiat rushed to Buckingham; the Duke intercepted James' dispatch to Carlisle and Kensington in Paris informing them of the termination of the affair, and then going to the King exerted all his influence upon him to persuade him to yield. The expedient was eventually devised of having the Privy Council consent to the relaxation of the recusancy laws.

Parliament, which claimed to be alone competent to suspend or dispense from legislation, would have to be confronted, but it was hoped to tie its hands with a *fait accompli;* Parliament would not be called together until after the ratification of the marriage treaty, which was completed on 10 November 1624.

If Richelieu felt complacent he had little cause. He had forced James into an impossible constitutional position, wherein the goodwill and future financial support of Parliament would be forfeited. In exchange for a major religious concession on England's part, he had made no commitment on behalf of Frederick of the Palatinate, and no contribution to Buckingham's anti-Spanish designs. In fact, he made it clear that France intended to persist in its neutral conduct, but did so only after the marriage was a commitment, and after Henriette Marie had been married to Charles, for whom the Duc de Chevreuse acted as proxy, outside the west door of Notre Dame. In March James I died, and the young girl, described by the Earl of Holland as 'the most charming creature of her country', and as 'a lovely, sweet young creature' whose 'shape is perfect'[3] was now Queen of England, though not yet in possession of her realm.

Buckingham had intended to be proxy for Charles I at the wedding, but James' death had prevented him. Now on an impulse he decided to go to Paris to receive the bride and escort her to England. While in Paris he would charm the French government into supporting his schemes against Spain. He arrived on 24 May 1625 and remained one week. What Richelieu, ever a good judge of men, observed was disquieting. England's leader was a dazzling man of thirty-two, a Rubensesque character of fine manners, splendid gestures and exuberant personality, but of intemperate enthusiasm and with the inconstancy of the wind. His extraordinary position as one of the two dukes in England and virtual master of the royal council, a man in whom the highest offices in the state were consolidated, he owed not to his brain, but to the accidents of handsome features and an athletic body, and to the weakness of graceless James I for these attributes. He now appeared at the French court in white satin studded with diamonds, and the ladies were stunned and the gallants amazed.

In three days he astonished the world by managing to wear twenty-seven suits of clothing, each richer than the other. The young Queen, Anne of Austria, found him seriously disturbing. Louis XIII had done his duty by her – the first occasion being an event gossiped about in the diplomatic dispatches from the French court – and had been rewarded by her miscarriages and little else. Neglected, starved of affection and even of admiration, volatile and in need of distraction, this not unattractive young woman with the Habsburg jaw and lip and the prominent brown eyes basked in the radiance of the English Apollo, who discoursed to her so brilliantly and complimented her, it may be taken, so outrageously. His fine nose, nobly cut mouth, piercing eyes, splendid brow, curling fair moustaches and pointed beard captured all women, and Anne was no exception.

The Palace of the Luxembourg had just been completed, and there Marie de Médicis gave a reception for Buckingham. The King pleaded illness as an excuse for absenting himself, but this did not prevent the affair from being the most splendid that Paris had seen since the days of Henri II. The guests were expected to admire, apart from Buckingham, the twenty-one vast canvases of Peter Paul Rubens representing the cavalcade of the reign of Marie de Médicis, which were then exhibited for the first time, and which now hang in the Louvre. What the more cynical and witty courtiers whispered to each other at this apotheosis of the matron is not recorded, but all were agreed that the great Rubens, who was there himself wondering when his payment would be forthcoming, had this time surpassed himself in the production of an overwhelming series of masterpieces. One may imagine the red figure of Richelieu inscrutably pondering the pictures of Marie de Médicis' escape from Blois and her reconciliation with Louis, and perhaps conclude that he was reflecting that the dukes around him who saw their turbulence thus dignified would hardly be discouraged from repeating the event by this immortalization of their disobedience.

Behind the glittering façade Buckingham was trying to captivate Richelieu and was finding the agreeable but impenetrable Cardinal a serious disappointment. Grandiloquently he proposed a joint Anglo-French assault on the Spanish Netherlands, which would gain for France the province of Artois. Richelieu received the proposal with scepticism, saying that 'it is for the English to see if their interests require such an effort'.[4] Shrugging off Buckingham's overtures, Richelieu told the Duke that England could go ahead and recover the Palatinate if she wished, but that no settlement in Germany could be effected without France's participation. As he sat for his portrait – the portrait which is now in the Uffizi – Buckingham poured his disgruntled sentiments into Rubens' ears and expressed his profound disappointment with the fruits of the French alliance. The subtle Rubens hinted that there were other allies that England might seek, a suggestion that Buckingham was to keep in mind.

The fantastic week was drawing to its close and Henriette Marie was to be escorted to England. Marie de Médicis and Anne of Austria were to accompany her as far as Amiens. By this time Buckingham's attentions to Anne, and Anne's responsiveness, were common gossip, and an officer of Anne's household reported that 'from the first day the freedom between them has been as much as if they had known each other for a long time'. The farewell ceremonies were to take place at Amiens, and the town surpassed itself in its reception. Five splendidly arrayed damsels were placed in five niches of the cathedral to represent the five daughters of France who had been queens of England, and to typify the descent of the English royal house from the twenty-two stone monarchs marshalled across the façade. There were theatrical performances and a *Te Deum* to attend, decorations to admire, and a discourse of the governor of Amiens to listen to. There was little opportunity amid all this activity for Buckingham to be close to Anne, but he was a determined and indiscreet man.

Mme de Motteville, one of Anne's ladies-in-waiting, recorded that he managed to be introduced into a garden where Anne was strolling in the evening, and which the King had ordered to be closed to everyone; it was on the banks of the Somme attached to the house in which the Queen was staying. With her was the Duchesse de Chevreuse, who, because she was involved with Buckingham's companion Lord Holland, possibly played a role in bringing the Duke and the Queen together. When Buckingham appeared, the Queen's equerry discreetly retired some distance. By accident or design Buckingham and Anne gave the others the slip down a trellis walk where they were obscured from view. Then the quiet of the twilight was pierced with Anne's cry, and the equerry was summoned and scolded by the Queen for leaving her.

What had happened under the trellis remains unknown, but the matter did not end there. When Buckingham took his public farewell of the Queen on departing with Henriette Marie for Calais he was observed to be weeping. Furthermore, overtaken by his impetuosity, he left the Queen of England *en route;* on the pretext of having received news from Charles I which required him to communicate again with Marie de Médicis, he rode back to Amiens, and, having discharged his alleged duty to the Queen Mother, sought out Anne of Austria. He was introduced into her chamber where she was in bed, and there, in front of her assembled ladies, he made an exhibition of himself. Falling on his knees, he kissed the bedcover with 'transports so extraordinary that it was easy to see how violent was his passion'. The old Comtesse de Lanoi, scandalized by this behaviour, told him 'with much severity' that this was not the custom in France, and that he should stand up. He snapped back at her that he was no Frenchman, and was not obliged to observe France's rules. Then 'addressing the Queen he uttered the tenderest things in the world'.[5] Anne, embarrassed and angry, ordered him out. He went, 'resolved to return to France as soon as possible'.

This intention Richelieu, when all this was reported to him, was determined to frustrate. Louis, more surly than ever at Buckingham's presumption, took severe measures, including the dismissal of the Queen's equerry and others of her staff. It was once more the story of the Spanish courtship. Buckingham's conduct had forfeited French as it had Spanish goodwill, while the French, in resisting the Duke's madcap schemes, had wounded Buckingham's vanity no less seriously than had the Spaniards. The Anglo-French alliance had started badly, and was shortly to end miserably. Within two months of Henriette Marie's arrival in England

Charles I had to face Parliament and explain the engagement to relax the laws against the Catholics. Buckingham added nothing to his credit in the eyes of the French, or even for that matter in those of his own countrymen, by trying to explain away the commitment as really no more than an elaborate ritual to quieten the conscience of the Pope in the matter of the dispensation, and that it was not intended to be taken seriously. This was disquieting to the French government, but worse was to come. There was serious trouble between Charles and Henriette Marie, both of whom were finding marriage a disappointment and attributing the cause to extraneous circumstances: Charles blamed the Queen's French household and sought to restrict its size and activities; Henriette Marie blamed Buckingham, whom she found dictatorial and interfering. Within a short time there were grounds for complaint that the treaty provisions concerning the Queen's entourage were being violated, while those concerning the Catholics remained totally unexecuted. An open breach occurred between the King and the Queen when the latter refused to participate in the Anglican coronation service.

This was disappointing enough to Richelieu, but almost equally disappointing was the lamentable failure of England as a military ally. In October 1625 Buckingham mounted his expedition against Cadiz. Eighty ships, some of which were Armada veterans, and most of which were pressed merchantmen, carried a motley rabble of untrained and ill-equipped troops into the harbour of Cadiz, but thereupon all initiative departed. After an effort to land which ended wretchedly, it was decided to abandon the attack on the port and lie in wait for the expected plate fleet from America. This slipped through the ambush, and the English returned home miserably at the end of November with nothing achieved. Shortly before their arrival Buckingham consummated his tactlessness with a public observation in The Hague that 'I acknowledge the power of the King of France. But I doubt his goodwill.'[6]

Richelieu, however, had need of the English alliance, for the civil wars in France had broken out again. The Peace of Montpellier of October 1622 had failed to put an end to the fanaticism of either the Huguenots or the Catholics, which the events in Béarn had unchained. Scarcely had the royal forces withdrawn when the mob raged through Montpellier, desecrating the reconsecrated churches, destroying the newly established Capuchin convent, and driving the clergy out of the walls. To awe these unruly enthusiasts a garrison was installed in the town and a royal citadel constructed – actions which were necessary but which violated the letter of the treaty. In Nîmes the property of Catholics and all the churches were burned and plundered and the whole Catholic population had to take refuge in Beaucaire. The same occurred in Alès, and there was not a Catholic church intact in Uzès. In some Catholic towns the bodies of Huguenots who had been buried in consecrated ground were dug up, but on the whole, because the royal writ ran in the Catholic areas, there was less opportunity for violence even if there was no less disposition towards it. The situation, then, when Richelieu came to power was one of mounting tension, and his advent was not calculated to alter it. Although he had in the royal council advocated a conciliatory policy towards the Huguenots in order to defend the realm against the accumulating pressures from without, he was known to them only as the tenacious apologist of Catholic doctrine, and therefore as an enemy. Neither was he likely to be able to moderate the Catholic zealots, the less informed of whom expected a crusade by a cardinal of the Church, while the better informed sought to push him into it to prevent his meddling with the Protestants abroad.

It needed only a stimulus for the Huguenot revolt to burst forth again, and this was provided by the Spanish siege of Breda in Holland. Benjamin de Rohan-Soubise, Rohan's brother and the man who had held St Jean d'Angély against the King in 1621 – 'infamous Soubise' as Richelieu called him – decided to create a diversion, and seized Blaret and Sables d'Oleron. In Blaret harbour lay six beautiful galleons, among them the *Vierge* of eighty guns, belonging to the Duc de Nevers, which had been built in Holland to conduct his crusading army to fight the Turks. On 18 January 1625 Soubise's squadron of ten ships anchored peacefully alongside them, and then in the dead of night boarded

and seized them. Simultaneously Rohan revolted again in Languedoc, and the citizens of La Rochelle, seeing Soubise off the Ile de
Ré with a fleet of seventy-four sail, joined him.

It was Soubise's violence which convinced Richelieu that his
policy of conciliating the Huguenots was unavailing, and which
led him to the decision that they must be eliminated as a political
factor. The event restricted his area of manoeuvre in the Valtelline dispute by requiring him to keep faith with Holland, to
which he turned for aid in chastising the rebels. The Dutch found
it incongruous that at the moment when they were on the point of
losing Breda to the Spaniards they should have to turn their fleet
against their Calvinist brethren, but self-interest persuaded them
that they had no alternative. They sent twenty-two ships under
Admiral Haultain de Zoete to join a scratch squadron of French
ships gathered together in Brittany under the Duc de Montmorency, and in due course the fleet appeared off La Rochelle. The
Dutch seamen, confronted by Soubise's ships, refused to fire on
their co-religionists, and peace overtures were made. Under cover
of the negotiations, however, Soubise had the maladroitness to
slip out of La Rochelle on 16 July 1625 with thirty-two vessels
and burn the flagship of Vice-Admiral Dorp with two fireships.
From that moment the Dutch thought only of revenge.

Among the ships under Montmorency's command were eight
English vessels which now became the subject of contention.
In the marriage treaty James I had promised to lend France twenty
ships to support Lesdiguières' siege of Genoa, and eight of these
had arrived in French waters while Buckingham was in Paris.
Their instructions forbade them to engage 'in the civil wars of the
French', and when Montmorency ordered Pennington, the English commander, to take on board three hundred soldiers to be
shipped to the Bay of Biscay, Pennington refused and took his
ships back to England. Richelieu put pressure on Buckingham,
and the latter, just back in London after his French visit, and still
glowing with his successes at the French court, yielded and
ordered Pennington to return to Dieppe and take the French on
board. Most of the ships were requisitioned merchantmen, and
their captains refused to sail 'to shed the blood of Protestants'.

Cajoled into going to Dieppe, the crews then mutinied, and not until August were the ships placed at the disposal of the French, though only one English sailor consented to enter their service. It was too late to save the Dutch, but not too late to attempt the destruction of Soubise. Montmorency, having collected seventy-six ships of all sizes, French, English and Dutch, caught Soubise behind a sandbank off the Ile de Ré and destroyed him. Soubise fled, leaving behind his hat and sword, and at Oleron managed to rally a dozen ships with which he sailed to Falmouth, there to become a Protestant hero to the Cornishmen and a provocation to Buckingham. The French gave chase and blockaded the Cornish port.

From that point Anglo-French relations rapidly deteriorated. At the end of the year English privateers seized French ships on the ground that they were carrying contraband goods to the Spanish Netherlands. The French demanded their restitution, and the English government replied that it would hold them until the eight ships of Pennington were returned. Charles I was in a recalcitrant mood. He told Louis XIII that he should respect the terms of the Peace of Montpellier, and if he refused to do this or to return the ships, diplomatic relations would be broken off. In fact, on the pretext of English opposition to the proposed subjugation of La Rochelle, which was no longer protected by Soubise's ships, the English ambassador in Paris, the Earl of Holland, was recalled. Charles went further and in July ordered Henriette Marie to replace certain of her French courtiers with Buckingham's relations, and when she refused he forcibly withdrew her from her chambers and locked out the French staff, who were told they would have to leave England. The Queen was so enraged that she broke the windows with her fist.

It was a serious situation likely to provoke an open breach with France, but Richelieu, whose virtue was patience, and who was in no position to add England to the number of France's enemies, counselled moderation. In September he sent the most agreeable cavalier in France, the Maréchal de Bassompierre, to England, and every effort was made to remove sources of friction. Henriette Marie was advised to compromise in the matter of her household;

and England was assured that the ships would be returned, that the demands of the Huguenots would be met, and that the French would further subsidize England's efforts to recover the Palatinate for Frederick. For a moment it seemed as if harmony would prevail. Henriette Marie was allowed to retain a sufficiently large French household, and Bassompierre even managed to secure the release of seventy priests held in English jails. On 15 November a great masque was held in Buckingham's residence, York House. Bassompierre accompanied the King on the royal barge from Whitehall, and was seated with him at Buckingham's table. Then in a neighbouring room was performed a living addition to the twenty-one tableaux of Rubens celebrating the glories of Marie de Médicis. She was shown as a goddess enthroned on the waters of the Channel welcoming her relations-in-law, the incongrous assembly of Frederick and Elizabeth of the Palatinate, Philip IV of Spain, Victor Amadeus, the son of Charles Emmanuel of Savoy, and Charles I. Affected by this fantasy, Buckingham suddenly announced that he had decided to go to France himself and heal the breach.

Bassompierre was agitated, for he knew that the Duke would be the last person in the world to receive a warm welcome from Louis XIII at that moment. Not only had he outraged the King of France by paying court to his Queen, but he was blamed for the estrangement of Charles and Henriette Marie and for the deterioration in Anglo-French relations. Richelieu, who had by now formed the opinion that he was a gadfly 'full of extravagance, violent and unrestrained in his passions', was in no mood to counsel Louis to hide his displeasure. For the moment there was nothing for Bassompierre to do but moderate Buckingham's enthusiasm until he could himself reach Paris and get instructions from the Cardinal. His return journey to France was delayed by frightful December gales, which blew his ship back and forth across the Channel for five days, and cast overboard two coaches which were being carried on deck, one of them loaded with a large quantity of rich clothing which Bassompierre had bought for his lady friends in Paris. When he finally arrived and reported that it was Buckingham's intention to appear in person, Louis ordered him to write instantly to the Duke to say he would not be welcome. Richelieu approved of this action, saying that Buckingham's presence would be 'prejudicial to the repose of the state, and not of much use in bringing the two crowns together'. Buckingham was, he added, by nature a conspirator, and there were already enough of these at the French court. The letter which was drafted to Buckingham was delicately phrased but firm.

Buckingham's wounded pride was not, however, the only or the main reason for the sudden crisis that now erupted between the two courts. Richelieu had for some months been seizing English ships as reprisals for the seizure of French ships by the English. Now the Duc d'Épernon, in order, so it was alleged, to exacerbate Anglo-French relations in the hope of bringing Richelieu down, seized a fleet of two hundred English ships carrying England's supply of claret for a whole year while they were waiting in Bordeaux harbour. There was an instant shortage of wine in England, prices rose, and on 3 December England retaliated with an Order in Council for the confiscation of all French ships and goods in English waters – which at that time extended several leagues from the coast.

Three months later, in March 1627, the crisis was deepened when Pennington swept up French shipping along the whole Atlantic seaboard and came back to England with a string of French prizes. Still Richelieu was for conciliation, but on this occasion he found Louis XIII unusually obstinate. The King demanded the restitution of the French household, and the release of the French ships. Buckingham informed Richelieu that Charles I considered himself no longer bound by the marriage terms in respect of the household, and had no intention of releasing the ships until France took initial steps towards peace. Fortified with the proceeds of the sale of Pennington's prizes, and the ships seized in English ports, Charles I was prepared for war with France, and Buckingham, now thoroughly offended at Louis' personal rebuff to him, was an eager abettor.

8

To Make the King Absolute
1626-7

Richelieu was at the pinnacle of power, but beneath him was sand. Not in recent French history had a first minister survived the resentment, intrigues and jealousies that gnawed continuously at the structure of government, and it was only to be expected that within months of taking office he would begin to sense the intensifying urge for his destruction, and observe the coalition of forces organized to this end. He knew that his survival, and the evolution of effective administration of the realm, depended upon eternal vigilance and ruthless counter-measures. He had witnessed the constant civil disobedience of the great magnates, and had seen it go regularly unpunished, even rewarded. This subversion of order and authority could not be permitted to continue, for it debilitated France and left her at the mercy of her neighbours; it had to be made clear that the risks of rebellion were out of proportion to the gains. For a period there must be a ruthless exercise of the royal power and a demonstration of its effectiveness. In the process, liberty would suffer and charity would be neglected, but the moral end of civil society made it necessary.

He summed it up in words that were intended to burn themselves into Louis XIII's memory:

Kings are true images of God. They cannot be too careful to acquire, by good deeds, the reputation of being liberal; it is thereby that they win over hearts. A king may pardon someone a fleeting intention to trouble the state, provided he is truly repentant and there is reason to believe that he will not lapse again. But where it is known that the man will continue in his evil design, the king is obliged in conscience to chastise him, and cannot fail to do so without being guilty of sin. If there is reason to fear that the overlooking of this fault will encourage others also to disobey, through his example, to the prejudice of national peace, the king is obliged to punish the crime, and cannot exempt himself from this duty without committing a graver crime.[1]

The Cardinal's predecessors had been brought down for reasons of spite, and inefficiency on their part and the ambition for power on the part of others. In his case there was a new factor introduced into the struggle, that of religion. Every enemy of Richelieu rallied under the banner of the Catholic zealots, and pretended that the Cardinal's unpopularity was due solely to his betrayal of the faith. This gave the subversive movement a solidarity and a moral aspect which made it doubly formidable and dangerous. And as Richelieu survived crisis after crisis and pursued his anti-Habsburg policies abroad with energy and determination, the frustration of his enemies made them ever more desperate. They tried to paint the Cardinal as a devil incarnate, sitting pale-faced in scarlet stroking his cats with the long sinister fingers of a mandarin, seeing all, knowing all, and forgiving nothing, the architect of evil, the possessor of the King, the enemy of God. It was the wildest caricature. The reality was a nervous, sensitive, conscience-stricken man, for ever overworked, compelling a frail and reluctant body by extraordinary will-power, for ever anxious and in peril, a man with some strange energy that drove him to reconstruct the state and make France a great power once again in the face of the most formidable obstruction, and at vast sacrifice to his own health and enjoyment of life. Richelieu's essential greatness is that he devoted himself to this thankless and emotionally exhausting task when almost anyone else would have succumbed to the pressure.

The shock to Catholic opinion of the French assault on the papal troops in the Valtelline produced Richelieu's first crisis, and his obstinate refusal to make amends until the political question had been solved deepened it. The usual way of effecting a *coup d'état* was to find some member of the royal family to head the movement: and ever since her fall as Regent, Marie de Médicis had been the easy victim of any aggregation of conspirators who sought to use her. A woman of uninformed piety, and an Italian whose political horizon failed to encompass the vastness of Europe, she believed simply in the Spanish claim to be the champion of Catholicism.

In the circles of Marie de Médicis trifles were magnified into major issues, and one such trifle was a quarrel among the Queen Mother's ladies-in-waiting which involved Richelieu's niece, Marie-Madeleine de Combalet, the daughter of his sister Françoise and her husband Pontcourlay. In January 1625 this girl, then aged twenty-one, and already a widow, was appointed to the royal bedchamber. She did not need to advertise that she was the Cardinal's niece, for the spiteful ladies of the court expected her to act above her station and radiate his conceit. Tongues wagged, among them that of the Princess de Conti, daughter of Henri, Duc de Guise, who had been assassinated by Henri III in 1588; she had her personal grudge against Richelieu because he had removed her nephew, the present duke, from his post as admiral in the Mediterranean. The members of the House of Guise were kingmakers by tradition, and were in no mood to bob the knee to an upstart Richelieu or suffer the pertness of a Pontcourlay daughter of a country-bumpkin squireen. Scandalized by Richelieu's tussle with Urban VIII, infected with the poison that those around her fashioned for his downfall, Marie de Médicis was transformed into an enemy; and as always with this woman of primitive emotions the issue was one of personality; the Cardinal was ungrateful; now that he had arrived through her agency, he spurned her; he was detestable, his pride was insufferable. Before the year 1625 was out Marie de Médicis was the focus of a vast conspiracy to remove the monster who made war upon the Pope.

As it happened, a more dangerous and more vicious royal enemy was emerging in the person of Louis XIII's seventeen-year-old brother Gaston, Duc d'Anjou, who bore the title of 'Monsieur'.

The historians of his own time and of subsequent generations have pictured him as a creature of despicable character, who
had inherited all of his mother's worst features, and few of his
father's good qualities. Gaston's motives, and the role he played in
events, are still so unclear that he may not, in fact, have been quite
as black as has been believed. His contemporaries found him
lively, charming and a good friend, but his pop-eyes, drooping,
thick lower lip, open mouth and puffy cheeks betrayed his limited
intelligence; and his constant grimacing indicated a temper that
was fretful, nervous and excitable. Although many of those who
associated with him were dragged by his intemperance to their
doom, it is not true to say that he altogether abandoned them.
Indeed, much of Gaston's conduct is to be explained by his efforts
to save his friends; and if he lent his authority to rebellion after
rebellion, it was largely because the ruthless execution of his co-
conspirators on each occasion led him to renewed disobedience.
In other circumstances Gaston might have been a patriot; he was
led to become a persistent traitor because Louis resented his
popularity, and because jealousy begot jealousy. It is also possible
that Gaston might have lived tranquilly had he not been tempted
by the serpent; and the serpent was the incandescent Marie,
Duchesse de Chevreuse.

This woman, who was to be in the centre of most of the
intrigues against Richelieu, was one of the vast Rohan clan, born
in 1600 the daughter of the Duc de Montbazon. She had hardly
reached adolescence before her delicate, aristocratic oval face and
vermilion lips, her blonde, silken hair, her mysterious, penetrating
eyes, and her svelte, supple body held in thrall the entire male
world; and she exclaimed prophetically, 'I believe that I am
destined to be the object of the folly of extravagant men!'[2] From
the age of fourteen she abandoned herself to the pursuit of love and
to intrigues, so that in later years Mazarin was to say that France
had been calm only when she had not been there. In 1617 she
married Luynes, he being then thirty-nine and she seventeen.
The Duc de Montbazon, in need of money, swallowed his Rohan
pride at this misalliance with the son of a petty Provençal seigneur,
and looked forward to acquiring more remunerative offices

through the influence of the royal favourite. Luynes was made a duke, and the new Mme de Luynes was thereby able to retain the tabouret to which the Rohans were accustomed. For Luynes she had no affection whatever, and although she provided him with a son and two daughters in remarkably quick succession his death was to her a matter of complete indifference.

At the age of eighteen this unscrupulous and subtle girl became superintendent of the Queen's household. Her influence over Anne of Austria, who was the same age, quickly became paramount, and the slow blood of the Habsburgs was stirred by the salacious poems which the new superintendent read to her. The papal nuncio, Corsini, was even led to report to Rome on the licentiousness of the Queen's court, and to intervene, as he said, 'with great precaution', with the Queen's confessor. Among the lovers whom Marie had taken even during Luynes' lifetime was the Duc de Chevreuse, and in a moment of pique with Luynes, Louis XIII had viciously said that he had told Luynes about it, and 'it gave me great pleasure to avenge myself on her, and cause him displeasure'.[3] Now that Luynes was dead the affair with Chevreuse was conducted publicly, and the nuncio, scandalized by the 'licentious discourse which passes the limits of decency',[4] intervened more decisively to have Marie removed from the Court. He found an ally in Marie de Médicis, whose return to Paris after her reconciliation with the King had aroused feelings of jealousy in Anne of Austria, which Marie de Luynes was quick to inflame. In April 1622 Mme de Luynes was given three days to leave the court. She immediately sent one of her officers to Chevreuse to propose marriage to him. The invitation reached Chevreuse when he was on his way to a pilgrimage and took him by surprise. He hesitated, questioning the officer as to what was behind it, and discussing it with his companions, who thought he would be extremely unwise to accept.

Claude de Lorraine, Duc de Chevreuse, was a scion of the Dukes of Lorraine. His great-grandfather had established himself in France and been made Duc de Guise by François I; his great-aunt was the mother of Mary Queen of Scots; his father was the great Duc de Guise of the Catholic League; his sister was the

Princess de Conti, married to a prince of the blood; his brother was the unordained Cardinal de Guise and archbishop of Reims, a man whose morality was as dubious as his own; and he was a first cousin of James I. Now aged forty-five, Chevreuse had avoided marriage because he had found no one of his rank. A valiant soldier and duellist, he was handsome, athletic and easygoing. Recently he had been made Grand Chamberlain of France, and he was in no mood to offend Louis XIII by marrying Marie de Rohan in the moment of her disgrace. Full of misgivings, he returned to Paris and went to see her, but, slave to her personality, he succumbed to her charms and her wiles, and within five days of her rustication from the court, and four months from the death of Luynes, Marie de Rohan was Duchesse de Chevreuse. 'I do not know what this will produce,'[5] Marillac wrote to Richelieu. In Louis XIII it produced rage, but in face of the whole race of Lorraine, which rallied to Chevreuse's support, he had to swallow his vexation; the marriage contract was signed by all the Guises, the Gonzagues, the Princesses de Condé and Conti, and the Duchesses de Mercoeur, Longueville, Elbeuf and Vendôme. Marie de Rohan was now a princess of Lorraine, and the châtelaine of Dampierre near Versailles.

It was Chevreuse who stood proxy for Charles I at the marriage with Henriette Marie, and his wife who, under his very nose, carried on an affair with the Earl of Holland and connived at Buckingham's courtship of the Queen – even prompting the latter to indiscretion. The Chevreuses went to England in the train of Henriette Marie, and there Marie continued her liaison with Holland, and, according to the French about the court, began another with Buckingham. Henriette Marie's chaplain wrote indignantly to Richelieu that he was ashamed 'of the imprudences of Mme de Chevreuse and of the simplicity of her husband', who appeared to be unaware of what was going on, or at least not to care. 'It is a public farce.' The English marriage had been contracted mainly to help the Catholics of England, but 'it seems that these women have come here to establish bastards rather than religion', the chaplain bluntly concluded.[6] In due course in Hampton Court Marie was brought to bed of a daughter who was later to be the abbess of Pont-aux-Dames. This event postponed her recall to France by a furious Richelieu, and it was not until July 1625 that she returned with her husband and the Marquis d'Effiat, bearing with her a letter from Charles I, thanking her for her company, and addressing her as 'our dear cousin'. To the friend of the Queen of France and the King of England Richelieu could not be other than amiable. None the less, though he was at pains to be polite and gracious to her, there existed between him and the Duchess a growing enmity.

Scarcely was she back at the French court when Mme de Chevreuse joined the frivolous ladies who mocked at the Cardinal. Worse, she spread abroad the notion that Louis XIII, who was always ill, had not long to live; Gaston would be king and Anne of Austria could marry him. The Queen listened to this dangerous talk and encouraged Marie in it. Suddenly the court was startled by an announcement that Gaston would marry a rich Bourbon of the Montpensier branch. The decision was taken by Marie de Médicis, who was gravely disquieted by Gaston's scandalous personal life. Anne of Austria was dismayed. If the King should die and Gaston be married, what would become of her? What indeed! exclaimed Mme de Chevreuse, and she resolved to incite everyone to exercise influence on Gaston to cause him to decline the match. Among those whom she approached was Gaston's governor, Colonel d'Ornano. This man was a Corsican whose father had led a band of Corsicans in the service of Henri IV during the Wars of Religion. Owing to his personal qualities and his firmness of spirit d'Ornano exercised over Gaston an extraordinary influence. What Marie said to him is not exactly known, but she was probably clever enough to disguise her real motives, with the argument that Louis XIII, so long as he was childless, would be weakened in his authority by Gaston's having children, and hence would welcome a postponement of the marriage. D'Ornano would thus gain credit from both Louis and Gaston; and Mme de Chevreuse promised him the Queen's backing.

Gaston, supported by d'Ornano's advice, declared he would not marry Marie de Montpensier, whom a contemporary described as being as 'proud as a dragon'. That the Queen was behind this

Richelieu knew from his informants, and, fearing the consequences of another upheaval in the royal family, involving, perhaps, another rebellion of Marie de Médicis, he took counsel of Père Joseph. The latter advised that d'Ornano should be won over, and as part of this plan he was nominated a marshal of France early in 1626. To Richelieu he said that he had not interfered in the marriage question in any way. According to Bassompierre, who recorded the matter in his *Mémoires*, Louis himself had ordered d'Ornano to prevent Gaston and Marie from meeting, and it is quite likely that the Corsican really believed that in participating in the cabal to prevent Gaston from marrying he was in fact serving the King. In the previous November Gaston had sought to be appointed commander of the army intended for the chastisement of La Rochelle, which was supporting Soubise's maritime adventures. Failing to receive a reply, Gaston had gatecrashed the council meeting in November, and had been told that his proper place was the hunting field. The incident had embarrassed everyone, and Gaston was nourishing a warm resentment. D'Ornano had been called before the King and told that Gaston should drop the idea of leading the royal army. Possibly at that meeting Louis had hinted that the marriage proposal should be abandoned, although it is unlikely that the cautious and tongue-tied monarch would have committed himself this far with a man he did not trust.

The King was not the only one who had a vested interest in Gaston's unmarried status. The princes of the blood, Condé, Conti and Soissons, all had their position on the ladder of succession to the throne. With them, and with all the restless magnates in the country, Mme de Chevreuse was in touch; and because she spoke with the Queen's voice they all listened. The Duchesse de Rohan promised the support of the Huguenots, the Duc de Nevers would raise troops in Champagne, Soissons would provide 400,000 crowns to support Gaston's opposition to the marriage proposal, and the Duke of Savoy would provide twelve thousand men. But the most ardent accomplices were the two royal bastards left over from the boisterous days of Henri IV, César, the Duc de Vendôme, and Alexandre, the Grand Prior of the Order of Malta, both sons of Henri's mistress Gabrielle d'Estrées. There was a mutual hatred between this pair and their half-brother the King. To d'Ornano Vendôme wrote complaining of the numerous injustices done to him by Marie de Médicis, and the King since the death of his father, and referring to the crown which Gaston would shortly wear; as soon as Gaston left the court all the conspirators would support him in open rebellion, as they had supported his mother; and the letter concluded that Gaston 'should use menaces and violence against Richelieu'. Vendôme hoped, in the outcome, to transform his governorship of Brittany into an independent principality.

Much of this was known to the government. In the royal council there was growing disquiet, and it was believed that the conspirators intended to assassinate the King. In so far as Richelieu's actions in this obscure and complicated intrigue are known to us, it seems that he had tried to avoid taking sides in what at the beginning was a sordid family controversy, and that it was Louis, not he, who had opposed Gaston's ambitions.[7] When Louis summoned him and Schomberg to Fontainebleau to discuss the evidence of a conspiracy he said that if Monsieur were to be separated from the plotters this would have to be done with circumspection to avoid throwing him into the latter's hands. Richelieu was staying at the château of Fleury not far from Fontainebleau, and it was rumoured that he was to be waylaid in the forest there and murdered. The King insisted that henceforth he should be escorted, and a regiment of the guards was ordered to come to Fontainebleau on the pretext of manoeuvres. It arrived on 4 May 1626, and that evening d'Ornano was arrested and removed to the château of Vincennes. His papers were searched and Vendôme's letter was discovered.

Gaston, as soon as he was informed of the news, seized his cloak and sword and angrily demanded to see the King. According to one account the latter refused to admit him; according to another the King accused him of trying to embroil Louis with his mother, whereupon Monsieur spat, 'I know the author of these calumnies, and I shall get my revenge!' The object of Gaston's revenge was Richelieu, but the manner of the revenge was as yet undecided upon. It was Mme de Chevreuse who again intervened at this critical point. For six days after d'Ornano's arrest she sat locked in her apartment, hourly expecting arrest like most of d'Ornano's friends and relations. When nothing happened she emerged to consult with Gaston about saving d'Ornano. She needed an instrument, and she found it in Henri de Talleyrand, Marquis de Chalais.

This man of twenty-eight was a charmer, an agreeable, athletic gallant very popular about the court where he was master of the royal wardrobe, but he was vain, lacking in honour and conscience, had recently killed a man in a duel, and he was firmly held in the toils of the Chevreuse, with whom he was insanely infatuated. Up to this point the object of his adoration had not yielded to him, and this, in the circumstances, was an advantage when she approached Chalais and asked for his aid. She said that if he would give his all to her, she would despise the rest of the world. Then she produced her trump card: the Cardinal, she said, was in love with her and was his rival. The siren had little difficulty in capturing the foolish fellow, but she was to find that her instrument lacked strength. He gossiped, and one of those in whom he confided was a Knight of Malta, Achille d'Éstampes, the commander of Valençay. Probably Valençay informed Richelieu, who decided to use Chalais to trap the real villains, the Vendôme brothers. At all events, Valençay persuaded Chalais to come to Fleury to confess, which he did on 10 May. What exactly he told Richelieu remains unclear, and there are several versions of it. One is that the Vendômes and Gaston were to assassinate Richelieu at Fleury, various pretexts being mentioned; another is that they were to hold a knife at his throat and force him to order d'Ornano's release. Whatever Chalais told Richelieu, the latter was moved to make a demonstration, and the following morning when Gaston awoke he found, to his astonishment, the Cardinal at the bedside awaiting the princely levee. Monsieur, in the presence of the devil, was overawed, as Richelieu intended he should be, and kept silent.

There followed the first of a long series of reconciliations between Gaston and his brother. But if Gaston was insincere, his insincerity, at least in his own eyes, was matched by that of Louis. For no sooner had Gaston taken his oath of fidelity and believed that all was forgiven and forgotten when the King struck: Vendôme and the Grand Prior were arrested. The former of the brothers had fortified himself in Brittany and proclaimed to the world that he would never again see Louis except in picture. The Grand Prior had sought to mediate, and, when the King threatened invasion of Brittany, persuaded Vendôme to come to Blois for a reconciliation. Richelieu was advised by Marillac that Gaston appeared to have received the news of their arrest with equanimity. Marillac was mistaken, for in fact Gaston was indignant that this arrest should be a prologue to his marriage with Marie de Montpensier, to which he had been forced to agree as part of the settlement. Mme de Chevreuse questioned Chalais, and quickly learned that he had been won over by Richelieu. She set about winning him back. Gaston, she said, should flee from France, perhaps to La Rochelle, preferably to Lorraine, and Chalais should organize the affair.

Chalais was observed to be closeted alone with Gaston for hours on end. They decided that when the court reached Nantes, where Gaston was to meet Marie de Montpensier for the betrothal ceremony, Chalais and five or six gentlemen would find a pretext for accompanying Gaston on horseback, and all would flee. A personal enemy of Chalais, Roger de Gramont, denounced him and on 9 July 1626 Chalais was arrested in the château of Nantes, and a judicial commission consisting of d'Effiat and Valençay was charged to inquire into the whole affair. Two days later, after Sunday mass, Gaston was on the point of taking flight when he resolved to confront Richelieu, who had also arrived at Nantes with the King. According to an eye-witness, 'the Cardinal with three preserves and two Genovese prunes made him forget all about the project which he had so long contemplated'. Gaston thought that by a new submission he would save the remainder of his suite from arrest, and, telling Louis that he was prepared to accede to Marie de Médicis' wish that he should marry Marie de Montpensier, he said 'it is necessary to save Chalais'. Before the wayward youth could change his mind again he was enmeshed in the bonds of matrimony. The ceremony was performed by Richelieu in haste, and almost in private, in the antechamber of the King in the château of Nantes: there was no music, and a witness thought he had never seen such a sad marriage. Newly invested with the Duchy of Orléans, which was richer than the Duchy of Anjou, Gaston was bedded with the proud dragon, only to be rudely disturbed by his mother-in-law looking for her pet dog in the nuptial bedchamber. Just over nine months later the new bride died in childbirth, though her daughter lived; she was to become the formidable Grande Mademoiselle of a later age.

Gaston's sacrifice failed to save Chalais. Gramont, becoming bolder every day, now came forward with new charges against him, and Chalais himself seemed only too eager to accuse everyone of almost any crime. How much of Chalais' confession is credible is difficult to say, for in his pitiable condition he answered in the affirmative every question that the commission put to him, and wrote long letters to Richelieu begging for mercy and saying that Gaston's entourage had destined for the Cardinal 'great blows of the dagger'. Of Mme de Chevreuse he said, 'all the conversation of that lady consists only of licentiousness, coquetry and oaths'. Yet he wrote to her protesting his love and asking for her support. After much hesitation she sought out Richelieu at the château of Beauregard, and interceded for Chalais. The Cardinal, perhaps not without some malice, produced the evidence that Chalais had given, and pointed out the passages where he had implicated and abused her. She fell into a frightful temper and accused Chalais in her turn.

The investigation complete, letters patent were issued constituting a chamber of criminal justice, one of the judges of which was François Fouquet, father of Louis XIV's famous minister Nicholas Fouquet. The Chalais who appeared in court on 11 August 1626 was a pathetic creature, his beard and hair unkempt, his eyes tormented. His trial has never been analysed, and there are features about it which call for investigation. For example, Gramont was rewarded with a pension of four thousand crowns for evidence which seems, at the best, hearsay, while Gaston's testimony is in the handwriting of Marie de Médicis' secretary,

Denis Bouthillier, who is not mentioned as being present at the interrogation, and it is not signed by him, though it is signed by Richelieu. Later, in a moment of rancour, Gaston was to proclaim to the world that Richelieu was behind his own proposals of escape, and that Chalais was merely the scapegoat. On 18 August Chalais was convicted of high treason and sentenced to be decapitated and quartered, and his heirs deprived of their nobility. It was profoundly frightening to all would-be plotters, for not in many years had conspiracy been dealt with in this very English fashion.

On the day of the execution the headsman was found to be missing, bribed, so it was said, by Monsieur to make himself scarce. There was no other to be found in Nantes, but the authorities were undeterred. Two condemned prisoners in the local gaol were promised their lives if they would act the part, which they undertook to do. Constantly kissing the crucifix on his rosary, Chalais laid his head on the block. The amateur executioners blundered; the first blow merely wounded, and the next three did no more than hack the victim about. The confessor, who had attended these events before, had to interrupt and explain to the bewildered fellows how it should be done. Chalais' eyes were still open, and the confessor said: 'If you are still conscious, indicate that your thoughts are on God.' The half-stunned Chalais said 'Jesus Maria!' Various estimates, ranging from twenty-nine to thirty-six, were made of the number of times the pair of gaol-birds chopped away at the bleeding and murmuring head before it fell off. The event shocked a France that thought it was callous.

There remained the problem of Mme de Chevreuse, and a council meeting was held at Nantes to discuss the matter. Richelieu described her as the worst of all the conspirators, recalling her part in the criminal enterprise of Fleury, her instigation of revolt among the Huguenots and the dukes, and her provocation of Gaston to disobedience. However, the arrest of a duchess was a thing unheard of, and would produce resentment on the part of the whole higher nobility; also, to provoke the Houses of Guise and Rohan at this moment would be dangerous.

It was decided, therefore, to send her into exile. She was ordered to a château in Poitou owned by her brother-in-law, the Prince de Guéméné, but she was not the one to tolerate a rustic retreat where she would no longer be able to intrigue, and where for lovers there were only the local squires. She departed secretly for the court of her husband's cousin, the Duke of Lorraine, where the occasions for conspiracy and sin were beyond computing.

In his *Mémoires* Richelieu argues that the execution of Chalais was necessary to protect the realm from new dissension. The end and object of his whole career, he explained to Louis XIII, was 'to make the King absolute in his Kingdom in order to establish therein order and rule, to which his conscience obliged him'.[8] First it was necessary to reduce the great nobles to loyalty, and to harness their energies in the service of the state. No state in Europe could exist on its public officers, but depended on the nobility. There must be only one noblesse – the royal noblesse. The aristocracy had failed to transform itself into a political oligarchy capable of resisting the encroachments of absolute monarchy. It consumed itself and the resources of the nation in the pursuit of phantoms of power and honour; and it was an impediment to the centralization of the state, upon which the grandeur of France depended. Richelieu wrote that:

... of all governments, the best is that in which the principal motive-power is in the mind of the sovereign who, though capable of acting by himself, has such modesty and good judgement that he never does anything without good advice.[9]

The King's counsellors must be firm of spirit, of solid judgement, prudent, and trained in history and letters. They must be able to anticipate evils and plan for the future.

The statesman must be faithful to God, to the state, to men and to himself. The probity of a public minister does not suppose a cringing or scrupulous conscience, for scruples can produce many injustices and cruelties.[10]

And he added:

Courage requires that a man be exempt from weakness and fear; it requires a certain spark which makes him desire and pursue great things with ardour commensurate with the wisdom of the judgement.[11]

These qualities he knew himself to possess.

The intriguers at the court were no match for this tenacious intellectual, to whom fear was by no means unknown, but in whom fear was dominated by courage, conviction and faith in God and manifest destiny. To him the logic of absolute monarchy demanded a minister who would be the King's servant and the people's dictator – the fountainhead of a bureaucratic system whose functionaries would be anonymous, loyal and efficient. Such a system existed in embryo, but Richelieu's predecessors had not been able to make it function effectively in face of the inertia of traditional institutions. France was not an entity, but a congeries of antiquated centres of administrative gravity. Threatened from without by the might of the Habsburgs and the instability of neighbouring countries, it could not tolerate egoistic and divisive influences from within.

The provincial governments were among the most significant of these. The provinces were ruled by governors, who were nominally for the Crown but often stood against it, and used the royal authority to become petty sovereigns; a contemporary called them 'satraps'. In certain of the provinces there were also provincial Estates, duplications of the States General, with the three orders, clergy, nobility and commons, meeting separately, though in most provinces the participation of the third estate was minimal. All the Midi had a vast degree of autonomy, and even in the centre and west the provincial Estates had not renounced their privileges and were engaged in a constant struggle with the Crown to defend them. Whenever the Crown proposed anything constructive, even the widening of the roads, it encountered the obstacle of provincial liberties, and men remembered the occasion when, in 1593, Provence had even refused subsidies to Henri IV to defend it from threatened invasion by Savoy. In addition, the cities, composed of oligarchies of men of the robe and of trade, had their liberties.

For two centuries the kings had sought to penetrate the

provincial administrative structure by creating officers answerable to themselves, who would duplicate and gradually absorb the functions of revenue-raising, defence, police and the courts. Henri IV had made use of a tradition of creating a royal lieutenant in each province who was supposed to assist the governor, but who in fact counterbalanced him, and also a professional commissioner who represented a central administration, and to whom various officers were made answerable. In the sixteenth century a commissioner of justice had been appointed in disturbed provinces, with power to determine all questions concerned with the pacification of a region, to discipline the army and secure its payment, and he combined in his competence the faculties of police and justice, both civil and military. After the armies had gone their way these commissioners had often remained, in face of protests from the provincial governors, judges and magistrates, who objected to their functions being usurped.

At first these commissioners' powers were expressly enumerated, and the commission itself was regarded as an extraordinary and temporary measure. Later, certain outpost areas were given permanent intendants – as Richelieu did in the case of Pinerolo. Not until 1635 did he succeed in issuing commissions on a more regular basis, and then only because war offered an excuse for extraordinary measures. They were made plenary in form, and the commissioner, now more often called an intendant, was given authority over the justices, officers and subjects of the Crown, with the power of resolution and decision of 'affairs concerning our service, repose and security, to receive requests, administer justice, preside over courts and police, and assist the governors and lieutenant-generals'. As a rule the commission over justice and police was included only after 1638, and the matter was not systematized until an edict of the council of 28 August 1642. Clearly the strength of the intendants depended upon that of the royal council, for if this were dominated by men, like Condé, who were at the same time provincial governors, the provincial institutions would be in a position to resist the royal functionaries.

The Parlement was the instrument for enacting royal decisions.

All legislation had to be registered by it, and it controlled the legal machinery. It was conservative, independent, and resistant to pressure. There were various techniques for overriding its obstruction, but they depended upon the strength of will of the monarch, or of his ministry. In eight of the provinces there were also duplicates of this body. At the time of Richelieu's accession the Parlement claimed that there was a fundamental law that all decrees were of legal effect only if approved by it, even if they were made in the King's presence. On this point Richelieu and the Parlement were to wrestle for the whole of his career, and he was to be most successful in gaining control of the judicial system. An ordinance of 1641 forbade the Parlement in future to concern itself with political questions, and restricted its judicial functions,[12] and in 1625 this would have been regarded as a constitutional impossibility. At that time the Parlement had an enormous reputation; it embodied the notion of judicial independence, it was patriotic, anti-Spanish, and gallican in religion. At the States General in 1614 it had delivered a memorial which stated its case as follows: 'Laws, ordinances, creations of offices, treaties of peace and other important affairs of the realm are sent to it so that it may deliberate on them, examine their merit and effect reasonable modifications in complete freedom.'[13] The standard work on the Parlement, written by Bernard de La Roche-Flavin in 1617, summed up its powers as follows: 'It has the function of verifying, ratifying, refusing, limiting or restraining'[14] legislation, and it was the pivot of a France composed of 'three sorts of government on the whole, that is to say, the monarchy, aristocracy and republic, so that one may serve as a brake upon and a counterpoise to the other'.[15] This thesis was anathema to Richelieu, who regarded the checks and balance system as an emasculation of the state, and who described the opposition which the Parlement presented to his measures as 'altogether beyond the bounds of reason'.[16]

The expression 'fundamental law' had appeared in the sixteenth century, and the notion was a Renaissance artifact which purported to be an eternal principle governing the life of the nation. It implied that behind the institutions of government was something unalterable by established authority, and it assimilated traditional privileges and liberties to the laws of God and nature. A leading commentator of the time, Charles Loyseau, put it as follows:

There are three sorts of laws which limit the power of the sovereign, without restricting sovereignty; they are, first the laws of God, since the Prince is no less sovereign for being subject to God; secondly, the rules of natural and not positive justice, because it is the characteristic of the supreme power of the state to be exerted, not at discretion, but according to justice; and finally, the fundamental laws of the state, because the Prince must exercise his sovereignty according to its own proper nature and the forms and conditions under which it is established.[17]

When it served the purposes of the royal authority to invoke fundamental law Richelieu was the first to do so. For example, when France acquired territory abroad by cession he argued that, since the fundamental law forbade retrocession, the question was diplomatically closed. But, in general, he found the notion an obstacle to his policies of intensifying the royal power throughout France.

The jurists who invented the notion of fundamental law – or perhaps derived it from the Spaniards who had inherited it from the days of El Cid – also took over from Roman law during the reign of François I the maxim 'What the King wills, the law also wills'. The two ideas were incompatible, and could be held in balance only so long as the king chose to exercise his authority conservatively, and did not seek to alter established institutions. By Richelieu's time the equilibrium between the concept of fundamental law and the concept of royal sovereignty had been seriously disturbed, as the work of Cardin Le Bret, published in 1632, makes clear. Sovereignty, he said, 'is a supreme power bestowed on an individual, which gives him the right to command absolutely, and which has for its end the repose and advantage of the public'.[18] Criticizing the anarchic character of feudal rights and privileges, Le Bret argued that all institutions and customs could be changed by the royal authority, 'for all persons, being equally subjects of the same King, are equally subject to the same law'. Sovereignty, however, was not yet detached from the medieval notion of the common good and the natural law, which laid down the boundaries outside which royal power ceased to be just, or the royal will obliging in conscience. Richelieu, in particular, still had his roots in St Thomas Aquinas, and he believed that the king was absolute only when he acted within the limits of Christian morality. 'The public interest,' he told Louis XIII:

... must be the only end of the prince and his adviser. It is impossible to conceive the good which a prince, and those whom he uses in his affairs can do if they religiously follow this principle, and one cannot imagine the evil which accrues to a state when they prefer the interests of individuals to those of the public.[19]

The concept of sovereignty introduced a gravitational factor into French political thinking without which Richelieu would have found it difficult to realize his policy of centralizing authority; the concept of reason added yet another. It was an age when men were becoming interested in mathematics and the physical sciences, and the structure of the state was conceived of in the symmetrical terms of geometry. Le Bret, in fact, used this precise analogy, saying that 'sovereignty is no more divisible than is the point in geometry'[20] – meaning thereby that no competition with the royal authority was possible, and that this was something ordained in the nature of things. Descartes in philosophy, Grotius in law, Corneille in drama, and Richelieu in politics were simultaneously demonstrating the faith that their age had in the power of human reason to perceive the true structure of things, and to delineate it without error, even down to its finer details. Richelieu wrote:

The light of natural reason enables everyone to know that, since man is endowed with reason, he must do nothing except by reason, for otherwise he would act contrary to his nature, and as a result, contrary against Him who is its Author.[21]

There is, in fact, in this thesis a paradox: Richelieu, like his contemporaries, is optimistic about the capacity of the mind to recognize the right and natural course of conduct. Again like his contemporaries, he is pessimistic about men's wish to do so. A strong emphasis on the sinfulness of man led to a greater reliance on God, and the king became a providential instrument. His absolutism thus derived on the one side from a belief in the institution of monarchy as a rational system of government, and on the other side from a belief in its necessary power to restrain the irrational tendencies in men; and the two beliefs were, in some measure, the antithesis of each other.

The tension in Richelieu's thinking between the power of natural reason to disclose absolute truth and the inadequacy of ill-informed minds to choose the best course of conduct made him at one and the same time the supreme theorist and the supreme opportunist. The king's ministers, he argued, since they were alone in possession of all the relevant facts, had a necessarily sounder judgement than those who argued from first principles:

> There are good reasons why those who have the direction of monarchical states say that in certain circumstances the subjects must blindly obey the prince; for often necessity constrains them to adopt policies which cannot be supported by abstract reason alone, but can be iustified only in the event.

Richelieu was an empiricist who adapted his policies to changing circumstances; and this flexibility, leading as it did to the exploitation of opportunity, enabled him to achieve his goal of the integrity and grandeur of France, just as it was the occasion of bitter disillusionment on the part of those whose expectations he disappointed. That he made adroit use of Marie de Médicis, the Catholic zealots, the Jesuits, the anti-Jesuits, the tolerationists and the anti-tolerationists, the pro-Spanish and the anti-Spanish, cannot be denied; but the view that his whole career was a contrived deception of all the world is as misleading as the opinion that, because he spoke and wrote in terms of theory, his politics were the product of inflexible doctrine.

Richelieu is an enigma only because he combined in a completely unique fashion an iron resolution and a gift for seeing both sides of a question. The one enabled him to pursue his ends with sublime disregard for the pressures exerted upon him from every side, and the other, reinforced by a sense of justice, led him instinctively to avoid extremes. Such a man was incapable of satisfying all opinions. While his awareness of the complexities of issues led him to gestures of moderation, his passionate devotion to the concept of order, coupled with his personal inclination to authoritarianism, prompted him no less often to betray the cause of liberalism. In the result, his theories and his practice frequently contradicted each other, just as the views expressed in the political pamphlets he sponsored contradicted each other because his policies changed; and this equivocation earned him the hatred of his contemporaries and the misunderstanding of historians, who have seen him as either all virtue or all vice, but rarely as a politician who was only more or less successful in his choice of goals and of occasions, and who, for all his opportunism, retained an acute sense of the problem of political morality. It was from the heart that he said that statesmen 'are like those one condemns to the surplice, with this difference alone, that the latter suffer for their faults, the others for their merits'.[22]

9

Red Eminence

1626-7

For twenty years Alphonse du Plessis de Richelieu had been devoting himself to silence at La Grande Chartreuse, where nothing had disturbed his contemplation of the divine, or his wonderment at the magical silver escarpments emerging like fairy castles from the mists above Grenoble. In 1625 his general sent him as visitor to the Charterhouse of Paris, which was located next to the Luxembourg, and while there he was plucked out of his monastic repose by his brother the Cardinal. In his *Testament politique* Richelieu wrote that a prelate should have a name which would convey authority, a record of exemplary conduct, piety which would provoke respect, and a culture which would attract esteem.[1] He needed Alphonse, for there were too few in high places in the kingdom on whom he could rely, and his brother would be the most reliable of all to help him to carry through a policy of ecclesiastical reform. Alphonse was dismayed at this plot to interfere with his plan of salvation, and he refused to yield. Both actors in the drama were Richelieus, and the tenacity of the one matched that of the other; but one Richelieu had the greater access to power, and a letter from the King to the general of the Carthusians sufficed. Alphonse was nominated archbishop of Aix, and consecrated in the Charterhouse of Paris. The Cardinal put on a splendid demonstration, borrowing tapestries and six great carpets from the Petit Luxembourg, where he was at the time living on the King's grace and favour, and paying six hundred *livres* to the widow of Condés chef to organize the feast. He also gave Alphonse, who, of course, had not a sol to his name, three thousand *livres* to buy robes and a carriage. Poor Alphonse suffered agonies of mind and immured himself in the Charterhouse until his departure for Aix, where he was given a tremendous reception which the Cardinal compared bitterly with his own at Luçon.

Despite the welcome, however, Alphonse found Aix a hostile atmosphere, for the Parlement of Provence was of an independent turn of mind, and was forever troublesome. Shortly afterwards, therefore, the Cardinal arranged for him to be appointed to the see of Lyons, where he was to prove a splendid and popular prelate. It was the practice when a papal nuncio was recalled from Paris for the King to ask for a cardinal's hat for him. Bagno was due to return to Rome in 1628, and the King said that on this occasion he wanted two hats, an ordinary one for the nuncio and a special one for his nominee – who was to be Alphonse – in consideration of the royal campaign against the Huguenots. Urban VIII invoked a bull of Sixtus V forbidding two hats to two brothers, although his nephews, the brothers Francesco and Antonio Barberini, had been made cardinals – but yielded in December; and on 7 January 1629 both hats were bestowed by the King in the chapel of the Louvre. Bagno arrived in a cortège of sixty carriages, followed by Alphonse in one of eighty. The hats lay in a silver basin, Bagno's being presented first, and a high mass followed. That evening the King gave a dinner to Bagno, and Richelieu gave one to his brother.

Richelieu the priest was as eager to reform the Church in France as was Richelieu the politician to reconstruct the state. The Wars of Religion had been over for only a generation, the implementation of the decrees of the Council of Trent had been delayed, and the great religious revival that had taken place had not been matched by changes in the archaic administrative structure of the Church. Richelieu himself at Luçon had been one of the first bishops to give practical effect to Trent, and it was his aim on assuming public office to extend his own scheme of reform to every diocese in France. The basic problem was the poverty and licence of the parish clergy, and almost the first thing Richelieu did was to consult several bishops, in whom he had confidence, on the measures necessary to deal with it.[2] He proposed that provincial councils of the clergy be held every three years to hear all complaints against clerics, but he was careful to respect the Holy See by reserving to it grave matters. He recalled the duty of bishops to reside in the dioceses, though in this matter he was not to be very successful, for as late as 1638 there were one hundred and twenty bishops who spent more time in Paris than in their sees. Although he kept some bishops away from their sees for administrative purposes, such as Sourdis, the excellent archbishop of Bordeaux, who was an admiral, and La Valette who was a general, on the whole he brought pressure to bear in this matter of residence, even writing to the Holy See to ask that specific bishops be ordered back to their dioceses.

He also insisted upon triennial diocesan visitations, proper payment of the clergy and their regular instruction, and examination of all candidates for benefices. This last was a subtle attempt to undermine the scandalous system of ownership of benefices by secular persons, of which he was himself the product. Nomination to benefices he did not object to, and, indeed, in the circumstances of the time it is difficult to see how he could have objected; but those who undertook· them should be made to qualify and reside, both of which requirements rendered the prospect unattractive to those unsuited for ecclesiastical office. The worst example of beneficial abuse was the case of Cardinal de Guise, who was ordered by the King, on Richelieu's suggestion, either to take holy orders or to renounce the archbishopric of Reims. Guise elected to resign and marry the Princesse Marguerite de Gonzague; whereupon Richelieu said to him with that scorching irony that made him so detested, 'What! You enjoy 400,000 *livres* in rents and benefices, and you want to renounce this dainty morsel for a woman! Others would sacrifice 400,000 women, if they had them, for what you want to leave!' This added yet another powerful figure to Richelieu's list of enemies.

Protégés of noble families who failed to pass their examinations for the priesthood were to be displaced, and for this occasion the patrons would lose the right of nomination. Finally, he recommended that the King appoint only proper persons to sees. He looked always for authority, especially that conferred by birth, and he wanted prelates who were capable of carrying this authority into the secular sphere; in this respect his views were fully shared by St Vincent de Paul, who liked his bishops to be noblemen. Richelieu's policy was not so much to make the Church a department of the state, as to make France a theocracy, with the Church interlocked with the state and permeating secular activity with its moral authority.

The dearest thing to Richelieu's heart was the idea of the diocesan seminary, which alone could provide adequate training for the clergy. In the Code Michaud, the vast scheme of administrative reform of which he was the architect, it was prescribed that there should be a seminary in every diocese in France, and that it should be paid for out of the revenues of the benefice. The desirability of this is borne out by a letter of Louis XIII to the Pope in which he asked for the right for the Capuchins to hear confessions in the parishes; this was necessary, he wrote, in order to bring back to the confessional those faithful in the countryside and small towns who had been alienated because of the incapacity and bad habits of the parish clergy. The penetration of the newer religious orders into the life of the parish occasioned a struggle, at times violent, between them and the bishops, who sought to bring them under their control. The Jesuits in particular were the target of numerous episcopal onslaughts because of their extreme ultramontanism. The struggle went on for the whole of Richelieu's career, and, backed by Père Joseph, he sought to mediate without in any way diminishing the influence of the orders.

If Richelieu's reputation were not in the field of politics he would be remembered as one of the more important reformers of the Church in France. The claim is bold, but it is justified. Certainly the re-establishment of their rule among the Benedictines is due in great measure to him, for early in his administrative career he set out to reform the older religious orders as well as to support the newer ones. His approach to the problem was typical. He believed in reform from above, by authority; and since the monastic orders were outside the authority of the bishops or the King it seemed natural to him that he should have himself elected general of the orders. It was a strange idea, and the Pope rejected it; he confirmed Richelieu's election as general of the order of Cluny, but refused bulls of confirmation in the cases of the orders of Citeaux and Prémontré. Richelieu tried, as general of Cluny, to unite this order with the congregation of St Maur, which was a principal channel of the Benedictine reform, but failed; and although his policy of reform was carried through with some success he proceeded from crisis to crisis, and from obstacle to obstacle, even on occasions using troops to dragoon the recalcitrant monks.

The reluctance of the Pope to support Richelieu in many measures, even at the cost on some occasions of leaving French churches without clergy, is attributed by French historians to his fear that Richelieu would become the head of a gallican church. It was constantly rumoured that Richelieu wanted to be appointed permanent legate in France, or even patriarch of Gaul, and Bagno reported as much to Rome. There was, true enough, no limit to Richelieu's ambition, but it must be remembered that this ambition stemmed less from human vanity, although he had enough of this, than from the conviction that he alone was competent to deal with what he believed, with justification, to be a crisis in state and Church. In face of the obstructions in the papal machinery, its formalism and caution – characteristics which have exasperated many another French prelate – it is not surprising that he sought to gain as much administrative autonomy for the Church in France as was compatible with the concept of papal infallibility.

In his *Testament politique* he complimented himself. Recalling that in his youth he had witnessed laymen in possession of the greater part of the priories, abbeys and bishoprics of France, and that in the monasteries and convents there were numerous scandals and much bad example, he asserted that 'these disorders have been absolutely banned', and that lapses from the monastic rule were now 'rare'. This, he said, gave him consolation.[3] He was by no means successful in all of his plans for reform, even in the matter of diocesan seminaries, but there can be no doubt that, but for his authoritarianism, the situation at his death would have been much worse than it was.

There were in Richelieu's own life a number of canonical irregularities. Early in his career as the effective first minister he secured from the Pope a dispensation from saying the divine office every day, on the ground of pressure of time. He was, however, careful to broadcast this so that those who had occasion to observe that he did not devote an hour each day to reading his breviary would not be scandalized. The main criticism which has been levelled at him is that of pluralism – the occupation simultaneously of several benefices in order to enjoy their revenues. In this he was not alone. His brother Alphonse, dedicated to his vow of poverty, found pluralism a necessary device for maintaining the establishment of an archbishop; and even a saintly prelate like Cardinal de La Rochefoucauld was no less guilty than Richelieu. It was the system that was at fault, and no one could find an alternative to it. Altogether it has been estimated that Richelieu aggregated benefices producing an annual revenue of one and a half million *livres* – certainly half a million crowns in 1639. We have, in fact a list of seventeen abbeys of which he was abbot, including Cluny, Citeaux and Prémontré, the total income from which was 274,653 *livres*.[4]

This pluralism was to lay him open to the charge of avarice, and it requires a good deal of understanding of the seventeenth-century mind and its environment to resist repeating it. There was no effective civil service or ecclesiastical administration, and the funds to employ the secretaries, messengers, secret agents, guards and police whom Richelieu found necessary to support his national and ecclesiastical activities did not come, at least to any great extent, from public sources. In effect, he was expected to maintain the administrative equivalent of a Prime Minister's department largely out of private means, which in 1622 he totally lacked. He was in no position to be more scrupulous than any of his contemporaries, and he cannot be blamed for failing to rise above the standards of the time. It was easy for Père Joseph to preserve his vow of poverty; his expenses were paid, very likely out of Richelieu's pocket. It was quite impossible for a cardinal to imitate a Capuchin, and in the eyes of the seventeenth century highly undesirable that he should try. Richelieu quietened his conscience with the thought: 'I wish to increase my benefices by means most advantageous to the Church so that those who come after me will have the occasion to pray for me.'[5]

Richelieu's total income has never been calculated, and only his expenditure accounts for the end of his life are available to enable an assessment to be made of the costs of his establishment. His governorship of Brittany brought him 100,000 crowns annually, his private estates about half as much again, and in his capacity of admiral he received anchorage dues from every port in France. He spent much of this magnificently on support of the arts, the collection of pictures, sculptures and jewels, the theatre, and the Sorbonne, but much of it too on governmental services, including the outfitting of whole regiments when France finally went to war with Spain, and on religious and charitable works. In 1639 it cost him roughly half a million *livres* to live, of which housekeeping took 175,500, stables 78,000 and the guards 103,000. Altogether one hundred and seventy-seven people ate at his expense, and a typical menu was two soups, two carp, one cod, two plates of eggs, and two omelettes for choice. Thirty-three coaches and one hundred and forty horses and mules were kept. The guards had been formed after the alleged threat to Richelieu's life at the time of the Chalais conspiracy, and at first numbered only thirty. By 1639 he was maintaining one hundred horse and a company of musketeers. The number of his secretaries is unknown, but they accompanied him wherever he went, night and day. His habit was to retire before midnight, sleep for three or four hours, then sit in bed writing or dictating to his secretaries until six in the morning. After two more hours sleep he would rise to begin his day's work. 'Nothing more striking could be conceived,' says a French historian, 'than the picture of this statesman fighting against sleep and death for every moment of his existence, in order to consecrate it to the glory of France.'[6]

In the state, as in the Church, Richelieu did not always triumph, and where he succeeded it was only by the exercise of consummate tact and prudence. He had always to persuade, he was rarely in a position to command, and he was much concerned with moulding public opinion in support of his policies. Several times he intervened in the paper debates, sometimes with his own pen, at others with the pens of his propagandists. The anti-Richelieu pamphleteers, the most notorious of whom, Mathieu de Morges, was forced to leave France, stopped at nothing in their onslaughts on the Cardinal. At times they ridiculed him, as when they poured scorn on the family tree he produced at the time he was made a duke in the early 1630s; at others they were malicious, as when they published an alleged exchange of letters between him and Alphonse in which he accused his brother brutally of stupidity and awkwardness, and Alphonse retaliated with charges of arrogance and pretentiousness. That Richelieu behaved towards Alphonse dictatorially there is no doubt – on one occasion he rebuked him for drinking chocolate which the Holy Office had condemned as the work of the devil because it was believed that sorcerers employed it as a drug; but this despotism is an insecure foundation for the legend that the two brothers were perpetually quarrelling.

Finally, his detractors descended to calumny, accusing him of debauchery and incest. His widowed niece, Marie Madeleine, lived in his household for a time; the pamphleteers accused him of keeping her as his mistress. The most unlikely stories were abroad; he had, for example, had affairs with Marie de Médicis and Anne of Austria; sixty years later some scribbler set out to prove that Louis XIV was his son. Secretaries, guards, doctors and clerics were with him every moment, even when he was in bed, and it is difficult to see how he could have found the opportunity for the sexual adventures of which he was accused without some solid evidence coming down to us. The only author of the stories who deserves even the slightest attention is the Cardinal de Retz who names two women as his mistresses, but de Retz was an irresponsible gossiper whose reputation as a reliable witness of events is slight.

Over and again in his writings and in his letters to the King, Richelieu reveals his conviction of the destiny of France. 'The

French,' he said, 'are capable of anything, provided that those who govern them are capable of teaching them what they should practise. Their courage, which leads them to battle in the four corners of the globe, verifies this proposition.'[7] The greatness of France resides, in his opinion, in the souls of the French, but the native genius must be stimulated by leadership. The monarchy embodies the spirit of grandeur, and is the visual expression of the virtues latent in the nation; it needs only a programme for the creative energies of France to be released in noble works and vast designs. Such a programme he aimed at providing. His excuse was the necessity to take some steps about implementing the resolutions adopted by the States General in 1614, and a second Council of Notables was summoned and sat through late 1626 and early 1627. Michel de Marillac, the Keeper of the Seals, was the minister responsible for laying proposals before the Assembly. He had been appointed to this office on Richelieu's suggestion as one of the Queen Mother's advisers, but now that Marie de Médicis had turned against the Cardinal, Marillac was suspect in Richelieu's eyes. The speech he delivered to the Notables was replete with pedantry and catalogued the advantages which France possessed in its resources, as well as the difficulties experienced by its traders, without rousing the Notables either to pride or indignation.[8] Richelieu seems, therefore, to have taken the matter out of his hands, and, in his capacity of minister of the navy and of commerce, to have argued his own case before the Assembly.[9]

Richelieu's opening remarks to the Notables concerned the grandeur of France, and constituted the keynote of his whole theme. His propositions, he said, were necessary, useful and glorious, not only to restore the navy in France to its original dignity but also to restore France, through the navy, to her original greatness. The revelations that followed go far to explain why Richelieu had become convinced that Spain's ambition was to strangle France. Spain was engaged in a desperate war upon the seas with the Dutch, and had instituted a maritime blockade of Holland. At that time the extent to which shipping could be interfered with on the high seas in order to control contraband was highly controversial, and the Spaniards, like the English, were responsible for the most exaggerated pretensions. They decreed that all shipping passing through the Channel should put into Dunkirk for examination; and if cargoes were found aboard destined for Dutch ports the ship and its cargo were forfeit. Spanish warships patrolled the Channel, forcing French ships into Dunkirk, where, according to Richelieu's information, the crews were bribed to disclose that the cargo was destined for Holland. The number of ships confiscated was steadily rising, the French merchants were calling on the government for protection, and the French wheat trade with northern ports, which constituted a basic factor in the French economy, was seriously threatened.

But the grievances of France against Spain did not stop there. The French property seized under Olivares' orders at the time of the Valtelline dispute was not restored for twelve months after the Treaty of Monzon had been signed. The prisons of the Inquisition were full of French sailors, who, coming from the western ports, were largely Huguenots, and who had often been in Dutch employ. Now the Spanish government had authorized the creation of a privileged company at Seville, consisting of Flemish and Hanseatic merchants, to ruin Dutch trade. Its fleets were to trade with northern Europe convoyed by two dozen warships, and it was given the right of visit and search over other nations, whose cargoes it could seize as contraband. This was virtually to create a trading monopoly in the North Sea; and to make matters worse, in September 1626 a Spanish ordinance forbade the transport of goods from Spain to Flanders, except in Spanish ships. Three years previously another had forbidden the import into Spain of all foreign manufactures, and a tax of forty per cent on French trade with Spain had been imposed, while Spaniards in France paid only two and a half per cent. Visas were demanded of French merchants trading with the Spanish Netherlands, to which were attached extortionate fees. That these were the measures of a country whose financial system was chaotic, and which sought to maintain stability of the currency and arrest the decline of home industries by extreme protectionism Richelieu did not understand. 'This nation,' he said of Spain, 'proposes to usurp sovereign authority over the sea, allowing no freedom to trade, not even to other nations between themselves.'

The French economy, depending as it did on the export to Belgium, Holland and the Baltic of wine, vinegar, brandy, prunes, nuts, and above all wheat, and the importation from the Levant of drugs, spices, silks, cotton, and linen, was vulnerable to Spanish interference. The Notables agreed to support a programme of reform, which had three principal aspects: the strengthening of French sea-power, the protection of French trade and the countering of Spanish economic aggressiveness by the creation of French trading companies of merchant adventurers to go across the seas and find new sources of raw materials and new markets.

The first of these projects was dear to Richelieu's heart, for his mind had dwelt on the problem of sea-power since he was bishop of the Atlantic town of Luçon. He had come to know one of France's leading seamen, Isaac de Razilly, and had listened long and attentively to his analysis of sea-power. Razilly was a Knight of Malta, had fought with the Order all over the Mediterranean, and had even been to the Amazon. In 1626 he wrote a long memorandum to Richelieu in which he argued that 'whoever is master of the sea has great power over the land. Look at the King of Spain; since he took arms at sea he has conquered so many kingdoms that the sun never sets on his lands.' Richelieu was impressed by the thought that the Dutch had been able to shake off Spanish rule because they had ships able to strike at the very foundation of Spain's apparent greatness – the plate fleets. Rubens was writing at this time that the plate fleet was carrying twenty millions in gold: 'It carries the fortune of Spain, for all our payments have been held back until its arrival, and we have pledged ourselves down to our shirts.'

Following receipt of Razilly's advice, Richelieu wrote a long memorandum in which he argued for the construction of thirty warships to ensure that the king's subjects would not be deprived of their goods and liberty. The cost of maintaining this fleet would be one million *livres* a year, and this could partly be raised by suppressing the offices of constable and admiral, which cost a quarter of this sum.[10] Later he was to write to the King saying:

'If Your Majesty always has in his ports forty vessels, well armed and well equipped, ready for sea at any moment when needed, you will have sufficient to guarantee you against injury, and to inspire fear at sea in those who have hitherto shown contempt for your forces.'[11] In 1624 France did not have a single vessel capable of standing against the English or Spanish warships, and since the French shipyards lacked the resources it was necessary to order such ships from Holland. In 1626 five first-class vessels were delivered from Dutch shipyards in time to deal with Soubise. One of them, the *St Louis*, was a sixty-gun ship of two decks, the equal of England's *Prince Royal*. By 1640, when Richelieu's nephew, Brézé, was winning sea battles against Spain, France had eighty-five units, sixty-three of them being ships and twenty-two galleys. The navy was a family affair: Amador de La Porte was in charge of the Conseil de la Marine, and Pontcourlay's eldest son, an extravagant young man, was admiral of the galleys.

Closely connected with the policy of sea-power which the Notables endorsed was that of commercial protection. 'Our neighbours,' Richelieu said, 'thought they had the right to sell us their goods at their own price and take ours for whatever they liked.'[12] While English drapery flooded France, French merchants had to pay double export taxes for English tin. If Spain and England protected their industry and shipping in this fashion, France would do likewise. It could not be expected that either Richelieu or the Notables would question the prevailing economic theory summed up in what was called 'the magic square' – free entry of raw materials, prohibition of the export thereof, prohibition of the import of manufactures, and free export thereof. Richelieu's economic knowledge was slight, and his plans for financial reform were confused, contradictory and based on suspect figures. He was undoubtedly influenced – as was his whole generation – by the views of a French economist Montchrestien, who thought of gold and silver as finite indices of national wealth, and who argued that France should be productively self-sufficient so as to avoid having to export specie to pay for imported goods. Following the meeting of the Notables an ordinance was issued which inevitably contributed to the economic crisis which Europe was experiencing: the loading of cargoes on foreign ships was forbidden if French ships were available; an exception was made in the case of salt, which, however, could only be exported from certain ports. In this way it was hoped to encourage French shipbuilding and provide employment for the two hundred thousand French sailors who, according to Razilly, were employed on foreign ships and who were now forbidden to work on other than French vessels.

The annual export to the Levant from Marseilles of seven million crowns which Montchrestien deplored was matched by an outward flow of gold to Spain. During the sixteenth century gold had accumulated in France, while in Spain the proportion of silver to gold imported from America had constantly increased; the result was that there was proportionately less gold to silver in Spain than there was in France, and this made gold coins dearer in Spain in terms of silver coins than they were in France; and French merchants naturally paid their bills in French gold. At first Richelieu's policy was to stop the expenditure of money on luxuries so as to limit imports and hence halt the drain of specie. He even went so far as to forbid all but the nobility to wear silk, and to restrict the use of carriages. Needless to say this design was quickly rendered abortive by a general recalcitrance.

The measure of the Cardinal's intellectual flexibility is indicated by the extent to which he was prepared, in the light of experience and contrary advice, to modify the aggressive concept of economic autonomy, which he derived from Montchrestien. Among the documents which came into his hands was an analysis of the Levant trade and its effect on the economy of Marseilles, written by a merchant of that city. In his *Testament politique* Richelieu incorporated for the King's benefit the arguments that he found therein, and to this source must be attributed much of his erudition in the matter of economics. It was pointed out to him that only about one half of the imports into Marseilles were paid for in silver, the balance being paid for in French exports; the imbalance would be rectified by developing the export trade, and this required the encouragement of French industries which could cater for Levantine demand, particularly in honey, wine, paper and cloth. Even this imbalance was not an absolute one, for many of the imports into Marseilles were re-exported to Spain, which paid for them in silver. So, Richelieu wrote, 'the silver that is carried to the East does not have its origin in France but in Spain, whence it comes to us through trade in the same goods that we bring from the Levant'.[13] It was an economic discovery which made nonsense of mercantilism, but the struggle with Spain, aggravating the money crisis, meant that not much could be done before Richelieu's death to take advantage of it.

The recognition that foreign imports could be paid for by increased export of national products led Richelieu to revise his views about the luxury trade. If the people wanted luxuries, let these be made in France, and be in part exported. Thereby a saving would be effected in coin, and more coin introduced. The Duc de Nevers had already attempted to introduce Venetian glass-making into France, and in 1626 privileges were granted which were to found the French glass industry. The tapestry manufacturing at La Savonnerie was begun the following year, giving employment to one hundred poor children who were offered a six-year apprenticeship. There was a silk factory at Tours, and because this city was near his own country Richelieu gave it every encouragement, until forty thousand people, so it was said, lived there on the industry, which spread to Lyons. The extractive industies also had Richelieu's attention: sugar refining was promoted in the north of France, and in 1627 a certain prospector, Baron de Beausoleil, who was suspected of black magic because of his experiments in base metals, was commissioned by Richelieu to undertake a survey of mines in the kingdom. Communications were not overlooked. In 1633 an engineer who was master of the royal works in Languedoc, one Antoine Baudan, wrote an opinion on the possibility of constructing a canal through the Midi to link the Atlantic and the Mediterranean. Richelieu seized on this idea, for it would enable shipping to be passed from the one side of France to the other without having to pass the Straits of Gibraltar in the event of war with Spain.

Inseparable from this policy of internal development was that of colonial expansion by means of trading companies. The first was the Company of Hundred Associates of Morbihan, and its articles of association, approved by Richelieu during the siege of La Rochelle, read in part like the introduction to a modern French treatise on France's overseas development. Multi-racism was a keynote:

The descendants of the French who colonize the said country, together with the savages who will be brought to a knowledge of the Faith and make profession of it, shall henceforth be considered native-born Frenchmen, and as such may come to live in France when they wish, and acquire property there, make wills, succeed as heirs and take gifts and legacies in the same way as true nationals and native-born Frenchmen, without being required to take out letters of declaration or nationalization.[14]

It was an act of remarkable enlightenment for its time, and set French colonial policy on a path which made the export of French civilization more likely and thorough; if France has affected the mind of much of Asia and Africa this is due in no small measure to Richelieu. Sully had despised Samuel Champlain's schemes for settling Canada because he thought the country had no gold; Richelieu gave them his complete support because a France Overseas would be a France more glorious and influential.

Whereas Canada's development was based on Brittany, that of the Caribbean was based on Normandy. French attempts at colonization in the West Indies would have occurred even without Richelieu's encouragement, but it needed his tenacity and financial backing for them to succeed in face of Spanish claims to monopolize the region, and of English and Dutch rivalry. In 1625 an adventurer named d'Enambuc, who for the previous dozen years had been wandering around the Caribbean, sought audience of Richelieu with a plan to grow tobacco on St Kitts. Richelieu was instantly intrigued with the proposition and launched the French West Indies Company, to which he subscribed 10,000 of the 45,000 *livres* capital. He gave the Company a monopoly of French trade in the West Indies and centred it on the port of Le Havre, of which he was governor – thereby, incidentally, increasing his own revenue. D'Enambuc was given a commission to

The face of majesty. Louis XIII. By Juste d'Egmont. For this rigorist and despot an implacable enforcement of the law substituted for justice.

The face of intemperance. Marie de Médicis. This canvas by Rubens portrays in allegory the escape from Blois of this florid harridan who became an hysterical enemy of Richelieu.

The face of belligerency. The Count-Duke of Olivares. By Velasquez. A dictator to whom power was a passion, he was obsessed by the notion of Richelieu's malevolence.

colonize St Kitts, and he sailed with three ships and several hundred settlers.

The enterprise was badly organized, and the colonists, who were mostly indentured labourers, were sadly reduced in numbers and in a desperate condition when they were finally landed on the beach at St Kitts. There they found the English already in possession, but negotiated with them a condominium of the island. The first tobacco crop had just been harvested when, in 1629, Don Federico de Toledo, who ironically had held a commission from the Spanish crown to help Richelieu against the Huguenots, descended on the settlement with thirty-five galleons. The English were in part condemned to the mines and in part sent back to England, and the French dispersed by flight to the neighbouring Caribbean islands, where they suffered shockingly, being deserted by their officers who made for France. For this cowardly act their leader was clapped into the Bastille by the furious Cardinal.

In analysing the reasons for Richelieu's distrust of the Habsburgs this affair at St Kitts must be emphasized, for it struck at once at Richelieu's pocket and at French access to tropical products. Richelieu referred the matter to Urban VIII on the basis that the Church's missionary endeavours were being hampered by Spain's claimed monopoly of the New World, and he coaxed out of the pontiff a bull authorizing the French Dominicans and Capuchins to service Guadaloupe, Dominica and Martinique. Both the exultant French and the outraged Spaniards regarded this as an implied rescission of the famous bull of Alexander VI which in 1493 had granted the New World to Spain. When in 1635 Richelieu's Company settled Guadaloupe this was under cover of missionary enterprise, and the fusion of religious and political motives was typified by the cross which was set up at the landing place, and which bore an escutcheon at its base painted with the lilies of France. Though their settlements were unexampled for misery, violence, treachery and vice, the French as well as the Spaniards could now claim Providential support for their policy of overseas expansion.

The Morbihan Company was stillborn because of provincial jealousy. The Parlement of Rennes had to register the decree creating it, and, since the Breton ports claimed that their commerce would be affected by the concentration of activity in Morbihan, it refused to do so. Despite this, the associated merchants continued to trade partly in cooperation, and Richelieu, not at all discouraged, tried to organize a new company. The result was the Company of New France, which Razilly was appointed to direct, and which was given a monopoly for fifteen years in respect of the exploitation of Canada, provided it introduced three hundred colonists every year into that country. As an added encouragement, it had at its disposal twelve titles of nobility. The venture started badly when David Kirke, an Englishman resident in Dieppe, blockaded Champlain and took him prisoner in July 1629; but steadily the penetration of the St Lawrence was pursued. François Fouquet, a judge in the Chalais case, was appointed councillor of state for overseas affairs and companies, and superintended such diverse fields of exploitation as Canada, Senegal, Cape Verde, Gambia and Spitzbergen. Richelieu was also working to extend French trade in Scandinavia and down the rivers into the heart of Russia. To this end he made his financial support of Christian of Denmark in the Thirty Years War dependent upon the latter opening the Danish Sounds so as to let French shipping into the Baltic. Whereas in 1628 no French ships passed the Sounds, in 1630 there were twenty and in 1631 seventy-two. The French entry into the war in 1635 was to stop the trade for some years.

Richelieu's vast horizon was due in great measure to the influence which Père Joseph exercised over him. France has always been prominent in the mission fields, but at this time it almost pre-empted them; and the Capuchins were among the most energetic of the religious orders. They were everywhere, in Senegal, in Ethiopia, in Syria, and even in Persia. There Shah Abbas gave them a house near his palace in Isfahan, where they were in close touch with the French merchants who were settled there and who controlled the export of carpets to Europe. From these diverse areas of the world the Capuchins poured information on to Père Joseph's desk, and he, in his capacity of superior of the missions, had perhaps the most cosmopolitan correspondence of anyone in Europe. His missionaries were able to act as un-official diplomats, negotiate trade agreements, introduce French merchants and gain privileges for them. Since the days of St Francis himself there had been French Franciscans in Morocco. Now their followers were able to secure for France a political as well as a religious foothold in the kingdom, and in 1631 the Sherif Abd-el-Malek signed a treaty opening Morocco to French merchants on the terms of the capitulations with Turkey. When the outbreak of war in 1635 made it impossible to export silver to pay for Moroccan leather and dates the French presence in the country was for a time terminated.

Without a system of regulations, all Richelieu's schemes of reform could not resist the inertia of established ways of behaviour. The resolutions of the Assembly of Notables and a large number of existing decrees were thus codified in detail in a document, known as the Code Michaud[15] from the fact that it appeared under the name of the Keeper of the Seals, Marillac, who lent his first name Michel to its title. Its drafting was delayed by the siege of La Rochelle, and it did not appear until 1629, when it bore the title of a royal ordinance to give effect to the complaints made at the States General in 1614, and issued on the advice of the Notables. It was a vast and comprehensive system, dealing with the production, protection and exploitation of corn and wine, encouragement of companies, public offices, the Church, the army and the navy, and even weights and measures.

It also dealt with the relationship between the council and the Parlement, with the courts, finance, public order and censorship of the pamphleteers, who were becoming daily more dangerous: the execution of a decree of 1621 provided for the demolition of all fortifications, and the implementation of a series of decrees against duelling. There was, perhaps, too much of an authoritarian element in the system, and industry tended to be over-controlled, this leading at times even to the murder of royal inspectors. On the other hand, much of the Code Michaud seems to have remained more or less a dead letter because of recurrent breakdowns in the administrative system. It became law only by promulgation in a *lit de justice*, because the Parlement of Paris refused to register it. The Parlement's reasons were typical. Richelieu had for years been preoccupied with the problem of finding some useful occupation for the swashbuckling offspring of the lesser nobility, whose estates could no longer support them – the class from which he sprang; and he sought in the Code Michaud to provide entry for them into the administration, particularly in colonial affairs, where their belligerence would be an advantage and their honour not too much offended by their participation in trade. But, since the administration was considered by the gentlemen of the robe as their exclusive prerogative, they saw in the Code Michaud only an attack on their privileged position. They therefore boycotted the whole instrument.

Whatever Richelieu tried to do, he found privilege an impediment. A man named La Paulette had proposed to Henri IV that judicial offices be made hereditary on condition of payment of an annual rent of one-sixtieth of the capital value. Thereby public office was transformed into private property, to be bought, sold and leased like any other property. The scandal persisted down to the Revolution, and the system was too entrenched in Richelieu's time for him to do much about it. The magistrates were exempted from capitation taxes, and in some provinces they, and other officers, ranked as nobles and sat in the Estates. They had landed property and took titles from them, and they were exempted from military service and the billeting of troops. In the first quarter of the century the capital appreciation in the price of offices was twenty-five per cent, and the holder could look forward to its continuing at the rate of one per cent each year. No wonder the Parlement, already viewing with dismay the large number of products from the new schools of the Jesuits who were forcing their way into the ranks of the gentlemen of the robe, was prepared to resist to the death the opening of those ranks to a horde of indigent cavaliers.

Despite his anxiety to find a way of life for the aristocracy, Richelieu did not believe in their capacity to govern. Himself half middle class, and comparing no doubt the virtues of his mother with the quarrelsome character of his grandmother, he advised against employing nobles in financial offices. They were, he said, vain and ambitious, and more tempted to venality than the bourgeois, who had probably less chance of escaping undetected. On the other hand, wherever the gentlemen of the robe claimed privileges which could not withstand close scrutiny they were dealt with. For example, in 1634 an edict was issued revoking privileges which rich families alleged they had acquired on the pretext of certain, largely imaginary, offices, and forbidding the collection of fees after the officer's functions had terminated. The struggle was to go on for the rest of Richelieu's life.

10

The Synagogue of Satan
1627-8

Peter Paul Rubens fancied himself as a diplomat, a man of the world busying himself with great affairs of state behind the veils of art. Handsome and extravagant, he revelled in intrigue, and his fine house in Antwerp saw much coming and going of diplomats and spies, official and unofficial; and in the gallery, where the visitors to his studio could watch his team working on the floor below like an orchestra under the master's brush, many a plot was devised. At this moment Rubens was acting as secretary of state of the Spanish Netherlands and was in Brussel. Buckingham, seething with hostility towards France, recollected Rubens' hint to him during their discussion at the sitting in Paris two years previously. Rubens might be used to effect an alliance of Spain and England against France; and there were plenty of trouble-makers on the borders of France who could also be stirred to action.

Buckingham was wont to employ the painter and connoisseur Balthazar Gerbier in his art transactions, for Gerbier, born in Holland of French parents and of English domicile, was the complete cosmopolitan. Under the pretext of negotiating a sale of a collection of antiques, Buckingham sent Gerbier to Rubens. The latter forwarded a report of the overtures to Olivares in an official dispatch of the governor of the Spanish Netherlands, and was immediately summoned to Madrid for discussions. His presence there, collecting commissions to paint while negotiating with Olivares, alarmed the French ambassador, the Comte de Fargis, who, when he was told that the government of the Spanish Netherlands was about to make peace with England, and that this would bind Madrid, took panic and on 20 March 1627 signed a treaty of alliance with Spain.

Madrid's motives in allying with France were a typical compound of the religious and the political. The two Catholic powers would, it was hoped, stand together against the heretic, whether he be in England, in La Rochelle or in the Palatinate; France, which was subsidizing the Dutch in return for the aid of their fleet against the Huguenots, would be detached from The Hague in return for Spanish naval assistance; and a French breach with England would involve lapse of French support for the Elector Palatine. Richelieu wanted Spanish support against La Rochelle in the event of that city being succoured by the English, and he hoped that Spain would stave off an English assault on France until at least the middle of 1628, but he had no intention of fulfilling Spain's expectations. In the outcome the alliance proved futile to both sides, who fell to indulging in recrimination, while the prospect of having to fight two major powers failed to deter Buckingham from a breach with France. The Duke proceeded with plans for a Protestant crusade against Louis XIII, in which he hoped, overlooking the incongruity in the idea, to implicate two of France's Catholic neighbours, Savoy and Lorraine.

While de Fargis was being frightened into making an alliance with Spain, one of Buckingham's companions, Walter Montagu, younger son of the Earl of Manchester, left England for Turin and Nancy. His official mission was to try to persuade these two courts to use their influence with Madrid to effect peace between England and Spain, but his real purpose was to gain their accession to a grand design against France. Charles Emmanuel of Savoy was the most cunning and the least scrupulous man in Europe; if he saw anything in the project for himself he could be counted upon to give it his support, but at the same time he would scrutinize the proposal carefully. Charles IV, Duke of Lorraine, was quite a different character, violent, brutal and unthinking, the perpetually sardonic smirk on his face betraying his arrogance and irresponsibility. He was later to say with relish, 'We princes are all cheats!' More than any other man he, by his intemperate conduct, was to drag France into mortal enmity with Spain; and it was Walter Montagu who gave him the initial prod.

Montagu was later to be converted to Catholicism, to become a priest, a French Benedictine abbot no less, and to attend Anne of Austria on her deathbed. He was at this time, however, a cold, haughty, Protestant English aristocrat. In London he had come to know Mme de Chevreuse, and he found her now in Lorraine's second capital of Bar-le-Duc. She had, to Louis xiii's fury, reached the Duchy and had been received by Charles iv as a cousin. Within days Charles was in her clutches, literally as well as metaphorically; and as Richelieu moaned, 'All begins with love!' At Easter 1627 a great fête was held in the ducal palace at Nancy where she was the heroine. Charles entered the courtyard in a magnificent costume, followed by a series of chariots richly decorated and accompanied by trumpets and torchbearers. In them were the princes and princesses of the House of Lorraine dressed as gods and goddesses on high Olympus, the ladies in scarlet and playing lutes. Charles, having donned his armour, then fought with other champions for a prize sword, which he won and laid at the feet of the twenty-six-year-old Mme de Chevreuse. To this court she now conducted Montagu, having, it is alleged, seduced him also *en route;* and as Richelieu wrote, the two had no difficulty in pushing the Duke 'to the precipice'. Montagu found Charles, then aged twenty-one, a large, bony young man with blond hair, and a body well developed by plenty of exercise, particularly horse-riding, at which he was adept. He was badly educated but had a natural intelligence and wit, was an endless talker, and was thoughtless, vain and wilful.

Charles of Lorraine was at odds with Louis xiii. Lorraine consisted in fact of two Duchies, Lorraine proper and Bar. In Lorraine the Salic law prevailed, which meant that only males could inherit; in Bar it did not prevail, which meant that more remote male heirs would be superseded by less remote female heirs.

The late Duke Henri had left two daughters, Nicole and Claude, and in order to preserve the unity of the inheritance Charles, his nephew, had married the elder of these. It was unfortunate for him that he could not marry both, for it was possible that the feudal law of coparcenary prevailed in Bar, so that the two daughters would inherit jointly. To complicate the matter, Bar was a fief of France, and the heir was required to pay homage to the French king before being invested; Lorraine was part of the Holy Roman Empire, but it was arguable that it was in addition a French fief; and in fact, Richelieu, basing himself on extensive historical researches and legal opinions, chose to treat Lorraine as a vassal state. Whatever the situation, Charles, as ruler of Lorraine and Bar, was a two-headed Janus, expected simultaneously to look to Vienna and Paris. When Louis XIII, in view of the dubious legal situation, made difficulties over Charles' investiture in Bar in 1625, the new Duke chose to concentrate his gaze to the east.

The matter was complicated by a long-standing dispute between France and the Emperor over the legal situation of the three bishoprics of Toul, Metz and Verdun. These, with their important fortresses guarding the vulnerable eastern frontier of France, had been transferred to the French Crown in the Treaty of Cateau Cambrésis in 1559, but whether they were held by France as fiefs of the Emperor, and were still imperial territory, was an open question. They were surrounded by the hereditary lands of Lorraine, and Bar, and the bishopric of Metz had certain feudal dependencies, two of which, Vic and Moyenvic, were second-class fortresses dominating the main road between Nancy and Strasbourg. Had these been included in the cession of Metz to France? If they had, then the French had several footholds deep in Lorraine and imperial territory. It so happened that Richelieu had set up a commission to investigate certain alienations of land from the bishopric of Metz, and when the commission reported it raised questions about French legal interests in Lorraine which the government of Lorraine had considered, or had hoped, to be dead.

Now Charles, looking for an excuse to make trouble with Louis XIII, ordered the bishop of Verdun to excommunicate the workmen engaged on the reconstruction of the fortress there, on the ground that they had demolished church buildings. Whatever rights Lorraine had over the dependencies of the bishopric, it had none over the town itself, unless the Treaty of Cateau Cambrésis was to be overthrown. Charles' action suggested that this, indeed, was his intention. The terrified bishop did as he was instructed, and the work came to an end. Richelieu promptly dispatched to Verdun a royal officer who proceeded to declare the excommunication null, and to recommence the work. The bishop was fined ten thousand *livres*. All this, the French government believed, was being instigated by Mme de Chevreuse, and what made the situation doubly dangerous was that she and the Queen were in constant communication.

In Turin Montagu found another ally, the Comte de Soissons, who had chosen this court for asylum. From here he went on to Venice and gained more promises of support from the Venetians, who were disgusted with the Treaty of Monzon and Richelieu's apparent betrayal of them. Meanwhile Buckingham, having sold the cargoes of the captured French merchantmen and pawned some of the crown jewels, had raised the money for an assault on France. His plan was to link up with the Huguenots in La Rochelle, who, he believed, would close their gates on the King as soon as he arrived. The city was the Geneva of the oceans, the 'synagogue of Satan', as Urban VIII described it when congratulating Louis on its fall. Here Puritanism had made a virtue out of trade, and Protestantism was a much more sombre affair than it was with Henri de Navarre and his feathered Gascon cavaliers. Rich, looking outwards to England and tremulous of Spain, it relished its traditional independence. In February 1626 it had been forced to submit to the King and to accept a royal commissioner, undertake not to arm its ships, restore ecclesiastical property, and accord liberty of conscience to Catholics. There were, in fact, Catholics now within its walls who constituted a nest of spies for Richelieu.

La Rochelle lies at the end of a channel which at low tide is mostly mud; and to the observer who stands on the remains of the dyke which Richelieu built to close it off from English help it still presents the same defiant fortified front. Its protected harbour, its quays, its fine arcaded streets and noble Renaissance town hall hidden behind a medieval curtain have changed but little. Across the white, flat waters which open out from the channel entrance can be seen two islands. The nearer, the Ile de Ré, is partially obscured by the northern headland. It is flat, and its trees are often detached from the shore as a result of refraction, The other, the Ile d'Oléron, is no more than a long line on the horizon to the south. Land and sea seem to merge into each other, and this sense of mutual accretion is intensified by reason of the long and rapid advance and retreat of the Biscay tides.

On 19 June 1627 (old style) Buckingham issued secret orders for an expedition, which, as Lord Admiral, he would command in person. Several regiments of infantry were to be transported to La Rochelle, and Buckingham would ask the citizens if they desired to have them. If they answered negatively, the troops would be returned to England; if affirmatively, they were to be placed under the command of Soubise, who had all along been fomenting trouble between the two countries. Once La Rochelle was garrisoned, the fleet would then sail to the Garonne to release the seized English wine-ships, and subsequently devote itself to seeking the Spanish plate fleet.

As with the Cadiz expedition, that to La Rochelle promised disaster. The troops were pressed men, a collection of 'base rogues'[1] and village yokels. There were insufficient supplies, the shortage of money was chronic, and arms and munitions were deficient. On 10 July 1627 Buckingham, the Lord Admiral's flag flown in the hopefully named *Triumph*, led one hundred and twenty ships, carrying six thousand troops, to anchorage off the forts of La Prée and St Martin on the Ile de Ré; and while Soubise went off to La Rochelle to ascertain the attitude of the city, Buckingham proceeded to land his forces on the island, which he considered would be an admirable base of future operations. Many of the mutinous men refused to disembark, or, having been forced on shore, bolted as soon as Jean de St Bonnet de Toiras, the governor of St Martin's fort, sent a troop of cavalry to oppose the establishment of a bridgehead. The situation was only saved by the great energy and bravery of Buckingham himself, who was quick to demonstrate that he had the capacities and instincts of a soldier even if he lacked those of a statesman. St Martin, however, was impregnable. Built on stony ground which made the opening of siege lines impossible, it could be reduced only by blockade. This could be a long business, and help and more munitions would have to be forthcoming if the French were not to raise the siege.

On the humid and stormy morning of 22 July 1627 Soubise, accompanied by Buckingham's secretary, Sir William Beecher, arrived at the gate of St Nicholas at La Rochelle and was denied entry by the sentries. It was pouring with rain and Soubise asked for shelter in the guardhouse while someone fetched the mayor to receive the important letters he was carrying. This concession was granted, and in due course the mayor, Godefroy, appeared. For the love of the churches he begged Soubise to go in peace. But inside the city was the mother of Rohan and Soubise, Catherine de Parthenay-Lusignan, Dowager Vicomtesse de Rohan, and this elderly Judith of the Protestant cause arrived in a great hurry, crying 'come in, my son, follow me without fear together with those you have with you. The House of Rohan will always wish for the welfare of La Rochelle, and will do all in its power to ensure it!'[2] A crowd had begun to gather and, swayed by emotion at this spectacle of reunion of mother and son, carried the delegation off to the town hall. The mayor began to waver, asking for time to reflect. Foolishly Soubise and Beecher accorded him this, and the following morning, having gained reinforcement from his colleagues, Godefroy announced that he could not take the responsibility of leading the churches into another revolt. Beecher then departed by ship to rejoin Buckingham, leaving Soubise with his mother. At the same time a citizen of La Rochelle, Sieur de Laleu, was sent to the King to say that the English would retire from La Rochelle if the King would agree to demolish the fort of St Louis, which had been built to save the city.

It was this qualified assurance that convinced Richelieu that the city fathers were insecure in their protestations of loyalty to the Crown, and strengthened his belief that they were being coy with the English only to give themselves time to assess the latter's strength. Richelieu was certain that if Buckingham took Fort St Martin, the Rochelais would revolt once more. His spies had long since acquainted him with Buckingham's designs, and even before the English arrived the machinery was in motion to eject him. Gaston d'Orléans was given supreme command in the area, though the effective commander was the Duc d'Angoulême; and on all the roads of France little groups of men with iron hats and carrying long pikes were plodding westwards, and small troops of horses were stirring up the dust; the feudal levies were being called out, and daily they swelled d'Angoulême's camp while the inhabitants of La Rochelle watched in growing dismay. By the beginning of August d'Angoulême had as many men and guns in position near the city as Buckingham had been able to land on the Ile de Ré. Louis XIII was ill, and at one moment it was even expected that he would die. Richelieu, in face of the prospect that Gaston might shortly be king, was anxious and hesitant about treating La Rochelle as an enemy. He decided to consult Père Joseph, whom he found in a crusading mood. With enthusiasm and eloquence Père Joseph set out to convince the Cardinal that it was his duty to take La Rochelle and stamp out this focus of sedition. He was in close communication with the Catholics inside, and had received from them information about the defences, the provisions and the dispositions of the inhabitants. At the end of July Louis was sufficiently recovered to appear at a council meeting. Any doubts about the course of action to be taken were now dissipated, for he made it quite clear that his will would prevail throughout the realm. The loyalty of La Rochelle would not be taken for granted; the city would be summoned, and unless it opened its gates to the King it would be besieged.

In August d'Angoulême stopped supplies entering La Rochelle, and the inhabitants now resolved to call on Buckingham for arms and help. Instead of La Rochelle aiding him as he expected, Buckingham found it a burden on his own resources. Within ten days of his arrival the beer ran out and being good Englishmen the troops refused to regard the local wine as a substitute. In England Charles I was making desperate efforts to raise reinforcements and supplies, but his system of forced loans was yielding money too slowly for effective measures to be taken in time. When troops had been collected there were no ships to carry them; when the ships were found the troops had deserted. In Fort St Martin Toiras' men had already eaten their horses, and rations were nearly exhausted; men were climbing over the walls at night to desert to the English; Toiras, overcome with fever, rose intermittently from his bed to rally the garrison. Buckingham sent in a letter, courteously worded, asking him to capitulate. Toiras responded with like courtesy saying that neither despair of succour nor fear of being harmed would move him to yield. He released an English prisoner, who, on being interviewed by Buckingham, said Toiras had expressed a longing for melons. Buckingham, ever gallant, passed in a dozen melons, and Toiras returned the gesture with a gift of flowers of oranges and Cyprus powder. At the same time Toiras sent off a swimmer in the night with a note hidden in a ball. It read: 'If you want to save this place, send me pinnaces on the 8 October at the latest, for on the evening of the 8th I shall no longer be in the place unless I have bread.'

Buckingham himself was only just hanging on. Storms continued to damage his siege-works and the waves broke his blockade booms. It became a race to see which of the rivals, the Duke or Toiras, could hold out the longer. Meanwhile Richelieu had been gathering a fleet of ships from all the ports of the west of France, overcoming the obstinacy and jealousy of the Bretons who were uncooperative, and hastening the building and fitting out of new vessels. These were now congregating in the area under the command of a redoubtable French seadog named Beaulieu-Persac who in 1609 had performed a most remarkable exploit in that with a single ship, supported by a dozen Spanish vessels, he had entered the port of Tunis and burned under the very guns of the forts no fewer than twenty-three Barbary corsair ships with a loss of five hundred and thirty-eight guns. The Cardinal had interviewed Beaulieu-Persac and had been impressed by his grasp of the tactical situation at La Rochelle.

On the night of 7 October Beaulieu-Persac set out for the Ile de Ré with forty-six vessels. It was dark, but a lantern burned on the fort of St Martin. As the English divined what was afoot they lit their own stern lanterns to confuse the pilots of the French ships. The latter, however, had carefully reconnoitred the route, and they navigated through the English vessels as they rode at anchor. Firing broke out in all directions, and Beaulieu-Persac, who was no more than decoy, drew the English ships around him. Eventually he was forced to strike his colours, but meanwhile the provision ships, twenty-nine in number, had grounded on the shore just below St Martin, and their crews were busily engaged in discharging their cargoes. At dawn the English beheld the garrison of St Martin's brandishing hams and beef tongues on their pikes. When Buckingham, who had spent the night in an open boat trying to organize his fleet, boarded the *Nonsuch* he found Beaulieu-Persac there. He told the Frenchman that his men must have been condemned criminals to have hazarded themselves in this fashion. Beaulieu-Persac replied that in his nation it was not the custom to employ condemned persons in important actions. 'Well then,' said the Duke, 'you have led the ships which have not yet discharged their cargoes; I am going to burn them now.'[3] Beaulieu-Persac had the satisfaction of seeing all Buckingham's attempts beaten off by the cannon of the fort, and the Duke reduced to impotence.

Four days later Louis XIII arrived in the royal camp to the thunder of salutes, and took up his abode in a village three miles south-east of La Rochelle. Richelieu established himself in a house at Pont-de-la-Pierre about a mile further away, quite near the shore, from where he could watch the rival fleets and the Ile d'Oléron, He was in an isolated position, and when the besieged in the city learned of his whereabouts they planned an expedition to the house to abduct him. Père Joseph, however, had excellent communications with the Catholics in the town, and as he sat in the draughty pavilion in the gardens of the Cardinal's house, which he had made his home and oratory, word came to him of the plan. When his kidnappers arrived they found the royal musketeers in ambush in the sand dunes and the King himself with a squadron of cavalry waiting to charge. October dragged into November without more activity, and the supplies in St

Martin were running down again. Buckingham's men were also in a sorry plight, reduced to a diet of overripe grapes, and waiting in vain for assistance from England, which adverse weather and the confusion in the English seaports forever postponed. Not knowing this, some members of the French royal council, particularly Michel de Marillac, were for abandong the Ile de Ré to Buckingham and concentrating on La Rochelle. Richelieu contested this, arguing that if the Ile de Ré were lost the Ile d'Oléron would also fall; and since La Rochelle could not then be blockaded from the sea it would be impregnable. He himself undertook the relief of St Martin.

The Cardinal now appeared in a weird half-ecclesiastical, half-military costume which excited the ridicule of the toughened veterans who plodded about the siege-lines in dirty buff coats and drooping hats faded by the salt air and the rain. Over black clothes he wore a metal cuirass of a natural steel colour, and over this in turn a prelate's starched collar. There was a feather in his hat and he carried a rapier beneath his cloak of cardinal red. With nine thousand men he prepared for a landing on the Ile de Ré, himself crossing to the Ile d'Oléron in a storm so violent that, as he wrote to Schomberg, every time one opened one's mouth to breathe one swallowed the sea. He arrived soaked through. From the Ile d'Oléron troops were passed over to the Ile de Ré at the same time as the others crossed from the small ports on the main-land north of La Rochelle. Every man had been ordered to go to confession and communion before embarking. With the French now in force on the Ile de Ré, and no sign of further aid from England, Buckingham was forced in his desperation to try an assault on Fort St Martin. This took place on 5 November 1627. Two thousand English rushed the French outworks and took them, but recoiled under the musketry from the defenders on the walls. As the assault party withdrew it was stormed by Schomberg, who had led the cavalry of the landing party from the beachhead.

In his dispatch to the King Schomberg proclaimed triumph-antly 'in one day I have landed on Ré, seen the seige raised and defeated and chased the English army!' [4] Led by three Capuchins who marched with crucifixes in their right hands – a crusading spectacle that would have caused Père Joseph to shiver with excitement – Schomberg with the troops of Louis de Marillac and the garrison of Toiras pushed the English into the salt marshes, where a road twisted through the rushes and crossed a stretch of water to the little island of Loix by means of a bridge. Here the English musketeers formed line, planted their forked rests on the ground and fired their matchlocks at the pursuing French while their comrades sought to scramble over the bridge. They were blasted away by a return salvo from the French musketeers, and then the French cavalry descended on them. Only three regiments had crossed the bridge before the English cavalry stampeded on to it, dislodging their own infantry. Hundreds of men in half-armour were flung into the water and drowned. On the Ile de Ré side of the bridge the remaining English were slaughtered. For Buckingham it was the end of the adventure, and having taken Soubise on board and recovered what he could of his army he set sail for England on 8 November. Of the troops who had set forth in June only half returned to Plymouth. Sadly Buckingham turned to his prisoner Beaulieu-Persac and said: 'Your Cardinal is the first man in the world!'[5]

As Buckingham was sailing for England Walter Montagu was making his way from London to Nancy. During his journey south some months earlier he had heard that Richelieu had ordered his arrest, and that a certain Montegni had been seized by mistake because of the similarity of names. Not daring again to cross France he had returned to England via Germany and Holland. After he had reported to Charles I rather pessimistically on the prospects of a European coalition against France, he was ordered to go again to Nancy to concert measures with Charles of Lorraine, and keeping off French soil as much as possible he was riding just inside the frontier of Bar. Two French spies followed him incessantly, and they were able to warn the French governor of Coiffy, near Langres, who sallied forth with a dozen men, and, without respecting the national boundary, overpowered Montagu and dragged him into France. Within hours Charles of Lorraine heard the news and vigorously protested at this violation of his territory, accompanying his protest with threats which Richelieu ignored. When Anne of Austria learned of Montagu's fate, from the circumstance that her musketeers were ordered to send a detachment to Coiffy to escort Montagu to the Bastille, she was terrified. In great distress she summoned her equerry Pierre de la Porte to her soon after midnight and told him to ride to Coiffy and find out what might be discovered in Montagu's papers which could incriminate her.

When he arrived at Coiffy La Porte found that he was expected to make a fourth at cards with the prisoner. He took the opportunity of communicating the Queen's anxiety to Montagu, and was reassured. But if there was nothing in Montagu's papers to implicate the Queen in Buckingham's plans there was plenty to implicate other crowned heads when the papers were examined by two finance officers Bullion and Fouquet – the latter the famous minister of the next reign. Charles of Lorraine had offered to raise fifteen thousand troops, and had asked the Emperor to add another seven thousand, and to garrison Vic and Moyenvic, the disputed dependencies of Metz. The Emperor had indicated his willingness to give armed assistance to the Bishop of Verdun, who he claimed was being unjustly oppressed by France. This threat to France's security at a moment when Louis XIII, at the Pope's exhortation, was battling with Protestantism and Richelieu was planning a relief expedition to help the oppressed Catholics in Ireland, produced consternation in Urban VIII who instructed Bagno, the nuncio, not to leave the King's side in case the latter might decide to abandon the siege of La Rochelle to meet the imperial threat from the east. There was further dangerous information in Montagu's papers. Venice would pay to raise ten thousand infantry, and Soissons and Rohan would command them.

That the Emperor should back Lorraine was understandable; but the Emperor was a Habsburg and so was Philip IV of Spain. Did this not imply that Spain was also a party to the plot? Buckingham's overtures to Olivares, coupled with the fact that Spain had not yet sent the expected help due to France under the treaty of March, caused Richelieu to suspect that it was. In actual fact Madrid and Vienna were at this time by no means close, and there is no evidence that the former was aware of Montagu's mission, though there is evidence that Olivares was dallying with the rebellious Rohan. At several sessions of the Spanish Council of State it was argued that Spain's interests would best be served by letting the Huguenot war consume France, and that they would not be served by helping Louis XIII to defeat his enemies, so leaving him free to interfere with Spanish designs elsewhere. When Philip IV, who took his claims to be the Catholic King most seriously, objected that he was under a moral obligation to help Louis defeat the Protestants, he was told that reason of state should prevail over ethics, and that it would be good for Spain if Buckingham took the Ile de Ré. Philip was indignant. He would not, he said, allow reason of state to prejudice religion, and if they sacrificed the former to the latter he was confident that God would give them 'great successes'.[6] Eventually Don Federico de Toledo was ordered to sail to help the French fleet at La Rochelle. He arrived at Morbihan two weeks after Buckingham had departed from the Ile de Ré, and, apart from providing an excuse for elaborate festivities, proved useless.

The winter was setting in and La Rochelle, expecting that with the spring a new English armada would appear, remained defiant. It was a town of formidable stellar defences, with bastions, demi-lunes, covered ways, moats and drawbridges, and the port was defended by two towers of unequal height between which a great chain was stretched. The roadstead extended seawards about two miles and was enclosed by two points of land, Chef-de-Baie on the north and Les Minimes on the south. Around this complex, and beginning a few hundred yards inside the roadstead on either side, was strung a siege line of enormous length, reinforced here and there with forts. Behind it, as the besieged could see, all manner of buildings were going up to house the troops and provide for their spiritual as well as their bodily needs, barracks, storehouses, tents, chapels. For Richelieu it was an anguishing time. Gaston d'Orléans exploded with indignation when the King his brother assumed supreme command, and shortly after Louis' arrival he deserted and returned to

Paris in a huff; Maréchal Bassompierre had a quarrel with the Duc d'Angoulême and refused for a time to cooperate with him; thereby he earned Richelieu's distrust and dug, if not his own grave, then at least his own cell; and Louis became ill and wanted to go home.

In February the siege-works were honoured with a visit from the most celebrated besieger of towns in Europe, the captor of Breda, Ambrose Spinola, Marqués de los Balbazes. This tall, thin, fine-looking Genovese was on his way from the Netherlands to Spain, where he had been appointed a member of the Council of State, and, in the company of the Marqués de Legañez, he appeared at La Rochelle. Louis XIII rose from a sick-bed to meet him, and Spinola greeted him with the charm of manner which Velasquez has immortalized in the picture of the surrender of Breda – the only one which shows the victor laying a consoling hand on the shoulder of the vanquished. Recalling that he had never had the honour of the presence of his King at any of his exploits, he expressed envy of the French nobility that they had their King to witness their achievements. Then he recalled that in 323 BC Antigonus, perceiving his enemy Eumenes, who was ill, drawn about the battlefield in a litter, had exclaimed, 'It is not the army I fear, but that litter!' Having examined the works with the eyes of a connoisseur Spinola went on his way, and Richelieu, who had accompanied him on his tour, wrote to Cardinal de La Valette that he was one of the best men in the world, and 'his goodness is equal to his capacity'. For the moment he was almost persuaded by Spinola that Spain had only one concern in the world, and that was to help France win this war. It is part of the poetry in history that it was to be Richelieu who two years later would occasion Spinola's death in his own Italy.

It was with great pride that Richelieu showed Spinola the huge dyke which he was in process of building across the roadstead in order to cut La Rochelle off from the sea. Two hundred hulks were collected from all parts of the coast and sunk in a line across the entrance. From both sides blocks of stones were laid, over which the sea swept consolidating the whole with sand and stones. Early in January 1628 the dyke broke and it was necessary to

recommence the work on a wider base. With the salt spray stinging his face the fragile Richelieu stood in the winter storms
watching with feverish interest the swarms of men engaged on
the work. On the seaward side of the dyke a row of boats was
placed to obstruct all passage through the remaining gap as it
gradually narrowed; and the soldiers halted for a moment to
enjoy the inspiring spectacle of the King himself in a gale carrying
stones to add to the obstruction. In February, however, Louis
decided to return to Paris. The prospect was gravely disturbing
to the Cardinal, for in Paris the King would fall under the influence of his mother, Cardinal Bérulle and Michel de Marillac, all
of whom had been hostile to Richelieu's Valtelline policy. He
feared that if anything went wrong at La Rochelle while the
King was absent they would blame him. What should he do?
Accompany the King or press on with the siege? Père Joseph
counselled him to stay where he was and do the work of God,
and this is what he decided to do. A premature spring sun warmed
him as he bade farewell to the King some distance out on the road
to Paris, and having, out of respect for Louis, omitted to carry his
umbrella he was mildly sunburned, and next day was in bed with
a fever and was bled five times.

Now effectively commander-in-chief of the whole operation,
Richelieu threw himself into the enterprise with renewed energy
as soon as the sickness was over. He had procured a life of Alexander the Great and was studying the details therein of the dyke
which that monarch had built before Tyre. This gave him new
ideas. The ships on the seaward side of the gap were arranged in
the form of a triangle, the apex towards the ocean. Above the
sunken ships there was still six feet of water at the equinoctial
high tide, and here he anchored beams of wood chained together
to form an obstacle. A jetty was built facing La Rochelle, and
cannon were placed upon it; and between the city and the dyke
fifty-eight ships chained together and armed constituted a floating
wall. In addition, thirty-six galleys and pinnaces were available
in the roadstead to attack any Rochelais expedition which might
be launched to destroy the dyke. Meanwhile the Catholics in La
Rochelle were passing out information, and even emerging with

it themselves. One day the Marquis d'Effiat brought to Richelieu the Sieur de Lizon, the royal lieutenant-general of La Rochelle, who was a Catholic. He had just slipped out of the city, and he mentioned that a canal existed on the eastern side of La Rochelle for the boats which gathered salt from the marshes there, and that this gave access to the city by means of a grilled water-gate. Salt collectors were found who could give information about the depth and width of the canal, and its conjunction with the waters of the moat. The grille, it turned out, was of wood, and hence could easily be destroyed. By night the position was reconnoitred from the counterscarp, and the moat was plumbed and found to be no more than three feet deep.

It was decided to attack secretly at night and blow in the grille by means of a petard. A party of petardiers was gathered, and its volunteer commander was one of Père Joseph's innumerable cousins, the Marquis de Feuquières, who was to become one of Richelieu's most able and subtle diplomats in the years to come. Feuquières went out on a reconnaissance on the orders of Louis de Marillac, and stumbled on a working party around some ruins half a mile from the city walls. On being told that these were some of the King's men, Feuquières advanced, when suddenly the air shivered to the flat roar of arquebuses, and the ruins exploded in flashes and clouds of white smoke. Feuquières' horse fell under him, and as he struggled to clear himself he found two muskets pressed against his chest. He was carrying on his person the orders for the attack on the water-gate, but while some royal cavalry skirmished with his captors around the drawbridge over the moat he made use of the distraction to tear the papers to little pieces beneath his cloak, and cast the remnants on the waters. Then, pretending to be exhausted, he staggered slowly through the Porte Maubec, observing the water-gate beneath, and memorizing every detail of the defences of the barbican and the two drawbridges. Even though a prisoner in the city, he managed to pass all this intelligence out to Père Joseph.

The assault on the water-gate was fixed for 12 March. Richelieu commanded the operation, inspected the petards, and supervised the embarkation in boats of some two dozen cavaliers who had attached themselves to him, including another future diplomat, the Baron de Charnacé. At ten at night in faint moonlight these slipped off down the canal. Behind the counterscarp were five hundred of Marillac's men, and behind them again fifteen hundred of Schomberg's. The idea was that, while one party blew in the water-gate and entered the city by boat, another would blow in the gate and enter by the barbican. In the middle of the moat stood a stone pylon, communicating with the counterscarp at one end by means of a drawbridge, and with the barbican at the other end by means of another. The assault party carried long planks, some of which would be used to bridge the first gap, and, when the pylon was gained, the others would be used to bridge the second gap. A petard would then be placed against the gate; and by means of special tools the two drawbridges would be lowered, the petard would be exploded, and the defences would be rushed. More reinforcements would be pushed through, and the city would be occupied. It was very cold, and Richelieu, waiting with a thousand horse and four thousand foot some two hundred yards away, grew impatient as the night dragged on in silence until dawn broke. The men carrying the petards had lost their way, and, failing to rendezvous at five in the morning with the assault party, had abandoned the enterprise. Richelieu was furious with Louis de Marillac, and his distrust of this man dates from this unfortunate episode.

The fate of La Rochelle hung upon the efforts of either Rohan or Buckingham, or of both. Rohan, a handsome man with fine moustaches and tuft of beard, was an intellectual as well as a soldier, one of the ablest political commentators of the age. His cleverness made him more dangerous to the state than other rebels. At that moment he was scouring the countryside between Nîmes and Albi recruiting zealous Protestant youths; but he was a long way from La Rochelle and was fully occupied with defending himself against Condé, operating in the Rhône valley.

Three deputies of the city of La Rochelle had accompanied Buckingham to England. Not for four months did they manage to communicate with their brethren, but in March a messenger got into the city with a note hidden in a button of his coat. The news was not good. The deputies had gathered supplies and shipping, but the English had not been able to provide a convoy of more than fifteen warships, and so they were still in Plymouth. Three weeks later a certain Captain David broke dramatically through the dyke defences at high tide, and amidst the thunder of guns, the leaping fountains of spray and the crash of splintering woodwork, reached the harbour. But, believing himself lost, he had cast overboard the dispatches from England which he was carrying, and these were fished out of the water and brought to Richelieu. They contained the news that Buckingham was sending his brother-in-law, the Earl of Denbigh, with sixty ships, but that shortage of money was holding them up. Clearly there would be time to complete the barrage, and then Buckingham could do what he liked. Ever the optimist, Buckingham was in fact quite sanguine. 'The French have no desire for peace,' he said, 'let all men beware of treating with them, for they are false.'[7] Money, however, was not his only difficulty; the nation could not be roused to an excess of pugnacity in the case of France as it could in that of Spain, and there was a universal clamour for peace.

The weak-kneed Godefroy had been ousted from the mayoralty of La Rochelle, and the new mayor was a fiery little fanatical seaman named Guiton, who every day climbed the tower of the church of St Bartholomew to look for the sails of the English ships. On 11 May 1628 he saw them. Bassompierre had invited Sourdis, the archbishop of Bordeaux, who commanded the French ships, to inspect his batteries and dine with him. Suddenly from the Ile de Ré he saw the signal flying that indicated the English were in sight. Louis XIII had returned to the camp on 17 April, and he and Richelieu met near the dyke to confer. In due course the English came around the southern point of the Ile de Ré and advanced in three columns towards the roadstead. As they came within range of his batteries on Chef-de-Baie Bassompierre opened fire, and while Denbigh studied the dyke with increasing dismay the cannon thudded and the shot fluttered the white sails and stripped them from the yards. After some time Denbigh withdrew out of range and anchored. The Rochelais managed to send a delegation on board his flagship, but received the discouraging reply that nothing could be done unless the barrage was broken. In desperation Guiton sent a message off to Denbigh: 'Do not leave your brothers whom you have, with such fine words, filled with promises: all Europe has its eyes on you.'[8]

Denbigh was at his wits' end to know what to do. He sent a petard on board a small boat to try to blow up the French ship-barrage, but the petard exploded prematurely and the celebrated petardier was hoisted with it. Then a 'rain of fire' was tried at night, which made a splendid sight, but proved abortive. On 18 May the whole English fleet weighed anchor and approached the defences. The townspeople thought that their relief was at hand and went wild with joy. The bells rang, the cannon thundered and flags waved. From the sides of the English ships flashes and clouds of smoke erupted and the sound of the cannonade rolled away in the sand dunes. Then one by one the ships drew off, tacked and slipped off to the corner of the Ile de Ré. Within a few hours they had quite disappeared from sight.

For generations the French were puzzled by this strange retreat, and Voltaire, as usual, had a romantic explanation: Richelieu, using Buckingham's love for the Queen, had persuaded the latter to write to the Duke to abandon the enterprise; and he, gallant as ever, had yielded to her entreaty. The real explanation was much more prosaic. Most of Denbigh's ships were requisitioned merchantmen, and their owners refused to take risks. Seeing that they were unprepared to take their vessels into the teeth of the fight Denbigh decided to withdraw a little and think the matter out. Some Rochelais ships misunderstood his signals as orders to sail for England, to which they turned; and the bulk of the fleet, nothing loath, followed them over the horizon. In England Parliament had had to be called together to vote the necessary supplies for a continuation of the war. It met in a mood of violent indignation, the outcome of which was the Petition of Right, followed by a Remonstrance against Buckingham; and finally the dissolution of Parliament. Through the Venetian Ambassador Richelieu made overtures for peace. There was trouble in northern Italy and he wished his hands to be free to deal with it. Buckingham responded favourably, contemplating that he and Richelieu might meet outside the walls of La Rochelle to negotiate a settlement. Nothing came of the suggestion.

There was now little hope for succour for La Rochelle, but it held out. On 24 May the besieged sought to get rid of useless mouths by pushing the women and children out of the gates; the royal soldiers pushed them back. The building of the dyke went on, but the Rochelais fired on the works, spattering them with the severed limbs of the workmen. Richelieu, with events in Italy preoccupying him, became more and more impatient. Bassompierre received from him a sarcastic letter concerning the dilatoriness of those bringing up supplies of building material:

> This letter is to learn if you intend to command this army or not. If you do so intend, you will please obey the order which I gave to M. de Rothelin to take the horses which are in your quarter so that he may fetch the powder at Saumur. If this is not your intention, since that of the King is different, your thoughts will not prevent me from being obeyed.[9]

Wounded by this letter, Bassompierre went off to see Richelieu and was coldly received. He gave his explanations and Richelieu relaxed and invited him and Schomberg to dinner. The King was much occupied with his religious observances, and, when his musicians failed him at Pentecost, prepared and himself conducted the choir in the camp. Someone was reminded, as he watched him participating at Vespers, of David playing the harp before the Ark of the Covenant. Inside the city they were praying too, and their faith in Buckingham was not less than that in God. When on 8 July 1628 Richelieu summoned the town and promised the King's mercy, Guiton read his letter to the city fathers, adding that he expected the English back at any moment. The poet Malherbe, pointing to a sentinel on the walls, remarked, 'See that fellow there. He suffers starvation and a thousand other miseries, and exposes his life every moment, because he wants to communicate under both species, and others want to stop him! Is not that a fine subject to trouble all of France?'[10]

By August the situation in the city was desperate. Mme de

Rohan had long since eaten her carriage horses, and begun on the carriage itself. When ordered to boil up the harness and leather springs her cook slipped over the walls and gave himself up to the royal forces, saying he would sooner be hanged than use his talents to make jellies out of boots and pâtés out of old shoes.[11] Bits of parchment were being minced up and boiled with leather in tallow and brown sugar to make bread. A dog's head cost ten ols, a pound of mutton dripping or one of donkey meat one *livre*, and a pound of horseflesh six *livres*. The inhabitants grew vegetables on the counterscarp and became targets for royalist marksmen; at night they prowled around the moat and the rocks at the harbour entrance scavenging for any sort of edible substance, however frightful. One of them, with dispatches for Buckingham, was caught slipping away to England and was put on trial for high treason. The Rochelais heard of this and demanded that he be treated as a prisoner of war 'according to the law of nations'. Richelieu replied that the law of nations had nothing to do with the matter; 'you are in no condition or state to treat with your master'. The Rochelais reminded him that they held Feuquières, and at this threat Richelieu suspended the proceedings against the envoy. After the siege was over they were recommenced, the accused was beheaded at Poitiers, and the head transported to La Rochelle for exposition on the Tour de la Lanterne.

Suddenly Buckingham was gone. On 2 September (new style) he met Soubise and the delegates from La Rochelle at Portsmouth to discuss further measures to relieve the city. Passing from the breakfast room where he had been talking to the Frenchmen, he was stabbed in the heart by a religious fanatic and disappointed soldier of fortune, John Felton. Charles I was determined to continue the war, but when Guiton told the people at divine service that he was expecting the English on 29 September, a woman cried out that she had eaten nothing for two weeks, and that her child and his nurse had died of hunger. Morale was breaking down, but Guiton remained defiant. As a gesture of his determination he flung his dagger at the table which still stands in the town hall, and the point of it chipped the marble surface. Eventually he was forced by his colleagues in the municipality to agree that two deputies should seek out the Cardinal. They found him conciliatory, for he wanted this tiresome business ended quickly. He told them that at the moment the King was disposed to leave the Rochelais their lives, property and religious liberties. And he added 'on my faith, the faith of a gentleman and a cardinal'. But, he warned, if the English came again things would be different. The deputies retired into the town with this admonition. There was silence. Then suddenly the Rochelais attacked the barrage and tried to burn it. They failed, but it was evident that they remained defiant.

This time Guiton was proved prophetic, for on 29 September the English fleet, now under the Earl of Lindsey, reappeared. Richelieu and Bassompierre drove quickly by carriage to the latter's headquarters at Chef-de-Baie. They were within range of the cannon on the walls, and these opened fire, throwing clouds of earth over the carriage as it moved quickly past. A little later they were joined by the King with his troop of musketeers. Night was falling and they resolved to pass it at Bassompierre's lodging. The following morning they studied the thirty-one English ships as they rode at anchor, then inspected the batteries at Chef-de-Baie. Early in the afternoon the English weighed, and began manoeuvring, while one hundred and twenty other ships rounded the Ile de Ré. From the coast cannonfire thundered and puffs of white smoke were blown to shreds in the sea breeze. By evening the whole fleet was anchored in a great semi-circle from Chef-de-Baie to Les Minimes. The following morning the ships began a bombardment of the barrage and the fortifications around it. In splendid order they followed one another like monsters engaged in some ponderous ballet, each of them bursting into flame and smoke as it discharged its broadside at the targets. Over three hundred shot whined over Louis XIII's head as he stood in the battery at Chef-de-Baie or himself applied the match to the touch-holes of the guns. It was said that the Cardinal had laid the first gun, pointing it at the beakhead of an English two-decker, and had seen with pleasure the great ship deflected slightly off course as the shot struck it.

From behind Chef-de-Baie the French galleys tried, without much success, to dart out and cut off the English stragglers. Their best trophy was a figurehead gilded with the arms of England which was floating amid a great mass of other debris on the sea. Louis, as soon as the English fleet had withdrawn out of range, rode off to inspect it, and claimed that he himself had shot it away. Next day the performance was repeated, and nine fireships and a ship full of explosives were sent towards the French fleet. They were snared by cables from small sailing boats, and drawn on shore where they burned. It was now quite evident that the barrage could not be broken by bombardment, and that the ships, their casualties mounting, were vulnerable to fixed shore batteries. Accordingly Lindsey decided to open negotiations. He had on board with him Walter Montagu, who had some time previously been released from the Bastille and allowed to return to England, and he and the delegates from La Rochelle, who were also on board, went ashore to parley. On 15 October Montagu dined with Richelieu and spent two hours trying to persuade him that the King's response to the overtures was too harsh. He left, saying enigmatically that at the first moment favourable to the English the French would learn what they could do. The best that they could in fact do was send Montagu two days later to meet Richelieu on one of the French ships. The latter put on a demonstration for him, taking him on a conducted tour of the barrage and the defences, and saying that it should be evident to him that England was being deceived by the Rochelais, and caused expenses which it could not afford. Montagu was impressed, and conceded, to the Cardinal's delight, that it was impossible to force the passage. It was decided to sue for peace, and that night Montagu set off with a safe-conduct for St Malo, whence he crossed to England.

The English fleet occupied its time with desultory bombardment until on 27 October six deputies from La Rochelle came out to one of the royal forts to parley. Hastily summoned, Bassompierre rode there at the gallop, and brought them to Richelieu, who called in the members of the royal council. The spokesman for the Rochelais were a pastor and a banker. They were ready,

they said, to capitulate, but they demanded their former privileges, franchises and immunities. Mme de Rohan and her sons,
who had been attainted of high treason and had their peerages
withdrawn and their properties confiscated, should be restored
in all their rights and honours. Furthermore, they wanted a treaty
of peace, not a pardon, and the garrison should have the honours
of war. 'Impudence' was Richelieu's reaction. There remained
no more of life in these 'shadows of living men',[12] he said, than
the mercy of the King might accord. The deputies now changed
their attitude and begged the Cardinal to intervene with the King
on their behalf. He replied that he would do so in eight days when
the King would return from an excursion. 'What, Monseigneur,
in eight days! In La Rochelle there are not provisions for three
days!'[13] Now that he had their resistance crumbling and found
the deputies abject, Richelieu pressed his advantage. With consummate tact and firmness he led them to see where the solution
to the problem lay, and the pastor returned to the city exclaiming,
'He is a great man!'

Next day there was a council meeting. Some members wanted
to raze La Rochelle; all were agreed that it was necessary to make
an example of it. Richelieu threw his weight decisively on the side
of mercy. If La Rochelle were to be obliterated, none of the towns
held by Rohan in Provence and Languedoc would ever yield;
Louis, as a great king, could on this occasion exercise clemency
which makes monarchs like unto God; Soubise in London had
been propagating the notion that Catholics would never show
mercy to heretics; it was desirable to give the lie to this argument.
On 28 October the deputies from La Rochelle reappeared and
signed the terms of capitulation. No one in the government
would sign for fear that this might later be construed as a treaty;
instead Hallier and Marillac, *maréchaux-de-camp*, signed for the
army. The Cardinal then invited these wraiths of men to a good
dinner, and stuffed with food the deputies' sons whom they had
brought along as valets in the hope of getting them a meal. Next
day the gates of La Rochelle opened and the drawbridge fell.
Twelve of the city fathers emerged and plodded, black figures
with balloon pantaloons and white collars under large black hats,

along the counterscarp towards the sea. Near Fort Louis they met Bassompierre, who dismounted, flourished his hat and was, as always, the perfect gallant. Horses were provided, and the deputies mounted, suffering agonies in their famished bodies as they rode to the royal lodging. Here they were received by the Marquis de Brézé in his capacity of captain of the guards, and taken to Richelieu, who, with Michel de Marillac, Bassompierre and d'Effiat, took them himself to the King. On their knees they made their submission and sought pardon. Louis confirmed the terms, and also invited the deputies to dinner.

On 30 October wagon-loads of food entered the city and the Huguenot soldiers marched out: there were only seventy-four French and sixty-two English among them. Later in the day Richelieu made his entry, accompanied by the papal nuncio and a great following. Guiton met him with six archers. He was promptly told that he was no longer mayor and could dispense with them. Everywhere there were emaciated corpses, the sight of which filled the Cardinal with horror, and spectres crept up to the carts to receive their rations. Over one hundred of them died that night from over-eating. Next morning was the feast of All Saints, and Richelieu celebrated mass in the city, giving communion with his own hands to the leading personalities of the court and army. It was a victory mass, followed later, when Louis XIII made his entry in a suit of armour covered with fleurs-de-lys, by a *Te Deum*. Père Suffren, the King's Jesuit confessor, preached the sermon, and it was thought that he gave Louis and God too much of the credit, and their human agents too little. It was noticed that the Cardinal raised his head as he heard Suffren exclaim, 'Sire, let your majesty recognize that your victory comes from God and not from your arms or your resolution!'[14] Louis looked at Richelieu, and the latter looked at him. People sensed the mutual shrug of their shoulders. They may also have grinned knowingly when a few days later a royal ordinance appeared in which the King acknowledged 'the efficacious succour of divine favour', but also the 'counsel, singular prudence, vigilance and laborious service of his very dear and beloved cousin, the Cardinal de Richelieu'.[15]

The same ordinance prescribed the liberties of Protestantism in the city. The most serious encroachment upon these was the transformation of the Huguenot temple, built by the Protestants in 1603, into the Catholic cathedral of a new bishopric. Cardinal Bérulle and Michel de Marillac wanted to proscribe the Protestant cult in La Rochelle altogether, but Richelieu insisted on the maximum religious toleration compatible with the suppression of the Huguenot political movement. Thereby he deepened the distrust of these two pious men, who increasingly regarded him as the great betrayer. Richelieu wanted Père Joseph, who all these months had huddled in his summer-house praying with the dawn and receiving his spies in the night, to be the first bishop of La Rochelle, but he refused. All Protestant clergy were confirmed in their appointments and their churches, and a royal commissioner of justice, police and finances was nominated. Guiton and fifteen of the city fathers were banished for six months: the former was in due course to become an officer in the royal army and to serve faithfully and honourably. Mme de Rohan and her daughter were put in a carriage and escorted by fifty horse to the château de Niort, where for a time they were imprisoned. The English fleet remained at anchor while all this was going on, and sailed for England on 10 November, just as the sea breached the dyke. It seemed as if everything was conspiring to make theatre out of the whole train of events before La Rochelle, the capture of which was a sensation in every city of Europe. And Richelieu's cynical comment summed it all up: 'They condemn me now in Rome as a heretic, soon they will canonize me as a saint!'[16]

An incident during the war with the Huguenots. The royal fleet engages the ships of the Protestant Soubise in the roadstead of La Rochelle and near the Ile de Ré.

The face of the irresponsible. George Villiers, Duke of Buckingham. By Rubens. This gilded Apollo's outrageous courtship of the Queen of France led to a war of personal vengeance.

The face of power. Richelieu. By
Philippe de Champagne. The eyes
and the sagging lines of the cheeks
alone betray the nervousness,
anxiety and bad health that the
mask of severe dignity sought to
disguise.

*Vraye effigie du R.P. Ioseph de Paris predicateur Capucin, Prouincial de Touraine,
superieur de missions és Estrangers et de Poitou, fondateur de Religieuses de
Caluaire. A rendu l'esprit entre les mains de ses superieurs le 18. decembre.1638.*

The face of theocracy. Père
Joseph, Richelieu's Grey
Eminence, keeper of his
conscience and his beloved friend,
nicknamed by him Ezechielly.
This religious mystic bridged the
gap between Church and state to
become the most guileful of
politicians.

11

Everywhere the French
Block Me

1629

During all the turmoil of the first decade of the Thirty Years War
one man had pursued a chimera with never-diminishing idealism
and enthusiasm. He was Charles de Gonzaga, Duc de Nevers.
For nearly twenty years, indeed, he had tramped all over Europe
exhausting his youth and resources in propagating his project of a
crusade; and all this time he had been urged on by his friend Père
Joseph, who never failed to lose his grip on reality when the Holy
Places were mentioned. Almost every Catholic prince in Europe
at one time or other had made use of this misdirected enthusiasm
and had deluded, not only Nevers, but also Père Joseph, into
believing that the quarrels in Germany could be ended if only the
energies devoted to them could be harnessed in a common assault
on the Turk. Much of the diplomacy in the years 1620-5 was
devoted to attempts to effect this improbable reorientation.
While Tilly and Wallenstein, Mansfeld and Spinola recruited
armies, Nevers recruited his crusaders; and at his own expense
he built a fleet to enable the combined operation in the Levant
to take place. To Dutch shipyards he paid out 50,000 crowns for
the construction of five of the finest galleons afloat, each of five
hundred tons and mounting between thirty and forty guns. His
own private army amounted to thirteen thousand men and he
collected the deserters from Mansfeld's wrecked army in Friesland

183

in 1623. The resources but not the dream were consumed in the French civil war, the five ships perishing miserably at the hands of Soubise.

Now, when Nevers was apparently discarded, and his cause abandoned by all but his Capuchin collaborator, he became a European problem. The Duke of Mantua, the worthless Vincenzo ii Gonzaga, was dying, as a result of his depravities, without direct heirs, and there were four claimants – Nevers himself, a cousin of the Duke; the Duke of Guastalla, another and more remote cousin; Marguerite Gonzaga, the Dowager Duchess of Lorraine; and that ever-eager interloper Charles Emmanuel of Savoy, who argued that his grand-daughter Marguerite, niece of Vincenzo, should inherit through the female line the marquisate of Montferrat, which was an appendage of Mantua only through an accident of descent. Mantua was a fief of the Holy Roman Empire, and by law the Emperor should judge the validity of disputed claims to its succession; but none of the interested parties was content to leave the question to the hazards of the law, or the vagaries of imperial politics. Richelieu instantly perceived the advantages to France of having a French duke in northern Italy; he was even more concerned to avoid the Duchy's falling to Guastalla, who was a Spanish puppet, for this would place a potential enemy on the flank of Venice, already overawed by the might of Spain, and vastly increase Spanish power in Italy.

Richelieu and Urban viii, their differences over the Valtelline forgotten, were of like mind on the Mantuan question, as they were on the Huguenot problem in France; the Pope, angered by recent Spanish accusations that he was pro-French, suspicious of Spain's Caesaro-papalism, and dismayed at Spain's tardy assistance to Louis xiii at La Rochelle, recoiled at the thought of a Spanish domination of Mantua. Secretly he and the French ambassador in Rome, Baron Philippe de Béthune, planned a *fait accompli* in favour of Nevers. The latter's son, the Duc de Rethel, was already in Mantua studying Italian manners, and the Pope prompted his marriage to Maria Gonzaga, Vincenzo's niece, who was also the niece of the Empress Eleanora, Vincenzo's sister. A French envoy in the person of the Marquis de St Charmont was sent to

Mantua to talk the dying Duke into executing a will in favour of Nevers. With the same end in view the Spanish governor of the Milanais, Gonzalo de Cordoba, sent the Conte Giovanni Serbelloni to Mantua in the interests of Guastalla, who was preparing to take the city by surprise. The struggle around the moribund Duke was won by St Charmont, who was abetted by the first minister of Mantua, a notorious enemy of Spain. A will was signed in great secrecy leaving the Duchy to Nevers, and with unseemly haste a marriage was contracted with a papal dispensation, and celebrated on Christmas Day 1627, between Rethel and the schoolgirl Maria, which would have the effect of negativing the claims of Charles Emmanuel. That evening Vincenzo died. Nevers, who was waiting in the shadows, stepped forth to occupy his Duchy.

Nevers' succession to Mantua was a minor issue compared with his claim to Montferrat. The Marquisate of Montferrat lay between Savoy and the Milanais, and its capital, Casale, dominated not only the upper Po but also the strategically important road from Genoa to Milan. Casale is reached from Turin across miles of flooded rice-fields hemmed in by dense groves of Lombardy poplars, and interrupted at intervals by wooded hills. At the western edge of the old city, and lying near the Po, is the citadel, upon which Gonzalo de Cordoba cast his covetous eyes. It was then the most important fortress in northern Italy. Walls of brick of great thickness constitute a quadrilateral, the north and south faces of which are extended to form each an apex where a gate and drawbridge over the moat give access to the wide, paved piazza separating the citadel from the buildings of the town. At each corner is an immense circular brick bastion; and from the embrasures on one of those rare days when it is brilliantly clear in Piedmont one has an unforgettable panorama of the whole Alpine complex from the Monte Rosa, Matterhorn and Mont Blanc to the Monte Genevra, standing as a great irregular purple silhouette against the turquoise evening sky. Whoever held this bastion held the whole Po valley.

By one of those accidents of history Gonzalo de Cordoba had long had a personal grudge against Nevers. Six years previously

Gonzalo had commanded the Spanish forces which had seized the Palatinate, and after the Battle of Höchst he had forced Mansfeld's army across the Rhine and into Alsace. At that time Nevers was governor of Champagne, and he had allowed Mansfeld to recuperate there. Mansfeld had employed this advantage wisely. Marching north from Nevers' territory he had fallen on Belgium behind Gonzalo's back, forced him into a premature engagement and defeated him at Fleurus, causing the Spaniards to raise the siege of Bergen-op-Zoom. Gonzalo had very good reason to distrust Nevers, and saw him as a Trojan Horse of the French in northern Italy. For months he had pestered Madrid concerning the impending danger, but Madrid had not reacted; Olivares was in one of his phases of depression and the government was in vacillating hands. Five days before Vincenzo's death Gonzalo wrote again, pointing out that, if Nevers were successful in establishing himself, the decline of Spanish power in Italy would be demonstrated to all the world; and he urgently asked for instructions. On the day after Vincenzo's death he wrote again, reporting that Nevers was taking possession without legal title, for it was the Emperor alone who could decide upon the rights of collaterals. Clearly the situation would be out of control by the time replies reached him from Madrid, so Gonzalo decided to take matters into his own hands. He turned to Charles Emmanuel.

Ever ready to sup with the devil, and never lacking a long spoon, Charles Emmanuel was nothing loath. Saying he had no liking to have the French on either side of him – for Montferrat lay just to the east of Turin – he had already let Guastalla know that he would support him. Now he suggested to Gonzalo that, since Philip III of Spain had renounced his pretensions to the fiefs of the Habsburgs north of the Alps, Spain was entitled to those south of the Alps. Gonzalo and Charles Emmanuel's agent, the priest Gaetano Coxa, took time off from celebrating Christmas to sign a treaty – on the very day Vincenzo died – by which Montferrat would be partitioned between Savoy and Mantua, in return for an alliance directed against Nevers. It was an act of spurious legalism, but that did not concern Charles Emmanuel. The House of Savoy had crept down the Piedmont, not by means of dramatic conquests, but by the digestion of small morsels; and Charles Emmanuel calculated that whatever the outcome of the impending struggle for Mantua, whether the Spaniards expelled Nevers or France propped him up, Savoy was likely to be bought off by the victor with a few more towns and a few more miles of farmland.

Gonzalo was a soldier, and he could envisage no other way of resolving the problem than by the sword. Two days after Christmas he wrote to the Spanish ambassador in Vienna, pointing out that there was no time to await instructions from Madrid, and asking him to secure from the Emperor approval to move the Spanish army into Montferrat in the Emperor's name. What he omitted to inform the Emperor was that he considered this a unique moment for a piece of frank aggression – the seizure of Casale. With the Milanais separating Mantua to the east and Montferrat to the west, there was nothing Nevers could do, Gonzalo calculated, to relieve his second capital.

Failing to comprehend the politics and law involved, Gonzalo was nonplussed when the Emperor not only refused his consent, but ordered him not to take up arms. Graf von Khevenhüller, the Emperor's agent, arrived in Milan and indulged in some very frank speech. Casale, he said, was at the disposal of the Emperor according to law, and what would the world say if the lieutenant of the King of Spain were, by seizing it, to do that which was alleged in the case of Nevers to be an act of treason? Philip IV would forfeit the confidence of the German princes and strengthen them in their view that 'in Spain reason of state prevailed over legal procedures, and might over right'.[1] On top of this admonition came a letter from the Spanish ambassador in Vienna, reporting that Ferdinand had been subjected to the pressure of the Empress, who had brought up Nevers' new daughter-in-law, Maria de Rethel, and was devoted to her, and who had shed floods of tears in front of her husband.

Gonzalo was the more bewildered in that Philip IV wrote to him on 16 January 1628, approving of his pact with Charles Emmanuel and commending his 'prudence'. For a month the situation remained static, while Madrid made up its mind.

Richelieu later wrote that Spain was intent on exploiting the French distractions in La Rochelle to gain an advantage over France; and that he was determined to frustrate this design. It is true that Gonzalo told Khevenhüller that while France was occupied with the Huguenots it would be easy to seize Casale and thereby prevent Nevers from handing it over to Louis XIII at a later date, but in none of the Spanish records nor in the correspondence between Gonzalo de Cordoba and Madrid is La Rochelle mentioned, nor does France appear except very incidentally. Spain's design was to secure Casale and oust Nevers in order to preserve military and political stability in Lombardy, and it was a design strictly limited. For this reason, Olivares could not comprehend the Emperor's attitude, and he persuaded Philip IV to write to Ferdinand on 15 February 1628 expressing surprise. The Spanish ambassador at Vienna was instructed not to seek the Emperor's permission for an attack on Montferrat, but merely to justify it when it was accomplished. At the same time instructions were sent to Gonzalo to proceed, and these were justified by the argument that Charles Emmanuel would not be able to take possession of everything, and should be helped by Spain pending the Emperor's decision on the succession question.

Even before he received these instructions on 2 March 1628, Gonzalo had commenced movement to support Charles Emmanuel, who had marched into Montferrat and seized Alba, Trino and Montcalvo. Gonzalo had been able to raise only about eight thousand troops, but since Casale was garrisoned with only a couple of hundred men of inferior quality he boasted he could take it without drawing his sword. Nevers had sent the Bishop of Mantua to Vienna to represent his cause, and when the bishop reported that Gonzalo had demanded that the governor of Casale surrender the fortress in the Emperor's name, Ferdinand was outraged. He told the bishop that Gonzalo had acted 'without orders and against my will'. The Aulic Council was summoned, and though there were not lacking voices who supported Spain, the outcome of the debate was the issue of an imperial decree sequestrating the Duchy of Mantua pending settlement of the succession issue, and appointing John of Nassau as the imperial commissioner to govern the territory. The Spanish ambassador, explaining these proceedings, reported that 'the Empress favours her niece in every possible way', and said that the imperial confessor, a Luxemburg Jesuit named Lamormaini, was entirely opposed to the war and was pro-French. This was not how it appeared to Richelieu. Since Nevers' claims were indisputably the strongest, the sequestration of the Duchy by the Aulic Council, most of whose members were known to be in Spanish pay, coming as it did on top of the Emperor's hostile policies respecting Metz and Verdun, convinced him that Vienna and Madrid were leagued in an aggressive conspiracy.

Richelieu's belief that Gonzalo de Cordoba's adventure in northern Italy was merely an aspect of a Habsburg design against France is understandable in the context of events. Three months before the Mantuan crisis burst upon him he found it necessary to write to Olivares reproaching him for the failure of Spain to honour its treaty engagement to assist against La Rochelle,[2] and later he reminded him 'that this was a matter of "conscience" '.[3] When Fargis' secretary reported to him that Spain would be unhappy if La Rochelle fell – and, as we have seen, this was the disposition of some members of the Spanish Council of State – he concluded that this delay was maliciously inspired.[4] His efforts to restrain the Spanish assault on Casale met with no response. In April 1628 he instructed Fargis to tell Olivares that Spain was obliged by the Treaty of Monzon and the Franco-Spanish treaty of alliance to negotiate the Italian question, and pending negotiations to halt military operations. Fargis was to proceed in this matter 'confidentially' and 'secretly'[5] – secret diplomacy being Richelieu's predilection – and he was to recall that Spinola, when he was at La Rochelle, had promised Richelieu that France would have satisfaction in Italy.[6] Madrid's only answer was to increase the Spanish army in Italy, and Richelieu decided that France had no alternative to supporting Nevers. But so long as La Rochelle held out this was impossible. It therefore became a race between the siege of La Rochelle and the siege of Casale.

Before Casale's stubborn brick ramparts Gonzalo de Cordoba's military reputation was now in the balance. The citadel and town showed no signs of yielding. Spain had poured over half a million ducats into Milan to support the operation, but the administrative system was such that only a small amount of this dribbled through to Gonzalo for the raising of fresh troops. His Italian regiments he found were hopeless. 'The Neapolitans,' he said, 'are the worst of men. They escape in shoals, and though I hang them and send them to the galleys in masses, it is to no effect.'[7] As time dragged on it became more impossible for Gonzalo to yield and yet save face.

In Vienna the Emperor's indignation was growing daily. Again the Aulic Council was called, and Ferdinand denounced the war as 'a declared injustice'. An imperial decree was issued requiring Nevers to submit to the sequestration, and stating that when he did so Spain and Savoy should hand their conquests over to the imperial commissioner. This was not at all to Charles Emmanuel's liking, and he began sounding out Richelieu. A Savoyard embassy arrived at La Rochelle and hinted that Spain would be abandoned if Richelieu would agree that Savoy could keep some of its conquests in Montferrat. Richelieu did agree. At the same time the Savoyard ambassador in Madrid asked Philip IV if Spain would go to war in the event of France forcing the Alps to raise the siege of Casale. Philip's reply was in the negative. Charles Emmanuel knew that he had little to hope for from Spain in defying the Emperor, and that it might pay him to cooperate with France. But as yet he remained a nominal ally of Spain.

The Pope's reaction to these events was one of dismay, and his efforts to bring about a reconciliation of the parties only earned him their distrust. He was already at odds with the Emperor over ecclesiastical affairs in Germany: Béthune reported to Richelieu that Urban's refusal to join a league of Italian princes and Venice to oppose Spanish designs was due to pusillanimity and parsimony, and Richelieu expressed his annoyance to Bagno, the nuncio in Paris; in Madrid the nuncio was cold-shouldered, Olivares would not consider an armistice, and he formed the opinion that Urban was secretly supporting Nevers. With customary hyperbole he proclaimed that there had never been a Pope so hostile to Spain, a sentiment echoed by Feria in the

Council of State. In the analysis of the breakdown in relations between France and Spain, which six years later was to lead them to general war, this discrediting of the baffled pontiff, tugged at as he was one way and then another by the rival factions, must be recognized to be a significant factor; for with the repudiation of his moral authority secular ambitions were released from ethical constraint.

So the year 1628 proceeded towards its close, while Richelieu, fretting at the length of time it was taking to reduce La Rochelle, played for time. It became clear that if Casale were to be relieved a winter campaign would be necessary, and officers were sent to survey the Alpine passes. A time-table was also formulated, which was in fact to be strictly adhered to. As soon as La Rochelle capitulated the army would march for Italy, leaving the pacification of the south of France until later; Casale would be relieved in March; the army would then proceed through Provence and deal with Rohan; and by the spring of the following year it would be ready to face Spain, either on the Spanish Netherlands frontier or in Italy, should Spain make the raising of the siege of Casale an occasion for a declaration of war.[8] First, however, it was necessary for Richelieu to salve his own conscience and that of the King, for this would not be a matter of upholding the law or defending the realm; it would in effect be international hostilities. His subtle mind was capable of effecting a satisfactory reconciliation between political need and moral duty, but the King was a pious and uneducated man who tended to see things in rigid and simple terms. It was necessary, to show him that the proposed course of action was not merely moral on the benefit-of-the-doubt standard, but that it was, in fact, morally obligatory.

To this end the aid of Louis' confessor was invoked, and while he worked on the King's conscience, Richelieu, having quietened his own, assaulted the King on a broader front. On 13 January 1629 he laid before Louis and the council a long and famous memorandum in which the question of the Mantuan succession was linked with the security of France, and with its grandeur – this word now coming to prominence in Richelieu's thinking, and acquiring in his argument the character of a moral end. The entire range of policy was reviewed. Internal fortifications, which served only the purpose of dissension, should be destroyed, and the frontiers should be fortified so as to enable the King 'to enter the states of his neighbours and guarantee them against the oppressions of Spain',[9] while securing the King's lands from reciprocal encroachment. It was important to be powerful at sea 'which gives entry to all the countries of the world'. Thirty galleys should be launched in the Mediterranean to defend the coast and threaten to interfere with Spanish communications to Genoa. The Franche-Comté should be outflanked by close relations with Geneva and the sale of the sovereignty of Neuchâtel to the Duc de Longueville.

Behind Richelieu's academic analysis lay other motives, which he did not commit to paper. It was important to unify the realm by providing external distraction. The great Huguenot warriors like La Force would rush to the colours if it meant war with Spain, as in fact they did; and with them would come the crowd of unemployed trouble-makers whom they used. It was necessary to suppress the mounting criticism of the Catholic zealots, and to this end the King's confessor should publicly approve of the proposed excursion to relieve Casale. Richelieu was not yet sure how far he could rely upon Louis' support, and it was desirable to distract the jealous young man from the whispers of Richelieu's enemies by conjuring up before him visions of glory for France and for himself – for Louis' piety was not inconsistent with a certain vanity – and by involving him in grand designs, the realization of which would make him quite dependent on the Cardinal. There was, in short, as much of an element of personal survival in Richelieu's approach as there was of survival of the nation.

When Richelieu finished reading this memorial to the council no one said a word. All eyes turned to the King. The latter, taciturn as ever, merely said that he was resolved to 'take advantage of the situation'.[10] He wanted no more talk of retreat. So it was decided. Up to this point Richelieu had kept his intentions to himself and a small group of associates. All Europe wondered whether he would follow up his triumph at La Rochelle by an invasion of England, but, knowing that Madrid must have cherished the hope that he would thus distract himself, he merely smiled blandly when ambassadors asked if this was his intention.[11] In fact, as soon as La Rochelle fell, the army released therefrom turned to the east, while Richelieu, tongue in cheek, wrote to Olivares saying he was sure that the latter would be delighted to hear of the city's surrender. The King left Paris on 16 January 1629, and all the way to Grenoble it was a triumphal progress. Near Dijon Richelieu received bad news. The Spanish ambassador in Paris, the Marqués de Mirabel was broadcasting that the Comte de Bautru, Richelieu's special envoy in Madrid, had signed a treaty handing over Casale to Spain. Recalling Fargis' propensity for unauthorized commitment, Richelieu groaned: 'I think the air of Spain is infected for negotiators.'[12] So upset was he by the news that he fell ill and had to be bled for an hour that night. As it happened Mirabel's rumour was false, but even before this was known Richelieu had made up his mind that no such treaty would be binding without full powers, and also without Nevers' agreement. The march into Italy went on.

Three movements were envisaged. One army corps under the Duc de Guise and Maréchal d'Estrées should be embarked at the mouth of the Rhône and shipped to the Ligurian coast, whence it would march north to Casale. A second corps should enter Piedmont; and the main army, commanded by the King in person along with Richelieu, should cross the Alps from Dauphiné and march straight for Casale. At the same time the troops of Mantua and Venice should march to Casale across the Milanais. In fact the King's operation was the only one which amounted to anything. It was a desperate undertaking. By the time the army struggled up the hill into the grey fortress of Briançon at the end of February 1629, the snow was deep, and Richelieu wrote with great understatement that the roads were not 'si beaux'. The pass over the Monte Genevra was closed to ordinary traffic and it was necessary to put everything, including the dismounted artillery and the carriages of the notables on sledges, and have them dragged over by gangs of local mountaineers. At Bourg d'Oulx, shivering in the miserable village which was constructed from local mountain

stones, he wrote to Marie de Médicis 'it is snowing here continuously. The place is the ugliest that can be found.'[13] From here
the road runs down into the valley which leads left to the Mont
Cenis, then Savoyard territory, and right to Turin. At Susa a
number of forts perched on elevations blocked access either way.
It was the first obstacle in Charles Emmanuel's domains.

No one quite knew where Charles Emmanuel stood. The
Spaniards were doing his work for him, and just then he was
seemingly neutral. Quite likely he would join the French, but only
after he had tried to extort some concession out of them. He sent
his son Victor Amadeus, the Prince of Piedmont and Louis
XIII's brother-in-law, over the mountains with the proposal that
Susa would be handed over to the French, provided that in return
a French town was handed over to Savoy. Richelieu's sense of
irony was aroused by this suggestion; perhaps Charles Emmanuel
would be satisfied with Orléans or Poitiers? At Embrun on the
way up the Alpine road there had been more conscience-salving
on the royal council. Richelieu had recalled all the nuisances
created for France by Charles Emmanuel, particularly his responsiveness to Montagu's proposals, and had argued that it would be
folly to trust him further.

So it was decided to attack Susa, and an officer was sent under a
flag of truce to the Savoyard commanding officer to ask for
lodgement for the King, as a friend of the Duke of Savoy. The
Savoyard, entering into the spirit of the thing, said, 'His Highness
is greatly honoured to accommodate His Majesty. But since His
Majesty has come with such ample company, you will be good
enough to allow me first to advise His Highness.'[14] Then he added
that the Savoyards would defend their passes, and reminded the
French, alluding to their repulse of Buckingham, that this time
they were not dealing merely with the English. The messenger
returned and the gallantry continued. Maréchal Bassompierre
rode through the snow, flourished his hat to the King and said:
'The violins have entered, the masks are at the door, and when it
pleases Your Majesty, we shall dance the ballet.'[15] Louis, who
had not lost his taciturnity even in this moment of excitement,
reminded him that they had not been able to transport many

cannon-balls over the pass. Did this mean, Bassompierre asked, that because the masks were not ready they could not perform the ballet? After Richelieu had said mass before the whole army and given communion to the King and the generals, the ball began. The French infantry, led by local guides, scaled the heights around the forts and enveloped them, closely followed, so the *Mercure* report tells us, by the King and Cardinal, and forced the Savoyards out.

Charles Emmanuel came to terms. At Susa he and Richelieu kissed each other on the neck and complimented each other. The Duke played the role of host and Louis XIII that of guest. But no one was deceived. France had Savoy at its mercy, and the best thing Charles Emmanuel could do was to try to turn the situation to his advantage. So he now proposed that the French should help him take Genoa. When this suggestion was rejected he had another: they should attack the Spaniards in the Milanais. Finally he even tried to persuade Richelieu to capture Geneva for him. Failing to divert the French from their objective he was forced to sign a treaty which allowed the French army to cross Savoy to Montferrat on this and on any future occasion, and which required him to victual Casale as soon as the siege was raised. In return he would be allowed to keep Trino, and Mantua would pay him 15,000 crowns rent in exchange for a renunciation of all claims to the marquisate. Meanwhile he undertook to leave Susa in the hands of the French as a gage of his good intentions, for Richelieu knew Charles Emmanuel too well to expect action on his word alone.

To Richelieu war was not the failure but an adjunct of diplomacy. Power was to be exercised when, and only when, a superior position was needed in negotiation; it was never to be a substitute for negotiation. When force should be disposed at critical points, when weaknesses should be exploited by manoeuvre, then the purpose of hostilities would be achieved and the negotiator could take over with a strengthened hand. Total war, as it was being waged in Germany, was to Richelieu a horrifying heresy and aberration. It is in the light of this theory that the expedition to Casale should be viewed. Overwhelming power had been brought to bear in the area, and it was unnecessary to proceed further than Susa, or engage in hostilities beyond the skirmish necessary to take that place. Gonzalo de Cordoba had no alternative but to submit to the power of events. He signed the Treaty of Susa on behalf of Spain and withdrew from Casale into the Milanais. The operation was over, and Richelieu could march the army back over the Alps to continue the pacification of the Huguenots, which had had to be delayed by the Mantuan question. The latter was by no means solved, but now that the military threat had, it seemed, been eliminated, it could be settled by legal and diplomatic means.

While Père Joseph set off to Mantua to begin the negotiations by securing Nevers' adhesion to the Treaty of Susa, Richelieu and the King, leaving a garrison in Susa, returned with the main forces across the Monte Genevra into France. The suppression of the Huguenot rebellion in Languedoc and the Rhône valley had become urgent, for Spain, all pious dedication to the victory of Catholicism in France forgotten, had been driven by Gonzalo's failure in the Mantuan War into responding to Rohan's overtures, and had on 3 May 1629 offered him 300,000 ducats to assist his rebellion, and paid Soubise a pension of 8,000 ducats. Richelieu's first object was Privas. This little town stands in the hills on the western bank of the Rhône, and its seizure by the Huguenots had been the occasion of the Huguenot rebellion five years previously. Since then it had been fortified, and had degenerated into a nest of saboteurs who regularly interfered with the traffic on the Rhône. It was now held by eight hundred men whom Rohan had thrown in to defend it. There was a murderous assault followed by fire and pillage, and by the end of May the Huguenots had been smoked out of all their strong places in the area. Huguenot resistance began to collapse everywhere as the news spread abroad that England and France had signed a treaty. With Buckingham gone and La Rochelle beyond succour, Charles I had decided on peace; in return for Louis' waiving a literal performance of the marriage treaty, he would abandon the Huguenots.

Richelieu was ill again, and at Privas he had struggled from his bed to try to exert some authority to stop the massacre of the inhabitants. Determination drove him on, and his dismay increased at the problem of reuniting this area of France, one-sixth of the realm, to the Crown. Everywhere the churches were in ruins, the Catholics expelled, the royal authority ignored. First the King's writ must once more be established and, then the process of conversion must be begun. The first was completed when on 28 June the Huguenots made peace and agreed to the abolition of all fortified places held by them, and to the destruction of their walls. Rohan retired to Venice where he became the Serene Republic's last *condottiere*. Montauban was still defiant, and while the King went back to Paris Richelieu undertook its submission. He was more successful than Luynes had been. Within one month the town that had held out since 1621 yielded.

Behind the advancing army came a flock of missionaries directed by Père Joseph, who had rejoined Richelieu before the sack of Privas. The Cardinal, consistently with his religious convictions, was insistent that there should be no conversion by force. However, it was necessary to provide protection for the friars and the Jesuits who were entering forbidden territory, and the spectacle of a group of soldiers trailing pikes and arquebuses after a barefoot missionary may have had an intimidating effect. Although constraint was employed, the majority of conversions were due to the tremendous impact made by the missionaries on the simple people with whom they were billeted. Two hundred and fifty families were converted in three weeks in Aubenas; within three months the entire populations of several smaller places were won over. Several leading Huguenot pastors became Capuchins. The nobility almost stampeded back to the Church, but often at a price. The Marquis de la Caze, a colonel-general of the Huguenots, announced he would become a Catholic and bring with him the gentry and towns in his jurisdiction, but asked for a pension of 6,000 *livres*. He got it. He also promised to bring with him the first consul of Montauban for whom he demanded the Order of the Holy Ghost.

The Catholic nobility were no less forthcoming. They sent their own private missionaries, paid for Père Joseph's Capuchins, and exhibited extraordinary zeal. Père Joseph was everywhere, reconsecrating churches and founding friaries. Within three months he had them operating in twenty towns, such as Nîmes, Uzès, Montauban, Mende and Florac. Administrative pressure was also applied to bring about the atrophy of Protestantism. All royal subventions for the education and maintenance of the Huguenot clergy ceased; royal commissioners were appointed to supervise the restoration of church property and revenues; foreign Protestant pastors were forbidden in France, although some Genevois managed to remain. The state within the state was no more.

By the end of August 1629 Richelieu was back in Paris and ready to deal with the diplomatic issues concerning Mantua. He was irritated by Nevers who, far from being grateful, was complaining bitterly at being forced to agree to an annual payment to Charles Emmanuel, and was making difficulties about the hypothecation of his revenues as security therefor. There were also disquieting reports from Madrid and Vienna. The former had received with dismay the news of the raising of the siege of Casale. The blow to Spanish pride was serious, but the undermining of Spain's military and political reputation was more so, when the whole Italian peninsula was restless at Spanish domination. Philip IV was moved to unwonted emotion, and eloquence. 'The King of France,' he wrote on the margin of a document, 'has had in mind to disturb me ever since he has been on the throne. Everywhere the French block me. Frenchmen in Brazil, Frenchmen in Genoa, Frenchmen in the Valtelline, Frenchmen in Breda, Frenchmen on the sea!'[16] On 29 April 1629 he called the Council of State into extraordinary session to debate the dispatches from Gonzalo de Cordoba. Everyone turned to its newest member, Spinola. The latter did not criticize his brother general Gonzalo, but restricted himself to pointing out that it was impossible, in the interests of Spain's future security, to accept the situation in northern Italy. He advised that Philip IV should make a declaration that he intended no action against Nevers or France, but that the French should withdraw their forces from Susa. Both sides, he thought, might find this a face-saving formula.

Olivares felt obliged to justify his whole Montferrat policy, and, despite the fact that Nevers was a Catholic and Richelieu a cardinal, he managed to do so on the basis of defence of the Faith. Since the Catholic monarchy was the right arm of the Church, he argued, whatever prejudiced it prejudiced also the Church. Philip IV had been offended by Nevers, and Nevers had to be punished for it. He even went further in the argument: the King would be guilty of sin if he allowed his reputation to suffer, for this would affect the service of God. It was this ability of the Spaniards to confound the will of God with the policies of Spain that justified Richelieu's deep distrust of them. He would have distrusted them the more if he could have witnessed the extraordinary religious exercise that was now about to commence. The Council of State determined on a show of force in the Milanais. For this they needed no moral justification; the justification was self-evident. But to finance it they decided to requisition privately-owned shipments of gold brought to Spain in private galleons; for this, justification was needed. So a commission of theologians was set up to quieten the King's conscience. The point seems minor now, but it was of major importance then, for the proposed action seriously threatened to disturb the basis on which the whole Spanish economy rested, that of the exploitation of America. What was really an economic issue was transformed by devious theological processes into a religious one.

Two things remained. The first was to appoint Spinola to command in Italy, and the second was to deal with Gonzalo de Cordoba. For the latter purpose a special and secret court of five members was set up. This was almost as extraordinary a proceeding as that of the theologians, for the five members were five members of the Council of State, including Olivares whom Gonzalo blamed for the whole fiasco, and the Padre Confessor. The wretched Gonzalo found the court consisted of judges in their own cause, but he courageously defended himself. He was found guilty, although the court recommended mercy. This was granted only after Spinola had consummated Gonzalo's failure, and the latter was then released to fight in Flanders.

Suddenly the Emperor took the initiative. Irritated beyond measure by Nevers' refusal to submit to the jurisdiction of the imperial commissioner, John of Nassau, he made the last and worst of a series of blunders – he ordered an army to enforce the sequestration and invade Venice. The imperialists, twenty thousand strong, marched from Feldkirch up the Rhine and into the Grisons, where they locked up the French ambassador and overawed the Swiss. Then they came down the Splügen Pass to Lake Como and drove all of Nevers' supporters within the walls of Mantua, to which they laid siege. Richelieu's ambassador in Vienna, who had been demanding that Nevers be invested in the Duchy, could do nothing but protest. He was bluntly told that it was the Duke's duty to hand the fief over to the Emperor for decision between the rival claimants; he had refused, and was now subject to the law. The Pope shared the alarm of all Italian princes, especially when the Swiss nuncio reported that the imperial soldiery included many Protestants who spoke openly of sacking Rome; and he sent 11,200 troops to the Mantuan frontier, thereby increasing Spanish and imperial indignation at the policies of the Holy See. France, Spain and Austria were trapped in a vortex which was to drag them eventually into total war.

12

Grey Eminence
1630

Spinola began preparing to besiege Casale while the imperial army was still before the gates of Mantua, and Richelieu was now faced with the decision to undertake a much more extended campaign in order to restore his superior bargaining position in the succession dispute. From September until Christmas 1629 he was in Paris engaged in consolidating the situation at home and preparing once more to march. He had, on acceding to office, bought the Hôtel de Rambouillet, which he was shortly to demolish to make way for his new official residence, the Palais Cardinal. There he gave a great fête for Christmas, attended by the King and the court, where plays, ballet and music – all of which he passionately enjoyed – were presented. It was intended as a demonstration to all the world that his position was unshakable – which was far from being the case.

On 29 December 1629 he set forth for Italy with the Duc de Montmorency, and at Lyons he heard that Charles Emmanuel was prepared to honour the Treaty of Susa and let the French army cross Savoy. Richelieu was pondering on the adage that 'Savoy hides a serpent in the flowers', and was determined to search it out before he walked into a trap. At Susa, where the army was assembling, the serpent manifested itself. Charles Emmanuel now wanted his claims to Montferrat arbitrated judicially – which would gain for him the Emperor's backing – demanded payment from France for six thousand troops which he said were to besiege Genoa, but which Richelieu had a suspicion would be used against him, and wanted certain Alpine territorial concessions. It was exasperating, but Richelieu was as ever charming and conciliatory, in the hope both of winning Charles Emmanuel over for the necessary time and of keeping him inactive while he assembled the necessary military power. In February 1630 the Maréchal de La Force, now the Crown's loyal subject, marched his army over the Mont Cenis. It was as difficult an undertaking as the King's passage the previous year over the Monte Genevra. La Force's eldest son wrote home that he was wearing a Hungarian fur coat, a cowl under his hat with double face-pieces, fur gloves and three lots of linen. He was quite comfortable except about the face, 'for the wind raises the snow so that it almost blinds one, and the wind is so biting that it cuts the face.'[1] He rode his horse with his hands stuck in a muff made of wolf's hair under lambskin, and it is not surprising that he fell off twice into the snow.

In March the army moved on Turin. At first it seemed that Charles Emmanuel would dispute its passage, but his troops withdrew within the walls of the capital. Richelieu put on a demonstration. Passing the city he rode with the cavalry, dressed in his improbable costume of black stitched with gold under a cuirass of the colour of water, a fine plume in his hat, a sword at his side and pistols in his saddle holsters. When the demonstration was over it began to rain and he took to his carriage. The not-so-fortunate soldiery, trudging in the mud and soaked through, groused as soldiers will, wishing the Cardinal to the devil. The Cardinal in his carriage overheard these maledictions as he trundled through the ranks, and stopping a major of the guards said to him: 'The guards are rather insolent. Don't you hear what they are saying of me?' The officer replied that he could hear well enough, but that it was usual for soldiers when they are miserable to wish to the devil those responsible for their sufferings. 'Well, none the less,' said Richelieu, 'you should forbid them to say so many stupid things.'[2] It is not given to some great men, at least of

France, to enjoy witticism at their expense, and on only one occasion is it recorded that anyone dared to be witty in Richelieu's presence. On that occasion Père Joseph was waxing enthusiastic about some tactical conception of his. Stabbing at a map with his finger he said, 'We shall cross here!' A Scots officer named Hepburn growled, 'But, reverend father, your finger is not a bridge!'

Richelieu did the unexpected. He struck, not east, but southwest, and seized the town of Pinerolo. This had been French in the Middle Ages. It would now serve as a major French base of operations, an advanced arsenal, and at the same time a gauge of Charles Emmanuel's goodwill. The French were poised over the valley of the Po with superior force, and nothing need now be done unless negotiations should break down. The diplomatic game began with the arrival of an agent of the Pope to demand the restitution of Pinerolo to Savoy. He was a dark-skinned Italian from the curia named Giulio Mazarin, and no one could have guessed that this was his first step in a career which was to make him Richelieu's successor. The ensuing negotiations were long and tedious, and they gave Charles Emmanuel the chance of cutting the French communications. To counter this move Richelieu advised the King to invade Savoy. In May Louis XIII crossed the frontier and took Annecy and Chambéry, the ancient capital of Savoy. Thither proceeded Mazarin and Richelieu, and in the great ducal castle of Chambéry the interminable negotiations continued.

The strategic situation was such as to give Richelieu little excuse for complacency. For as the French army crossed the Alps in the spring of 1630 France's flank was turned by the appearance of imperial troops in Lorraine, so that the French strategic frontier had in fact pivoted on the intersection of the Rhône and the Alps. Mme de Chevreuse and Walter Montagu had pushed Charles of Lorraine into seeking imperial forces with which to threaten France. It had taken eighteen months for these to make their appearance; suddenly they were found to be occupying Vic and Moyenvic, which, though they were in Lorraine, were claimed by France to be French territory. Charles' role in a vast Habsburg conspiracy was now, Richelieu concluded, plain to be seen; and as the pendulum of power swung in France's favour in Italy, the diplomatic advantages of this were cancelled out by the imperial counterthrust in the opposite direction in Lorraine.

The concept of limited war, meanwhile, was being falsified by events in Italy. While Montmorency was moving his army to join that of La Force at Javenne, fifteen miles north-west of Turin, he was surprised in a defile by eighteen thousand Savoyards. He fought his way out, capturing six hundred prisoners and seventeen colours, and went on to beat the Savoyards at Avigliana. The great Wallenstein himself, victorious in Germany, was marching to the succour of Charles Emmanuel, and his lieutenant, Collalto, was already in Italy burning with the desire to put an end to the diplomatic charade. On 18 July 1630 Mantua fell by storm. Seventy soldiers in barges managed to surprise one of the water-gates, the imperialists burst into the city, and for seventy hours they pillaged it, the Lutheran soldiers of a Catholic army desecrating the churches and stealing the chalices. Nevers and Rethel were both captured, and the ducal palace was stripped by the plunderers. To this end was the Emperor's police action come. Now the imperial general Piccolomini, together with Collalto, joined Spinola who had laid formal siege to Casale in May. Although Casale had one of the finest citadels in Europe, heavily defended with artillery, it had no outworks or trenches, and Spinola described it as a body without members. While Richelieu argued in Chambéry, the trenches were steadily advanced right up to the citadel. The besieged financed themselves by means of cheques drawn by Lyons bankers on a Casale merchant, named Rossi. But Rossi ran out of coin, and it was necessary to melt down cannon and make coinage out of gunmetal. The people would not accept the coins, and the economy of the defence began to collapse. Fever attacked the garrison, while the food supplies came under strain.

Charles Emmanuel died during the summer, and the new Duke of Savoy, Victor Amadeus, was married to Christine, a sister of Louis XIII. She was entirely pro-French, and had advised Richelieu that the Savoyards were quite capable of forging letters with his signature and sending them in to the governor of Casale to deceive him. Now she persuaded her husband to lend his support to the peacemakers. The plague was raging in Milan and all the armies were infected; a mood of languor settled over Piedmont in the steamy heat; the great Spinola caught the disease beneath the walls of Casale and died in a castle nearby; the French Marshals, La Force, Marillac and Schomberg, were at the bridge of Carignano but were too weak to raise the siege. Richelieu tried to persuade Victor Amadeus to add his forces to those of the French and to help in a final effort to relieve Casale, but the Duke refused. The Cardinal was now faced with, at best, a military stalemate, at worst the loss of his bargaining position. On the diplomatic side it became vitally important to succeed, and the diplomatic scene shifted to the battlefield and to Germany.

The diplomatic move on the battlefield was made by Mazarin. He was at that time the secretary of the papal nuncio in Turin, Panciroli, and the only status he had was that of an agent, really no more than a messenger, of the nuncio in the latter's capacity of peacemaker among Catholic princes. His origins could not have been more obscure. It was said that his father, of Jewish descent, had been an itinerant seller of rosary beads in Palermo who had fled to Rome to avoid his creditors; and while this is only one of the stories about Mazarin's antecedents, all accounts do agree that his father was a Sicilian who had married in Rome a girl above his station, and that Mazarin had been born near the papal city in 1602. He had advanced himself at school and in the Church by a remarkable intellect, which commended him to Richelieu when the two began to work together for a settlement in Italy. Mazarin now set off to Casale from Lyons, where Louis XIII was detained ill with dysentery, and by dint of charm and persuasion he secured an armistice which was to extend until October. The town was to be turned over to the imperialists and the Spaniards, while Toiras, the hero of the Ile de Ré, and now the governor of Casale, would retain the citadel. If the latter was not relieved at the expiry of the armistice, it would surrender.

The expiry of the armistice was thus a deadline for the French envoys who sought from the Emperor himself the imperial

investiture of Nevers in the Duchy. It so happened that the
Emperor had summoned the Electors to meet at Regensburg on
3 June 1630, his main intention being to have his son elected King
of the Romans, thereby ensuring the succession of the imperial
crown in the Habsburg line. It was Richelieu's intention to defeat
this proposal, and he hoped to persuade those Catholic and
Protestant states in Germany which were jealous of Habsburg
ambitions to constitute a third force to contain the quarrel
between the Emperor and Frederick of the Palatinate. To this end
France would send a plenipotentiary to the meeting, and Charles
Brûlart de Léon, the French ambassador to the Swiss, was selected.
Brûlart, however, was merely to be a front to cover the back-
stairs intrigues of Père Joseph, who was to accompany him. It
has generally been believed that the Capuchin was to appear
merely as one of Brûlart's staff, but he was armed in fact with
credentials, signed by Louis XIII at Grenoble on 29 June, which are
to be found in the archives at Vienna.[3] Père Joseph left Richelieu
at Grenoble on 2 July 1630, and a week later joined Brûlart at
Solothurn. The two envoys crossed Lake Constance and proceeded to Memmingen, where Wallenstein was encamped.
Père Joseph talked to him at length of his plans for a crusade, and
of his design to create an independent power in Germany as a
preliminary to the peace, without which the crusade could not be
launched. He found Wallenstein responsive. At Ulm the two envoys took a boat on the Danube, and reached Regensburg on
29 July 1630.

Regensburg was crowded with richly clad delegations, and the
Emperor was there, exerting himself in the conference room of
the Electors in the town hall to persuade them to proceed to the
election of his son. For a moment Père Joseph must have thought
that he was dreaming of his crusade, for in the archives of the
French Ministry of Foreign Affairs[4] is a description of the scene in
Regensburg which makes it clear that the French felt they might
as well have been in Trebizond. The Emperor brought with him
two thousand horsemen and three thousand in his suite, of whom
only twelve hundred could be lodged in the town, most of them
Hungarians who painted their necks and arms red and were

dressed like Turks in long red or blue robes, tied in the middle and buttoned up the front, over which they wore soutanes of damask, satin or velours of different colours. They had long boots of soft leather or red sheepskin and did not remove their enormous spurs even when inside. Their cylindrical fur hats with feathers, their short fur pelouses and their silver saddles were remarked upon with astonishment.

The French had no comment to make about the Emperor himself, but plenty about his family. The King of Hungary, then twenty-two, had, they found, a long thin face, large, beardless chin and moustaches in the Spanish style. His cloak was golden in colour with black lining. The Empress Eleanora was thirty-five, 'fresh, gay, plainfaced but with black eyes and perfectly white hands, teeth and skin'. Her two daughters were 'pale and blonde à l'allemande'. The streets of Regensburg were decorated with arches of triumph, and over one of the gates was a painting 'in the form of emblems surrounding a cap of triumph in which was an arm holding in the hand a crown of gold with the device *legitime certantibus*; and on the opposite side were the other words *mihi unica erit*'. As Père Joseph passed beneath this tableau the motto gave him cause to ponder.

He found his reputation had preceded him. The Emperor was out hunting when he arrived, and was informed of his presence on his return. He was seen to be disturbed, and sat with his councillors until three the next morning. When Père Joseph made his courtesy call on the Bavarian general Tilly, one of the latter's staff named Perlo de Flemal followed him and said:

Are you Père Joseph? So you are a Capuchin, which means you are under an obligation to help to make peace in Christendom, and what do you do; you loose a bloody war between Catholic sovereigns, between the Emperor the King of Spain and the King of France. You should blush for shame!

Tilly's chamberlain threw the offensive fellow down the staircase, and Tilly himself came out to apologize, but Père Joseph, says Graf von Khevenhüller, who recorded the incident,[5] was convinced that the affront was premeditated, and he nursed his resentment throughout the negotiations that followed. It was expected that he would prove as slippery as an eel, and therefore the imperial plenipotentiaries, led by the Abbot of Kremsmünster, were determined to pin him down. But, protested Père Joseph, he had no powers to negotiate, and no instructions. None the less, he was told, he was Richelieu's right-hand man and he was expected to speak in the name of Louis XIII.

Brûlart was armed with full powers to treat, and with general instructions which he could exhibit publicly. He also had additional secret instructions, all dated 28 June 1630 from Grenoble, on how to conduct himself in negotiation with each of the Electors. A copy of the full powers exists in Latin in Vienna,[6] and they gave Brûlart 'power to treat of a general peace in Italy', and to this end to 'confer, negotiate, and treat', and to 'conclude, and sign' in the King's name 'all written articles, treaties, and agreements for the said peace, promising the faith and word of the King' respecting whatever Brûlart might 'do, negotiate or conclude'. The secret instructions ignored the Mantuan question altogether, and the official instructions referred to it only in the context that the French should resist the Emperor's suspected efforts to gain the Electors' support for his Mantuan policy.

It seems that when the documents were drafted Richelieu considered the Mantuan issue as very incidental to Brûlart's principal mission of persuading the Electors not to elect Ferdinand's son as his heir, and not to yield to the Emperor's demands that they should go to war with all his enemies, Holland and Sweden in particular, instead of limiting it as they sought to do to the German Protestants. By the time Brûlart and Père Joseph began their negotiations, however, Mantua had been captured, Nevers ousted, and the Mantuan situation had become critical and its settlement their paramount interest. Brûlart's instructions were inadequate, and it was unclear whether 'peace in Italy' might not include, as a condition for a satisfactory settlement of the Mantuan question, concessions by the French elsewhere in Europe.

On the interpretation of Brûlart's instructions and his full powers the issue now turned. In the early seventeenth century the international law rule concerning treaty-making was still in its formative stage, but there were reasonably established conventions. If a diplomat was armed with full powers to sign, and he did sign, the faith of his prince was committed and the latter could not refuse ratification – which in this instance would be an empty ceremony. If, on the other hand, the full powers were merely to negotiate, and they stated that the prince's ratification would be necessary before a treaty should be concluded, the signature would be the empty ceremony, and it would be the ratification alone that would be effective. Further, it was possible for an envoy armed with full powers to sign provisionally none the less by a clause in the treaty making the signature conditional upon ratification. Obviously the scope of full powers was a matter of vast importance, and no one proceeded to conclude a treaty without an elaborate examination of them. In fact the scrutiny of full powers of the negotiators at the peace conferences in Westphalia at the end of the Thirty Years War lasted for two years – largely because of the French experience at Regensburg.

Père Joseph was granted an audience by the Emperor on 3 August, and finding present the Emperor's confessor, Père Lamormaini, whom he knew to be opposed on moral grounds to the war in Italy, he himself raised the question of the investiture of Nevers in Mantua. The Emperor then asked if the envoys had full powers to treat. Père Joseph replied that Brûlart had full powers to accept reasonable conditions, but that before any treaty could be concluded it would be necessary to have the approval of the King. This was not strictly true, and the reply was a deception to give the French freedom for manoeuvre in the coming negotiations.

Not until 11 August did Brûlart and Père Joseph sit down with the imperial plenipotentiaries, Kremsmünster, Nostiz and Questenberg. At that meeting the French were merely asked what they proposed, and their discourse respecting the Mantuan situation was listened to. Next day they were asked to produce Brûlart's full powers. This they did, and the transcript of the meeting does not indicate that the imperialists found them in any way limiting or defective. But Brûlart and Père Joseph had a rude awakening. They had come to Regensburg to sow some seeds of dissension, and now they discovered that the Emperor's negotiators were not averse to sowing a few themselves. The latter hinted that no settlement in Italy would be possible so long as France continued to support, in one way or other, the Emperor's enemies elsewhere. Therefore, any treaty must contain a commitment that Louis XIII would, in effect, abandon Venice, the Dutch, Denmark and Sweden. This was unexpected, and Brûlart pointed out that his powers did not extend so far. He would have to write for further powers.

Did this mean, the imperialists asked, that the negotiations should be postponed until they were received? Not at all, said Père Joseph, the discussions could continue and the area of possible agreement be ascertained. As to a general peace in Europe, yes, of course France sought it. He protested that France was not in league with other European powers against the Emperor, and he denied that Richelieu was even then negotiating with the King of Sweden. Next day, when he had thought the matter over, Père Joseph announced that even the new powers which Brûlart had asked for would not cover a general peace, and that yet further powers would be necessary. While these were being sought, he said, there would be no harm in discussing the general questions raised, without, however, any commitment on either side. In this way he hoped to preserve the maximum freedom of movement.

A messenger was dispatched by Brûlart to Richelieu explaining the situation and asking for further full powers. While he was awaiting these Père Joseph busied himself with the main purpose of his visit to Regensburg, intriguing with the Electors against the Emperor. Ever since his accession to power Richelieu had been pursuing two policies simultaneously in order to weaken what he imagined was a Habsburg stranglehold in Europe. The first was the encouragement, by means of subsidies, of the enemies of the Habsburgs, notably Holland and Denmark, to pursue open war against them; the second was the effort to create a neutral third party in Germany. To some extent the two endeavours were mutually contradictory: the first tended to link the Protestants together in a more cohesive effort against the Emperor, and this meant that the second could succeed in the main only with the Catholic states of Germany. In principle the latter were by no means unwilling to play the role ascribed to them by Richelieu, but the more the Protestant cause was consolidated the more they were thrust by force of circumstances into the Emperor's hands. Richelieu and Père Joseph do not seem to have grasped the intricacies of German politics. Much attention was devoted to persuading the German princes to adopt courses of action on which they were already fully resolved, or which anyone acquainted with the matter would have recognized to be beyond the bounds of possibility. Père Joseph's role in frustrating the Emperor's intentions at Regensburg was overvalued by himself because he failed to realize how little real influence France had on German events.

Among the Electors Père Joseph selected two who might constitute the nucleus of a neutral third force. They were Philip von Sötern, the Archbishop Elector of Trier, and Maximilian of Bavaria. The former of these was on the line of the Spanish advance from Belgium to the Rhine, and the treatment accorded to him by the country that called itself the right arm of the Church had already disposed him to seek French protection. For a pension of 36,000 *livres* his support was bought. Richelieu's main hopes reposed in Maximilian, whose Bavaria had been cultivated by France as a potential rival to the House of Habsburg since the reign of Henri IV. In recent years, however, France had given Maximilian reason for disquiet. The English marriage, which Maximilian had done his utmost to discourage, made him fearful that France would support England's demands that Bavaria's Electoral dignity be restored to Frederick of the Palatinate; and at the time of the Treaty of Monzon he was panic-stricken at the thought that the French armies released from the Valtelline might attempt this by force. Reassured by events, he was none the less disappointed to discover that France's break with England was not followed by French recognition of his Electoral dignity, for Richelieu, obliged to keep a modicum of faith with his Protestant allies, who were fighting in theory for Frederick's cause, sought to compromise; he suggested that the right to elect the Emperor should rotate between Bavaria and the Palatinate.

As Richelieu became deeply involved in the Mantuan affair both he and the Pope began to see in Maximilian's growing independence of the Emperor a solution to the problem of Habsburg hegemony. The Emperor's armies had just reached the Baltic, and he had issued the Edict of Restitution, in virtue of which all Church lands which had been secularized since 1555 were to be restored. This reversal of nearly a century's history threatened to disturb boundaries and established economic and political interests all over Germany, and to affect the security of Catholic no less than Protestant princes and cities. Maximilian, anxious at the thought that a Catholic victory might turn out to be a Habsburg one, resentful of the ambitious role played by Wallenstein and of his apparatus of military charges and war contributions, and angry at the Emperor's scheme of incorporating the army of the Catholic League in the imperial army, so making it an instrument of the centralization of the Empire on Vienna, was disposed to see himself as a counterpoise to the Habsburgs.

It was Père Joseph's principal task at Regensburg to capitalize on this fortuitous Franco-Bavarian harmony of interests. But when he raised with Maximilian the question of the election of Ferdinand's son as King of the Romans he received the disquieting reminder that imperial law forbade any prior engagements with respect to elections. The fact is that Père Joseph did not realize that Bavaria and the other Electors were committed to the courses of action which France wished to see pursued, and resented being made to appear to be French puppets. Even before Père Joseph arrived in Regensburg, Ferdinand had already decided to yield to their demands that Wallenstein be discharged, in order to gain support for his son's election; and the French had no influence on the election proceedings, for the Electors had already made up their minds not to be influenced by this concession of the Emperor. On the face of things Père Joseph had succeeded in his mission; but it might have been better had he not been in Regensburg, for Maximilian's victory over Ferdinand made Bavaria the less dependent on France, and the more critical of French policies. To his surprise, Père Joseph suddenly found Maximilian putting pressure on him to sign a treaty of general peace with the

Emperor so as to prevent Richelieu from subsidizing the Protestants to continue the war. From being the persuader Père
Joseph became the persuaded.

The issues then that in June Richelieu had thought to be of
primary importance had proved by September to be illusory,
and by way of compensation the Mantuan question, with the
armistice at Casale due to expire in October, had become dominant. Brûlart's new full powers reached him on 3 September.
There is a mystery about this document; no copy of it exists in
Paris and there is no record of what it contained. However, from
a number of different clues it can be deduced that it was no more
than a copy, possibly this time in French, of the full powers of 28
June, and even bearing that date.[7] Wherein, therefore, did it
differ from the document that Brûlart considered to be insufficient? The answer appears to be that the second full powers
carried the King's signature, whereas the first carried only Claude
Bouthillier's, as secretary of state for foreign affairs. In a report to
the Electors dated 18 September the Emperor said that he had
taken objection to the defect of signature, and that 'some days
later' Brûlart had handed over another set of full powers 'of the
same date and contents and in the same form, but signed in the
King's hand'.[8] If Richelieu had merely repeated the scope of
Brûlart's powers he had clearly limited him to the signature of a
treaty concerning 'peace in Italy'.

This conclusion is substantiated by the new instructions which
Richelieu drafted on 3 September and which reached Brûlart on
19 September. They did not authorize Brûlart to make a 'general
peace', though he might negotiate to this end on the implied but
not express assumption that he would refer back before signing a
treaty of 'general peace'. Brûlart should negotiate 'discreetly' the
question of France's undertaking not to support the Emperor's
enemies with troops, munition or money; and if there was to be a
general settlement, then the question of the disputed legal position of the dependencies of the three bishoprics of Metz, Toul and
Verdun should be settled, and the Emperor would have to withdraw his forces from Vic and Moyenvic. If France was to be
required to abandon the allies who helped to preserve the balance

of power in Europe and to withdraw from Italy, this must be conditional on a removal of the factors which threatened to upset that balance; the imperial commitment to Lorraine was one such factor. Richelieu was insistent that the Treaty of Monzon be honoured, though the Emperor had made it clear that this was a matter for Spain and not for him; and also that France retain Pinerolo, though Père Joseph in the negotiations had undertaken that it would be evacuated.

These instructions were already outdated by the march of events, and they were found more confusing than helpful. The Emperor was no less anxious than Richelieu to see an end to the Mantuan affair, for the build-up of imperial troops in Italy had postponed a proposed assault by Wallenstein on the Netherlands, and had occasioned the loss of 'sHertogenbosch and Wesel; whereas at the end of 1629 there were twenty-nine thousand imperialists in Italy, there were now fifty-five thousand. The Swedes had invaded Pomerania, and it had become a matter of urgency to disengage the forces committed south of the Alps, and also to prevent the French from giving their support to this new enemy on the Baltic. The imperial plenipotentiaries increased the pressure on Père Joseph and Brûlart to sign a treaty which would achieve both these ends; and, to their dismay, the French envoys found that the Electors had turned on them and were supporting the Emperor's demands. Père Joseph, being a saintly man according to his own lights, found himself under increasing moral constraint to make a general peace and prevent his master from meddling with the Protestants; and the constraint increased as the armistice in Italy ran out.

It was just at this critical moment that Richelieu lost control of the situation. Louis XIII, having contracted dysentery at Grenoble, had retired sick to Lyons and was there at death's door; and the Cardinal, suffering from the sickness himself, saw a chasm opening beneath his feet as Marie de Médicis and Gaston d'Orléans seemed to be on the point of assuming control of the state. The events in Regensburg suddenly seemed to him to be of minor importance. After 19 September Père Joseph had no word from Richelieu, and all that the two envoys knew was that the loss of

Casale was imminent. They were not told that Marshal Schomberg with the army of Champagne was even then crossing the
Alps to join La Force and Louis de Marillac in an all-out effort
to relieve it; and they did not know that Richelieu's silence was
due to the King's apparently mortal illness and his own distraught
condition.

On the main point, the investiture of Nevers in the Duchy,
the Emperor was agreed – he had never in fact had any other
intention – and it seemed that a moral and satisfactory peace
could be made. There is a danger that negotiators, after spending
weeks in debate, will be reluctant to dissipate their efforts by
insisting at the last moment on points on which no agreement is
possible. Rather than put in jeopardy the advantages gained in
negotiation they tend to compromise these points, and the pressure to do so becomes irresistible. Brûlart and Père Joseph decided
to exceed the letter of their instructions and sign a treaty. To them
it seemed a good one. In Italy, the Spaniards would withdraw
from Casale and the imperialists from Mantua, while the Emperor
adjudicated the succession question. Once satisfactory provisions
had been made with respect to the compensation and indemnities
to the other claimants, Nevers would be invested in the Duchy.
The French would withdraw from all Italy except from Susa and
Pinerolo. Nevers would take possession of Casale without fortifying it. Savoy would keep Trino, and the revenues of Montferrat
would be hypothecated to pay him an annual rental of 18,000
crowns. On the obverse side, article 1 provided that France would
not in any way assist the enemies of the Emperor; there was no
settlement in Lorraine – on the contrary, the Duke of Lorraine
was brought into the treaty, although he had not been party to
the negotiations, and this implied the right of the Emperor to
supervise matters in the Duchy.

Brûlart alone had powers to sign, and Père Joseph at first
refused to add his signature. The Electors and the Emperor's
plenipotentiaries, however, were insistent that he, as a man sharing
Richelieu's mind, should do so. On 13 October 1630 at nine in
the morning Brûlart and Père Joseph affixed their seals. Within
hours an imperial courier was on the way to General Collalto

with a copy of the treaty and orders to permit Casale to be revictualled and reinforced, and instructions to cajole the Spanish into accepting the terms agreed upon. At the same time Père Joseph's brother-in-law, St Etienne, left Regensburg for the French camp with a copy. It reached Schomberg before he heard anything of it from Richelieu. Observing the terms, he shrewdly guessed that Richelieu would disavow it; and even if the Cardinal did not, he reckoned, the Spaniards before Casale would. If the French withdrew now, the Spaniards could have Casale for the asking. Schomberg therefore decided, against Mazarin's protests, to march on.

The 26 October 1630 was a beautiful soft autumn day, and the French army made a brave sight, as with banners flying, and the sunlight glinting on armour and the forests of pikeheads, it approached the Spanish trenches before Casale. The Spaniards about-faced to confront them and the garrison of the citadel sallied forth in their rear. The French lines halted to pray, and there was a profound silence which not even the birds disturbed. Then a single cannon shot thudded and the French began to advance. Suddenly from the Spanish lines appeared a cavalier, in black, who rode obliquely across the confronting armies,, madly waving a piece of paper and crying *Pace! Pace! Alto! Alto!* [9] The French halted. It was Mazarin. He had news, he said: the Spaniards were prepared to negotiate on blank paper. In full view of both armies a conference of the generals was held. Nobles in gilded armour flourished feathered hats to one another, there were gallantries and compliments, and finally signatures. It happened that even before Père Joseph left for Regensburg the Marquis d'Effiat had been armed with full powers to negotiate with Collalto, who also had full powers from the Emperor. Communications between d'Effiat and Brûlart had been too intermittent for any coordination to be possible, and, as the concurrent negotiations continued, the likelihood of contradiction increased. Richelieu had kept both sets of negotiations going in the hope that one or other would yield fruit. Both had, and there were now two treaties between which to choose. The new agreement provided for the return of Casale to Nevers, and for the French to evacuate Montferrat when the Spaniards and their artillery train and baggage had been embarked upon the Po.

The Cardinal heard of the Treaty of Regensburg from a résumé by Brûlart on 20 October when he was about to leave Lyons for Paris. He was delighted, and announced that it would be ratified. The dispatches containing the full text arrived two hours after the court had left Lyons, and caught up with it only two days later at Roanne, where the King and Richelieu were about to take a boat down the Loire. Richelieu was stunned as he read the instrument, and raising his hands to the sky in a gesture of frustration he declared he would refuse ratification. To the Venetian ambassador he said he would resign his office and retire to a monastery. The King signed the same day a blistering letter to Brûlart, expressing his 'extreme displeasure' at his disobedience of his instructions, and pointing out that article 1 involved him in a breach of his faith, which he had up to this point kept inviolate, and that article 6 had conceded too much to imperial claims in Lorraine.[10] And Richelieu sent a dispatch to the marshals in Italy ordering them to take no account of the treaty and to continue their operations.[11]

Marie de Médicis, who had been left at Lyons because of an indisposition, arrived at Roanne on the evening of 26 October. She appears to have regarded Richelieu's proposal to disavow the treaty as the ultimate step in perfidy, but cold-shouldering her, Richelieu took to his desk, and, pen in hand, worked out all the possible attitudes he could take. He could ratify with reservations, he could disavow the treaty while laying down terms for further negotiation, or he could await news from the army in Italy. He decided for the moment to adopt the latter course, and when finally he heard of the Treaty of Casale he was reinforced in his decision to refuse ratification of that of Regensburg. Michel de Marillac was in favour of ratification with protocols of interpretation, and a difference of opinion between them on this point further embittered their feelings towards each other. Richelieu was also angry with Brûlart and Père Joseph, and even years later in his *Testament politique* he recalls his chagrin at the latter's indiscreet commitment.[12]

The Treaty of Regensburg, as it stood, was quite unacceptable. It purported to tie France's hand with respect to her friends and allies who were opposed to the Emperor, and would appear to the Dutch and to the King of Sweden, with whom Richelieu was negotiating, as a piece of double-dealing. At the same time, it was an insufficient guarantee to France that these friends and allies would not henceforth be needed, for it left the Lorraine question open without removing all cause of friction in Italy. Instructions were sent off to Brûlart to go to Vienna and deal with the protocol aspects of the refusal to ratify, giving as a justification the floating and contingent character of the clauses concerning the settlement of the Mantuan question. There were too many qualifications, and no commitment of Spain or confirmation of the neglected Treaty of Monzon.

The news that France and the Emperor had made a general peace treaty was travelling far and wide. In The Hague and in the camp of the King of Sweden there would be dismay; in Catholic countries there would be satisfaction, and there a disavowal of the treaty would be deemed a serious breach of faith. This is the last thing that Richelieu wanted, for a king's reputation for honour was the most valuable of his assets.

Kings [he said] must take care as to the treaties they make, but when they are made, they must observe them religiously. I know that many political writers teach the contrary, but without considering at this point what the Christian faith can furnish against their maxims, I contend that, since the loss of honour is greater than the loss of life, a great Prince should risk his very person rather than the interests of his state, and rather than go back on his word, which he cannot violate without losing his reputation, and, consequently, losing the most important attribute of sovereigns.[13]

To explain away the treaty to the Protestants, and to explain away the refusal to ratify to the Catholics, dispatches were sent all over Europe, and the official reason given for the disavowal was that Brûlart had been instructed to settle the Mantuan question and nothing else. On this Richelieu stood on firm ground. Although the treaty did not contain a clause making it conditional on the King's subsequent consent, the full powers had made the Emperor aware of Brûlart's limited authority; and according to the conventions of the time the treaty could therefore be considered null. When Brûlart reached Vienna, however, and communicated the instrument of repudiation to the Emperor, the latter took the stand that the treaty was binding, on the ground that authority to make 'peace in Italy' comprised authority to make a 'general peace'. He expressed his bitterness about Père Joseph, whom he regarded as the architect of his deception, and said he should be banished from a Christian realm. He demanded an explanation from Louis XIII,[14] and for a moment considered breaking with France. Time and again he was to reproach Louis for breach of faith, and he was to exert considerable diplomatic pressure on France from all quarters to compel performance of the treaty. In March 1631 he was to write to the Pope protesting at the French violation of article 1 of the treaty[15] when Richelieu signed a treaty of subsidies with Sweden; and in August, when Gustavus Adolphus was tramping through Germany, scattering the imperial armies, he was to ask the Electors, in vain, to take joint action against France to compel execution of this article.[16] For the next five years the Emperor and Philip IV were to insist in every piece of negotiation that the treaty be honoured, and it became a pivot around which every discussion revolved, and a diplomatic encumbrance ever more formidable and inert. Even in this early period of the history of international law, political issues tended to assume juristic form; thereby they rooted themselves in principle and reinforced convictions, and so were rendered the more intractable and the less negotiable. In the history of the Thirty Years War the Treaty of Regensburg is a major event, the turning-point, indeed, in France's relations with the House of Austria.

Richelieu's dispatch to the army in Italy, telling it to ignore the Treaty of Regensburg, arrived after the marshals had negotiated their own treaty under Mazarin's auspices. It was a most insecure arrangement, for on the field the generals were as little disposed to allow a written document to dominate the situation as was Richelieu in the domain of diplomacy. Mazarin, who was far from being a neutral negotiator, and was leaning ever more to the

French side, told Schomberg that the Spaniards were planning to surprise the citadel of Casale while the peace kept the French inoperative. Schomberg decided to anticipate this contemplated treachery, and, in direct violation of his engagement, he put a French garrison in the citadel. Now the Spaniards were able to broadcast that the French had twice in the same month broken their solemn engagements. But there was little they could do beyond expostulating, for Casale was now beyond their military power. This gave Mazarin the opportunity to press for a final settlement of the whole Mantuan question, and he achieved it in two instruments signed at Cherasco in April and June 1631, known as the Treaty of Cherasco. According to this new arrangement Nevers was to be invested in the Duchy, and all the armies would withdraw from his territories, and the French also from Susa and Pinerolo. The Emperor, that ever unlucky man, had been compelled to concede everything save abstract acknowledgment of his superior title in Mantua; and in the outcome his folly in enforcing the sequestration lost him the Thirty Years War.

It might have been expected that Richelieu would regard his achievement with some satisfaction; in fact it awoke in him only further anxieties. He had checkmated the Spanish move to cut France off from aid to Venice, or from interference with the Spanish traffic in the Valtelline; but the elimination of Mantua as a factor in the balance of power negatived this advantage. The Duchy was in a frightful condition. Sack and plague had reduced its population from 170,000 to 40,000; the Duke's two remaining sons, Rethel and Mayenne, were among the victims. The currency, formerly one of the strongest in Italy, had collapsed. The Duke found his palace stripped and he had to borrow pieces of furniture from other Italian princes. He tried with little success to recreate a cultivated court life – Guido Reni refused to paint for him because the proferred fee was too little. The remaining five years of his life the Duke devoted to prayer and the rule of St Francis. As an ally of France he proved useless.

The evils of the Mantuan war must have convinced Richelieu of the futility of power politics, but he and the Habsburgs were caught in a logical trap from which there was no escape. The pendular power swing in Italy had disturbed the perilous equilibrium between France and the House of Austria; thereby Ferdinand and Philip had been forced into a dangerously close relationship, which previously had existed mainly in Richelieu's imagination. The situation in Italy was inherently unstable, and the only chance Richelieu had of stabilizing it was by distracting Spain and Austria elsewhere; the imperialists were in Vic and Moyenvic threatening France's rights in the eastern borderlands; and the fiasco at Regensburg had aggravated the situation to the point of mortal danger. So Richelieu turned to the King of Sweden; and this opportunistic move was to compound the problem.

People of our Rank
1629-32

History is a pattern of accidents, and chief among these is the accident of personality. Had Gaston d'Orléans behaved himself Charles of Lorraine might not have provoked a crisis; and in this event the papal effort to reconcile France and the Habsburgs might have been successful. Following the deplorable events of the Chalais conspiracy Richelieu had exerted himself to be friendly towards the royal heir, not only in the interests of harmony in the court and in the nation, but also as a personal insurance should the heir become the King. Gaston responded with flippancy. Announcing to Richelieu the pregnancy of his wife, he said that if it was a son he wanted him to be a cardinal. 'Why?' asked Richelieu, whose sense of humour was not his strongest point. 'Because,' replied Gaston slyly, 'in France the cardinals run everything.' At La Rochelle he performed creditably. His appointment to command the army was due to a sudden and serious illness of the King who had been on the point of conducting the siege, and to the importunities of Marie de Médicis who brought pressure to bear on Richelieu. The relief of the forts on the Ile de Ré was largely due to his enterprise and activity in collecting ships and passing in supplies, and Richelieu wrote him a letter acknowledging the fact. Gaston's contentment was, however, shortlived. His mother upbraided him for hazarding his person in front-line skirmishes; the King reproached him for wasting the lives of his soldiers; and when Louis eventually arrived before La Rochelle and took the chief command away from Gaston, the latter retired in pique to his drinking and philandering in Paris. The execution of one of his bosom companions, the Comte de Montmorency-Boutteville, for duelling added to his discontent.

Marie de Médicis had intervened to get Gaston appointed to the army on his promise to remarry, this time to marry her niece the sister of the Grand Duke of Tuscany. Now that he had been superseded by the King, Gaston announced that he no longer regarded himself bound by this undertaking. Instead he began to interest himself in the delightful eighteen-year-old Marie de Gonzague, the daughter of the Duc de Nevers. The latter had earned the eternal enmity of the Queen Mother by an odious comparison he had drawn between the origins of the Gonzagas and the Medicis, and she resisted the proposed match with passion. When Richelieu proposed to march to the relief of Casale, Gaston was enthusiastic to champion the rights of his lady's sire, and asked for the command of the army. His first overtures were coldly rejected by the King; and when Gaston asked Marshal Bassompierre what Louis thought of the marriage project he was told that the King had too much on his mind to think about it at all. It was due to Richelieu that Gaston was in fact given the command he sought, and this threw Marie de Médicis into a high fever. The Cardinal was apparently abetting Gaston in his courtship, and this made her the less inclined to enjoy the spectacle of Richelieu humiliating the Spaniards in Italy. From this point relations between Richelieu and the Queen Mother seriously deteriorated.

Even the sardonic Cardinal must have been surprised at the course of events which now leagued Gaston and his mother in a common and violent enmity towards himself. Only one week after Gaston had been appointed to the army of Italy, Louis announced that he intended to lead it. Richelieu tried his utmost to dissuade him, not only because he expected a repetition of Gaston's conduct when superseded before La Rochelle, but also because he wanted Louis in Paris to keep control of the political atmosphere there, which was increasingly hostile to the Mantuan expedition. The King, driven by the urge to compensate by military glory for the defects of personality which made him feel inferior to Gaston, was adamant. Gaston displayed an insane resentment, crying that he was being deprived of all responsibility, that Richelieu was running everything, and that the King would collect all the honour. Characteristically he deserted, at first returning to Paris to prevent Marie de Gonzague from leaving for Mantua, and when he learned that on Marie de Médicis' orders she had been taken to Vincennes into what amounted to custody, he retired to his principality of Dombes. There, instead of venting his wrath on his mother he began to intrigue with her against Richelieu, and his interest in Marie de Gonzague was gradually superseded by a passionate resentment of the Cardinal which entirely devoured him. Not surprisingly Richelieu concluded that the marriage project was no more than a farce played out between mother and son to conceal their alliance against the King and his minister.

Leagued against Richelieu were three of the Queen Mother's intimates, Cardinal Bérulle, Michel de Marillac and Louis de Marillac. To these might be added Bassompierre, for he had indicated his opposition to a conflict with Spain in Italy by the enigmatic remark that he would be a fool to take La Rochelle – meaning thereby that the siege should be protracted so as to keep the army tied down. All four were of a generation older than Richelieu; their outlook had been formed in the days when the Catholic League had been allied with Spain, and they failed to grasp the fatal significance for France of this entanglement, or to understand how the outlook of a new generation could be different. The Venetian ambassador reported on 6 November 1629 that 'it was Bérulle who was the author of all the Queen Mother's distaste for Richelieu', but Bérulle died during the Mantuan war, and his place as leader of Marie de Médicis' faction was taken by Michel de Marillac. He was now sixty-seven, and had been the Queen Mother's man since the days when he was her superintendent. He was intensely religious and had written books on piety, and he was withdrawn and grave. His half-brother, Louis de Marillac, was ten years younger, and because he had married a Catherine de Médicis, cousin of the Queen Mother, he became firmly attached to the latter's cause. He was captain of her guards, had worked closely with Richelieu to effect her reconciliation with Louis in 1620, and had conspired with her to assist Richelieu's rise to power. It was through Richelieu that he was made a marshal after the taking of Privas. He was less intelligent than Michel but more gallant and agreeable. His fault was a devotion to luxury; he was a collector of *objets d'art* and fine clothes, and he occupied his time with trivialities.

It was the loss of her predominant position on the council that was the real source of Marie de Médicis' vexation with Richelieu, and it was her plan to have him replaced by Michel de Marillac who would be the docile instrument of her will. To this end Marillac was pushed more and more into opposition on the council. At the meeting held on 26 December 1628 to decide whether or not to relieve Casale he supported Bérulle in arguing that priority should be given to crushing the Huguenots in Languedoc, to conserving the treasury, which was deplorably low in specie, and to doing something to help the miserable peasantry who lived on oatmeal and were for ever being provoked into violence by the desperate efforts of the tax collectors. If there was to be war with Spain in Italy, he argued, it would be perpetual war, and two of Marie de Médicis' sons-in-law would be enemies. When in February 1629 the army was in fact across the Alps he wrote to Richelieu expressing doubt whether the blessing of God would be on the enterprise. The apparently brilliant success of Richelieu's first entry into Italy, followed by his elimination of the Huguenot menace in the south, only increased the hostility of his frustrated enemies in Paris, and when he returned there in September 1629 he sensed that his absence had been used to advantage to turn the King against him. He found the whole council 'agitated as though in perplexity about some great design'.

During the Chalais conspiracy Richelieu had gone anxiously to the King and offered his resignation, and Louis, in one of those rare moments when he was both articulate and tender, had refused to accept it, saying in words that have no doubt been paraphrased,

I have every confidence in you, and it is a fact that I have never found anyone who could serve me to my satisfaction as you do. I beg you to have no fear of calumnies. Be assured that I shall never change, so that, whoever may attack you, I shall support you.[1]

Now Richelieu wrote to Marie de Médicis saying that if he had offended her he was willing to resign, and he followed this up by a visit to her. He found her glacial. 'How are you?' she asked. 'I am better,' he replied, his lips trembling with anger, 'than many people here would wish.' And prepared now for a showdown he accused the Princesse de Conti and the Duchesse d'Elbeuf of showing spite to his niece, Mme de Combalet. Marie de Médicis snapped back that he was insupportable. At this Richelieu withdrew and handed in his resignation to the King. A reconciliation was effected by Louis, who demanded that Richelieu retain his office, but required him to write a letter of apology to the Queen Mother. Nothing, however, was solved, and incident followed incident. To stifle the opposition the King invented the title of first minister for Richelieu, but in fact he thereby only succeeded in provoking his mother's faction still further.

When Richelieu in the autumn of 1629 returned from Italy to conduct his campaign against the Huguenots in Languedoc, Gaston d'Orléans took fright. He had received a cold and menacing letter from Louis, and now that Richelieu, the devil incarnate, was back in France he felt himself in peril. Announcing that he intended to take the waters at Spa he crossed the border of Lorraine with a group of his staff and threw himself into the arms of Duke Charles. He was well received, but he was short of money, and he sold his gold chains to maintain himself. That the heir to the throne of France should be in exile was a constitutional novelty and Gaston's bargaining position was strong. Within two months he was able to negotiate a settlement with Louis which gave him the government of Orléans and 200,000 livres with which to pay his debts. In February 1630 he was back in Paris, again courting Marie de Gonzague and at the same time fomenting his mother's wrath against Richelieu. In the summer she went off to Dauphiné where Louis and the Cardinal were supervising the Mantuan operation, and he was left virtually in control of Paris until the court returned towards the end of the year.

Richelieu's absence in Italy from February 1630 gave everyone the opportunity to conspire against him. Marillac was complaining about the 'miseries and afflictions of the people of France, who languish under great and incredible poverty',[2] and was arousing general indignation at the extravagance of a foreign policy of glory. The campaign against the Cardinal was adjourned to Lyons. There Marie de Médicis settled down, refusing to join the King and Richelieu at Grenoble or St Jean-de-Maurienne where the interminable negotiations with Mazarin were being conducted. Louis' invasion of Savoy, the country of his own sister, roused the Queen Mother's indignation even further; and as Mantua fell and the stalemate before Casale showed no signs of ending, and everyone's temper shortened in the summer heat of the Rhône valley, the Cardinal's policy became ever more questionable. No one, not even Richelieu, knew what was in the King's mind: Louis remained for him, as for everyone, an enigma. He still did not, it seems, like Richelieu, and it is doubtful if he ever came to like him, but his respect for Richelieu's ability had increased his confidence in him and his dependence upon him. Richelieu's main weapon with Louis was the threat to resign, for the King knew that with the Cardinal gone his own problems would be increased a hundredfold. But who could tell when this recalcitrant monarch, who had shown himself incapable of constancy in his human relations, might lose the confidence in his minister which was the only bond between them? If he listened to Richelieu's arguments and weighed them up before acting, why should he not listen to arguments against the Cardinal which he might find equally cogent? And when the King turned against someone oblivion was the mildest of possible fates.

In July 1630 Louis contracted dysentery, and departed for Lyons, leaving Richelieu alone in Dauphiné. In his weakened condition the King was scarcely able to resist the constant assaults made upon him by his mother and the anti-Richelieu faction, led by the Princesse de Conti. Incessantly they paraded the Cardinal's vices before Louis' fevered eyes, and with mounting hysteria they demanded the minister's dismissal. In September the King's life was despaired of, and news reached Richelieu that Louis had summoned his courtiers and, amid a general flood of tears, had begged their forgiveness for the offences he might have committed. While Alphonse de Richelieu was giving the King the last sacraments, Guise, Bassompierre and Louis de Marillac were meeting to decide what should be done with Armand-Jean de Richelieu when King Gaston I was proclaimed. Guise, it was said, was for exiling him, Bassompierre for imprisoning him for life, and Marillac for his death. Not improbably Richelieu was informed of this; and as he felt the forces of revenge, spite and detestation closing in around him he found his last reserves of emotional energy drained. The King's recovery was an immense relief, but the experience he had been through left Richelieu tense, suspicious and more than ever wary.

There is, perhaps, nothing that adds to Richelieu's credit so much as his decision to refuse ratification of the Treaty of Regensburg. It would have been so easy, considering the perilous situation in which he found himself, to take the line of least resistance on this occasion. His integrity forbade it. The outcome, as might have been predicted, was a wail from Marie de Médicis, and a significant shaking of the head by Michel de Marillac. The long voyage in the Queen Mother's company down the Loire from Roanne must have been a nightmare to him, for Marie de Médicis chose to assume a benign role which he knew was intended to deceive him as to the hate gnawing away inside her; while he perhaps disguised his apprehension by playing the guitar to her. From the Loire the travellers crossed to the Yonne in order to pass into the Seine, and at Auxerre the King took Richelieu aside and told him everything that the Queen Mother had said against him. When the Court reached Paris in November Richelieu took his pen and composed a letter to Marie de Médicis, which was dignified yet deferential, and which subtly reminded her that his scarlet gave him a certain dignity and immunity. It was in vain. With Marillac and Madeleine de Fargis, the wife of the erstwhile ambassador in Madrid, she had secret meetings at a Carmelite convent to draw up an accusation against him, the main charge of which was his squandering of the treasury on the Italian adventure. Within two weeks, she expected the first minister's fall would be accomplished.

Since the Louvre was under repair, Louis took up his residence on his return to Paris in Ancre's former house, now called the Hôtel des Ambassadeurs. This was close to the Luxembourg, where Marie de Médicis lived, and the King had only a short walk to her apartments. Disquieting reports reached Richelieu that mother and son were often closeted together. We do not know what pressures she was exerting on the King to secure the Cardinal's dismissal, but it is clear that Richelieu felt his position crumbling. On the pretext that she was taking medicine, Marie de Médicis cancelled her levee for 10 November, and by a curious coincidence Michel de Marillac offered the same excuse for refusing an appointment with Richelieu for that morning. Apparently by previous arrangement, the King, accompanied by his close friend Saint-Simon, the father of the famous narrator of the next reign, walked across to the Luxembourg and disappeared into the Queen Mother's cabinet.

There are seven separate accounts of the day's events, and since they differ in detail it is difficult to know exactly what happened. Saint-Simon told his version of the story to his son, who recorded it, and this is the only thing approximating to an eye-witness account. Saint-Simon says that the King had gone to Marie de Médicis to hear her acknowledge her desire for a reconciliation with the Cardinal, but all the other accounts, including that of Gaston d'Orléans, who recorded what his mother said to him after the event, are agreed that she had called the King to her to demand his dismissal. Certainly the behaviour of everyone concerned bears this out, and Bassompierre, who was apparently in an ante-chamber, is quite emphatic that the Queen Mother's intentions were hostile.

Richelieu's cousin, La Porte de la Meilleraye, the captain of the Queen Mother's guards, was excluded from Marie de Médicis' chamber as Louis and Saint-Simon entered. A moment later the Cardinal's niece, Mme de Combalet, appeared in her capacity of lady-in-waiting. There followed a scene, for Mme de Combalet, seeing the icy look of the Queen Mother, dropped on her knees and began to express sentiments of humility. Marie de Médicis' coldness gave place to scorn, anger and bitter reproaches; and while Saint-Simon sat with his eyes fixed on the ground Louis retired behind a mask of almost Confucian dignity. Eventually he rose, put his hand on Mme de Combalet's shoulder and told her he had heard enough and asked her to withdraw. When she had gone Louis made some reproachful observation to his mother, and then they began to discuss the Cardinal.

The latter, meanwhile, had been informed by his spies that the King had gone to the Luxembourg, and sensing that the crisis was upon him he could not resist the impulse to find out what was going on behind his back. Undoubtedly he experienced spasms of terror in his heart, and, as usual in moments of strife when he found it necessary to collect his thoughts, he sat down, seized his pen, and jotted down some notes to organize his argument when he should be face to face with the royal pair.[3] Then he betook himself nervously to the Luxembourg, where he encountered grey-bearded Marillac awaiting in a corner the outcome of the conference in the Queen Mother's chamber. Unable to control his ironic tongue, Richelieu exclaimed: 'Oh, monsieur, you are here! And you said you were sick!' A moment later he found Mme de Combalet in tears and probably heard from her what was going on. Doors were barred, and the *huissier* forbade entrance, but somehow or other, probably by a back corridor, he gained access to Marie de Médicis' chamber, and pushed open the door.

In the cabinet were Louis XIII and Marie de Médicis, she, it may be gathered from the sparse accounts, reiterating in her loud voice her charges against the Cardinal, he sitting silent. The King's eye was perhaps attracted by a disturbance of the arras, or the opening of a door; and as the devil of whom the Queen Mother was speaking manifested his presence he cried out, 'There he is!' Richelieu, trying to seize command of the situation, advanced saying, according to Bassompierre, 'I am sure you were speaking of me.' 'Not at all,' lied Marie de Médicis. 'Admit it, Madame.'⁴ The Queen Mother, her large bosom heaving and her voice rising with excitement, then attacked him with anger and bitterness, and the shock of this onslaught broke the stony façade of Richelieu's presence, and it seems that his whole nervous system reacted. The story that he met the Queen Mother's assault with a reproachful aloofness is less likely than the story that he fell on his knees, trembling like a leaf. She, it is clear, behaved like an enraged harlot, screaming, taunting him, dragging up from the past real and imagined slights, and shocking Louis and Saint-Simon with her demonstration of uncontrolled vulgarity. Richelieu managed to expostulate that he had never intended to hurt her feelings, but now that she had the arrogant monster in an abject and humiliated situation at her feet, she responded to his anguished pleas and apologies with no more than gestures of contempt.

Louis, to whom the dignity of the monarchy was sacred, sat in embarrassed silence, until, according to one account, he tried to intervene on Richelieu's behalf. Then Marie de Médicis flew at her son, accusing him of preferring a valet to herself. Perhaps the King motioned Richelieu at this point to leave, or perhaps he merely permitted him to leave without a further word. The pathetic creature staggered out of the royal presence, and one can conclude from the accounts that, not daring to go home to the silence of his thoughts, he hung about the courtyard of the Luxembourg in the hope that when the King came out he might by a word or a look indicate his feelings: too many minsters had Richelieu seen on their way to the Bastille or some château on the Loire. In due course the King emerged, but his countenance betrayed nothing, and Richelieu returned home convinced that his career, probably his liberty, and possibly his life, were in peril. Marie de Médicis was triumphant. Calling Marillac in she announced gleefully that shortly he would be taking Richelieu's place. Quickly the Luxembourg filled with excited courtiers complimenting and flattering the Queen Mother and her following, until the crush became so great that no one could move

Within hours it was rumoured all over Paris that the Cardinal had fallen.

The King was smouldering with resentment at his mother's conduct as he regained his lodging. Already a crowd of courtiers had collected, aware that something was happening, and as they bowed their backs and flourished their hats at his entrance it was obvious that they were seeking to draw conclusions from his mood. Accompanied only by Saint-Simon, who told the story to his son, Louis entered his cabinet, and threw himself on a couch. He was so inflated with anger that as he drew his breath the buttons on his doublet burst and scattered on the floor. There was a period of silence, and then he asked Saint-Simon what he should do. Saint-Simon, though a frivolous dilettante, was not devoid of perception, and he gave him an intelligent résumé of the state of France and of Europe, and drew a horrifying picture of what was likely to happen if at this critical moment the guiding hand were to be removed. Louis needed little of this to reassure him as to the course he should take, and he told Saint-Simon to require Richelieu to attend him that evening at Versailles, whither he would immediately go. When Saint-Simon bowed himself out of the royal presence he found the ante-room crowded with excited cavaliers. Spying M. de Tourville, who had married one of Richelieu's nieces, a daughter of Brézé, he called him into a window-corner and gave him whispered instructions. Tourville set off for Richelieu's house and found the Cardinal closeted with Cardinal de La Valette. It seems that Richelieu was planning to leave Paris, perhaps for Le Havre, of which he was governor, and that he was packing his works of art, fearing they would be pillaged by the mob when they learned of his downfall; and that La Valette was trying to persuade him not to do anything until he had confronted the King and ascertained his intentions. Now suddenly there came the royal summons, and late in the afternoon, accompanied by La Valette, who was proving a calming and consoling influence, he made his way to the tiny hunting lodge which constituted the royal retreat at Versailles.

It was a cold November evening when he was ushered in by Saint-Simon. Falling on his knees before Louis he said the King

was the best of masters. For once in his cold life the King had
been moved by the Cardinal's wretchedness; he described him
as the most faithful and affectionate servant in the world, and
assured him that his position was secure. Then, inviting Richelieu
to stay the night, he told him that he had ordered Marillac's
arrest, and that the Marquis de Châteauneuf, whom Marie de
Médicis hated as much as she hated Richelieu, would take over the
seals. Marillac was living near Versailles, and when he learned that
Richelieu had arrived at the hunting lodge and was with the
King he became alarmed. There was nothing, however, he could
do, but go to bed and await events. The following morning he
received the King's orders to hand over the seals, and a little later
he was taken under escort to Lisieux, where for several weeks he
was confined in an inn, paying his own accommodation bill. Then
he was incarcerated in the donjon of Châteaudun, where he
devoted the remaining few months of his life to prayer.

When Marie de Médicis heard the news she was stupefied.
According to Gaston d'Orléans she groaned that, but for her
neglect in barring the door to the back passage, she would have
brought Richelieu down. The Comte de Serrant, expressing the
cynical amusement of the court at the bewilderment of the Queen
Mother and her following, called it 'the day of dupes'. But the
Venetian ambassador was more perspicacious. She and Gaston,
he reported, were each a colossus difficult to beat down. 'I do not
know,' he wrote, 'if the Cardinal will succeed.'[5]

Richelieu was a shaken man. It took days for him to recover
from the shock, and it was reported that he had been seen in
tears, at which Marie de Médicis savagely commented that he
could turn them on whenever he liked. In her fury she boycotted
the council meetings, saying that she would rather die than sit
at the same table as Richelieu. 'I'd rather be damned than fail to
make him feel the effects of my revenge,'[6] she spat. The situation
became more hysterical when Anne of Austria began shedding
tears, alleging that Richelieu was mistreating her. She refused even
to mention his name, calling him by the impersonal 'on'. There
was wild talk that Richelieu was planning to poison both Queens
so as to end the Spanish connection altogether. In fact he was

making desperate and sincere efforts to placate Marie de Médicis and prevent a fatal breach between her and her son. A procession of envoys, including Père Suffren, the King's confessor, attended at the Luxembourg, and eventually on 27 December she appeared at the council, but only as it turned out, to intervene in the deliberations concerning the withdrawal of the Spaniards about her court and that of Anne of Austria, the restriction of the Spanish ambassador's rights of entry, and the administration of her affairs.

As Richelieu well knew, it was Gaston who held the key to the situation. If he should flee to the provinces, or again to his friends Charles of Lorraine and Marie de Chevreuse, there would be another civil war. Gaston's intimate companion, Antoine de Puylaurens, had fallen in love with the Princesse de Pfalzburg, one of the young sisters of Charles of Lorraine, during their sojourn in Nancy the previous year and was anxious to return there. Richelieu decided to coax him by a large bribe to keep Monsieur docile, and for a moment it seemed as if Puylaurens had been successfully bought. Gaston was never one to play a passive role, however, and apart from multiplying his protestations of loyalty and goodwill, he took to courting Mme de Combalet. This drew from Richelieu a warning letter in which the Cardinal thought he was not obliged to thank Monsieur for including his niece in the list of women in whom he indicated an interest. It was only a question of time before the apparent harmony between Gaston and Richelieu became threadbare. On 30 January 1631 Gaston appeared at Richelieu's residence, on the site of the Palais Royal, with a retinue of fifteen gentlemen; and curling his thick lower lip, he treated Richelieu with outrageous impertinence. 'If your quality of priest had not stopped me,' he said, 'I would already have treated you as you deserve. But you might as well know that it will not guarantee that in future you will not receive the chastisement due to those who offend people of our rank.'[7] Then he announced that he was retreating to Orleans or Blois to get out of Richelieu's way.

After his departure Richelieu sent a messenger at the gallop to Versailles to inform the King. The latter, indignant at his brother's behaviour, came immediately to Paris, and let it be generally known that he intended to support Richelieu. It was discovered that Marie de Médicis, even before Gaston's call on Richelieu, had given Gaston the jewellery she had inherited from Marie de Montpensier, and this suggested that she and her son were in league. With the precious stones Gaston could raise a formidable army of rebellion. The King thereupon decided to visit Marie de Médicis and reproach her, but he encountered only a 'vomit of fire and flames against the Cardinal', and further demands for his dismissal.[8]

It now became dangerous to leave Marie de Médicis at liberty to become the focus of another rebellion, and, using her secret relations with the Spanish ambassador as an excuse, Richelieu wrote a memorial of thirteen pages to the King explaining why she must be removed from every sphere of influence.[9] It was a carefully drafted document, in which the author avoided any indication of vengeful motives, and which was concerned solely with considerations of public safety. The King needed little convincing, and on 22 February 1631 he issued an order for her rustication. She chose the château of Compiègne for her retreat, and there she was to be guarded by the Maréchal d'Estrées, who as the Marquis de Coeuvres had conquered the Valtelline.

The busybodies around her were also dealt with: the Princesse de Conti and five duchesses shared her fate, various of her court officers were arrested, and Marshal Bassompierre was put in the Bastille, where, despite his great services to the crown in the matter of the English marriage and the Italian campaign, he was to remain for twelve years. Richelieu sent him a rosary with a letter informing him of the indulgences he could obtain with it, and reminding him that the remission of temporal punishment for sin is only possible after the guilt has been removed by absolution. There followed a homily on the state of grace, and a request that every tenth Hail Mary be offered for the Cardinal. 'However,' Richelieu added, 'if you think this is too much I shall be content with every twentieth, for I consider, as you do, that the first Hail Mary which no doubt you will say with devotion is worth more than thirty others which have a strong chance of being said with distractions.'[10] No doubt this was the sincere gesture of a friend and priest, but Bassompierre will be pardoned if he considered the Cardinal to be a sanctimonious humbug. The truth was that there was nothing against Bassompierre except suspicion, and even this was based on the trivial circumstance that a letter to him from the Maréchal de Marillac in Italy had fallen into Richelieu's hands. It disclosed nothing more than some warmth of feeling between two men who had been well-known enemies, and Richelieu thought that 'this was not for nothing'.[11]

Surrounded by conspirators, Richelieu was fighting the constriction with almost paranoiac frenzy. Every thread linking people was traced and regarded as sufficient reason for arrest. Later Richelieu was to justify this in words that distress the modern conscience:

Laws are quite useless if they are not followed by enforcement, which is so absolutely necessary that, although in the ordinary course of affairs justice requires authentic proof, the same is not true of those which concern the state because in such cases persuasive inference must sometimes be held to be sufficient, for parties and cabals which are formed against public security ordinarily act with such cunning and secrecy that there is never any evident proof save in the event, when the matter is beyond remedy.[12]

Attention concentrated on Louis de Marillac. He was then lodged with Marshals Schomberg and La Force in the castle of Foglizzo, which lies some sixteen miles north-east of Turin, and which was then French general headquarters in Italy. On 20 November 1630 he received a letter from his brother, written on the Day of Dupes, in which Richelieu's downfall was announced. Even in front of Schomberg, who was loyal to the Cardinal, he could not conceal his joy. In the same mail he also received orders from the King appointing him commander-in-chief in Italy. The next day further dispatches arrived, and they were handed to Schomberg in the presence of Marillac and La Force. Expecting that they contained orders for his dismissal, Schomberg held up luncheon, which was about to be served, in order to open up the packet in the seclusion of a window. La Force, his long white spade beard and bristling moustaches making him seem an even more formidable old man than he was, joined him, and over his shoulder saw in the King's handwriting an order to arrest Marillac. Seizing the letter, and dragging Schomberg after him, La Force disappeared down a corridor to his room. There the two marshals, luncheon forgotten, discussed what they would do. Marillac was not only their superior officer, he was commander of the army of Champagne, which was officered by his friends and relations, and it was encamped all around Foglizzo. Guards were called, the drawbridge raised, and the two marshals waited outside Marillac's room while he finished lunching. When he emerged Schomberg handed him the King's dispatch. In silence Marillac read it, and then uttered a string of oaths.

The experience was painful for his colleagues, especially for La Force, and there is some reason to believe that they might have connived at Marillac's escape. But Marillac behaved with dignity and would not demean himself by flight. He was brought under escort from Italy and locked up in a room in Ste Ménéhould where the windows were so firmly shuttered that he could scarcely breathe, and the chimney so tightly grilled that it smoked. There was nothing in Marillac's papers or conduct on which a charge could be brought save that his lieutenant had locked the gates of Verdun against the King's forces; Marillac had ordered them to be opened only after being placed under arrest. Why Richelieu persisted in prosecuting the Maréchal in a fashion which appears almost vindictive is unclear. It has been suggested that he hoped to get him sentenced to death, and then exchange his pardon for Marie de Médicis' cooperation; but Richelieu's own journal discloses that he was more concerned to save the government's face, for if Marillac were to be released his arrest would be attributed to the Cardinal's personal spite, and the opposition would be encouraged. Marillac had to be sacrificed in the public interest.

Meanwhile, what was Gaston plotting? No one quite knew, but all manner of precautions were taken. Toiras, twice a hero, was in Paris, and he received a letter from Gaston, which he sent on to the Cardinal; it was not to do poor Toiras much good, for he attracted Richelieu's lynx-like eye, was shortly afterwards disgraced, and went off to live on charity in Rome. Vendôme was released from the Bastille on condition that he left France. And it was decided to draw the Duchesse de Chevreuse away from Nancy, where she was likely to be the yeast in a situation that threatened rapidly to ferment. On the pretext of a general reconciliation between Richelieu and Anne of Austria she was recalled to the Queen's side, and returned triumphantly to Paris, charming even Richelieu with her sweetness when she called on him.

Cardinal de La Valette was sent to Orléans to negotiate with Monsieur, but Gaston was irrevocably committed to the plans of Puylaurens and his colleagues. At the end of March 1631 he suddenly quitted Orléans at the head of a troop of four hundred cavaliers, and made for the Spanish town of Besançon in Franche-Comté. In April he was once more in Nancy. The King followed him with his cavalry but halted at Dijon, where he had to control his impatience. He tried to have the members of Gaston's staff who had followed him outlawed, but, although the Parlement of Burgundy registered the proclamation of outlawry, that of Paris refused, the lawyers arguing that it was not treason for the officers to follow their master. Louis was angry, and summoning the Parlement to the Louvre, he tore up the file with his own hands. The King's anger was increased by the rumour that Gaston was again set on marriage, this time with the pale, timid, eighteen-year-old Marguerite de Vaudmont, the second sister, none the less, of Charles of Lorraine, who hoped, some day, to see her Queen of France. Through Charles, Gaston was in touch with the Infanta Isabella, Governor of the Spanish Netherlands, who promised him subsidies to raise an army for the invasion of France. The commander of Valençay was sent by Gaston to Rubens, who was then secretary to the Infanta's privy council, with the proposal that Spain should support the twin causes of Monsieur and his mother, and create a diversion on the French coast with the Spanish fleet. An envoy from Lorraine also asked that the Infanta receive Marie de Médicis, who, it was proposed, would escape from France.

The lady herself, furious with Richelieu at the indignity she was now suffering, had no wish to accommodate him or alienate French opinion by leaving France altogether. Instead, she resolved to seize one of the frontier fortresses in France, and with the aid of Gaston's friends raise rebellion. It so happened that the Baron du Bec, son of the governor of the fortress of La Capelle, the Marquis de Vardes, was among Gaston's intimates, and he undertook, when his father should be absent, to open the gates to the Queen Mother. To effect this conspiracy, however, much coming and going was necessary, and when Richelieu learned from his spies of cavaliers riding between La Capelle and Monsieur in Nancy, and of coaches parked in obscure forests, and heard that the Marquis de Vardes was in Paris on the King's business and away from La Capelle, he divined what was afoot. Du Bec was summoned to Paris to explain. He arrived there, but, knowing that Marie de Médicis' escape was imminent, secretly left again. This indicated that events were moving quickly to a crisis, and the Marquis his father was dispatched back to his fortress and told to shut the gates. He arrived there just before Marie de Médicis left from Compiègne.

It was another of those occasions of drama which she so much enjoyed. On 15 July 1631 a carriage emerged from the château loaded with what the concierge was told was the baggage of a lady-in-waiting. Three days later the empty carriage of the lady concerned departed, accompanied by a cavalier who kept his face masked with the corner of his cloak. Then the concierge was asked to keep the gates of the château open until late at night as some gentlemen were bringing in a large bag of animals from the hunt. At midnight the concierge was disturbed by a troop of horsemen who were passing out through the gate with a veiled woman in their midst. He recognized among the party Marie de Médicis' confessor. Someone told him that one of the ladies-in-waiting was eloping, and then generously tipped him to keep quiet. The party disappeared into the night. Some distance through the forest of Compiègne the masked cavalier appeared and conducted Marie de Médicis to the carriage, which was standing on a side-road.

Changes of horses had been prepared and everything went as planned on the road between St Quentin and Maubeuge until the cortège appeared before La Capelle and found the gates firmly bolted. There was now nothing to do but pass on to the Spanish Netherlands, and the garrison of the fortress watched the carriage and riders move in that direction. They had had no food for many hours and Marie de Médicis was in an excited condition when the first Spanish town, Avesnes, was reached. Twenty times she told everyone of her adventures, continuously she up-braided du Bec for a blackguard. The dignified Spaniards, when she arrived in Brussels, were delighted, but very likely did not know what to make of this hysterical creature. Richelieu's reactions were mixed. With the Queen Mother now also in the enemy camp, the Spanish capacity for mischief was increased. On the other hand, France, and he himself, were well rid of her. In fact she was never to return to France, but was destined to drift from one court to another for the next twelve years, ever less welcome, boring everyone with her recriminations against the Cardinal, and writing long, incoherent letters to Louis and the Parlement, full of insults and blame. To the first of these Louis coldly replied in words dictated by Richelieu: 'I have every proof of the affection and sincerity of my cousin the Cardinal de Richelieu; the religious obedience which he renders me, and the faithful care which he has for everything concerning my person and the good of my estates testify to this.'[13] The Spanish am-bassador sarcastically observed that the Cardinal was giving so many proofs of his virtue because he was angling to get himself canonized before his death.

Marie de Médicis' flight sealed the fate of Marshal de Marillac, for to release him at this moment when rebellion again threatened would be an encouragement to the unruly. It is doubtful, how-ever, if the trial of Marillac did anything but further disturb the realm, for it became the occasion of a bitter tussle between the lawyers and the Crown. Marshals of France had the right to be tried by the Grand Chamber of the Parlement, and in February 1631 it granted him leave to appeal to it. A decree of the royal council quashed this, whereupon the Parlement of Paris sum-moned all the chambers into plenary session and issued a remon-strance to the Crown, in which it prohibited Richelieu's chosen judges to proceed further with the instruction, or to interrogate

the prisoner and witnesses, which in French law was the preliminary to trial. The King retaliated by forbidding all court
officials to give effect to the Parlement's action, and turned to the
Parlement of Burgundy, which was more submissive. This
undertook the role of instruction through a commission of two
men, one of whom, Laffemas, was a sinister member of the judicial service, whose ruthless conduct of political trials had earned
him the nickname 'the Cardinal's hangman'.

The idea of a trial for treason was quietly dropped and the
commission proceeded to examine evidence which might support
charges of embezzlement during the fortifying of Verdun, bad
government of the army, illicit profits in the purchase of munitions, false accounting, and general peculation. The Marshal
objected to the commission and refused to answer questions,
whereupon the Parlement of Paris issued a new decree forbidding any commission to proceed with the instruction. This
was again annulled by the royal council. Gaston d'Orléans,
hoping to get the Parlement on his side, now intervened. Writing
to the commission from Nancy he said that 'the prodigious ambition and the frightful audacity of the Cardinal de Richelieu,
had reached this excess'.[14] The Queen Mother followed this up
by a public demand for Marillac's acquittal. In November 1631
the royal council issued an edict ordering the commission not to
meet again, and reserving the charges for the King personally.
As in the Chalais affair, Marillac was now to be tried by irregular
methods, and the lawyers were in a state of indignation.

While the deplorable proceedings dragged on, Gaston had been
busy collecting troops, and the King and Richelieu moved into
Champagne with an army ready to deal with him. In the course
of this operation the court reached Verdun, where Marillac was
held, and the Marshal sought an audience with Richelieu. The
Cardinal replied that the interests of the King were his only consideration; the proceedings would shortly be finished, and they
were none of his concern. In fact, however, they were very much
his concern. A decree of the royal council nullified all Marillac's
legal protests, twenty-four judges were appointed, and the trial
was held under Richelieu's eye in his own château of Rueil. The

President of the Court was the new Keeper of the Seals, Châteauneuf, so that executive control of the process was guaranteed. There was enough established on the charges of peculation to justify a conviction, but Marillac defended by saying that in fact he had paid out more than he had received in the royal service. In any event, everyone knew that his was a peccadillo in that age of universal corruption, and that the trial was only a pretext. On 8 May 1631 he was sentenced to death. He appealed on the solid legal ground that the offences for which he had been convicted were not in law capital, but the appeal was rejected by a slight majority. Marillac's family now sought to intervene with Richelieu personally, but he shrugged them off, 'M. de Marillac is in the hands of the judges. It will soon be finished.' And without more he entered his carriage. When he was again approached his only comment was, 'Go and see the King. He is good.'[15]

In his *Mémoires* Richelieu tries to gloss over the Marillac affair. He does not mention the public good, except to refer to the necessity of making an example for the benefit of others who might be disposed to break the law, and he confines himself to accusing Marillac of vanity and lack of rectitude – faults which Marillac possessed, but which certainly did not warrant the death penalty. It has been suggested that Marillac was the victim of a theme of vengeance which inspired the contemporary playwrights. This is, however, to attribute to Richelieu a passion which as a priest of indisputable sincerity he could not have tolerated, and which as a cold-blooded rationalist he would have repudiated. Marillac was sacrificed to the needs of the state, which Richelieu understood to be a moral end superior to the liberty of the individual; and it was the Marshal's misfortune to be on trial at a moment when the security of the state was seriously imperilled from within and without. Richelieu laid before the council a memorandum in which he said:

Spain, the Empire and Lorraine are joined against France; the design is formed, ready to be hatched if their projects can succeed. Letters taken from Brussels and Nancy indicate that there are many adherents in France that we do not know about; we must hasten the Marillac case.[16]

At the end of 1631 Marshal de La Force was ordered to invade
Lorraine and disperse Gaston's troops. These were pursued into
Luxembourg, and the opportunity was taken of occupying
Sedan, the seat of the Duc de Bouillon, who was then in Holland.
The Dowager Duchess, with French guns trained on her palace,
was forced to take an oath of fidelity to Louis XIII. Gaston, ejected
from Lorraine, appeared in Brussels in an angry and dangerous
mood, and found his mother there trumpeting her hatred of the
terrible Cardinal. The governor of the Spanish Netherlands was
an ageing and sensible lady, the Infanta Isabella, daughter of
Philip II. For Olivares' bellicosity she had little sympathy, and
Monsieur's arrival placed her in an embarrassing position. Her
own council considered it to be a wonderful opportunity to sow
discord in France, but she herself was sceptical. Monsieur and his
mother, she reported to Madrid, claimed to have a host of supporters, but this remained to be demonstrated. A little later she
wrote that Gaston had really no effective partisans in France, and
the only following he had in Belgium was that paid for out of
Spanish money. Nothing, she recommended, should be done by
Spain except in the name of the rebels; for instance, if the French
were to be ejected from Sedan, this should be done in the name of
Marie de Médicis.[17]

Despite this private reticence on her part, the Infanta felt
obliged publicly to support Gaston. On 27 January 1632 she
wrote to Philip IV saying that Monsieur had asked for asylum;
this she could not refuse, and, although she had no money with
which to support him, she would treat him with every deference.
Gaston was, in fact, lodged in the apartments of the Infanta's
deceased husband, the Archduke Albert, and she paid for his
accommodation while he went about organizing revolt in France
and raising troops. In Madrid the news that French forces had
entered Luxembourg in pursuit of Gaston threw the Spanish
court into a fit of indignation. It was proposed that Wallenstein
should be employed to lead an army into France in support of
Monsieur, and the latter was offered 20,000 crowns a month if he
would agree to invade his own country. Isabella was instructed to
raise as many troops for his support as she could. She coldly

replied that Monsieur had told her that he knew that Spain intended to invade France, and that if it did so he would take the side of his own country. This was somewhat discouraging, but Olivares did not shelve his plans to help Gaston, and Isabella was instructed to prepare a considerable army in Alsace for a diversion in France and 600,000 ducats were credited to her for this purpose. A rupture with France, she was informed by Madrid, was 'probable'.

Much of this was known to Richelieu, for regular reports were received from the French envoy in Brussels, culled mainly from information supplied by an informer in Gaston's suite. When, therefore, the question of commuting Marillac's death sentence was laid before Louis neither he nor Richelieu felt inclined to make a demonstration of either mercy or weakness. A delegation of the Marshal's friends was coldly received by the King, who merely said, 'I shall reflect on what is to be done. In the meantime, retire.' On 10 May 1633 Marillac, without having been told of his fate, was removed at six in the morning from Rueil to Paris. He believed that he was being taken to the Bastille, and did not become aware of the sinister purpose of his journey until the carriage passed the fortress and proceeded down the Rue St Antoine to the Hôtel de Ville on the Place de Grève. There the scaffold had been erected, and the square was dense with people. The Marshal was taken into the Hôtel de Ville, and the death sentence was read to him while he knelt before a crucifix. The day was spent in preparing his soul for death, and disposing of his temporal affairs. At three he took a little wine, toasting the executioner, priests and officials who were present with the words 'Your health, Messieurs, for the last time!' His lovelocks were then cut, and at four he mounted the scaffold. One blow with the sword severed the head from the body of a man who was still bewildered at the fate which the implacable monarch whom he served had prescribed for him.

The memorable example made of Marillac served, not to quieten opposition, but to stimulate it, for fear of the Cardinal as well as indignation stirred persons more important than Marillac to join the ranks of Gaston's following. Chief among these was the Duc de Montmorency, the governor of Languedoc. This splendid nobleman was then thirty-five, one of the most powerful men in France, member of a family that had given the country five constables and seven marshals, brother-in-law of Condé, and related to the royal family in several ways. In his capital, Toulouse, and in his magnificent châteaux scattered throughout the province, he held almost royal state. Fifty gentlemen and thirty pages accompanied him wherever he went, and he was a patron of letters and art, the protector of poets and of liberal thought. He was gracious, charming and universally adored. He was also a fine soldier who in 1630 in Piedmont had captured nineteen colours in the battle of Avigliana. And it happened that he was nursing a private grudge against Richelieu who deprived him of his office of Admiral of France for quite valid administrative reasons, but had failed to compensate him with the office of Maréchal-de-camp-général in Italy, which he considered to be his due.

Montmorency was also the vehicle of a public resentment against the Cardinal in Languedoc, which was one of the five provinces enjoying a special tax régime. Whereas in the rest of France the *taille* was a tax imposed directly on revenue, and fixed arbitrarily each year, in these five provinces it was payable only on land. Those persons who had no land paid nothing: manorial land was exempted, although this did not mean that the nobles were necessarily exempted, for if a noble bought non-manorial land he was liable to taxation; conversely, if a peasant bought manorial land he was exempted. The government in Paris did not levy the tax directly. It merely notified the provincial Estates of the total amount which the province was expected to contribute, and the Estates then proceeded in complete liberty to decide upon measures for raising the required sum. There was much abuse in the system, and the suppression of the Huguenot rebellion in Languedoc in 1629 seemed to Richelieu the occasion for ending the anomaly. An edict was issued requiring that in future financial impositions could no longer be levied by the Estates with the consent of the provincial governors, but by royal officials operating, in Languedoc, from twenty-two regional offices.

These royal officials were not bureaucrats in the strict sense, but more like private contractors, recruited mainly from the legal profession, and they were universally hated. The introduction of this system into Languedoc caused bitter resentment, and the whole official class of the province took shelter behind the seemingly impregnable façade of 'provincial privileges' and 'fundamental law'. The Parlement of Toulouse quashed the edict creating the offices of royal tax collectors, and Montmorency, in his capacity of governor, went to Paris to negotiate. The outcome was satisfactory neither to Richelieu nor to the Estates of Languedoc, for the compromise which was reached neither preserved provincial liberties in their entirety nor assimilated the province to the rest of the country in the matter of revenue. In October 1631 Richelieu struck again, appointing two royal commissioners to undertake the raising of taxes in the province. The Estates seethed with hostility, and when, six months later, the tax was levied in spite of them, the bishops and barons protested violently. Montmorency tried to act moderately, but the pressures exerted upon him by every interest in the province became irresistible. Little by little he was pushed into the camp of the factious.

The evil genius in the course of events was the bishop of Albi, a Florentine named d'Elbène, who was a creature of Marie de Médicis, and who had two nephews in Gaston's entourage in Brussels, one a priest, the other the captain of Gaston's guards. The latter travelled secretly to Albi, and, after his visit, d'Elbène set himself to use the tumult in Languedoc to push Montmorency, and with him the whole province, into supporting Gaston's rebellion. To the wavering Duke he painted a glowing picture of his own position in France should the Cardinal be brought down. As d'Épernon had won immortality by bringing Marie de Médicis out of Blois, he suggested, so would Montmorency by bringing her out of exile. He would, undoubtedly, succeed to his father's office of Constable, which Richelieu had abolished after the death of Lesdiguières. Two days after Marillac's execution Richelieu received a report from Brussels which indicated that Gaston, Charles of Lorraine and Montmorency were leagued together. Montmorency had compromised himself in several respects, and a private conversation between him and his wife, in which she tried to dissuade him from any dangerous course of action, was reported to Richelieu by a lady's maid who had eavesdropped. The Cardinal was watching Montmorency with a disturbed eye as the spring of 1632 advanced towards summer.

A week after Marillac's execution Gaston moved. From Brussels he went to Trier, where he assembled a force of about 2,500 horse, and with these he proceeded to Nancy, where Charles forgetful of his recent chastisement, supported him. The results for Lorraine were disastrous: instantly La Force descended on the Duchy and reached the outskirts of Nancy. Charles, stupefied by the rapidity of the French action, came to terms at Liverdun on 26 June 1632, and on 8 July he came in person to pay his respects to Louis XIII and ask for his pardon. The price he had to pay was the transfer of the County of Clermont to France. Gaston, deprived of his Lorraine base, passed into France with his little force, which was quickly reduced to the number of eight hundred by desertions. *En route* he issued an inflammatory proclamation calling on all Frenchmen to revolt and overthrow 'Armand-Jean, Cardinal de Richelieu, disturber of the public peace, enemy of the King, dissipator of the state, usurper of all best offices in the realm, tyrant and oppressor'. The recipients were, however, too canny to take this document seriously, and everywhere the towns closed their gates on Monsieur, who, with Marshal Schomberg in pursuit, disappeared into the wilderness of Auvergne, where he managed to rally about three hundred of the country gentry. On 22 July he passed through the Tarn gorges into Montmorency's province of Languedoc, and on 30 July he and the Duke joined forces at Lunel.

Richelieu had already taken steps to deal with Montmorency, but the plan had miscarried. It was proposed that the Duke be lured into Montpellier and there seized. When Montmorency arrived, however, rumour that he would be arrested was circulating and the townspeople thronged about his *hôtel* and enabled him to escape. He was now in open rebellion, but the speed with which Schomberg moved into Languedoc, and the ruthlessness which he employed, stunned the province. Rebel officers were dragged to the scaffold protesting that they were prisoners of war, not criminals; the old care-free days of civil war had gone for ever. Montmorency was declared a traitor, the Duchy was attainted and reunited to the Crown, and all the Duke's property was sequestrated. Proceedings were filed against him in the Parlement at Toulouse, and all associated with him were given fifteen days in which to disavow him or be outlawed. It took just one month to end the affair. At Castelnaudary Montmorency was forced to a half-hour action by Schomberg. The grey horse on which he was mounted was stabbed in the flank and fell dead, throwing Montmorency in full armour on the ground; bleeding from seventeen wounds, his teeth knocked out by a bullet, he was taken prisoner.

Gaston, blockaded in Béziers, but looking to Spain for help, tried to gain time by negotiating with Schomberg, who was reluctant to employ force on the royal brother. However, Schomberg blocked the roads from Roussillon and the Spaniards did not move. Louis XIII and Richelieu advanced to Montpellier and took over the negotiations. Gaston was merely required to renounce all factions inside and outside the realm. He was still arrogant, demanding the release of Montmorency and a host of benefits to himself. While the negotiations were going on he broke out of Béziers and occupied the castle of Olonzac, near Carcassonne. There he was forced to submit, and, as Richelieu had never doubted, he abandoned Montmorency, and signed the necessary articles. At the last moment he demanded that they include permission to marry Marguerite, the sister of Charles of Lorraine. The King forbade it. Gaston with a smirk asked what they would do about it if he did marry without Louis' consent. He was told the Pope would dissolve the marriage. It was Montmorency who made the sensational disclosure: Gaston had been married secretly to Marguerite de Vaudmont on 3 January.

There remained only the process against Montmorency. Richelieu weighed the face-saving advantages to Gaston of pardoning the Duke against the dangers of leniency, and it was decided to proceed. When the judges were delivering their sentence in Toulouse, Montmorency's eyes rested constantly on the crucifix in the courtroom. He behaved throughout with his usual charm and dignity. When crowds in the streets shouted for mercy for him, Louis' reply was 'I should not be King if I had the sentiments of individuals',[18] and he continued quietly to play chess while everyone else was in a state of high excitement. Montmorency was beheaded on the Place de Salin in Toulouse by means of a primitive sort of guillotine. It was said that his blood splashed the statue of Henri IV, but since this stands in a niche at the second-storey level the tale is probably a baroque ornamentation of the event. Dozens of others followed him to the scaffold, and the effigies, and sometimes even the portraits, of those who had fled were 'executed'. The Duchesse de Montmorency was exiled to the convent of Ste Jeanne de Chantal in Moulins in central France, and there some years later she was to erect a pompous mausoleum for her husband, which escaped the frenzy of the Revolution because someone recalled that the deceased had been a victim of the monarchy.

The court went off on a triumphal tour of the south of France, and at Bordeaux there was news. Gaston had bolted again, and was with his mother in Brussels. As soon as he had heard of Montmorency's death he had put his Order of the Holy Ghost in his pocket, donned his cloak and said to his companions, 'I would not leave the Kingdom if I had any security for my life.' Then he wrote to Louis saying that he had submitted only in the hope of saving Montmorency: he now regarded himself absolved from all fidelity.

14

The Unleashing of the Lion

1631-2

Among the numerous sightseers who came to watch the siege of
La Rochelle was one with a military and diplomatic bent, Hercule
Girard, Baron de Charnacé. He was a gentleman of means and
leisure who, finding himself inconsolable after the death of his
wife, had gone on a long voyage to the East. He had been in
Egypt, Arabia, the Holy Land, Turkey and Greece, and had
returned across Poland and Germany. Knowing of Père Joseph's
schemes for a crusade he sought him out in the royal camp at La
Rochelle and discussed with him the situation in the Balkans.
When Père Joseph reported that Charnacé had met Sigismund the
King of Poland and Gustavus Adolphus the King of Sweden,
Richelieu asked for Charnacé to be brought to him. He wanted to
know what opinion Charnacé had formed of the two monarchs,
who had been at war for more years than anyone could count, and
whether he thought that they could be reconciled so as to release
the Swedish army for more useful activities elsewhere. Charnacé's
analysis so impressed Richelieu that he was offered employment as
a special envoy to the two kings. He accepted, and his instructions
were issued in January 1629 when Richelieu was about to cross
for the first time into Italy. They required him first to mediate
between the Catholic League and Denmark, whose King was in a
condition of lethargy and despair after a thorough defeat at the

hands of Wallenstein, and then similarly to act as mediator between Sigismund and Gustavus Adolphus. Charnacé left for the Baltic immediately and was to become France's leading ambassador of the next decade.

The first mission was doomed to failure, for Richelieu's pensioner, King Christian of Denmark, was too exhausted to make further efforts. Christian agreed to a hard peace on Wallenstein's terms and withdrew from the war. Charnacé, armed with further instructions from Père Joseph, then went on to Poland, and reached Marienburg on 1 July 1629. He was not well received by the Poles, who had good reason to be suspicious of Richelieu's motives. Only recently had France been trying to create a political link between Denmark and Russia to obtain for France the monopoly of the Caspian trade on the Narva, and this had developed into a proposal to ally Czar Michael Romanov with the Transylvanian Protestant, Bethlen Gabor, in a league against Sigismund. Nor was Charnacé's mediation proposal received with enthusiasm by the Swedes, whose preoccupation during recent years with adventures around the Pripet marshes had not disposed them to view with great alarm the fate of their co-religionists in Germany. It was not the least of Charnacé's triumphs that he contrived a compromise truce between Poland and Sweden, and brought hostilities to a temporary halt. He was not, however, to find the harnessing of the energies of Sweden such an easy task. Gustavus Adolphus was a great man of bold conceptions and vast designs: he was bluff, likeable and country-squirish, but he was convinced that he was the instrument of God, and was of thunderous disposition and almost barbaric lack of balance. He would be nobody's creature.

Richelieu had set out to cultivate Gustavus with very little understanding of the man or his motives. The appearance of Wallenstein on the Baltic, his assault on Stralsund, and the overthrow of Denmark, filled Gustavus with apprehensions concerning the security of the Baltic, which he treated as his own private sea; and on 3 November 1629, a week before Charnacé arrived in Uppsala, the Swedish royal council resolved on war with Ferdinand and a claim to the succession to Pomerania, whose ageing duke was without heirs. At that meeting Gustavus, embroidering his speech as was his wont with dog-Latin and classical irrelevancy, had argued that in taking such a step he had no other intention than *patriae utilitatem*; and he had concluded, paraphrasing St Augustine, 'for myself I perceive that I need look for no rest, until I find it in the rest eternal'.[1]

The Swedish King was determined upon intervening in the Thirty Years War whether France prodded him to do so or not. Already he was sending offers of alliance to Saxe-Weimar, Hesse-Cassel, Hesse-Darmstadt and the Mecklenburgs, and was planning a rising of the Protestants in Bohemia, and even in the Swiss cantons. Most of the recipients of his overtures were coy, but Gustavus' booming declarations of religious fervour and Protestant solidarity had the psychological effect among the ordinary people of Protestant Germany of the coming of the Messiah. Charnacé recognized immediately that this passionate man needed no subsidizing to assault the Habsburgs, and would not be easily controlled; and accordingly he left Uppsala with nothing accomplished save the truce with Poland. At Elsinore in January 1630 he was halted on his journey home by a dispatch from Richelieu. France was about to march for the second time into Italy, and Gustavus' intervention in northern Germany was needed as a diversion, especially to counter the imperial thrust into Lorraine. With the dispatch was a draft treaty and full powers to Charnacé to sign it if Gustavus would agree.

Charnacé thereupon returned to Uppsala, and now the contradictions in Richelieu's policies became evident. Gustavus wanted a clause in the treaty which would commit France to supporting the restoration of Frederick v in the Palatinate, whereas Richelieu wanted one which would guarantee the Electorate to Maximilian, who, he hoped, would emerge as the leader of a third force in Germany. Gustavus wanted a perpetual alliance which would guarantee French support for all his future projects; Richelieu wanted an alliance for only six years because he thought in terms of the immediate need to confuse the Emperor's policies. Gustavus wanted to remain neutral vis-à-vis Spain because Sweden's Spanish trade, especially in timber and minerals, was important; Richelieu wanted the Spaniards out of Germany and intended that Gustavus should perform this service. On these issues Charnacé and Gustavus indulged in stormy debates, and finally the negotiations broke down on the issue of the amount France would pay to Sweden to support its armies in the field. Gustavus valued his services too highly; Richelieu tried to buy him too cheaply because he did not want to give him the economic means of escaping beyond his control. Charnacé broke off the discussions and took his leave.

Gustavus for a time tried to manage on his own resources. By heroic efforts he contrived to recruit 72,500 men, although for want of shipping he was able to land at Peenemünde with only 14,000. He was a harassed and overworked man, tormented with a violent temper; and his inability to distinguish religion and politics, coupled with his tendency to act on impulse, made him as much a danger to his friends as to his enemies. Upon landing in Germany he had only the vaguest of objectives, and he was vastly discouraged by the poor response from the Protestant princes, who regarded him personally with distaste, and his designs with suspicion. It was evident to him that if he was to push these reluctants once more into the fight he must have money, and France alone could provide it. As his financial situation deteriorated and his mercenaries became restless about their arrears of pay, Gustavus was forced to humble himself and reopen negotiations. None the less, Charnacé found him more disposed than ever to place an absurdly high value upon himself and his efforts. He would not, for example, have his name mentioned in the recital of the parties to a treaty after that of Louis XIII; it was easy to ridicule the pretensions of the Goth who boasted of his descent from Alaric, and on the basis of it asserted his precedence over the descendant of Louis Capet, but a shrewd observer could have deduced that Gustavus was not likely to be easily managed, and that to leave him any loopholes in a treaty would be to invite trouble.

The King and the ambassador engaged in tempestuous debate, and then Gustavus decided to approach Richelieu directly. He sent one Lars Nilsson Tungel in July 1630 to talk to Richelieu at St Jean de Maurienne, where he was supervising the Mantuan war. The Cardinal had just signed an agreement with Venice pursuant to which the Republic would pay one-third of any subsidy which France might offer to Sweden, to a limit of 400,000 *livres*. Charnacé had been instructed to offer this sum in the event of peace being made in Italy, and less if it were not made, but Nilsson Tungel found the Cardinal quite indifferent towards his mission, and so preoccupied with his peace discussions with Mazarin that he had no time for the Swedish envoy, who afterwards claimed that he was so neglected at the French court that he would have starved to death had he not fended for himself. Nilsson Tungel went home with a dismal report on the prospects of a French alliance, but also with the mistaken notion that Charnacé had been authorized to offer more money than he admitted. Gustavus was so enraged that he broke off negotiations with Charnacé, and even denied him a safe conduct.

The disastrous outcome of the Regensburg discussions, fraught as it was with new hazards for France, disposed Richelieu to press once more for a Swedish diversion, and Charnacé, then in Berlin, was ordered to proceed to Gustavus' camp and reopen the matter. By this time both Gustavus and Richelieu had become so anxious to effect an alliance that the self-assertion of the one and the canniness of the other were both seriously compromised. There came a point in the negotiations when, in order to secure agreement, they were both willing to forget about big issues, or to be agreeably vague about them. This is a common phenomenon in diplomatic history, and for this reason treaties are often less contracts in which the parties state their undertakings clearly than patchworks of glosses which conceal a hope that suspected difficulties will not materialize. If Charnacé's negotiations with Gustavus alarmed Maximilian and his allies, Père Joseph's presence at Regensburg had alarmed Gustavus. To add to the general disquiet, Père Joseph had returned from Regensburg with the horrifying notion that Gustavus and the Emperor might seek an accommodation. Upon both Gustavus and Richelieu there was mounting pressure to conclude a bargain.

The final negotiations between Charnacé and Gustavus were constantly interrupted by Gustavus' bursts of administrative energy. The Swedish army, like a plague of carrion crows, was busy stripping Pomerania bare, and Gustavus was desperate to control it, keep it fed and billeted, and hold at bay both the imperialists and the unhappy Duke Bogislaw of Pomerania. Not until they were at Bärwalde, some distance up the Oder towards Frankfurt, did Charnacé and Gustavus reach agreement. There, on 23 January 1631, a treaty was signed, news of which filtered through only slowly to shock Vienna, Madrid and Rome. The stated objects of the Franco-Swedish alliance were common defence, the security of the Baltic, and liberty of trade – the maintenance, in effect, of France's important privileges in the Sounds. Gustavus would maintain thirty thousand foot and six thousand horse in Germany; he would respect the law of the Empire concerning religion, and would guarantee freedom of worship for Catholics in Germany. The price of this religious concession, by which Richelieu hoped to minimize the impact of Gustavus' intervention in the war, had been forced up, and France undertook to pay to Sweden an annual subsidy of 400,000 imperial thalers.

The disastrously weak clauses in the treaty were those which Richelieu compromised in the hope, vain as it was to prove, of keeping the Lion of the North on a short chain. The question of the transfer of the Electoral dignity from the Palatinate to Bavaria was left open, and Gustavus agreed to respect the integrity of Bavaria and the lands of the Catholic League only 'in so far as they sincerely observed neutrality'. In other words, should Maximilian and his following choose not to stand aloof and let Gustavus whittle away at the imperial structure, or attempt the restoration of the Palatinate, the latter was released under the terms of the treaty from any constraint respecting them. And, since both sides undertook to make no separate peace for five years, and much could happen in five years, Gustavus would have ample time to nullify any efforts which Richelieu might continue to make to entice Bavaria into neutrality. Within months the Protestant hero was, in the eyes of Catholic Europe, to reincarnate Alaric – an Alaric paid by a cardinal of the Church to scorch the lands of the counter-reformation. Richelieu had become Faust.

If the Emperor's Mantuan policy had been an error, Richelieu's

Swedish alliance which it provoked was an even greater one. French money gave Gustavus Adolphus momentary independence, and, far from chaining him, in fact unleashed him. The Treaty of Bärwalde was a flimsy document, dependent for its operation on too many contingencies, and open to too much liberty of interpretation. Richelieu was excessively optimistic as to the possibility of keeping Bavaria neutral in the struggle between Gustavus and Ferdinand; and until he had Maximilian committed to a neutral course of action it was folly to leave Gustavus free to do whatever impulse suggested to him. Richelieu's major fault was his deliberate disturbance of the equilibrium in Germany in order to regain equilibrium in France's borderlands, for the one was disproportionate to the other. In fact, as events were to demonstrate, the violent displacement of power in Germany, consequent upon the Swedish onslaught, was to prove more dangerous to France's security, and to drag her more irresistibly into the abyss, than the pendular swing of power in Italy.

While Charnacé was negotiating the Treaty of Bärwalde other French envoys were busy trying to persuade both the Protestant and the Catholic princes to remain neutral. In addition, the support of the Catholics was sought in the matter of the disputed dependencies of the bishopric of Metz. At Leipzig there was a meeting of Protestants, and in Dinkelsbühl one of Catholics. Both meetings consolidated the respective parties, the one in opposition to the Emperor, the other in support of him. The Protestants agreed on general resistance to the execution of the Edict of Restitution; the Catholics found themselves supporting the Elector of Cologne, who had called on the Spaniards to suppress his rebellious subjects in the bishopric of Liège, and thereby took the first step towards abandoning their neutrality in the Spanish-Dutch conflict. They also referred the question of ecclesiastical property to the forthcoming Diet of Frankfurt 'on the basis of religious peace and the Edict of Restitution' – which implied their support for the latter. The forces of Protestantism and Catholicism were thus coalescing in a new mutual antagonism at the very moment when Gustavus' intervention made the whole situation in Germany fluid once again.

The dangers of this situation were obscured by Maximilian's sudden decision to seek the protection of France. Had he taken this decision when Père Joseph had urged it on him at Regensburg the Treaty of Bärwalde might never have been negotiated. Now, too late, Maximilian, at the Pope's behest, fearful of the Swedish threat, and equally fearful of Spanish designs in Germany, agreed to a Franco-Bavarian defensive alliance for eight years. The Treaty of Fontainebleau, signed in May 1631, provided that both France and Bavaria would work for neutrality between the Catholic League and the Dutch, and that neither country would assist Spain. On the face of it this instrument did not contradict the Treaty of Bärwalde; in practice it did, for it failed to neutralize Bavaria against Sweden; and, while it encouraged Maximilian to expect French constraint upon Gustavus, it left him free to fulfil his obligations to the Emperor. Since Gustavus had taken no steps to recognize the transfer of the Palatinate Electoral dignity to Bavaria, Maximilian had serious reason to doubt whether his neutrality in the coming struggle between Sweden and the Emperor would be in any way to his advantage; if France were unable to protect him he would, in the last analysis, be compelled to rely on the Emperor. But under the Treaty of Bärwalde France could not protect him unless he remained neutral. Richelieu was snared in his own dilemma, and it might almost be said that he shut his eyes and hoped that the impending disaster might be averted.

The hurricane built up slowly. Only the city of Magdeburg declared for Gustavus Adolphus, and when Wallenstein's successor, Tilly, laid siege to it, no help was forthcoming from the other Protestant states. Tilly was an imperial general, but he was also commander-in-chief of the Bavarian army, and his presence at Magdeburg was in itself sufficient to exempt Gustavus from his undertaking to respect the integrity of Bavaria and the territories of the Catholic League. In fact Richelieu warned Küttner, the Bavarian negotiator of the Treaty of Fontainebleau, of this when the latter invoked against Sweden the mutual defence provisions of the treaty. While Gustavus bullied Saxony and Brandenburg into letting him pass through their territories to the relief of

Magdeburg, Tilly pressed on with the siege, and on 17 May 1631 took the city by storm. His army, totally out of control, turned the victory into Armageddon. The corpses of twenty thousand of the inhabitants poisoned the Elbe or provided food for the dogs and magpies scavenging in the wilderness of sulphurous ashes. The holocaust shocked a Europe that had grown accustomed to frightfulness, and threw the Protestants into Gustavus' hands. Within two weeks Holland signed a treaty with him supplementing the French subsidies, and two weeks later George William of Brandenburg, with Gustavus' cannon trained on the palace of Berlin, was forced to sign another placing the resources of the Electorate at Sweden's disposal for the duration of the war. Gustavus was now poised for an onslaught on central Germany and the Rhineland.

Strategic considerations during the Thirty Years War had ever to be sacrificed to logistics, and armies became monstrous organisms with no other purpose than survival through exploitation of the environment. In 1630 the situation after eleven years of war was bad enough, but as general war developed it became desperate. Armies stripped the fields of unripened corn and ate the livestock. There was no seed for the next harvest, nor stock animals for breeding, and the shortages became cumulative. In time even roots, acorns and berries became difficult to find. Murder was followed by plague, and the peasants, even when they had something to plant, were too famished for the task. The whole economy of Germany, already perilous before 1618, collapsed. Trade broke down, the rich cities devoured their capital but did not replenish it. The soldiers, brutalized by deprivation and mistreatment, burned haystacks for sport, strangled and roasted peasants in the hope of extracting from them their hoarded silver or food, and begot a terrible revenge when the peasants could gain the upper hand. So the movement of armies was like a random game of chess, in which pieces migrated into unexploited territories with no aim save sustenance and no achievement save ruination; and as one territory after another was eaten out the scale of the movement became ever larger.

After Magdeburg Tilly's army was in a frightful condition, and he turned to the Rhine in a hunt for food. This move brought him towards Hesse, and the Landgrave cried to Gustavus for help. Tilly was forced to turn back and throw himself on the resources of Saxony. John George the Elector tried to play for time, but Tilly's men had no time. Steadily they ate their way into the Electorate, and on 11 September 1631 John George joined Gustavus. A week later Tilly was defeated at Breitenfeld by the combined Swedish and Saxon armies. It was the turning point of the war. Gustavus had liberated Europe from the Habsburgs, and no longer would Protestantism be on the defensive. Also no longer, though only a few like Richelieu could see it, would the war be fought on a doctrinal premise. With the Pope hostile to Austria's religious policy, and with a cardinal in league with the Protestant hero, the intellectual coincidence of Catholicism and Habsburg supremacy had been destroyed; and with Gustavus' mind concentrating on the idea of Swedish political expansion in Germany, Protestantism was no longer the only, or even the main, cause of the enemies of the Habsburgs.

Richelieu's satisfaction at the news of Breitenfeld was short-lived, for now Gustavus burst into the 'Priests' Alley', the aggregation of Catholic bishoprics and abbacies in central Germany. By 5 October he was in Würzburg, and there he issued an ultimatum to the Catholic rulers which made their neutrality impossible. Among other things he demanded from the ecclesiastical Electors 40,000 thalers a month with which to fight their co-religionists. At the moment they were all attending the Diet at Frankfurt, called to discuss the Edict of Restitution, and as the Swedes came down the Main they fled, scattering in all directions back to their states, or in search of charity if their states were no longer theirs. To the Protestants in Frankfurt Gustavus, the first foreign conqueror ever to occupy the city, was the new Gideon. Just before Christmas he burst into Mainz and put the Elector to flight.

Even before the Swedish army came to a halt on the Rhine Richelieu had been active on three fronts, in Italy, in Lorraine, and in the Grisons: and although these movements were fundamentally unconnected with the Swedish advance, and were purely coincidental, they appeared to Vienna and Madrid to be part of some vast Franco-Swedish strategic design. The first move was taken in September in Piedmont, only two days after Gustavus' victory at Breitenfeld. All during the summer of 1631 imperial, Spanish, French and Savoyard commissioners had been supervising the execution of the Treaty of Cherasco. The last step was the handing over of Pinerolo to Savoy in their presence. This occurred on 20 September, when Victor Amadeus made a solemn declaration that France had fully and punctually executed its engagement to evacuate the fortress. In Spanish eyes the matter was finished. In Richelieu's eyes, however, it was far from finished. In the previous March, three months before the peace of Cherasco, Victor Amadeus had signed a secret treaty by which he had agreed to cede Pinerolo to France. The author of this engagement was Mazarin, who had been sent by Urban VIII to Richelieu to persuade him to ratify the Treaty of Regensburg, but who had instead plotted with the Cardinal to secure for France a permanent foothold in Italy in order to checkmate Spanish designs there.

The Treaty of Cherasco contradicted this engagement in spirit if not in actual terms, and Richelieu had pondered long over this problem. As he said in his *Mémoires*, if Pinerolo were to be held by France it would guarantee that France would always be the arbitrator and master of Italy; if it were to be delivered up, all thought of this would have to be abandoned for ever. It was the Spanish reaction to the peace of Cherasco that perhaps decided him. The first treaty, signed in April, had been disavowed by the Emperor; the second treaty the Emperor had ratified in order to disengage his army in face of the impending threat from Gustavus Adolphus. But Olivares, full of moral indignation though he was at Richelieu's refusal to ratify the Treaty of Regensburg, had exhibited no scruples about urging Ferdinand to repudiate the second Treaty of Cherasco, which he protested had been made over Spain's head.

When the Spanish and imperial commissioners inspected Pinerolo they failed to detect the presence of two hundred French troops hidden in the fortress cellars, who, after the departure of the commissioners, proceeded to take possession of the place once again. The evacuation had been nullified by a piece of sleight of hand; and when Feria, again Spanish governor of the Milanais, learned of this charade he threatened that the investiture of Nevers would be declared null and void unless Richelieu honoured the Treaties of Regensburg and Cherasco article by article.[2] In this way the questions of the French occupation of Pinerolo and of French support for Gustavus were diplomatically assimilated. Richelieu replied that Spain was breaking the Treaty of Monzon in moving the troops released at Casale through the Valtelline to Flanders; in August alone 5,800 had made the passage. If Spain continued to violate the Treaty of Monzon, France would repudiate that of Cherasco. At Mazarin's urging, Paris and Turin resolved to allay Spanish wrath by publishing an agreement whereby France would be granted occupation of Pinerolo as a gage for only six months. But a secret article confirmed the treaty of March, so that in fact France had sovereignty over Pinerolo in perpetuity.

The Pinerolo deception hardened the diplomatic situation; the second move, also motivated by developments only distantly connected with the Swedish alliance, hardened it still further. This was the invasion of Lorraine, which was decided upon as Gustavus' army was descending the Main. Its primary objective was the dispersal of the troops which Gaston was raising with Charles' support for an invasion of his own country, but it promised other results: the imperialist garrisons in Vic and Moyenvic, which constituted a continuing threat to France's rights, could be chased out while the Emperor was distracted by the defeat at Breitenfeld; and a French presence in Lorraine would deter Gustavus Adolphus from crossing the Rhine to batten on this as yet unexploited territory, so carrying the war into France's borderlands. Charles of Lorraine had furnished Gustavus with ample excuse for such an action. The Emperor had given Charles a commission to raise troops in the Duchy; Richelieu believed they would be used to support Gaston's adventures; in fact Charles had sent them at the Emperor's request as reinforcements to Tilly after Breitenfeld, they had been caught up in Gustavus' advance down the Main, and were at this moment in disorderly retreat before the Swedes. Charles had gratuitously made himself an enemy of Gustavus.

The nuncio, Bichi, did his utmost to restrain Richelieu from this hostile action, but the latter, with his penchant for history and law, developed elaborate arguments about the supremacy of the French Crown in Lorraine, and the right of Louis XIII to assert his jurisdiction there. La Force's army encountered virtually no opposition when it crossed the Lorraine frontier; Gaston's force fled into Luxembourg and the imperialist garrisons in Vic and Moyenvic capitulated. Charles came rushing back from his uncle Maximilian of Bavaria to make his submission in person to Louis XIII at Metz, where French general headquarters were established. There he signed an agreement by which he gave France transit rights across Lorraine for the purpose of aiding the Catholics in Germany, thus securing for Louis the line of the upper Moselle.

In the first days of 1632 it looked for a moment as if the French would march on to the Rhine and occupy Alsace. The suzerain of this imperial province was the Archduke Leopold, and it was he who had invaded the Grisons and was busily fortifying this French-protected territory. This afforded an excellent excuse to seize his government of Alsace and thereby both prevent an imperial invasion of France across the vulnerable frontier of Lorraine and impose a solid obstacle to Gustavus on the left bank of the Rhine. At a council meeting on 6 January at Vic Richelieu proposed this move.[3] The nuncio heard of it and descended on the Cardinal in indignation. A war against Austria, he said, would be fatal to the Church, and he was sorry he needed to remind the Cardinal of his superior obligations of religion. Richelieu replied that Louis would enter Alsace only to protect the Catholics there from the fury of Gustavus, but Bichi said that no one would be deceived by this flimsy excuse. He added bluntly that it was not for a prince to confide the government to a cardinal of the Church in order that he should direct an enterprise against Catholicism. Next morning Richelieu saw Père Joseph who also threw his weight against the projected invasion. Such an action, he argued, would alienate France's friends in Germany, who were being enticed to declare themselves neutral in order to hold Gustavus within the bonds of the Treaty of Bärwalde. Richelieu yielded to the pressure and the French forces withdrew to French territory. Hardly had they done so when news arrived that Gaston had returned to Nancy. Although this was as yet unknown, on 3 January he had secretly married Charles's sister Marguerite.

The third movement of French forces was into the Grisons. The flood of Spanish and imperial troops through the passes to reinforce Tilly was alarming, and, in Richelieu's eyes, in violation of the Treaty of Monzon. It was resolved, therefore, to send Rohan to command a Grisons army, and the Venetians were persuaded, albeit grudgingly, to give their commander-in-chief leave of absence for the purpose. Rohan appeared at Chur and was now actively engaged in the task entrusted to him. As Richelieu's anxiety concerning Gustavus' intentions mounted he began to see Rohan in the role of a defender of Swiss neutrality, not only against the Spaniards and Austrians, but also against Sweden, and thus as an obstacle to an incursion by Gustavus into Italy. In Rohan he had picked the wrong man, for the redoubtable Huguenot was shortly to lend his support to Gustavus' schemes to bring the Swedes into the Valtelline, thereby threatening to substitute Swedish for French protection.

The new year of 1632 saw Europe in a state of the utmost excitement. The terrible Goth had come to a halt on the Rhine and was busy turning Mainz into a great base for the operations of the spring. Where he would next turn no one knew. At the French court there were the wildest speculations. If he found himself blocked on the Moselle he might come over the Vosges, ravage the imperial territories of Alsace and Lorraine and threaten France; or he might make peace with the Emperor, march through the Swiss passes, and, like his ancestor Alaric, storm Rome. In Spain there was frantic activity. Shortly after Breitenfeld the Council of State met and resolved to defend the Palatinate against Gustavus, and prod Poland into breaking the truce with Sweden and cutting Gustavus' lines of communication. It was even suggested that Spain reach an accommodation with England on the restoration of Frederick to the Palatinate, and persuade the Emperor to revoke the Edict of Restitution in order to quieten the German Protestants. Olivares proposed that all Spanish diplomatic missions proclaim that this was a political and not a religious war, and that Gustavus was ambitious for himself and was not the saviour of Protestantism. France, he said, was the real enemy, and it should be distracted in every possible way, in particular by the Emperor making a diversion into France from Lorraine, and by fomenting sedition within France.

This admission by Spain that the war was political and not religious did not advance Habsburg credit in Rome when Madrid and Vienna tried to drag money out of the Pope. When first told of the Treaty of Bärwalde Urban refused to believe it, and when presented with the unpleasant fact instructed Bichi to persuade Richelieu to repudiate it. After Breitenfeld he renewed his plea, begging the Cardinal to send a mission to Gustavus to convince him that he must respect Catholic goods and persons. Richelieu's only reply was that Charnacé was already instructed to secure the neutrality of the Catholic League; and when Bichi indicated that this was insufficient he became indignant and, with a scandalized air, disclosed that he knew the Emperor to be negotiating with Saxony and Sweden an agreement of which the first victims would be Bavaria and the Catholic League. The Protestants, as part of the bargain, would keep the territories which they had occupied, and Frederick v would be restored in the Palatinate. Then, becoming confidential, he confessed that, in truth, it was very difficult to restrain Gustavus. As the latter reached the Rhine a papal bull was issued calling on all Catholics to pray for the success of Catholic armies, and Urban renewed his pleas to Richelieu to act to restrain Gustavus, urging him to distinguish between the cause of the Habsburgs as a political matter and the fate of Catholics in Germany as a religious one. This did not satisfy Olivares, who told the nuncio that, since heresy was everywhere in triumph, the Pope should use the papal treasure in Castel St Angelo to equip new Spanish armies.

In the French general headquarters at Metz that January there was intense diplomatic activity. Charles of Lorraine was there to make his submission, the nuncio was badgering Richelieu to break with Gustavus, and the Cardinal himself was preoccupied with the problems raised by Gustavus' appearance on the Rhine. If France was not to be subjected to contradictory demands under the Treaties of Bärwalde and Fontainebleau, Bavaria and the Catholic League would have to be persuaded to declare their neutrality. Richelieu hoped that the shock of the Swedish advance would effect this end, and Charnacé was sent off to both Maximilian and Gustavus as a mediator. His instructions indicate the extent to which Richelieu's policy had created a world of fictions. He was told that, if Maximilian was not prepared to declare his neutrality in writing, Charnacé should try to persuade Gustavus to accept it orally. If neither Maximilian nor Gustavus was prepared to trust the word of the other – which was found to be the case – Charnacé was to guarantee them both against violation of their undertakings, provided each would agree to defend France against imperial retaliation for the attack on the Emperor's garrisons in Lorraine. If Maximilian invoked against Gustavus the mutual defence provisions of the Treaty of Fontainebleau, Charnacé was to tell him that the *casus foederis* would only arise if Gustavus refused to observe Bavarian neutrality; and it would not arise at all if Maximilian did not, in fact, remain neutral.

Charnacé's mission was doomed to failure because it was based upon a misconception of the respective situations of Maximilian and Gustavus. Maximilian and his allies were not unwilling to declare their neutrality – in fact their agents flocked into Metz all eagerness to do so – but their conception of neutrality did not coincide with that of Gustavus. They wanted guarantees that Gustavus would recognize Maximilian's Electoral dignity, restore to the Catholic League all its territories, and permit the imperial troops free retreat across them to the Habsburg hereditary lands. Gustavus rejected these terms outright, and all Charnacé's efforts to preach moderation to both sides were wasted on the wind. Threats achieved nothing more. When Charnacé hinted to Gustavus that France was obliged by the Treaty of Fontainebleau to defend Bavarian neutrality, Gustavus lost his temper and told him he would make peace with Ferdinand – a reply that nonplussed Charnacé, who achieved nothing more than a temporary truce between Sweden and Bavaria to enable the discussions to continue.

Richelieu was mainly concerned with the problem of getting Gustavus back over the Rhine, for the advent of the Swedes on the western bank had brought them into contact with the Spanish forces in the Palatinate, and had created a serious danger of a power conflict between Spain and Sweden in this area. The neutralization of the ecclesiastical electorates was thus a matter of paramount importance and urgency. When the Comte de Bruslon, Richelieu's envoy, reached Trier just before Christmas 1631 he was welcomed by the Elector, Philip von Sötern, as 'an angel from heaven'. Sötern was terrified and, far from needing to be persuaded to declare his neutrality, solicited the protection of a French army to guarantee it against both the Spaniards and the Swedes. The coterie of ecclesiastical refugees congregated in Cologne, who included the Elector of Mainz, and the bishops of Würzburg, Worms and Osnabrück, also persuaded the Elector of Cologne to make a proclamation of neutrality on the last day of the terrible year of 1631, and the bishop of Würzburg was dispatched to Metz to enlist French protection.

The council meeting of 6 January at Vic decided that Charnacé's mission to negotiate the neutrality of the Catholic League needed to be supplemented by a mission to secure Gustavus' recognition of the neutrality of Trier, Mainz and Cologne, and restoration of their lands to Catholics. To this end Richelieu's brother-in-law the Marquis de Brézé, was sent to Mainz.[4] He was captain of the guards, and he took with him twenty-five gentlemen of distinction in the hope of overawing Gustavus with baroque splendour. The Swedish King was quite unimpressed by either the display or the argument. When he remained obdurate Brézé resorted to threats: France, he said, had forty thousand men ready to march; whereupon Gustavus flew into one of his rages and roared at him: 'Let your King go where he will; but let him have a care not to come too close to my armies; if he does he must look for an encounter with me!'[5]

When he had cooled down Gustavus said he was prepared to be conciliatory about the lands on the left bank of the Rhine but about nothing else. He would return to the Electors of Trier and Cologne whatever places of theirs he held, except Speyer, but he was not prepared to deliver up any other conquests to the Catholics. On the contrary, he demanded that all Protestant places taken since 1618 in Lower Saxony be restored, and the armies of the Catholic League be virtually disbanded. This meant, in effect, evacuation of Lower Saxony by Pappenheim's Bavarian army and the consequent removal of the one major danger to Gustavus' lines of communication. Neither Maximilian nor the other Catholic rulers could be expected to make so great a strategic concession when they had no confidence whatever that Gustavus would respect their interests; and when Charnacé brought Gustavus' ultimatum to Metz on 25 January 1632, Richelieu considered his terms so unreasonable that he resolved not even to communicate them to the German Catholics. A week later, however, he summoned the bishop of Würzburg, who had been hovering about Metz for a month, and told him that he was sending Charnacé back to Mainz to try to persuade Gustavus to be more sensitive to the fears of the Catholics, but that if this time Charnacé failed in his mission the Catholic bishops would be compelled to accept Gustavus' conditions pending a more general agreement.

With nothing but vague promises of help to console him, Würzburg left Metz on 7 February and returned to Cologne. It appeared to the Catholic rulers huddled there in peril that Richelieu was trying to cajole them into committing political suicide, and they turned in their desperation to the Emperor. Maximilian, too, realized that neutrality was a farce, and three weeks later sent an agent to Vienna seeking help from both Ferdinand and Spain. While ordering Pappenheim to continue winter operations against the Swedish communications in Lower Saxony, he connived at Tilly's dramatic expulsion from Bamberg of the Swedish general Gustav Horn. Gustavus Adolphus was enraged at what he regarded as a breach of faith during the truce and made it clear to Charnacé that he was entitled to exploit the loophole in the Treaty of Bärwalde. For Bavaria there was now no hope save in imperial arms.

15

War is the Road to Peace
1632-4

On 3 March 1632 Gustavus Adolphus began to march. It had never been his intention to leave a neutral Bavaria athwart his line of advance from Mainz to Vienna, and in order to secure his communications he felt compelled to eliminate it as a military power. He knew that Richelieu was not prepared to break with him, and exploiting that knowledge, he resolved to leave his rear exposed to the French, and to sweep Maximilian into oblivion on his front. His plan was to seize the as yet untouched triangle of rich farmland between the Danube, the Lech and the Alps, with its two important Protestant cities of Ulm and Augsburg. This territory would feed him, provide him with cash to pay his troops, and constitute the economic base for the overthrow of the Habsburgs. By 26 March he was at Donauwörth, and when he took the hill of the Schellenberg, which overlooks the town, and directed his artillery at the vulnerable defences, the imperial garrison fled across the Danube. Although Donauwörth was a Protestant town the Swedes thoroughly plundered it, and murdered all who were armed, and many, too, who were defenceless. A joyful massacre occurred on the bridge of 'Jesuits and Monkes', as the Scottish mercenary Monroe records, the Swedes 'making great booty over all, where ever they came, hanging the Papists by their purse, not sparing to torment their shinnes'.[1]

The Lech flows swiftly into the Danube just across the bridge and a little downstream from Donauwörth. At this time it was brim full with the water from the melting alpine snows, and Tilly had all bridges over it destroyed and all boats removed. On its other side the fields were intersected with watercourses and then, as now, there were extensive scrubby woodlands. The Swedish generals advised Gustavus not to attack over the Lech, but he went ahead himself to reconnoitre, exchanging insults with the sentries of Tilly's army which he found ranged on the other side. The houses of a nearby village were demolished to make floating bridges; under the cover of a smoke screen from burning damp straw and gunpowder, these were launched on the surging stream, and on 5 April 1632 the Swedes established a bridgehead on the other side. Standing in the tangled brambles Tilly was wounded and lost control of the situation. His army had no defence in depth, but had relied on the river to protect it, and there was now nothing to do but extricate it and withdraw to Ingolstadt.

In the great gothic church-hall of Ingolstadt, whose tower is curiously set at the diagonal, Tilly died to the thunder of Gustavus' siege guns. It was Gustavus' intention to hold Maximilian in Ingolstadt while he advanced on the southern bank of the Danube and took Regensburg, but the Bavarians anticipated him, and by the end of April Maximilian was securely in possession of the city. There he called on the French ambassador to Bavaria, Père Joseph's brother-in-law St Étienne, and asked him to open negotiations with Gustavus. St Étienne knew his Gustavus even less than did the other French negotiators. When he tried to persuade the King of Maximilian's sincerity Gustavus replied in typically expressive language that even the louse is not devoid of virtues; and when St Étienne descended to the same level of discourse Gustavus rebuked him for his familiarity, and told him his mission was an impertinence: if Maximilian was not prepared to accept his terms, which were virtually those of unconditional surrender, he would harry Bavaria from end to end. St Étienne, like his predecessors, then threatened French displeasure, and Gustavus, as ever in such circumstances, flew into a temper and told him that he was quite indifferent to French feelings. For all he cared Louis XIII could send his forty thousand men to Maximilian's aid.

St Étienne's mission was a failure, and Gustavus proceeded to do exactly as he had promised. Everywhere the churches were plundered and burned, the smoke hung over the wake of his advancing army and the bodies grew bloated in the ditches. The Protestant city of Augsburg had a Bavarian garrison which it expelled as the Swedes approached its gates. The burghers had a rude shock, for their deliverer had only one purpose in mind in occupying the first city of the south, and that was systematically to milk it to support his army. Furthermore, he made the unprecedented demand that they take an oath of loyalty to himself. Augsburg, which had already fallen on evil times with the failure of the banking houses of the Fugger and the Welser, was reduced to ruin, while Gustavus took time off to have his bust carved by the city's greatest sculptor, Georg Petel.

On 6 May Munich capitulated, and St Étienne took the credit for persuading Gustavus not to plunder it. The Swedish army staggered into the city under the weight of immense loot, which it proceeded to auction off in the streets at bargain prices. While his men were thus recouping their fortunes, Gustavus set out to enjoy himself. He prowled around the Residenz, which he contemplated removing stone by stone to Uppsala, located the one hundred and nineteen pieces of artillery which had been buried by the garrison before its surrender, and showed the workmen how to excavate them. He extracted from the city half the cash he wanted, but supplemented it with the Electoral treasures. He was in the capital of the Counter-Reformation and determined to make the most of the experience. The Jesuits here had refused to be stampeded, and to their celebrated church and college of St Michael strutted Gustavus, in a gay and inquisitive mood. He enjoyed the experience much as Père Joseph would have enjoyed observing the Moslems in the Dome of the Rock had he ever realized his ambition of conquering Jerusalem, but perhaps with less fascinated horror. To disquiet Richelieu further he now entered into negotiations with Rohan and the Swiss to operate jointly with them in order to block the Splügen and

the Bernina against Spanish help. This was a dangerous encroachment on France's traditional rights in the Grisons, and it seems
clear that Gustavus had in mind to oust French influence there
and replace it with his own. Gustavus found Swiss neutrality
ridiculous, especially when the fields of Switzerland were full of
corn and cattle. Fortunately he managed to frighten the Swiss as
much as he frightened Richelieu, and they rejected his overtures.
At the same moment he was receiving an envoy from Gaston
d'Orléans, who tried to enlist his support against Richelieu with
some scheme of reconciling Gustavus and Ferdinand. There
seemed no end to the mischief which Gustavus was capable of
creating for France. Suddenly, Gustavus' plans were interrupted
by news of disaster. Wallenstein, restored to command after
Tilly's death, took Prague on 15 May, and the Saxons, in full
retreat, were negotiating. If they made peace, Gustavus' communications would be in peril. He was therefore forced to march
north, and around Nürnberg in the summer of 1632 there was a
long period of skirmishings and wanderings.

In the French state papers there is little to indicate that this
wrath of God disturbed Richelieu or the French government as
much as it horrified the other Catholic states of Europe. The
explanation for this detachment was the French preoccupation
with the problem of Gaston d'Orléans. Not three months elapsed
from Charles of Lorraine's submission to Louis XIII when he was
again supporting Gaston's plans for an invasion of France. Spain,
outraged by Richelieu's subsidization of Gustavus Adolphus, and
by a report from the Spanish ambassador in Paris, the Marqués de
Mirabel, who had penetrated the secret of the Pinerolo deception,
resolved to give its full encouragement to Gaston's schemes.
At a meeting of the Council of State on 23 January 1632 Gonzalo
de Cordoba, restored to favour and recently made a member,
made a bellicose speech to his fellow councillors. Louis XIII, he
argued, should be dethroned, and Gaston, with Spanish arms,
should replace him. The papal nuncio reported to Rome that
Madrid reposed great hopes in Gaston, who, it was thought,
would distract France and divert the subsidies that would otherwise go to Gustavus. Feria was also proposing from Milan that

he should support Gaston by an invasion of France across the Alps. Philip IV wrote a letter to the Emperor in which Richelieu was accused of being the instigator of all the 'commotion' in Europe.

In July, while Gustavus Adolphus was fencing with Wallenstein, the second French invasion of Lorraine began, the outcome of which was the Treaty of Liverdun, in which Charles submitted for a second time. At the same time French and Spanish troops were finally coming into collision. Philip von Sötern of Trier, under pressure from Richelieu, had agreed to allow France to garrison his fortresses of Philippsburg, at the junction of the Rhine and the Saal between Heidelberg and Karlsruhe, and Ehrenbreitstein, which covered the confluence of the Moselle and the Rhine at Coblenz. Both were in Spanish hands, as was Philip von Sötern's capital, Trier, and the Spaniards would have to be prised out. Gustavus, only too eager to embroil France and Spain in hostilities, detached Swedish troops to help the French take Ehrenbreitstein, which capitulated on 12 June. Philippsburg was to resist for the next two years, but the Spanish garrison in Trier was expelled by La Force in May. While the French were distracted with the pursuit of Gaston into Languedoc the Spaniards returned and installed themselves in Trier once more. On 6 August the French laid formal siege to the city and captured it two weeks later. This was sufficient reason for Spain to go to war, but the moment was inopportune: Gaston had been forced to submit; the Emperor was in no position to contemplate adding France to his list of enemies, and therefore held back; Spain herself was unable to undertake alone the burden of a general war, for the plate fleet, for the third time in a decade, had been lost. Of thirty ships which began the voyage from the Spanish Main only two reached Havana, and neither of these was carrying bullion.

The ambiguities in Richelieu's German policy are evident in the instructions which he gave St Étienne concerning the French actions in Lorraine and in Trier. St Étienne was to propose a suspension of arms for three months between Gustavus Adolphus and Maximilian. He was to inform Gustavus of the French chastisement of Lorraine and the occupation of Trier, and was to entice him to regard this as part of a common effort meriting his good graces. To Maximilian he was to represent it as aimed at the preservation of the Catholic lands of the Electors, and to persuade him to regard France as the ally of the Catholic League. But should Maximilian take this too literally and again invoke the Treaty of Fontainebleau, St Étienne was to recall that it was Bavaria which in January had violated the truce with the Swedes. To compound this double game – or perhaps merely because France did not have the specie – the subsidies to Gustavus were quietly discontinued, while St Étienne was authorized to offer Maximilian 100,000 crowns, pleading France's deplorable financial state as an excuse for not making it more.

The struggle between France and the Habsburgs in 1632 was only intensified by the inept diplomatic moves made by both Madrid and Vienna. The Spanish Council of State decided that Gonzalo de Cordoba should take command of the armies of the Spanish Netherlands, with a view to driving both the Swedes and the French from the Rhine. The problem was how to get him to Brussels in a hurry. The easiest route was across France, but unless the new commander-in-chief was to be invested with diplomatic immunity it would be difficult for him to travel through what was virtually enemy territory. When the French ambassador in Madrid handed Olivares a secret memorandum concerning a proposed reconciliation between Louis XIII and his mother this seemed to afford sufficient excuse to send the general on a mission to Paris *en route* to Belgium. Gonzalo arrived there on 15 March and was received with great courtesy. Next day he had an audience with Louis XIII and saw Richelieu. The latter, as usual, talked a great deal. He had subsidized Gustavus, he said, in order to create a diversion in Germany while Spain was troubling the peace in Italy. Gonzalo did not respond to this frankness, but was laconic and made no serious effort at negotiation. He made a few vague observations about Pinerolo and the Swedes in a detached way which suggested that neither he nor his masters were in the slightest degree interested in discussing peace, and two days later he departed for Brussels. Richelieu recognized from the general's conduct that his diplomatic role was a disguise, and this did little to mitigate his deep distrust of Spain. Matters were not helped when at about the same time an imperial envoy arrived in the person of Baron von Schwarzenberg to announce the creation of a Habsburg League between Ferdinand II and Philip IV, and to assure France that it was directed not against her but against Sweden. He behaved, as the papal nuncio reported, more like a charlatan than a negotiator.

To Spain the issues raised by the events of 1632 were simple in the extreme: Richelieu was the evil genius who had brought the frightful Nordic heretic to scourge Christ. The most effective way of dealing with him, it seemed to Madrid, was by means of canonical sanctions, and to this end a dramatic campaign was mounted in Rome. Olivares' agent there was a man not unlike himself, a violent, proud man, convinced of the providential role of the Habsburgs. He was Cardinal Borgia, a descendant of Alexander VI and the bearer of a name reminiscent of aggressiveness and ambition. Among his following he counted Cardinal Ludovisio, a nephew of Gregory XV, Cardinal Borghese, a nephew of Paul V, and Cardinals Ubaldini, Lante, Crescenzi, Saint-Sixte and Sachetti. As soon as he heard of Richelieu's coup at Pinerolo, Borgia went to Urban VIII, accused Louis XIII of preparing a new aggression in Italy, and contrasted his duplicity with the loyal and just conduct of Philip IV. When he demanded that a legate be sent to France to compel Louis to return to Christian ways Urban could only observe that not much had come from the mission of Cardinal Barberini as legate in 1626. He undertook, however, to send a letter to Richelieu, pleading with him not to break the peace, and to instruct Bichi the nuncio to say that the Pope had no other intention than to keep the peace between Catholic powers. He added that he would pass on to Richelieu all of Borgia's complaints, and would inform Borgia of Richelieu's reply. In the letter which he wrote to Bichi the Pope instructed him not to lose sight of the interests of Catholic Germany, and to try to open Richelieu's eyes to the wide horizons and ambitions of Gustavus' mind, with a view to detaching France from Sweden. At the same time he instructed the nuncios in Vienna and Madrid to restrain the respective courts there from anti-French activities.

Louis' reply to these overtures was dictated by Richelieu, who, as usual, took refuge in legal arguments. Pinerolo was now under French sovereignty; Savoy had freely sold it; it was part of the domains of the Crown, which, pursuant to French fundamental law, were inalienable; hence it was legally beyond negotiation. Bichi reported to Rome that this was a 'ticklish question'.[2] Louis further explained that Pinerolo had been accepted to prevent the Spaniards from molesting the Italian princes, including the Pope. When this argument was disclosed to Borgia he treated it with contempt, asking Urban to grant Philip the privilege of crusade in Naples, which meant in effect the transfer to Spain of the revenues from the ecclesiastical benefices there. The Pope refused, but offered some financial help to Ferdinand. The latter let it be known that he would take all he could get, but that he expected a lot more than he was offered. At the beginning of 1632 Urban's mind was turned to the idea of a conference between Richelieu and Olivares. Richelieu replied that Olivares was trying to have him assassinated – a notion that had some little foundation in Spanish support for the various conspiracies against the Cardinal. When this was passed on to Olivares he indignantly exclaimed that he was merely a servant of the state and had nothing personal against Richelieu.

Olivares had the deepest suspicions of Urban VIII. The Pope was, indeed, a Francophile in culture if not in politics; he had been nuncio in Paris at the time of Louis XIII's birth, and had held the monarch at the baptismal font; and he loved France with that intensity of feeling that only France can generate in the hearts of aliens. Spanish complaints to Vienna about Urban's pro-French policy grew ever more bitter. He was accused with some truth of being the author of the Treaty of Fontainebleau and, with less truth, of conspiring with Richelieu to put Maximilian on the imperial throne. In vain he defended himself against these charges, and his indignation knew no bounds when he learned that Borgia's excited faction in the consistory were accusing him of rejoicing in Gustavus' victories. Borgia was personally rude to him, telling him to his face that he was neglecting his duty as the Vicar of Christ in failing to bring canonical sanctions against

Richelieu. Early in 1632 he and his following gained audience with the Pope and demanded that he declare himself for the Emperor, and accord the right of crusade which Philip wanted. Urban coldly replied that if the Pope were required to fight every Catholic prince who allied himself with heretics he would never cease to have weapons in his hands. He would agree to nothing more than renewed efforts for reconciliation and the grant of ecclesiastical subsidies to be raised from the Spanish clergy.

Borgia and his party were sarcastic about this limited financial support. The Pope, they muttered, always had plenty of money to build palaces or the baldachino in St Peter's, and to plaster everything with the Barberini bees, but none to save Catholicism. At the end of February they were reinforced by an imperial envoy, the Duke of Savelli, who was sent to complain about Richelieu's support of Gustavus, and to demand more money. He failed totally with Urban, whereupon Borgia decided to make a public protest at the consistory to be held on 8 March. He wrote out his speech, intending to say 'if the Catholic religion suffers any harm, it will not be because of the King of Spain, a most pious and obedient sovereign, but because of Your Holiness'. He was not allowed to get so far in his declamation, for when he began by saying that 'evil grows day by day and Your Holiness does nothing', he was told to be silent. Put off balance by this interruption from the Pope Borgia halted for a moment, and then tried to continue. 'Are you speaking as an ambassador or a cardinal?' asked the Pope. Borgia opted and said he was speaking as a cardinal. 'But cardinals,' said the Pope, 'may only speak in consistory when asked.' Borgia opted again. He would speak, then, as ambassador. 'In that case,' exclaimed Urban, triumphantly completing the scholastic dilemma, 'you have no place in this assembly.'

Borgia waited a second and then boldly continued to read his speech. Again he was told to be silent. 'Hold your tongue, we order you,' cried the Pope, 'you deserve to be ordered to leave.'[3] At this point Urban's brother, the Cardinal St Onuphre, got up, and crossing to Borgia laid his hands on him to push him back into his seat. This caused a commotion; Borgia shouted that he was being assaulted, and there was a sudden flurry of red silk on the floor of the consistory. Cardinal Spinola became so enraged that he lost his voice and beat his arms about helplessly. Cardinal Colonna called the Swiss guards, who entered and restored order. The consistory was closed, but Borgia had his speech printed and circulated throughout Rome. The Bishop of Catania compared him with St Paul, who had stood face to face with St Peter.

When Philip IV received Borgia's dispatches the Spanish Council of State resolved to back the Cardinal against the Pope. Olivares said that Catholicism was on the point of ruin, and that the King of Spain was the sole pillar of the Church. On him could not rest the full responsibility for all the disasters in the world; it rested on the head of the Church. A threat was made to suspend the rights of the papal nuncio and seize ecclesiastical revenues. Some members of the Council even wanted to demand reparation from the Pope for the insult to Borgia, but Olivares decided to waive this if Urban would agree to recall Louis XIII to his duty. The Pope saw that the situation was getting out of hand, and he was prepared to be conciliatory. He told Philip that it was only out of regard for him that he did not excommunicate Borgia. Now he would demonstrate his devotion to his duty by making a great effort to unite all against Gustavus Adolphus, and on 1 April a bull was issued asking all the Catholic world to pray for this end.

The Borgia affair provided troubled waters in which Richelieu could not forbear to fish. Referring to Borgia's 'insolence',[4] he told the Pope he would support him against Borgia in every possible way. Urban's reply was disconcerting. He intended, he said, to be a father to all. Richelieu was persistent. He persuaded Mazarin, who was then in Paris as the papal representative, to try to reconcile Louis and his mother, to suggest to Cardinal Francesco Barberini in a disinterested way that the best means of covering Italy from attack by Gustavus would be to create an Italian defensive league including the Pope. The latter was receptive to the idea, provided the league was strictly Italian and strictly defensive; but when the proposal was made to bring the Swiss into it Spain saw this as a move to close the Valtelline and protested violently. Urban decided that the best course would be to lapse into neutrality. At this point another imperial envoy arrived in Rome, Cardinal Pazmány, the Primate of Hungary. He had a double mission, the first to secure more money, the second to protest that the Emperor was scandalized to hear that the Pope no longer supported him in the policy of the Edict of Restitution. Pazmány laid before the Pope the documents in which the latter was supposed to have agreed to the Edict. He also argued that Italy was as much menaced by Gustavus as Germany was. Pazmány's instructions were that if the Pope remained immovable he was to return home. In fact he partially accomplished his mission, for he dragged out of Urban another 300,000 thalers, of which 50,000 were earmarked for Maximilian.

The news of the fall of Munich was received by the Pope with sadness and dismay. The Blessed Sacrament was exposed for three days in Sta Maria de la Victoria, and the Forty Hours Devotions were prescribed. When Wallenstein took Prague Urban's spirits rose. A *Te Deum* was sung, and the Pope, though crippled from gout, hobbled through a solemn pontifical mass. His relations with Borgia, however, did not improve. The Cardinal went around Rome showing everyone a letter he had received from Philip IV approving of his condict. Urban tried to avoid him, even retreating down the corridors of the Vatican so that he would not have to speak to him. Borgia put it around that if the Pope did not mend his ways all the Spanish cardinals would withdraw from Rome.

On 7 June Borgia received his credentials as Spanish ambassador. The Pope refused to accept him, but Borgia intended to be treated as the accredited representative of his country. He arrived at the Quirinale grandly attended in a cortège of twenty-seven coaches. When this was of no avail he arrived the next day in a cortège of seventy coaches. All the Spanish diplomatic mail came to him. Whenever their coaches met he snubbed Cardinal Francesco Barberini. The Pope had had enough of him, and, disturbed at the scandal he was creating, ordered him to reside in his see of Seville. Borgia replied that he was an ambassador and refused to go. The Pope then took the matter up with Philip IV, who demonstrated his intention of supporting Borgia by appointing Borgia's lieutenant, Cardinal Ludovisio, as governor of Milan, although he too had been ordered to reside in his diocese. Borgia then announced that he would retract his accusation against Urban only if the latter entered into a defensive league with Spain in Italy, and supported Spain in execution of the Treaties of Regensburg and Cherasco – which meant requiring the Pope to compel Louis XIII, under pain of canonical sanctions, to break with Gustavus and evacuate Pinerolo. The Pope, naturally, refused, and relations between the Holy See and Madrid worsened.

Suddenly the situation was transformed: Gustavus Adolphus was dead. At Lützen on 16 November 1632 his body was rolled about under the hoofs of cavalry horses, and though his troops, with the courage of despair, went on to defeat Wallenstein there was no longer an apocalyptic figure to champion the Protestant cause. The news was received in Rome, Madrid and Vienna with unexampled joy. Cardinal Barberini wrote to Bichi that 'the Pope has received with the delight you can imagine the news of the disappearance of this serpent who tried to poison the whole world with his venom'.[5] Urban VIII said a mass of thanksgiving in Sta Maria dell'Anima, but his omission of the *Te Deum* incensed Borgia and the Spanish faction, who considered the firing of cannon from St Angelo an insufficient acknowledgement to God for His intervention on behalf of His Church. Madrid was illuminated, and Olivares could not forbear to demonstrate his satisfaction to the French ambassador. At the meeting of the Council of State on 9 January 1633 he said the time had now come to sow division in France. 'We must wish it all possible evil; the more France suffers the more Christendom will be tranquil and the more Catholicism will be in repose.'[6] He proposed a new league, consisting of Spain, the Emperor, Lorraine, Gaston d'Orléans and Marie de Médicis, to be backed by the Spanish armies from Italy.

When the news of Lützen reached Paris Richelieu was ill in Bordeaux. He had decided after the suppression of Montmorency's rebellion to take a long-needed holiday at the château of Richelieu, and so had not followed the court to Paris. His health broke

279

down before his own departure, and now at this crucial moment his advice was not available. The council met on 4 December, and it is evident that relief at the removal of the uncontrollable Gustavus Adolphus and anxiety at the military vacuum created by it were present in equal degree. It was recorded that Louis XIII thought that France had 'not, perhaps, lost very much by the death of the King of Sweden', but other reports indicate that he was so agitated that Léon Bouthillier had to calm him. While a messenger was sent to Charnacé instructing him to urge Gustavus' Chancellor, Axel Oxenstierna, to go on fighting, another was sent to inform Richelieu of the changed circumstances.

Richelieu wrote of Gustavus, with some truth though a good deal more self-justification, that his sense of justice, his mildness towards the conquered and his severity towards the excesses of his own army, placed him in a category apart from the other combatants in this war; and that his army, compared with the disorderly, mutinous rabbles of the Emperor, did little to outrage peoples. To Louis he wrote from Bordeaux that had Gustavus lived for only six months longer France would have been much more secure, but that, provided diligent efforts were made to hold the Protestant powers together, France need not fear unduly the ill will of its enemies.[7] Forcing his rebellious body to endure the discomforts of the journey he set off for Paris, and there on 3 January 1633 he wrote a long memorandum to the King in which he argued for a continuation of his previous policies. The war should be kept going in Germany with French subsidies; France should continue to keep out of it, but, if the Swedes withdrew and the Protestants weakened, it might be necessary to consider direct military intervention. For, he concluded, once peace was made in Germany the Habsburgs would attack France on all sides. Considering the infidelity of the Habsburgs, 'war would be a road to a sure peace'.[8]

Every day the pamphleteers issued their broadsheets, generating violent public controversy about international affairs. The worst critics of the Cardinal had been silenced or exiled and the stage was occupied by those who reminded the nation of Spanish designs. 'The Spaniards,' wrote one of them, 'all pretend to serve religion, but in fact they follow the precepts of Machiavelli.'[9] This was the worst accusation that could be made against a nation, for in the revived moral atmosphere at this time the doctrines of the celebrated Florentine were regarded by all factions as quite reprehensible. French public opinion had become dangerously excited, even before Gustavus' death, at the news that Feria was assembling an enormous army in the Milanais preparatory to marching through the Grisons to confront the Swedes in Bavaria. It now became known that Feria had received instructions to occupy the whole line of the Rhine, on the Alsatian as well as on the Black Forest side. Ostensibly to discuss reconciliation, but in reality to find out what 'evil designs' Olivares had, Richelieu sent a special agent named Bautru to Madrid. Bautru reported that Olivares had no inclination 'but for war and blood'; and, deciding that he was wasting his time, he returned to France. Olivares concluded that Richelieu had no intention of treating honestly, and resolved to intensify his efforts to support Gaston.

The major restraining influence upon Olivares was the Infanta Isabella, who remained unconvinced of the utility of subsidizing Gaston and his mother. Marie de Médicis she regarded as a nuisance, and she would have sent her off to Aachen but for fear of rousing her animosity. She cleverly tried to make Spanish support for the troublesome exiles conditional on a more general European movement. Rubens was instructed to try to get the Savoyard ambassador in London to interest Charles I on their behalf, but it quickly became evident that England had no intention of becoming involved: whereupon Isabella reported that she had given orders to pay the Queen Mother any sum of money she asked for, for money was now the poor woman's only consolation, but that she had no funds to support another invasion of France by Gaston. Only two-thirds of the necessary cash to maintain the administration had arrived from Spain, and so much crown land had been sold to balance the budget that revenues were no longer sufficient to pay ordinary salaries.[10]

It is evident that Richelieu, mesmerized as were most of his contemporaries by the apparent might of Spain, discounted the economic impediment of Spain's making war on France. The

Spanish economy was in an even more desperate condition than the French, with a decline in the first thirty years of the century of seventy-five per cent in the tonnage of shipping between Spain and the Indies, of sixty per cent in the sheep population, of seventy-five per cent in the number of textile manufacturers, and an absolute decline in the population. Erroneous economic policies raised the price of goods and services above the level in the rest of Europe, and wild inflation led to currency depreciation. Piet Hein's capture of the plate fleet aggravated the problem while the Mantuan war was in progress. Whenever Olivares contemplated directly opposing the Franco-Swedish threat with force he was checked by lack of money, and was driven to support of Gaston as the only alternative. In April 1633 he wrote to the Infanta Isabella instructing her that Gaston and Charles of Lorraine were to be given every assistance so that they might be employed to cover Feria's advance down the Rhine. Wallenstein was asked to lend Gaston seven thousand troops to lead into France, and a month later Isabella was told to add another six thousand Germans to these, and to pay Gaston 60,000 crowns a month for six months to enable him to raise yet more troops.[11]

Thus encouraged, both Gaston and Lorraine began recruiting, and Richelieu was shaken by the thought that when Feria reached the Rhine he might add his Spanish troops to theirs in an attempt to induct Monsieur into France and on to the throne. Yet a third French invasion of Lorraine became, in his reflections, a necessity. As it happened, the Swedes were concentrating in the Palatinate in preparation to meet Feria, and Richelieu persuaded Oxenstierna to extend the range of his operations into northern Alsace, where he was certain to come into collision with Lorraine troops. In July 1633 the Swedes accordingly laid siege to Hagenau, and when Charles marched to its relief he was crushed in open combat at Pfaffenhofen. With the Lorraine army scattered, the French were able to enter the Duchy unopposed, on the pretext of Charles' continued refusal to do homage to Louis XIII for the Duchy of Bar. La Force laid siege to Nancy, and on 20 September Charles came to terms at Charmes.

The Treaty of Charmes contained a provision designed to hold both Gaston and Charles in check: Gaston's wife Marguerite was to be handed over to Louis XIII. When, however, Louis made his solemn entry into Nancy on 25 September she was found to have disappeared. Her flight had been contrived by her brother, Cardinal François of Lorraine, the unordained bishop of Toul. When La Force had opened his siege-lines around Nancy, François had emerged from the city to negotiate on behalf of his brother Charles, and at Château-Thierry he had met Richelieu, who found him a calm, gentle but quite determined youth, prepared to confess, but also to justify, his own role in the marriage of Monsieur to Marguerite. So that François might continue the negotiations which he hoped would put Nancy in French hands without a siege, Richelieu provided him with a pass to come and go across the French lines in his carriage, accompanied by a stated number of persons. When François next emerged from the gates of Nancy and reached the French outposts he was allowed through without much scrutiny of his retinue. Sitting beside him in his carriage was a young cavalier in black, sword at side, large plumed hat and false lovelocks shading a face darkened with a mixture of saffron and gunpowder. It was Marguerite; and as the coach trundled through the French lines François meditated what he would say to Louis XIII when his stratagem was discovered. He decided that he would argue that nothing in his pass forbade him to bring out a woman; the pass mentioned only a certain number of persons; what else had he done?

In a wood through which the road ran to Louis' headquarters three gentlemen were waiting with a remount. Leaving the carriage, Marguerite rode with her escort to Thionville, where, this time disguised as a chambermaid, she accompanied a nobleman on the route to Brussels. A courier rode ahead of her with a letter to the Infanta Isabella asking for asylum, and another to Gaston's favourite, Puylaurens, saying 'I am saved by the grace of God!' In Brussels there was general delight at the news. Marie de Médicis declared that it was the happiest day in her life – mainly because the Cardinal had been outwitted. Gaston was radiant until the Abbé d'Elbène, nephew of Richelieu's enemy the ex-bishop of Albi, warned him that this escapade might cost him his right to the throne. His countenance suddenly darkened, Gaston went to a Jesuit, and asked him if he thought the King could deprive him of the succession, or the Pope annul the marriage. Reassured on both points he brightened again, and set off for Namur at the head of two hundred horse to meet his wife.

As the cortège bringing Marguerite neared Brussels, the Infanta Isabella went a league outside the city to meet her, indicating thereby the importance Spain attached to Monsieur. Marguerite entered the old lady's carriage and accompanied her into the capital to the booming of cannon and the shouting of the populace. She was taken direct to her mother-in-law, who met her at the door of her salon, saying 'there you are, oh there you are!' and lumbered into the room with her, a mountain of flesh and black taffeta and velvet. The Infanta did not cease to hold the young girl's hand, and after the brief interview with Marie de Médicis led her to the quarters of her late husband, which were at the disposal of the royal refugees.

When Louis XIII heard that he had been outwitted he vowed vengeance, and to avoid his wrath and try to salvage his Duchy Charles abdicated in favour of his brother François and fled to Germany, where he took command of one of the imperial armies. As feudal overlord of the Duchy of Bar, Louis refused to recognize François' succession, for Bar was the inheritance of Francois' two female cousins, Nicole, the wife of Charles, and Claude, her unmarried sister. On the pretext of preserving the rights of the princesses, Richelieu decided to retain Nancy in order to complete the quadrilateral of great fortresses, Nancy, Verdun, Metz and Toul, which protected the French eastern frontier, and would constitute a barrier to an invasion from Alsace. He failed, however, to reckon on the astuteness of François, who carried Claude and Nicole off and locked himself up with them in Lunéville. La Force was ordered to seize Lunéville and the three refugees. As his army approached the city in overwhelming strength, François conceived the notion of further outwitting Richelieu by marrying Claude and claiming Bar in her name.

In the early winter's evening while La Force was before the gates, an anxious discussion took place between François and two theologians from the neighbouring abbey of the canons-regular of St Rémy. As a lay cardinal the twenty-five-year-old François was competent to marry, but in canon law he would require two dispensations, one from the publication of banns, the other to contract a marriage with his first cousin. The clerics were agreed that, as bishop of Toul, he could dispense himself from the publication of banns, but they were not so sure about the dispensation *in secundo gradu*, because this was normally reserved to the Pope, and bishops had jurisdiction in canon law only in cases of pressing necessity. And what necessity, asked François, could be more pressing than this? He would, then, give himself both the required dispensations, and later have the Pope ratify the second of them so that Louis XIII would have no argument to nullify the marriage.

The decision was no sooner taken than it was executed, and the marriage was celebrated on the spot by one of the canons. Under canon law, however, it would be irrevocable only when consummated, and, with La Force about to burst through the door at any moment, this act became a matter of urgency. Claude exhibited qualms about the matter; it seemed to her that François' manipulation of canon law smacked a little too much of expediency, and she preferred to await the papal dispensation. Her resistance, however, was overcome by her persuasive cousin, and the canonical requirements were hastily met before La Force appeared and locked the spouses up in their respective chambers. Next day the old marshal carried them, and also the Duchess Nicole, off to the ducal palace at Nancy. From there François wrote a letter to Richelieu informing him of his marriage, and signing it 'François Duc de Lorraine'. Richelieu was shocked. The conscience of the King would not permit that François and Claude be left together until the papal dispensation was received. Claude and Nicole should therefore be brought to Paris.

The Cardinal, however, was once more outmanoeuvred by the astute François. Before the removal of the princesses could be accomplished, the papal dispensation, rushed through by the Lorraine agents in Rome, and carried across Europe at breakneck speed, was placed in François' hands. To put the matter beyond all doubt, François dragged a parish priest out of bed and went through the form of marriage a second time at three o'clock in the morning. The French governor of Nancy, the Comte de Brassac, when informed of this, was so enraged that he pulled off his perruque and flung it on the ground. On 31 March 1634, late at night, François, his lovelocks gone, his head cropped, disguised as a valet, and accompanied by a real valet, walked past the French sentries on to the streets of Nancy. At the same time a gentleman of the Lorraine court passed the gatehouse accompanied by a page carrying a flaming torch. He was in a temper on account of some misdemeanour of the page, and amused the sentries by the way he scolded the youth, who seemed quite overwhelmed. The page was Claude, and she was also swallowed up in the darkness of Nancy. Not until midday the next day did Brassac, suspicious at the silence in the suite of the Lorrainers, investigate and discover that his charges had flown; and not for some weeks did Richelieu learn that they were in Florence with Christine of Lorraine, the Grand Duchess of Tuscany, and sister-in-law of Marie de Médicis.

The fugitives from the Houses of France and Lorraine were now leagued in a European-wide conspiracy against Louis XIII, which Spain was prepared to back in every possible way. The problem of Marie de Médicis and Gaston was a sufficient complication in Richelieu's delicate dealings with Urban VIII. Now it was made vastly more complex by the Pope's espousal of the cause of François, whom, as a Catholic prince, he considered to have been wronged. The terrible Charles of Lorraine, whose debaucheries and philanderings were a scandal in Catholic Europe, merited little sympathy from Urban, but François was an innocent to be protected. In all the subsequent diplomatic negotiations the issue of French recognition of François as Duke of Lorraine was to be prominent. The Spanish ambassador in Paris felt outraged. Feigning sickness he refused to speak to Père Joseph, packed his bags and went back to Madrid, having delivered an impassioned lecture to the nuncio, Bichi, on Richelieu's rogueries and spirit and intrigue. In Madrid Olivares exclaimed, 'We must reply to violence with violence!' He believed that Richelieu intended to occupy the whole Rhineland, and he renewed his efforts to create a European league to support Gaston.

Two months after the arrival in Belgium of Marguerite of Lorraine the Infanta Isabella died. Almost with her last breath she begged Gaston never to desert his mother, whom she pitied but did not respect. With her passing was removed the principal restraint to the ambitions of Olivares, who appointed as her successor one of his own creatures, the Marqués de Aytona. Henceforth the Spanish Netherlands was to be more directly ruled from Madrid and to lose much of its autonomy: even when Ferdinand the Cardinal-Infante was shortly afterwards made governor he was told to follow Aytona's instructions. This development was ominous to Gaston, who was now treated as a pensioner of Spain and not an honoured royal guest as he had been. The Spaniards made it quite clear that they trusted him as little as Richelieu did, and were watching his every move. Richelieu's policy was to detach Monsieur from his mother, whom he was determined to leave in Brussels, and entice him back to France and out of the Spanish clutches. By devious routes he was in touch with the Abbé d'Elbène and with Puylaurens. Whether the Spaniards detected this or not is unknown, but on 3 May 1634 someone tried to assassinate Puylaurens, and rightly or wrongly Gaston blamed his hosts. As Puylaurens ascended the staircase of the palais royal in Brussels with several cavaliers, twenty-five balls were discharged at him from an arquebus, and with blood pouring from a bullet wound in the cheek he gained the top of the stairs where he found Gaston with drawn sword.

Whether or not Olivares was an accomplice to the assassination attempt it is clear that he had already decided to make demands on Monsieur: the latter would accommodate himself more closely to Spanish policies in future, or he could expect trouble. Gaston was in a dilemma. If he returned to France at that moment it would be on Richelieu's terms, and these were unacceptable. Legal proceedings had been instituted before the Parlement of Paris for a declaration that his marriage was in violation of the fundamental law of the realm, and was invalid; and a Parliamentary inquiry had been instituted into the 'abduction of Monsieur by the Duke of Lorraine'. Although Louis was prepared to pardon his brother and restore him to his dignities and estates, he was adamant that he would not recognize the marriage. Gaston had sent a letter to Richelieu, reminding him of his 'favourable offices', and asking him to intervene with the King in the marriage affair. Richelieu had shown the letter to Louis and had replied graciously but in a noncommittal way.

Desperate, Gaston now succumbed to Spanish pressure, and on 12 May signed a treaty with Philip IV – the ratified copy of which fell into Richelieu's hands some months later when a Dutch ship forced a Spanish vessel to ground herself near Calais and a Spanish courier was arrested. It was a highly treasonable document. Gaston undertook not to treat with Louis without Spain's consent; in the event of war between France and Spain he was to take the side of Spain; and in the event of the Spanish army occupying France he was to cede to Spain certain French towns. In return, Spain undertook to provide twelve thousand troops for an invasion of France by Gaston, half of them to be Spanish and the other half French, plus three thousand horse: the invasion was projected for September 1634. Gaston would also be paid 70,000 francs for the raising of troops, and 45,000 crowns a month for their maintenance, and 15,000 for his own private expenses. Also found on the courier were full powers to Aytona to declare war on France should this become necessary.

16

The Logic of Commitment
1634

Richelieu was no more and no less than anyone else the creature of his time, and it is not to be expected that he would stand outside the established framework of ideas and strategy. The period of the Thirty Years War was one intermediate between one system of political organization and another. The feudal structure of Europe had broken down and had not yet been effectively replaced by the structure of the Enlightenment. The smaller states and vassal territories had lost the guarantees which feudal law and the pressures of morality had afforded, and international law was as yet too frail an instrument to substitute for it. Behind the façade of the Franco-Habsburg quarrel lay incompatible views on the future of the smaller states. It was the Habsburg ambition to achieve discipline and order in central Europe by reasserting and intensifying imperial authority so as to make of the Empire a unitary political tapestry; to the French the Empire was an organization of sovereign states whose political integrity was their primordial right. The French view was to prevail in the Peace of Westphalia, but, as in the case of the American Civil War, the validity of the constitutional arguments of each party could be determined only by the sword.

All political writers of the period believed that the problem of international peace was best resolved upon a theory of equilibrium.

France and the Habsburgs were seen as two poles evenly balanced. So long as the balance remained undisturbed the smaller border states, like Mantua or Lorraine, Savoy or Trier, were guaranteed, and it was axiomatic that any depression in the balance in one part of Europe had to be compensated for in another part if this guarantee was to be maintained. As Philippe de Béthune, the French ambassador in Rome, and a leading political theorist, wrote, 'The security of states consisting principally in an equal counterpoise of power, and the aggrandizement of one prince implying the ruination of his neighbours, it is wise to prevent it.'[1] Reflecting upon Richelieu's attempts to neutralize the Catholic states in Germany, he argued that neutralism is impossible of accomplishment, for a neutral state is hated by all its neighbours and can depend upon the protection of none of them; it is thus destined to disaster. Rohan, who in addition to being a general and a religious leader was one of the most eminent political philosophers of the time, also wrote that 'the equality of these two powers, France and Spain, supports all the others. These latter therefore have a paramount interest in maintaining it, for they would be easily overcome by whichever of the two remains superior to the other.'[2] Both writers exerted, we know, considerable influence on Richelieu's political convictions.

The theory of equilibrium appealed to an age attracted by scientific parallels in the realm of political and social ideas. The Spanish adventure in Montferrat was seen as a disturbance of equilibrium in Italy; Richelieu's retaliation reversed the thrust; the imperial entry into Vic and Moyenvic acted as the counterpoise to this. But at the end of 1632 the whole apparatus of equipoise had been overthrown by the French possession of Pinerolo in the south and of Trier, Ehrenbreitstein and parts of Lorraine in the north. French theorists naturally expected Habsburg counter-moves to restore the balance, but, since France wanted the struggle carried on vicariously by stipendiaries and pensioners, and as far away from her borderlands as possible, such moves had to be resisted by propping up the border states and extending the system of alliances. Spain became ever more convinced that the most effective method of opposing France was by the promotion of internal subversion and the crushing of French satellites, such as Trier, by overwhelming force. The time was rapidly approaching when the policy of struggle by proxy would be bankrupted, and it is evident that each side, without wanting general war, was being dragged by the logic of its position deeper and deeper into commitment.

Feria's army left Milan in August 1633 and marched over the Splügen Pass, down the cleft of the Upper Rhine to Chur, and after five weeks made its appearance at Lindau on Lake Constance, whence it proceeded along the northern shore, delaying for a short time while it cleared the Swedes out of certain fortified positions in southern Württemberg. Its arrival caused panic among the princelings who had territory on either side of the Rhine between Basle and Coblenz, and stimulated Richelieu to take measures to protect them. La Force, the conquest of Lorraine just completed, was reinforced with twelve new regiments, bringing his total army to twenty-two thousand men. For the moment he was ordered to remain west of the Vosges so as to give Feria no excuse for an invasion of the Duchy, but when the Duke of Württemberg asked for French protection for his County of Montbéliard, one of his Alsatian possessions, La Force entered it on 10 October. The advance guard of Feria's army made its appearance on the Alsatian bank of the Rhine two weeks later. In December the Count of Hanau-Lichtenberg also asked for French protection, placing Ingweiler, Neuweiler and Buchweiler in French hands. The Bishopric of Basle and the Abbey of Lüders followed suit, and then in January 1634 Count Salm, afraid of both the Swedish attack on Hagenau and of Feria's wrath, sought to save his territories by placing Hagenau in La Force's possession. Thus France had thrust towards the Rhine at both the southern and the northern ends of the Vosges.

Richelieu's Alsatian policy was entirely one of expediency. The local rulers had offered him a strategic advantage in this imperial territory, which would increase France's area of manoeuvrability. It was not his intention to attach Alsace permanently to France, for his concept of territorial sovereignty was legalistic and moralistic. German historians of the nineteenth century, preoccupied with the emotive issue of Alsace-Lorraine, saw Richelieu as the inventor of the theory that the Rhine was France's natural boundary, and the architect of a policy of French expansion to the river. The thesis has been hotly contested as well as defended. There were contemporaries of Richelieu who argued that France should occupy its natural limits, and one of them even sought to defend France's claims to Vic and Moyenvic on the argument that Caesar's Gaul extended to the Pyrenees, the Alps, the Rhine and the two oceans,[3] but there is no evidence that Richelieu based his policies on a geographical premise. His own statements of objective are delphic. On one occasion he referred to the ambition of Henri IV 'to make the Rhine the boundary of France, fortifying three or four places there'.[4] In the course of his celebrated policy statement on the eve of the first expedition to relieve Casale he proposed an advance to Strasbourg so as to acquire an entry into Germany. This was a year before the Emperor put troops into Vic and Moyenvic, although after it was known that Lorraine had asked for them. Does this indicate an aggressive intention on Richelieu's part which contradicts the thesis that his every move was in response to Habsburg encroachments? In view of his warning that such an advance implied 'lots of time, great discretion and quiet and disguised conduct'[5] it is clear that he was formulating, not an immediate policy of action, but a long-term objective.

Even then it is arguable that this objective was not predatory but restitutionary in character. Richelieu followed the prevailing argument of the lawyers that, since the Crown held territory only in trust for the nation, it could never lose it. Whatever rights the kings of France had in the borderlands were therefore still viable. On this argument Richelieu satisfied his conscience over the Pinerolo fraud, and on it he probably based his proposition to the Dutch that France and Holland should partition the Spanish Netherlands, France taking Artois, Hainault, Ostend and Luxembourg.[6] His memorandum on the invitations of the Alsatian rulers to occupy their territories discloses no ambition to supersede these in actual government, but only an ambition to resist the policy of the intensification of Habsburg power in territories which were as dubiously imperial as they were dubiously French.[7] 'The Emperor,' said Richelieu, 'under various pretexts of specious character, but without foundation, set about making himself master of Germany and subjecting it to an absolute monarchy, annulling the laws of the German nation on which the imperial authority is based.'[8] If the Habsburgs could manipulate the public law of Europe in this fashion so could Richelieu, who even went so far as to institute in 1641 an enquiry into the rights of the French monarchy in Milan, Naples, Sicily and Piedmont.[9] It may be that his policy was expansionist, but its generating principle was a legal one, and it did not matter how ancient the legal pretension was. The French delegates who tried to persuade Gustavus Adolphus not to cross the Rhine argued that the Rhine territories had been French from the time of King Dagobert. And in a work dedicated to Richelieu in 1632 Jacques de Cassan argued that the antiquity of rights cannot diminish their vigour, but on the contrary augments it.[10]

Richelieu's sense of insecurity in 1633 was due not only to the expectations he had of renewed Spanish support for Gaston d'Orléans, but also to his lack of confidence in France's allies, the Dutch, the Swedes and the German Protestants. He feared that all these might withdraw from the war, leaving France alone to face a Habsburg move to place Gaston on the throne. Both the Belgians and the Dutch were weary of the struggle, and there were moves afoot to negotiate peace between Brussels and The Hague. No one was sure that Oxenstierna would persist in Gustavus' policy, and if he did not do so the German Protestant movement would collapse. Already Saxony and Brandenburg, unwilling partners of Gustavus, were weakening after military reverses in Bohemia, and they were shortly to begin peace negotiations with the Emperor. To sustain the allies four energetic diplomatic missions were mounted in January 1633: Charnacé was sent to Holland with offers of further financial assistance to the Prince of Orange; Père Joseph's cousin, Manasses de Pas, Marquis de Feuquières, the prisoner of La Rochelle and now military governor of Vic and Moyenvic, was instructed to give similar encouragement to Oxenstierna and the German Protestants:

St Étienne was to renew his efforts to achieve the neutrality of Maximilian; and the Maréchal de Créqui, governor of Pinerolo, was to go to Rome and make yet another effort to persuade Urban VIII to join a defensive league of Italian states.

Scarcely had these missions departed when a Spanish mission arrived in Paris. The new ambassador was an arrogant man named Benevente y Benevides, who acted like another Borgia. At his first audience he made a categorical demand for reparation for the breaches of the Treaties of Regensburg and Cherasco, and he refused to discuss matters further until Richelieu put France's requirements into writing. To require a negotiator to place everything on paper is to require him to commit himself; thereby the area for manoeuvre is minimized. Richelieu, who could be as cold as stone or as agreeable as the sunshine according to the circumstances, aloofly replied that in France it was the custom to negotiate *viva voce*, and he was not prepared to depart from it. For a time there was an impasse. Père Joseph took Benevente aside for a stroll in the gardens at Fontainebleau, and in a shady corner tried to talk him into being reasonable, but to no avail. Eventually Bichi, the nuncio, intervened in order to get the discussions going again and persuaded Richelieu to make the concession which Benevente demanded. Richelieu prepared a superficial document, containing nothing new, reiterating the charge that the Treaty of Monzon had been constantly violated by Spain and requiring Spanish recognition of French sovereignty in Pinerolo. These were non-negotiable issues in Spanish eyes, and Benevente became violent, blaming Louis XIII for all the troubles in Europe. Richelieu drew the conclusion that negotiations with Spain were unavailing.

Olivares had long since drawn the reciprocal conclusion. Richelieu, he said, 'is so full of venom and devoid of ideas, just as is everything emanating from that Court.'[11] He told Barrault, the French ambassador, that Spain was far from reduced to impotence in face of France, and it would avenge itself. 'The Emperor,' he added, 'is also in a position to defend his honour and his interests, and if necessary he will penetrate into the heart of France.' This bullying was disquieting, and it disturbed the Pope

as much as it did Richelieu. Cardinal Barberini commented that
'neither the Emperor nor the King of Spain would agree to permit the King of France to re-establish peace in Germany, for they
are frightened that Louis XIII might enjoy an exaggerated influence there'. Richelieu summed up his feelings in an interview
with Bichi, in which he said: 'Have I not always said that the
Count-Duke had perverse intentions, and that he wished, not the
conclusion of peace, but the ruination of Christendom, and to
become master of all?'[12] The mission of Benevente had made
matters worse, and at a critical moment when the political and
military situation was changing rapidly it is tragic that France and
the Habsburgs ceased to comprehend each other's motives, and
even ceased to be able to continue the dialogue.

When Charnacé reached The Hague he quickly recognized that
his task of keeping Holland in the war would be a difficult one.
The Dutch had been receiving one million *livres* a year from
France, and had undertaken not to make peace without France's
consent. Charnacé was now instructed to raise the subsidy by
fifty per cent, to offer four thousand volunteer soldiers to assist the
Dutch army, and in case of need to reinforce the latter by a
French army of fourteen thousand. Already, then, early in 1633,
Richelieu was contemplating the possibility of intervening mas-
sively in the war. There was a violent struggle between the pro-
peace and pro-war factions in The Hague, which went on all
through 1633, and not until the end of the year did Charnacé's
efforts begin to show results. In December the delegates of the
Spanish Netherlands who had been negotiating peace terms were
ordered to leave The Hague, and in February 1634 Charnacé
was authorized to offer three million *livres* a year. This was
accepted and the Netherlands was kept in the war.

St Étienne's mission produced no result, for Maximilian was by
now too committed to the Habsburg cause by the Swedish
devastation of Bavaria to find any merit in a proposal that he
should head a third force in Germany. Créqui's mission to Rome
was no more successful. He arrived there in March 1633 and
made a splendid entry into the city. His fine speech, on the theme
of the loyalty of Louis XIII to the Holy See, was much admired,

but it was a disappointed man who reported to Richelieu that he no longer believed the Pope to be pro-French. 'It is true,' he said, 'that all these words which I have had with him are to the advantage of France. But when it comes to having any effect there are always obstacles which it is impossible to surmount.'[13]

Feuquières' instructions were to keep the Swedes and the German Protestants in close alliance, but to place their combined forces under some malleable German leader whom France could control. To this end he should contrive an allied high command, which would agree to regard the western bank of the Rhine as France's sphere of influence, and would avoid carrying the war there. Feuquières found Oxenstierna a man almost as obdurate as his late master. The Swedish Chancellor would make no commitment about the Rhine, was not at all conciliatory about the preservation of Catholicism in Germany, would not agree to a three months' truce with Bavaria so as to give St Étienne some chance of completing his mission, and made it quite clear that if he was not to have the supreme direction of the war he could withdraw his forces. The Protestant rulers were meeting in Heilbronn, and here Feuquières sought to gain two ends – to achieve a defensive alliance between France and the Protestants, and to support the latter in their resistance to Oxenstierna's claims to head the alliance. With remarkable skill Feuquières sought to arouse German fears of Swedish hegemony, but in April 1633 he was forced to concede defeat and sign on France's behalf a defensive alliance with the newly formed Heilbronn League, without gaining any concession from Oxenstierna save his undertaking to respect the Bärwalde conditions concerning Catholicism.

The news of this pact was received in papal circles with renewed dismay, for it was concluded at the very moment when the German Catholics were again being flayed. The Swedish general Horn and the ablest Protestant general, Bernard of Saxe-Weimar, whose object was to carve out a principality for himself, were ravaging southern Germany, and Maximilian was again invoking the Treaty of Fontainebleau. The Treaties of Heilbronn and Fontainebleau were in spirit if not in terms incompatible, and Maximilian, disgusted with France, threw himself finally and completely into the arms of Spain. In August Père Joseph was agitated by reports that his brother Capuchins in Frankfurt, Mainz, Speyer and Augsburg were suffering at the hands of the Swedes, and Feuquières was instructed to recall to Oxenstierna his engagement at Heilbronn to respect Catholicism. A gentleman of the Court, Varennes, was also sent to the Swedish Chancellor to say that 'the King believes it to be in our common interest not to give any excuse for contending that this is a war of religion, as one would have us believe'. Bichi was scandalized by the Protestant alliance, and finding Richelieu again ill in bed told him bluntly that his sickness was an act of Providence. Richelieu replied that Spain had forced him to ally with the heretics, and argued that a Catholic prince always has the right to assure the independence of his state, and for this purpose to seek the alliance of sovereigns differing in religion.

Saxony and Brandenburg had held aloof from the Heilbronn negotiations, and Feuquières was instructed to go to Dresden and Berlin with offers of separate alliances and money. With Saxony the mission was a complete failure, but Feuquières had temporary encouragement in Brandenburg. Here the Catholic minister of the Calvinist ruler of a Lutheran state, Schwarzenberg, happened to be sympathetic to France. Brandenburg felt isolated in Germany and needed French support to achieve some independence of action. But the Elector had an interest in the Pomeranian succession question, and in the end chose by remaining aloof not to compromise his credit with either side. Richelieu's German policy of creating a counterpoise to Vienna was recognized even by himself to have utterly failed, and after the middle of 1633 the Cardinal virtually abandoned his diplomatic offensives in Germany and concentrated on consolidating the French position on the left bank of the Rhine and on maintaining French influence within the Heilbronn League.

He was also drawn into an attempt to suborn Wallenstein, who had been put into communication with Feuquières. Wallenstein wanted to know what protection Louis XIII would give him, what conduct was expected of him, and against whom and where he should march his army. When Feuquières reported these astonishing overtures to Richelieu a council meeting was held, and instructions were sent to Feuquières which were encouraging to the conspirators. Should Wallenstein raise the standard of revolt against the Emperor, France would support his pretensions to the throne of Bohemia. By the time he was in possession of these instructions Feuquières had formed the impression that Wallenstein was playing, not a double, but a triple game, and that he was a man whose mind, resolution and grip on reality were in decay, and he privately resolved to handle him with caution. There followed some occult communications and then the affair was suddenly over. Wallenstein had been discovered, and in the house of the Burgomaster of Eger he was ignominiously done to death on 25 February 1634.

Wallenstein's death was almost as much of a sensation as that of Gustavus Adolphus. There was astonishment at the revelation of his treason, mingled with relief that he had been discovered in time. Olivares seized the occasion to push the Emperor into declaring war on France, and pretended to be scandalized when he refused. Ferdinand, in fact, was quite conciliatory, telling the Spaniards that he was prepared to recognize French sovereignty over Pinerolo if France would leave the Valtelline open. The death of Feria in Munich on 11 January 1634 meant that two of the leading imperial generals had been removed, and this checked all action for a time. On 13 April, therefore, the Spanish Council of State decided to postpone a declaration of war on France. It was in this month that Charnacé's year-long efforts ended in the renewal of the Franco-Dutch alliance. The new treaty was kept a close secret, but in July the Spanish arrested a courier sent from the Prince of Orange and the States General to the Dutch ambassador in Paris, and on him was found a copy of it. Olivares affected to discover in this a concerted Franco-Dutch plan to attack Dunkirk, Gravelines and Mardyck, though in fact no such plan existed, and again laid the evidence of Richelieu's villainy in triumph before the Pope. The effect of this was somewhat mitigated by a French disclosure. When Bichi came to say farewell to Richelieu on his recall to Rome the Cardinal produced a copy of the treaty which Gaston and Philip iv had made on 12 May, and Bichi took this to the Pope as evidence that virtue was not all on the Spanish side.

The renewal of the Dutch alliance coincided with a meeting of the Heilbronn League at Frankfurt, where Feuquières found himself in a key position. Oxenstierna's domination of the cause had bred resentment among princes who had no wish to substitute one master for another, and his control over the united armies had begun to weaken as Bernard of Saxe-Weimar became more self-assertive; he was also confronted with a mutiny which demonstrated to all Sweden's allies the extent to which Swedish power had declined since Gustavus' death. Feuquières offered the Heilbronn League greatly augmented French assistance if the members would agree to place under French control the fortress of Philippsburg, which had recently been taken from the Spaniards by Swedish troops, who had then garrisoned it. It was his hope that Oxenstierna would find himself unable to refuse without provoking a breach with the Heilbronn League: either France would gain control of the fortress or it would break Oxenstierna's leadership of the cause. The Heilbronn League, however, was not as ready to make concessions to France as Richelieu expected, and by July the Cardinal had almost reconciled himself to getting nothing more significant out of the Protestants than Colmar.

Suddenly, in the late summer of 1634 the military situation became critical. Philip IV's brother, Ferdinand the Cardinal-Infante with an army of twenty thousand men reached Lake Constance from Italy and began clearing the Black Forest. The Emperor's son, the King of Hungary, had taken the supreme command of the imperial armies after Wallenstein's death, and he began to move at the same time along the Danube to cut the communications of Horn and Bernard of Saxe-Weimar, who had an army, also of twenty thousand men, near Augsburg. Regensburg, which Horn had taken a few months previously, opened its gates to the imperialists, and the latter continued their advance up the Danube, while the Cardinal-Infante proceeded down it to meet them. As the gap between them narrowed, the Protestant army retreated across the river to the north bank. It seems to have been at this moment that Richelieu privately concluded that it would be necessary to go to war with Spain. When Donauwörth fell to the Emperor, all resistance of the Heilbronn League to Richelieu's demands collapsed, and on 26 August 1634 the League members agreed to hand Philippsburg over to France. When this was reported to Richelieu he wrote on 11 September to Feuquières instructing him to inform the League that French forces would enter Germany in May 1635. This dispatch had just left Paris when news arrived of the destruction of Horn and Bernard. At Nördlingen, north of the Danube, they had rashly tried to interfere with the junction of the Cardinal-Infante and the King of Hungary. Outnumbered by fifty per cent they were systematically demolished on 6 September 1634 by the Spanish *tercios*, leaving between twelve and seventeen thousand dead on the field, and Horn and six thousand other prisoners, most of whom joined the imperial service.

The almost total destruction of the two principal armies holding the field against the Emperor was as much a matter for alarm in Paris as in Frankfurt or Uppsala. Richelieu went immediately to discuss the matter with the King. Next day he had a conference with Père Joseph, at which it was agreed that there was now no alternative to a French declaration of war, although this could be postponed until the following spring. Three members of the council were then called in, Bullion, Séguier, and Bouthillier, and they supported the decision. A total army of ninety-five thousand men would be raised; the Heilbronn League would immediately be furnished with fourteen thousand men provided it would undertake to capture Breisach, the important fortress which controlled traffic on the Upper Rhine, and hand it over to the French. Dispatches were then drafted to Feuquières setting out under what terms France would agree to enter into closer relationships with the Heilbronn League: she would have an equal voice with Sweden and the League in the political as well as in the military direction of the war: guarantees respecting Catholicism were required. As it happened matters were taken out of Feuquières' hands by the arrival in Paris of Jacob Löffler, Oxenstierna's delegate, and Philip Streif von Lauenstein, councillor of the Count Palatine of Zweibrücken and delegate of the League.

They were to seek a French declaration of war, or at least the dispatch of troops to their aid.

The two envoys found Richelieu standoffish and disposed to negotiate only on his own terms. Louis XIII they found even more difficult. He said he would refuse to treat with them at all unless the Protestants undertook to give reparation for the damage they had caused to Catholicism. Löffler and Streif were in anguish at this reception, and on 1 November 1634, after a very short negotiation, they signed a treaty in which they yielded to all Richelieu's demands. France did not commit herself to war, but gained equal voice in the Protestant councils and the delivery into French hands of the places held by the Swedes in Alsace. Catholicism was to be restored in all states where it had enjoyed liberties before 1618. The treaty struck Sweden hard, for it deprived it of the supreme direction of the war and of the disposition of the French subsidies, and when Löffler and Streif brought the instrument to Worms, where Oxenstierna was meeting with the Heilbronn League, there was a crisis. Löffler was dismissed and Oxenstierna announced he would refuse ratification in the name of the infant Queen Christina of Sweden: most of the German Protestant delegates recognized, however, that they had no alternative but to accept France's terms.

Oxenstierna withdrew from Worms, but he quickly found that events were throwing him into Richelieu's hands. In order to consolidate his garrison troops in a new army he had to hand over the Alsatian positions to La Force, and to concede the latter's entry into the Palatinate, whose delegate, afraid of the withdrawal of the Swedes and the impending arrival of the Cardinal-Infante, asked for French protection. On 15 November 1634 Bavarian and imperial troops laid siege to the Palatinate capital, Heidelberg. Feuquières was instructed to withhold French support for its relief until the ratifications of the Treaty of Paris had come in, and he was given complete authority to order La Force to act when he was satisfied that the political conditions had been fulfilled. Oxenstierna and Bernard of Saxe-Weimar tried to persuade Feuquières to act promptly in order that France would be committed to war. It became a question of whose resolution would weaken first, for Heidelberg's security was no less vital to France than to the League. It was Feuquières not Oxenstierna who weakened, for early in December, without waiting for the Swedish ratification, he ordered six thousand French troops to advance from Mannheim to raise the siege. When the imperialists withdrew from before Heidelberg he then recalled the French on to the western bank of the Rhine, whereupon the imperialists returned and renewed the siege. By this time all the princes of the League had ratified the treaty, but the cities and the Swedes resisted. To increase the pressure on the latter Feuquières withheld the French subsidies, but again he was forced to weaken and order the French across the Rhine. On Christmas Eve La Force and Brézé relieved Heidelberg and began to march up the Necker. Richelieu was carrying the struggle deep into Germany.

The strategic conception of equipoise was now to be demonstrated. As the French left wing thrust forward, the imperialist left wing did likewise, so pivoting the whole front on the junction of the Saar and Alsace. Charles of Lorraine, with an imperial army, crossed the Rhine at Breisach, thrust through northern Alsace, and surprised the French in Philippsburg. By the beginning of 1635 he was in Speyer. At the same moment the Spaniards in Luxembourg advanced on to the Moselle and entered Trier, where they took prisoner the Elector, Philip von Sötern. The French army on the Necker had to return to Mannheim, where it contemplated with none too much satisfaction its principal lines of communication in enemy hands. Early in April Charles of Lorraine began a systematic occupation of Alsace as a preliminary to a triumphal return to his own Duchy. La Force was ordered to expel him, but considering his troops to be too exhausted he retired as far as Metz. Richelieu had committed himself to belligerency, and there was now no retreat for him.

17

The King's Reputation

1634-5

Hugo De Groot, or Grotius as he called himself, was one of the savants of the age, and traditional father of international law. In fact De Groot the man of history and Grotius the genius of legend are almost two different people. Born in Holland in 1584 he was a prodigy and bookworm who published Latin verses in infancy and expounded encyclopedic knowledge in his youth. He was a doctor of laws at fifteen, having already defended theses on mathematics, philosophy and jurisprudence, and he pleaded his first case at the bar at the age of sixteen. At the age of nineteen, with published Latin tragedies behind him, he was official historian of the States General and at twenty-four Advocate General of Holland. Like other infant prodigies, however, his knowledge was disorganized and his self-esteem considerable; his enormous reputation was due to immense industry which enabled him to reinforce his writings with a crushing weight of academic authority and precedent; and it was this reputation which gave him his pre-eminent place in the science of international law.

In 1619 Grotius became involved in a political and religious schism in Holland, and found himself condemned to life imprisonment in Lovenstein castle. His indulgent jailers allowed him to import books by the trunkload, which, after their contents had been devoured, were returned to the libraries. One day

303

in 1621 the trunk went out of Lovenstein with Grotius inside instead of the books. Shortly afterwards he appeared in Paris, and there he wrote his most famous work, *De jure belli ac pacis*, which he published in 1625 with a dedication to Louis XIII. Its hallmark is eclecticism, its ideas were extensively borrowed from the writings of the Spanish Jesuit Francisco Suarez, and it is philosophically confused. But it revolutionized the society of nations and assisted in transforming it from a bear-garden into a system of relationships which, if it did not abolish war, at least made human survival more likely. Gustavus Adolphus was immensely taken with the work, being of a bric-à-brac turn of mind himself, and dragged the massive tome with him wherever he went. It did very little to modify his conduct of the war, but, like the Bible which accompanied it, it furnished him with material for endless discourse with foreign ambassadors.

The book had just appeared when the paths of Richelieu and Grotius first crossed. It has been supposed, without much evidence, that the two men took an instant dislike to each other. Perhaps it was no more than the usual case of the jealousy of scholars, perhaps it was the intolerance of conceit in others that opinionated men often have, but, whatever it was, it seems that they failed to get on, and in 1631 Grotius left Paris because the pension granted to him by Louis XIII was unpaid. Three years later, when he was fretting in Hamburg without his books, he made contacts which led to his being employed by Oxenstierna. Now, at the end of 1634, when Oxenstierna hoped to get a better bargain out of Richelieu than Löffler had managed, he appointed Grotius as ambassador to Paris.

When Richelieu heard the news he shuddered, and presumably he vented his feelings to the King, for we find Louis writing to Feuquières that 'no one will treat with Sieur Grotius, and he will be promptly sent home after his first audience'.[1] Obstinacy, however, was a characteristic of both Oxenstierna and Grotius, and the latter arrived in Paris, and survived there as ambassador for nine years, despite Richelieu's reiterated demands for his recall. He believed, and rightly so, that the French reverses in Alsace, the loss of Philippsburg, and the imminence of a peace between

Saxony and the Emperor would make Richelieu a little less intractable, and secure for Sweden much better terms than Löffler had been able to obtain. Oxenstierna in fact hoped to push France into war; and there is something to be savoured in the situation of the founder of international law and a cardinal of the Church engaged in ruthless bargaining to extend a war which had already magnified almost without parallel every human depravity, cannibalism not excluded.

Grotius had to wait nearly a month for his first audience with the King; it is clear that Richelieu was anxious to avoid having to negotiate with him at all, and he was told that he had no powers to discuss the question of a treaty. His treatment was in contrast with that accorded to the Dutch envoys who were settling the details of the new alliance with France when Grotius made his appearance in Paris. The court was preoccupied with balls and spectacles in their honour, and both the King and Richelieu were engaged in their planning, as if they were unaware that their country was on the eve of a war which they both knew would squander its resources. Louis XIII himself wrote and produced his Ballet of the Blackbird, and the *Gazette de France* of 22 March 1635 recorded that he 'devised the dance figures, the music, and designed the costumes', though he 'hardly spent more hours than the number of days normally required to compose the ballet'. The hunting of the blackbird with falcons was one of the King's favourite distractions. In the first *entrée* two lackeys entered carrying caged falcons, and in the subsequent *entrées* they were followed by the *chef de vol*, the chief falconer, his aide and two pages, and Louis himself in the role of the wife in female costume of Master Pierre of the Cross of Lorraine, dealer in lures and little bells. He was followed at the fifth *entrée* by Thomas the Butcher, whose function was to feed the falcons, and at the sixth by the crossbow carrier, the *porteur d'émerillons*, who carried the special small falcons which were used to catch blackbirds, and the *porte merles descapés* carrying captured blackbirds. The hunters, of absurdly antiquated manners, made their *entrée* to an old-fashioned gavotte, and Spring announced the end of the hunting season:

Me voici dessus l'horizon
Où je viens rajeunir le Monde
Je fais voir la belle saison
Qui réjouit la terre et l'onde . . .
[L'hiver] . . . me voyant fuit ce séjour
Où je viens établir l'empire de l'amour

Finally in the *grand ballet* riders on horseback performed, at the conclusion of which the performers stepped forth to invite the ladies to join in the dance, which then became a ball. The first performance was given at Chantilly on 15 March 1635, followed by a second at Royaumont two days later.

When Grotius finally managed an audience with the King he was received with the barest formalities and in a strikingly unfriendly fashion, Louis, apparently impromptu, expressing his astonishment that another nation should presume to dictate to him:

I believe I am free to dispose of my money and my troops! If the Catholics are not permitted to practise their religion nothing is possible between us; I am not hostile to anyone on account of religion, for mine is dear to me, as yours is to you, but I am not able to disinterest myself in the question.[2]

On 14 March Grotius met Léon Bouthillier and Père Joseph at the convent of the Capuchins, adjacent to the Tuileries, and debated with them the law of treaties. This time Père Joseph was on the other side of the Regensburg argument. He contended that, since Löffler had signed a treaty which did not reserve ratification, but which, on the contrary, recited Oxenstierna's full powers, the treaty was binding on Sweden. Grotius, whose mind ran alike to precedent and a touch of malice, recalled the disavowal of the Regensburg Treaty. Père Joseph was piqued. He protested that before signing that engagement he and Brûlart had taken care to point out that several of the terms exceeded their powers, and he could produce evidence of this. Grotius retaliated by arguing that Löffler had done likewise. Père Joseph then accused the Swedes of having diverted the French subsidies intended for the Heilbronn League, and at this Grotius expressed indignation. Tempers became frayed, and Père Joseph threatened to report Grotius to Oxenstierna, to refuse to have any further dealings with him, and to have Feuquières protest to the Heilbronn League against violation by the Swedes of their engagements. When Grotius remained obdurate Père Joseph tried conciliation, but to no avail. The meeting broke up and the Capuchin reported to Richelieu that there was nothing to be done with a faithless ally, and to Feuquières that it was useless trying to talk to a man as obstinate as Grotius.

Two weeks later Grotius and the Cardinal came face to face, and there was almost a repetition of the scene. Père Joseph was present, and when he and Grotius fell into an argument Richelieu had to intervene, saying, 'Come, come, I see that you and the reverend father do not understand one another.'³ Grotius replied that Oxenstierna himself would come to Paris to conduct the negotiations. The Cardinal had nothing to say to this except that the Swedish Chancellor would be very welcome, but that a meeting with him would do more harm than good unless it was based on a revision of the Treaty of Paris. In the midst of the discussions despatches arrived from Germany announcing that Oxenstierna was on his way to Paris. On 2 April he left Worms with a suite of two hundred, including the generals, cooks, smiths, tailors, grooms and secretaries necessary to support his dignity as Regent of Sweden. At the head of his cortège as it lurched across Lorraine to the burgeoning poplars of the Marne were the *maître d'hôtel*, trumpeters, drummers and cavalry; and the impact made on the popular imagination by the frightening Swede whom no one knew whether to take as friend or enemy is recorded in the nursery verse recited to recalcitrant children:

> *Prie, petit enfant, prie,*
> *Autrement viendra le suédois,*
> *Autrement viendra Oxenstiern.*
> *Il trouvera le moyen de te faire prier.*

The bogy disturbed the nights of the Cardinal as well as of the children of France. On 22 April, when Oxenstierna was nearing Vitry-le-François, Richelieu called Père Joseph, Bouthillier and

Charnacé into conference to discuss the news from Germany and 'see what they could do' about negotiating with Oxenstierna in the light of it.[4] In fact events were placing Richelieu in the hands of the Swedish Chancellor, though the latter was unprepared for the conciliatory reception which was being planned for him. The news of the loss of Philippsburg had been received in Paris with dismay and disgust, and Richelieu had written to La Force that he was 'extremely vexed'.[5] Then the Saxons had disclosed an imperial plan to go to war with France. Now the Spanish arrest of the Elector of Trier, which took place on 26 March, was a shocking affront as well as a strategic defeat. As soon as the news of it reached Paris Louis XIII ordered his carriage and hurried to Richelieu's château at Rueil to consult with him. A council was called, at which Gaston d'Orléans, recently returned from Brussels, resumed his seat, and it was resolved that the 'King cannot avoid taking arms to avenge the affront which he has received by the imprisonment of a prince who has been placed under his protection'.[6]

Grotius set out to meet Oxenstierna at Soissons, missed him and was eventually located by a Swedish search party, which conducted him to the Chancellor at Meaux. At Crépy-en-Valois the Swedes purchased quantities of plumed hats, gloves and hose so as to smarten themselves for their appearance at Compiègne where the King and Richelieu awaited them, and near Compiègne on 26 April they encountered the French *chef de protocol*, the Comte de Bruslon, with several royal carriages to be placed at Oxenstierna's disposal. At the gates of Compiègne Oxenstierna was met by the civic dignitaries, and he made his entry through crowded and decorated streets. The principal houses of the town had been requisitioned for the Swedes, and that allotted to Oxenstierna had been richly furnished. Here Richelieu's cousin, the Marquis de la Meilleraye, greeted the Chancellor on behalf of the King, and a committee of local notables presented valuable gifts as well as cordial greetings.

Next day Oxenstierna paid his official call on the King, Grotius acting as interpreter. The changed mood of the French government was indicated by the fact that the King's own carriage was provided for the occasion, and that Louis greeted Oxenstierna as 'cousin'. The audience lasted half an hour, and then Oxenstierna called on Richelieu. He was received by the Cardinal's guard in scarlet and met at the door by the Cardinal, who even permitted him to precede him into the house. No business was discussed, and Richelieu was at his most charming, trading witticisms and felicitations in Latin. It was during Richelieu's return call the following day that the question of the treaty came up. The Cardinal found the Chancellor to be just what he expected, a man who negotiated in a 'gothic' fashion.[7] Mutual need drove both parties to a rapid agreement after only three hours of discussion, and Richelieu immediately left Compiègne, apparently because he wished to have no further relations with the 'cunning' Swede. At Monchay he drafted detailed instructions for a treaty, and within twenty-four hours Oxenstierna, his mission accomplished, and a ring on his finger worth 60,000 *livres* which the King had given him at his farewell audience, began his return journey to Germany, with some incognito sightseeing in Paris on the way. By the Treaty of Compiègne which Richelieu and Oxenstierna had negotiated, both parties undertook to assist the evangelical party in Germany by recourse to arms; neither would conclude a separate peace or armistice; and the usual provisions about Catholicism were incorporated, except that the Swedes might retain the episcopal revenues in the territories held by them. There is some indication in Richelieu's correspondence of his vexation at having to yield on the question of supreme French direction of the war, and at his distaste of an alliance forced upon him by necessity and at which he took no pleasure. The deed was done and there remained only the question of an ultimatum to Spain.

On 16 May 1635 the French herald Gratiollet left Neuchâtel-sur-Aisne with the declaration of war, and arrived at Brussels three days later. He appeared before the gates of the city in his heraldic tabard, with the fleurs-de-lys of France quartered with the chains of Navarre, and with his floppy herald's cap on his head and his baton in his hand. Accompanying him was the trumpeter-in-ordinary of the King, who proceeded to blow *chamades* in the customary fashion. The burgomaster of Brussels, accompanied by the King of Arms of the Low Countries, the latter wearing the robes of the Golden Fleece, hastened to the gates, and Gratiollet formally demanded audience of the Cardinal-Infante, who was the new governor of Belgium. The burgomaster tried to persuade him to leave his regalia at the gates, and, when Gratiollet refused, he departed leaving him to make his entry into Brussels unattended.

There now followed a ludicrous episode. Gratiollet was instructed to make a solemn declaration of war, but could find no one to whom to issue it. His insistence on an audience with the Cardinal-Infante met with requests to wait, which were repeated hour by hour until evening. In fact the Cardinal-Infante had summoned his council to discuss whether or not he was obliged to give audience to the herald, and the debate seems to have dragged on until Gratiollet, weary of waiting, rode down to the Place du Sablon and, as he reported, tossed the declaration of war 'to the winds'. There was a large crowd of curious Belgians there, and two Flemish heralds, who apparently had been shadowing Gratiollet, cried to the people 'with all the force of their lungs' not to pick up the parchment.[8] Gratiollet thereupon forced his horse through the crowd, followed by his trumpeter, and left Brussels. On the way he was surprised by a carriage blazoned with the arms of France and Navarre, which he himself was wearing, and recognizing the occupant as Marie de Médicis – no doubt as surprised as he at the encounter – he doffed his velvet cap with heraldic flourish and went his way. At the frontier next morning he affixed a copy of the declaration to a post, made *chamades* with the trumpet to a single goggle-eyed peasant whom he dragged out of a church for the purpose, and crossed into France. It was the last time that a declaration of war was to be made with heraldic ceremonial.

A Belgian official, Vincart, who wrote an account of the year's events, describes Gratiollet as a 'so-called herald' who could produce no credentials; and it seems from this that the Cardinal-Infante's excuse for not receiving Gratiollet was that there was

The face of the papacy.
Urban VIII. By Andrea
Sacchi. Badgered by the
Spaniards, misinformed
about Richelieu, this
baroque pontiff strove
nobly to preserve peace.

The face of the Lion.
Gustavus Adolphus.
The bust carved in
Nuremburg by Hans
von der Putt after the
Swedish king, having
broken Richelieu's
leash, had descended
apocalyptically on
Catholic Europe.

The face of the fractious.
Gaston, Duc d'Orléans. By Van
Dyke. Brother of the King, his
vindictiveness and jealousy led
him into repeated rebellion and
treason, and finally brought
France and Spain into mortal
combat.

Grand banquet of the Knights of
the Holy Ghost in the presence
of the King. By Bosse.
Richelieu, newly consolidated in
power after the Day of Dupes is
at the head of the table on the
left.

no proof that he was not a fraud. Spain did not declare war until August.

The declaration, if anyone on the Spanish side ever removed it from the post, read:

I am summoned here on the part of the King my master, my one and sovereign lord, to inform you as follows: Since you have failed to release the Archbishop of Trier, Elector of the Holy Empire, who had placed himself under his protection, when he was unable to receive it from the Emperor or any other prince; and since contrary to the dignity of the Empire and the law of nations you are holding as prisoner a sovereign prince with whom you are not at war; now therefore His Majesty declares that he is resolved to avenge this offence by force of arms, for it is of concern to all the princes of Christendom.[9]

It was a declaration addressed to Spain only, and efforts were made to limit it to Spain. To Maximilian of Bavaria it was stated that the attack on the Bavarians at Heidelberg had been made only because they were assisting the rebel Charles of Lorraine. If Bavaria should turn against the Emperor, France would supply twenty-three thousand troops to help it. Needless to say this overture fell on deaf ears.

The French decision to declare war had been opposed with all possible vigour by Urban VIII and his agents, particularly Mazarin who was then in Paris on a special mission. Louis XIII had agreed in principle to a peace congress under papal auspices, and until the arrival of Oxenstierna in Paris Ferdinand had avoided any steps which might make this impossible. On 7 April a letter arrived in Madrid from Ferdinand asking Philip IV to name plenipotentiaries. Philip secretly instructed the Cardinal-Infante to do so, provided France and the Emperor both did so, but made it clear that he none the less expected and wanted war. He wrote: 'If in the year which has just passed we had disturbed the French to the slightest extent in their own country, the imperialists would without difficulty have reconquered the Empire. If this year the war is not taken into their own country, everything will be finally lost.'[10] He told Vienna that, since there was no chance of France's participating in a congress, action and not talk was necessary. The

Emperor was urged to make peace with Saxony so that the imperial army would be free to act against France. Poor Ferdinand, for ever a prey to conscience, was having a disturbing time. Father Quiroga, his daughter-in-law's confessor, and a violent Espanophil, told him he would mortally sin if he failed to conclude peace with the Saxons. The papal nuncio and his own confessor Lamormaini said this was nonsense. Ferdinand set up a commission of twenty-four theologians to go into the question, and acting on their decision he agreed to make peace with the Saxon heretics at Prague on 30 May 1635. The most important Protestant power thus withdrew from the war ten days after France entered it.

The more belligerent members of the Spanish Council of State rejoiced at the French declaration of war because now the Emperor would have to take action against Louis XIII, but their satisfaction was not shared by Olivares, who, despite his pugnacious remarks, would never, in the opinion of the English ambassador in Madrid, of his own accord 'break with France'.[11] Already involved in a struggle with the Catalans and the clergy over military taxation and billeting, dismayed at his declining resources and the continuing inflation, he had shrunk from the fatal decision. The outbreak of war was in fact followed by public and secret negotiations for peace between Olivares and Richelieu, and by renewed efforts of Mazarin to call a peace conference. This suggestion was anathema to Sweden, and Mazarin and Grotius came into collision. The latter reported to Sweden that Mazarin would tell any tale to detach France from Sweden, and had even gone so far as to attest that the Habsburgs had in fact nominated plenipotentiaries.

Richelieu had not been alone in making the decision to go to war; it was the unanimous decision of the council, a body not as subservient to the Cardinal as has been supposed, and one quite capable of independent judgement. It was a decision which he had tried desperately to postpone for personal as well as national reasons. His health had broken down regularly in recent years under the strain of office; he had been more or less seriously ill ever since the anxious year when Gustavus Adolphus rampaged through Germany; and he seriously doubted if he could withstand the additional pressures of a major war. He no longer felt young, he was a worrier, and already every moment of his life was occupied. War would be a serious, perhaps fatal, interruption of the task of transforming and consolidating France; and as Bullion, the capable intendant of finances, warned him, the cost would wreak havoc with the economy and the fiscal system. Gloomily he told Mazarin that he would have given half his fortune or an arm to have avoided war.[12]

Once convinced of the necessity of war, however, Richelieu did not shrink from it. His whole training, and the intellectual environment of his time, justified him. History played the mannerist role in politics which eclecticism played in literature and art; it was part of the humanistic approach to affairs; and it demonstrated to Richelieu that a state which is not prepared to defend its honour is inevitably lost. Two concepts play an almost mystical role and have the character of moral goods in his doctrine, that of national repose and that of national grandeur: 'Man's greatest obligation is the saving of his soul'; that of kings is 'the repose of their subjects, the conservation of the state as a whole, and the reputation of their government'.[13] This concept of reputation dominates Richelieu's thinking. 'The slightest loss of this kind,' he wrote, 'means that a great prince has nothing else to lose.'[14] In considering whether or not Richelieu was the slippery, untrustworthy politician that tradition has represented him to be, it is necessary to recall that he would act in no way to diminish France or Louis' honour. True, he was devious, but his reputation for deviousness surpassed that of contemporaries because he showed greater cleverness, determination, and subtlety than they. He always gave himself the benefit of the doubt, but he did not deliberately flout his engagements.

There is in Richelieu's writings a hard-headed approach to human affairs, that coexists in a state of tension with the moral directives to his conscience. In this respect he was, again, a man of his time. It was an age of little faith in human goodness, and though Richelieu was far from being a jansenist he was not a little infected by the jansenists' scepticism about natural virtue. He was pessimistic about humanity, convinced that the evils of the age derived from fallen nature and a consequent propensity to sin. Freedom in the early seventeenth century meant in practice licence, and therefore freedom in theory had to give place to the concept of order, a notion which appears more often than any other in Richelieu's writings. In national and international affairs this approach gave rise to a double moral standard. 'There is a difference,' he wrote, 'between civil and political prudence, and this is so great that the moral order really makes two separate virtues of them.'[15] And again:

> In the course of ordinary affairs justice requires clarity and evidence of proof. But it is not the same when one is concerned with affairs of state, where one is dealing with the *summa rerum*, for often conjectures must stand in place of proof, considering that great designs and important undertakings can never be verified except by their success or outcome, which is beyond remedy.[16]

Such was Richelieu's moral position as a statesman. He recognized that it was a position of danger, for exaggerated emphasis on the moral good of the state could result in eliminating the moral good of the individual. A balance had to be struck between the two goods, and this required a judicious and penetrating judgement. For mediocre spirits the way of Richelieu, so he himself said, was the way to tyranny, and for this reason mediocre spirits had to be kept out of politics.[17] It goes without saying that Richelieu was not a mediocre spirit; at the same time this dictum explains why he considered himself indispensable to France.

This theory of the morality of statecraft, with its emphasis on the benefit of the doubt, accommodated itself readily to the theory of the just war, which figured prominently in Catholic writings of the period. A contemporary of Richelieu, Le Bret, wrote that 'undertakings must be judged just or unjust according to the utility or the harm which the state derives from their execution'.[18] The problem of determining whether an action is moral or immoral was resolved by almost all contemporary theologians on a formula known as 'probabilism'. According to this it was permissible to follow a solidly based opinion in favour of liberty of action, even though the opposing view might be the more probably correct one. The jansenists considered that probabilism led to laxity, and their opposition to Richelieu's war with Spain had its ethical basis in their resistance to the 'benefit of the doubt' theory. Their voices were added to those of the Catholic zealots in a frenzied protest. Richelieu commented that 'such opinions, founded on reasons of piety, and full of reasonable doubts and fears on all sides show clearly what strength and firmness of courage were necessary to maintain the King's reputation in the matter, and to end the affair with conditions that would be glorious for France'.[19]

Violent disagreement about the morality of public action is a recurrent phenomenon in the history of Catholicism. Once it is conceded that the moral system imposes restraints upon political activity, dispute is easily generated about whether or not the politicians have overstepped the boundary. From the same moral premise widely divergent opinions can be derived as the ethical norm is applied in concrete circumstances. There will always be a Catholic party disposed to see events in the simple terms of black and white; the enemy is defined as he who is intent on the overthrow of Catholicism or of the moral order, and there can be no truck with him at any level. Attempts will be made to drag the Church institutionally into opposing policies which in any way accommodate the devil; and political issues, such as recognition of a government deemed to be intrinsically evil, participation with it in international conferences, even trade with it, cease to be morally neutral. Catholics who fail to concede the compulsive requirements of religion and ethics in these matters, and who prefer to retain a degree of political manoeuvrability and subtlety, are apt to be denounced as more unregenerate than the enemy itself. So it was with Richelieu. From Olivares down to the Left-Bank scribblers Richelieu was the betrayer of Christ, the Judas of his age.

18

Await the King's Grace

1635

France began the war at a serious disadvantage. The enemy was tactically poised on the Moselle, the Meuse, the Saal and in the Vosges, and held command of the sea on the Mediterranean littoral. The reconstruction of the French army which Richelieu had undertaken was incomplete; the Code Michaud, the important reform document which dealt with every department of government in France, dedicated a section to army administration, but it was not really effective. The recruitment was antiquated, being rooted in the system of medieval levies, reinforced heavily with employment of mercenaries, and the commissariat was primitive. Richelieu wrote of the latter:

In 1631 we found to our cost that it was necessary to have a single commissariat for all the armies. We need at court a man of high rank, living on the spot, who could exercise the general supervision of supplies. The supervision of supplies must be in the hands of people of rank, whose vigilance, loyalty and capacity is known, since thereupon depends the subsistence of the armies, and quite often even of the state.[1]

The system functioned badly, with rapid changes of commissaries, until in Sublet de Noyers Richelieu found the man he wanted. The Spanish army, vastly experienced, was much better than the French in three important respects: engineering (the Spaniards were famous for bridging rivers), tactics on the field (at Nördlingen the *tercios*, as a result of superb drilling, fell on their knees as the Swedes fired so that the bullets flew over their heads), and speed of movement (in the Low Countries the movement of rearward echelons enabled them to gain rapid tactical advantages).

On the outbreak of war France had an army of twenty-five thousand around Mezières – Sedan, and another of nine thousand in Picardy. La Force had fifteen thousand in Lorraine and on the Rhine, and a new army of twenty thousand was being formed at Langres under Cardinal de La Valette: this cleric needed a dispensation for the purpose from the Holy See, and Richelieu's brother Alphonse, then ambassador to Rome, had some difficulty in coaxing it out of the Pope. Twenty-one new regiments were being raised; in June twelve thousand Swiss were recruited, and fifteen thousand were in reserve. All nobles were called to the colours and brought out their feudal levies. Another army of twelve thousand was placed under Rohan. This doughty Huguenot had compromised himself badly in Richelieu's eyes by his negotiations to bring Gustavus Adolphus into the Valtelline, and early in 1633 Richelieu had secured his dismissal from the Grisons. Rohan had returned to Venice for a while, and then went to Baden where he wrote a classical work on the Swiss constitution. Now Richelieu summoned him and ordered him to clear Alsace of the troops of Charles of Lorraine, lead his army into the Valtelline to block the passes against Spanish traffic, and eventually besiege Milan. The Duke took over his command, shouldered Charles aside into northern Alsace, crossed Switzerland into the Grisons by the route Basle, Brugg, Zürich, St Gallen, and Chur, and came down the Bernina in early summer to defeat the imperialists at Lavino and Tirano, and later at Morbegno. The Emperor exclaimed at this alleged violation of the Treaty of Monzon, and when it was learned that Rohan had overthrown the Catholic administrations in Chur and the Valtelline, and melted down the church-bells, his indignation knew no bounds.

While Rohan was entering Alsace, Brézé led the army of Mezières-Sedan down the Meuse to join the Dutch at Namur, and by the end of May 1635 the combined forces were at Maastricht. Here they turned west to march on Brussels, which they were threatening by the end of June. At Tirlemont they desecrated a famous shrine and committed atrocities; and Louvain, to which they laid siege, was in a high fever of anxiety. Then their momentum gave out; the army sickened and logistical problems became overwhelming, while the imperial general Piccolomini, moving with speed through the Ardennes from the east, cut the French communications at Namur, and pushed the Franco-Dutch forces north as far as Nijmegen: Brézé's army disintegrated, and the maddened Belgians took a horrible revenge on the scattered survivors, bags full of severed ears being delivered in triumph to a shocked Aytona, who issued orders that these horrors should cease. At the same time Charles of Lorraine burst through the gap north of the Vosges and by the middle of summer was back in the heart of Lorraine, having interposed himself between the armies of La Force and La Valette; another imperial army under Gallas crossed the Rhine, pushed Bernard of Saxe-Weimar into the Saar, took Worms, Landau and Kaiserslautern, and began the siege of Zweibrücken. Here Gallas was checked by La Valette, who had been ordered to help Bernard, and pushed back over the Rhine at the end of August. La Valette, however, had outrun his supplies, and when Gallas counter-attacked he was forced to retreat all the way up the Moselle to Metz, both sides suffering great losses.

By September France was in a condition of crisis. Its northern frontier was exposed by the swallowing up of Brézé's army in the Netherlands; the eastern frontier was about to be invaded. Worse, the Swedish government refused to ratify Oxenstierna's signature of the Treaty of Compiègne, and the Swedes were largely inactive. Sweden's main interest was in the succession to Pomerania, and France's entry into the war seemed to afford it the opportunity of entering into an accommodation with the Emperor by which his support for this ambition could be bought. Also, the withdrawal of Saxony from the war, the lack of interest of Brandenburg, and renewed threats from Poland tended to concentrate Swedish interest less on the Rhine than on the Baltic. Oxenstierna, described by Père Joseph as a 'terrible man', had used

Richelieu as Richelieu had sought to use Gustavus Adolphus, and now that the French alliance seemed unlikely to produce any dividends for Sweden there was a tendency for it to be quietly abandoned.

Later Sweden was to find that this opportunism was unrewarding, but at the end of 1635 Richelieu felt himself abandoned. This did not make Grotius' mission any easier, and there is no doubt that the learned man's diplomatic essay was a complete failure. Sedentary by inclination, loving his books and always collecting precedents, he could not bear the itinerant habits of the French court, which was for ever migrating, and he resisted being dragged around like the other ambassadors. The result was that he became ever more ineffective. In the French Foreign Ministry archives there is a delightful document in which Richelieu comments tartly on Grotius' draftsmanship of an armistice agreement to which the Swedes hoped Richelieu might agree.

Not only the Swedes appeared to have abandoned France; the Dutch were equally unreliable. In August the imperialists had dispatched a force by boat down the Rhine and the Waal; their troops had scaled the walls of the fort of Scheinck and massacred the garrison. Dragging Brézé with him, the Prince of Orange retired into the depths of the Netherlands to defend his capital, and did little further. Brézé became suspicious that Orange was, in fact, negotiating with the Spaniards. Meanwhile, the terrible evils of the war which had ravaged Germany were now being imported across the Rhine. Gallas in his retreat before La Valette employed a scorched-earth policy, so that quickly the French cavalry was reduced to eating the leaves of the vines, while the troopers ate bread only every fourth day, and subsisted on cabbages and roots. Bread in some places cost a crown a pound, and the young Turenne had to sell his silver mug to buy it. The French army in Alsace was on the point of mutiny, and deserters from it, as well as from the broken Protestant armies in Germany, roamed the countryside in search of food, for all the world, as one writer puts it, like bands of foraging baboons. The city of Strasbourg, inundated with ragged and emaciated soldiery, thrust three thousand of them out of the walls to die in the ditches. La Force, aged seventy-seven, had just lost his wife at Metz and seemed devoid of all energy.

These blows hit Louis XIII harder than they did Richelieu, and he became ill and more morose than ever. Léon Bouthillier went to Richelieu and warned him to keep away from the King, who, however, vented his feelings, as was his wont, in two nasty letters which he wrote to the Cardinal. He wanted to take command himself in Lorraine, but Richelieu, knowing how desperate the situation was becoming, and fearing the King's reaction when he should experience the demoralization of his army (which Richelieu had already witnessed during the Italian campaign), firmly sought to oppose his wishes. Matters were not made any better when the Cardinal urged the King to appoint the Comte de Soissons to command on the Belgian frontier. The King grew hot with rage and fell into tears of vexation. He resolved to proceed to Lorraine with a convoy which was taking wheat to Nancy and dragged Richelieu along to St Mihiel, which had revolted in favour of Charles of Lorraine, and which Soissons was besieging.

Soissons, as jealous of his honour as the King was of his, was piqued at being thus superseded. Richelieu forestalled an explosion between them by securing the surrender of the place, just before the King was forced by Gallas' threat to Metz to withdraw to St Dizier, where he gave an impression of misery and hesitation. The Lorraine officers of the garrison of St Mihiel were confined in the Bastille, and the thousand other ranks condemned to the galleys; seven hundred of them, however, escaped from their chains to add to the numbers of desperate vagabonds now plaguing the roads of France. When the news reached Louis he suffered a bilious attack. The year ended ingloriously for France, and in his *Mémoires* Richelieu does not hesitate to attribute the failure of the marshals to their jealousies of one another, the indiscipline of the nobility, and the political and religious divisions in the army.

In the Mediterranean and Italy things were proving no better. On 13 September twenty-two Spanish galleons under the command of the Marqués de Santa Cruz appeared before Nice, surrounded the Iles de Lérins, and frightened the governor of the fort on the island of Ste Marguerite into evacuating it with his arms and baggage. Next day the Spaniards landed on St Honorat, and after a preliminary bombardment persuaded the governor there into surrender without the honours of war. By the time they were ready to attack Cannes, however, its forts had been sufficiently garrisoned, and they therefore contented themselves with making the Iles de Lérins a powerful base. The famous abbey of St Honorat was thoroughly despoiled to build bastions, and the Spaniards were to prove irremovable for several years. The governors of Ste Marguerite and St Honorat were both arrested, but they were acquitted of cowardice by the Parlement, an event which added to the affront to Louis' dignity.

While the Côte d'Azur was thus in turmoil, the French were suffering reverses in Italy. There the alliance between France, Victor Amadeus of Savoy and the Dukes of Mantua and Modena was producing few advantages for anyone. It had been intended that a Franco-Savoyard army should march on Milan from the west while Rohan attacked from the east, but Créqui, who had set off from Pinerolo, was checked at Valenza and came to a halt. Victor Amadeus, apt like his father to follow the shifts of the wind, appeared in the French camp and announced that if in ten days he had no indication from France that something was being done to retrieve the situation he would take 'the road by which he had come'. When the Spaniards managed to reinforce the garrison of Valenza, Créqui accused Victor Amadeus of connivance, and the latter accused the marshal of negligence. At the end of October Créqui abandoned the venture altogether for that year.

As the winter of 1635-6 descended upon Europe military activity was stilled on all fronts. But Richelieu had a new battle to wage – with the Parlement of Paris concerning the war charges that were being imposed. The Parlement's behaviour at the time of the Marillac trial had outraged Louis XIII, who described the Parlement's attitude as 'insolence'.[2] Richelieu, who knew how entrenched was the institution of the Parlement in the French way of life, and being partly himself of the bourgeois of the robe, recognized that an outright onslaught upon it by the King would be explosive. For this reason he counselled patience and moderation. His enemies sought to use this against him, urging the King to destroy the powers of the Parlement, in the hope that the resultant crisis might bring about the Cardinal's downfall. However, the Parlement's constant scrutiny of legislation submitted to it by the council, and its regular refusal to register it on the ground that it offended some archaic privilege or other, gradually exasperated Richelieu; and on 3 August 1631 he wrote himself to the president saying, in effect, that the King's patience was exhausted; the Parlement claimed to be able to do everything without the King and he able to do nothing without it. 'Must I also warn you,' he added, 'that His Majesty cannot dispense himself from taking up and consecrating rights as sacred as those.'[3] For the moment this warning had some effect, and a number of decrees which the Parlement had been holding up, including that creating the Cardinal a duke and peer, were registered.

It was the function of the Keeper of the Seals, the Marquis de Châteauneuf, to deal with the obstructions of Parlement. This man had none of Richelieu's adroitness, and his short career from the day when he took over from Marillac was hardly distinguished for prudence. His public utterances made him obnoxious to the Parlement, while his private intrigues and indiscreet association with Richelieu's enemies roused the latter's suspicions – suspicions which Père Joseph, to whom Châteauneuf was anathema, energetically fostered. Public opinion was hostile to Châteauneuf for his presiding role in the courts that condemned Louis de Marillac and Montmorency, and his enemies worked for his downfall without scruple. His Achilles' heel was his philandering instinct, for it led him into the clutches of that ubiquitous siren Mme de Chevreuse. She was now thirty-one, he fifty-four. It was obvious to all observers that she was snaring Châteauneuf for some dubious end, exciting his jealousy, inflaming his desire until he was her slave. When Gaston fled to Brussels after the execution of Montmorency the conclusion was drawn that the Chevreuse, her friend the Queen, and by implication Châteauneuf, were involved in this new conspiracy. Richelieu, gliding with feline stealth in the shadows of the affair, could not disguise his disquiet, and thereby he gave the Chevreuse the opportunity of hinting to Châteauneuf that the Cardinal was jealous. And since the Cardinal was seven years younger than Châteauneuf did not the latter also have the occasion for jealousy? The letter in which she told of her hatred for the Cardinal came in due course into Richelieu's hands. 'The Cardinal's tyranny grows from moment to moment. His vainglory is not only insupportable to me, but odious.'[4] Richelieu had ordered her to break with Châteauneuf, she said, and had gone so far as to tell her husband that her conduct was intolerable for a man of spirit such as he.

At Bordeaux, on the way home from the Montmorency trial at Toulouse, Richelieu fell ill of kidney trouble, and was thought to be near death. Châteauneuf, unlike the other ministers, did not wait at his bedside, but, on the pretext of a summons to join the Queen, set off for Paris. He could not resist the temptation to receive the honours intended for the Cardinal by the towns *en route*, and provoked the comment that he was already acting as if he had superseded him. This conduct outraged the King, who, on 4 February 1633 wrote to Richelieu saying that the insolence of the Parlement and the antics of 'these two persons', meaning Châteauneuf and Chevreuse, had piqued him 'extraordinarily'.[5] Châteauneuf was arrested and an investigation produced proof that, prodded by the Chevreuse, he had warned her of a proposed attack on a place in Lorraine, and that she had in turn warned Charles of Lorraine; that he was in liaison with Gaston; and that he had been free with council secrets. He was gaoled, and the Duc de Chevreuse was told to take his wife away to Couzières, near Tours, and keep her there.[6]

Châteauneuf's disgrace was received by the Parlement with delight, and for once Richelieu was popular with its grave but troublesome members. Indeed he found his relationships with them so harmonious that he decided to take them into his confidence and win their support for his policies. On 17 January 1634 he expounded to them his whole theory of government in a long speech, in which he recited the troubles of the realm, the war situation, the measures he had already taken and the measures he contemplated.[7]

The imposition of war taxation, however, provoked a new crisis, and on 4 January 1636 several members of the Parlement were arrested for refusing to register the necessary legislation, whereupon the Parlement refused to register forty-two edicts creating new charges. Richelieu wrote to the King that the Parlement had behaved in an 'extremely insolent' fashion, and the King forbade the Chambers to meet until they were prepared to yield to his will. The crisis was overcome, only to be repeated every time money was involved, until Louis issued an ultimatum saying 'I will be obeyed', and Richelieu followed up with 'you will await the King's grace, for he insists on being obeyed'.[8] With remarkable flexibility and skill he managed the Parlement, negotiating and temporizing again and again. The struggle, however, was exhausting to a man overburdened with accumulating problems, and it was with a justifiable touch of bitterness that he wrote that 'without money nothing can be done; but as soon as you propose any extraordinary means of raising it, the Parlement objects and raises an outcry among the people. However, one must be above this sort of thing and ignore the calumny.'[9]

With the fall of Châteauneuf Richelieu eliminated all personal opposition and factions within the government, and thereafter until his death the ministry worked as a team, often uncomfortably it is true; and it is not the least of the Cardinal's achievements that he was able to keep in control a group of power-hungry men and direct their ambitions to the good of the state. He appointed the key men, and once he had confidence in them, conceded them a large measure of autonomous activity. It is difficult to say who was the author of many decisions that were taken, and the Cardinal resisted the tendency of Louis XIII to pin responsibility for all actions upon him. On occasions the councillors, Bullion especially, appealed over Richelieu's head to the King. The latter concerned himself with all the details of government, was vexed when not consulted prior to action, complained when Richelieu was not present to open dispatches, and often impatiently opened them himself – which gave Bouthillier, Séguier and Sublet de Noyers spasms of alarm for they often included in official correspondence their own letters full of court gossip and personal comments.

The inner council, consisting mainly of these men and Richelieu, met informally, without minutes, in anybody's room as
might be convenient. In the outcome there was no absolute
division of functions, and internal and foreign affairs were inter-
mingled. Everything of importance was signed by the King; he
had a unique respect for tradition and the rights of his subjects,
and had to be persuaded of the necessity for every administrative
change. If Richelieu dominated his colleagues, Louis dominated
the whole structure and was held in awe by the councillors, who
trembled before his fits of bad temper and phases of depression.
The ministry thus constituted a conspiracy to keep bad news away
from the King and to protect one another from the King's wrath.

The most loyal of Richelieu's colleagues were the Bouthilliers,
Claude the father and Léon the son, who was shortly to become
the Comte de Chavigny. Claude's father had been a clerk in the
law office of Richelieu's grandfather, François de La Porte, and in
fact took over the practice after La Porte's death and acted as
lawyer to Mme de Richelieu. Claude and his brother, Denis,
were recommended by Richelieu to Marie de Médicis and
became her secretaries, and Claude's appointment as secretary of
state in 1628 was regarded by the Queen Mother as a victory for
her party. In the subsequent crisis between her and Richelieu,
Bouthillier remained loyal to the Cardinal, and on d'Effiat's
death in 1632 became, jointly with Claude de Bullion, superintendent of finance. Léon Bouthillier, then only twenty-four, had
attracted Richelieu's attention. He followed his father in the
department of foreign affairs where he performed brilliantly, and
his big nose, haughty brow and shrewd eyes dominate French
diplomatic history. The Earl of Leicester, English ambassador,
found him a typical Frenchman, and sniffed disapprovingly:

He is as hard to be found as a mouse in a barne; he lyes sometimes at
bathing houses and sometimes in other places, and is so much a man of
pleasure, as it is a wonder to many, that the great Apollo of this state
will put so many and so great businesses in his hand. By my faith, they
say they drinke hard here now some time.[10]

He was ever on the move, negotiating with Gaston, whom he

kept under control for five years, touring battlefields, and controlling political prisons, the royal household and the grant of pensions. The King treated him as he treated Richelieu, sometimes amicably, sometimes irascibly.

Chavigny was jealous of the other ministers, and on one occasion Richelieu had to intervene and say, 'For God's sake do not let your jealousy affect the government of the country!' His was the task to prepare the texts of letters and treaties and read aloud to the King dispatches from other nations, and he demonstrated that he was a masterly draftsman: Richelieu had merely to sketch out the contents of a document in general principle. He was devoted to Richelieu, called his son Armand and daily reported to the Cardinal the King's disposition towards him, but after Richelieu's death he made the mistake of backing Gaston against Mazarin and was disgraced, dying at the age of forty-four. No one regretted this slippery man, who was servile to Richelieu and arrogant to his inferiors.

Bullion, aged about seventy when he died in 1640, was a flat-faced, corpulent, gouty man who was humorous, clever, experienced, wily and independent. He had survived in the government from the days of Ancre, and had early befriended Richelieu, who borrowed money from him. If he disagreed with the Cardinal's policies he ignored them, not hesitating to brush aside express directions. There was a constant struggle between Richelieu, who placed ends above means and foreign affairs above internal affairs, and the conservative superintendents of finance, who had to extract money out of the people by traditional methods which were inadequate to the demand. Unfairly, the Cardinal placed the blame on the shoulders of the tax-collectors for the disorders that resulted from attempts to push to the absolute limit the existing means of raising revenue, and on Bullion for military defeats which he considered to be due to insufficient expenditure: 'I have been preaching to Messieurs des Finances for a long time that there are certain privileged things where you must see ahead of events before a catastrophe makes us recognize the peril. For one crown that it was necessary to give at the right moment, it will now take ten.'[11] Bullion, no less unfairly, blamed

Richelieu for not being more violent with the Parlement in the matter of its obstruction of financial decrees, particularly those devaluing the currency and creating new offices for sale – which came to be the last financial resort. In 1638 Bullion's independence was in theory curbed by a regulation making him more subject to the council,[12] but he treated it light-heartedly, as he did the Code Michaud, which he admitted he did not even bother to consult.

Ferret-faced Sublet de Noyers was forty-four in 1632, in which year he wrote a paper on money which discussed the problem of the drain of gold and silver from the realm. He was first introduced to Richelieu by Feuquières, and was distantly related to Richelieu's mother. His power increased enormously after 1635, for even licences to import goods from enemy countries came under his jurisdiction. Commanders in the field received almost daily information from him about the political and military situation, and were expected to furnish regular returns on the basis of which Sublet calculated the necessary supplies of food and ammunition and the pay-rolls. He seems to have been a pious, austere, friendless man, for whom neither Richelieu nor the King had much affection, and despite his care, industry and adroitness he was to be dismissed within two months of the Cardinal's death. Among his functions was the supervision of public buildings and in 1638 he saved Fontainebleau from ruin, the whole building having leaked like a sieve. He also patronized Nicolas Poussin after the painter's return from Rome in 1640.

The government of France was conducted in haste, and the ministers moved from one crisis to another without ever having the time to plan ahead or reflect upon their problems. They worked all hours of the day and night, were for ever on the move about France, and were constantly having to postpone decisions. Over and again Richelieu remonstrated with them for failing to act quickly enough, or to act at all. To save time Richelieu often gave verbal instructions, copies of correspondence were sometimes not filed, or instead of fair-copies being made the mauled drafts were used, so compounding the problems of the researcher. As far as possible Richelieu kept aloof from direct negotiation, and even from routine work. He described his role as that of a 'supervisor of diligence',[13] and he saw himself as a coordinator of policy. His personality pervaded the whole administrative structure, and though he appears often only a shadow in the background of events his was a shadow recognized by all to be of vital significance.

The greatest administrative achievement of Richelieu's career was the completion of the process whereby the secretaries of state ceased to be mere secretaries – originally in fact no more than scribes – and became departmental heads controlling the provincial intendants, whose activities intensified after 1635 under the cloak of emergency war measures. One of the secretaries of state was always with the King; in this he acted the traditional role of secretary, but was subtly transformed into the channel through which the royal control of the whole machine was ensured. Liaison between the secretaries and Richelieu was close, so that the King and the Cardinal were able to harmonize their activities without necessarily consulting in person. But because the geographical divisions in the administration remained rigid, most documents had to be countersigned by the departmental head concerned, thus imposing a check on authoritarianism and a limitation on flexibility. The Cardinal respected these divisions because 'contradiction in orders is something which can cause much harm'.

Richelieu changed very little of the form of French administration; rather he effected a subtle transformation of emphasis. Whereas the King had traditionally relied on a counterbalance of rival factions to conserve his authority, Richelieu substituted the concept of ministerial responsibility to the Crown. Without structural modification, therefore, the government was tightened and rendered more bureaucratic and less personal. The great offices of state, held by the princes and the dukes, declined, while lesser offices, such as the secretariats, increased in importance. The outbreak of war was an event of major significance in the history of French government, for it provided the excuse for emergency administrative measures which were to become permanent features of Richelieu's system of government.

19

In Conscience Bound

1634-6

Urban VIII was an ageing man, and the constant assaults made upon him by Spanish and imperial agents with a view to canonical chastisement of Louis XIII and Richelieu had become wearisome. For years he had expended great energy in trying to reconcile the Catholic powers, but had seen recriminations substituted for negotiation. Sadly he had observed that the pendular swing of power in the Rhine districts inevitably extended the commitment to military operations; and that the drift from limited hostilities for diplomatic advantages to general war was not likely to be arrested. Towards the end of 1632 he had sent special missions to Madrid, Vienna and Paris with a view to bringing the three governments to the negotiating table. His choice of envoy to France, however, was unfortunate, for he was identified in Spanish eyes with the pro-French party in Rome, and the envoy to Spain thus found it impossible to convince Olivares of the sincerity of the Pope's endeavour. At Vienna developments were more hopeful, but Ferdinand was sceptical about Richelieu's willingness to settle outstanding issues; what, he asked, could be expected after the experiences of Regensburg and Cherasco? In fact Urban had no more confidence in Ferdinand than the latter had in Richelieu, for the Emperor was even then negotiating for peace with Saxony and Hesse-Darmstadt in order, so it was believed, to be free to deal with France. 'In Vienna,' the nuncio reported, 'they think only of treating with the heretics.'[1]

When at the end of 1633 the Spaniards discovered that Richelieu had been playing their own game of political subversion, and was involved in the conspiracy to raise rebellion in Belgium, they sent the evidence to Rome and laid it with a scandalized air before the Pope. Now would Urban threaten Louis with ecclesiastical censures? The Pope reminded Philip IV that these had not proved very salutary in the past, instancing the cases of Henry VIII and Elizabeth I, and recalling that such censures against Henri IV had delayed the implementation in France of the decrees of the Council of Trent. Philip described this objection as 'frivolous'. The poor Pope, by now desperate for some expedient to prevent open war between the leading Catholic monarchs, offered the pathetic suggestion that everyone should pool resources for a crusade against the Turks. Richelieu's devastating comment on the irrelevancy of this proposal was that Constantinople was a long way away.

If Olivares failed to understand the Pope's predicament, so did Richelieu, who went his own way in the expectation that Urban would always yield to his importunities, and then expressed himself aggrieved when he did not do so. For example, he conceived the idea of extending French political influence down the Moselle by having himself nominated coadjutor archbishop of Trier. After all, did not prelates like the Elector of Cologne gain political strength by having themselves elected bishops of sees like Hildesheim as well? When the proposal was made to Philip von Sötern several technical problems arose, but he indicated that he was prepared to nominate Richelieu coadjutor of Speyer. One of the Trier bureaucrats was sent to Rome to secure the Pope's consent, but the Spaniards, who knew all about the matter, recollected that he was a Luxemburger, and, as such, one of their subjects, and set to work in Rome to intimidate him. As it happened they were wasting their time for Urban VIII was not to be persuaded that there was any advantage to the Church in this outrageous pluralism, and rejected the appointment. 'This is against the German concordat,' he protested. 'What would the

French say if a German prelate were appointed in their country?'[2]
It is the measure of Richelieu's limited understanding of the position
of other sovereigns that he could not see that the Pope, in face of
Spanish accusations of partiality, could not possibly waive the
decrees of Trent for what was, after all, nothing but a political
design to gain a footing in the Habsburg empire.

The reasons for the tensions that developed between Richelieu
and Urban VIII have been misunderstood. In no way did Richelieu
depart from traditional Catholic doctrine on the supremacy of the
Holy See, and the difficulties that arose between Paris and Rome
were diplomatic and political, and only on one occasion doctrinal.
This was the occasion of Gaston's marriage to Marguerite. After
the abdication of Charles of Lorraine and Marguerite's flight to
Brussels, legal proceedings were commenced in the Parlement of
Paris to declare Monsieur's marriage null, and to chastise the
House of Lorraine for its misdemeanours. On 5 September 1635
the Parlement decreed that the marriage was null, and that:

... all the feudal property belonging to Charles, Nicolas-François
and Henriette of Lorraine, held from the Crown of France mediately or
immediately, are declared returned, reunited, and incorporated there-
with, and all and every their other goods situated in France, moveable
and immoveable, are acquired and confiscated by the King.

To put the issue beyond doubt in canon law, Monsieur went
through the form of marriage again with Marguerite before the
archbishop of Malines, but his defiance of Louis weakened as his
resentment of Aytona's treatment of him increased. He sent
d'Elbène to Paris to negotiate the conditions of his return. Carefully baiting the trap, Richelieu told d'Elbène that if Puylaurens
should persuade Monsieur to return to France, he, Puylaurens,
would be made a duke and a peer. Puylaurens, however, knew
his Richelieu too well, and suspected that the road to Paris would
be the road to the Bastille; he therefore demanded concrete
assurances. To his surprise he was offered them in the form of a
proposal from Richelieu that he should marry the Cardinal's
cousin, Mlle de Pontchâteau. This decided Puylaurens, and it
remained only to find sufficient enticement for his master. Gaston

was told that should he return he would be restored in his property and given a sum of 400,000 *livres* to pay his debts; and that his marriage should be judged 'according to the laws of the realm'. Since the Parlement had already in fact done this, the formula really implied that Monsieur should desert his wife.

Gaston was on an excursion on the Scheldt, and actually playing cards, when a message was brought on board saying that the Cardinal-Infante had won a great victory at Nördlingen. Black with anger he rose, overturning the table and casting cards and money into the river. Probably he feared that now the Spaniards would invade France and require him to honour his treaty with them. His mind was made up. On Sunday 2 October 1634 he and his friends went on a foxhunt, after arranging for a late mass to be said on their return. Aytona was at the château of Tervueren some thirty-five miles away. The party left Brussels for the open country and rode until Monsieur's horse dropped dead beneath him. At nine that night they reached the frontier fortress of La Capelle, and in answer to the challenge of the sentries Gaston shouted out that he was the King's brother. The governor, Baron du Bec, appeared and was cautious. An officer was sent across the counterscarp to inspect Monsieur's papers, which included a pass issued by the King, and Gaston was admitted to the officers' mess. Give us supper,' he groaned, 'we have not eaten nor drunk for eighteen hours.' On 21 October 1634 he was received by the King at St Germain in the presence of the whole court. In the midst of the proceedings, and late probably by design so as to make his presence the more dramatic, appeared Richelieu. 'My brother,' said Louis, 'I beg you to love Monsieur le Cardinal.' 'I shall love him as myself,' said Gaston, 'and am resolved to follow his counsels.'[3]

The reconciliation, as usual, was shortlived. Almost as soon as he had settled down, pressure was imposed on Gaston to concede the nullity of his marriage. Gaston was intractable. Surrounded by theologians who advanced every possible canonical argument, he listened silently. Finally all turned to hear the husband's point of view. All this law, he said, was over his head, but one thing he was clear about, and that was that there was in his marriage no vitiating element of force or seduction. So far as he was concerned he was married to Marguerite until the Church, not the state, should declare otherwise. Obviously, then, there had to be a canonical process of annulment, and this, as Richelieu knew, would have to be carefully managed, for important political issues were at stake.

Meanwhile, having participated at the marriage of Puylaurens, now a duke, to Richelieu's cousin, Gaston betook himself to Blois to settle down with his seven-year-old daughter, who was taught to sing naughty songs about the Cardinal. There he was occupied with a building programme, wherein he employed the newly fashionable architect François Mansart. In February 1635 he and Puylaurens went to Paris to attend a ballet that was being much talked about, and Puylaurens found himself alone with Richelieu in one of the rooms of the Louvre. The Cardinal seemed to be in a malicious mood, and after some time he excused himself to go to the King's cabinet. Puylaurens remained for a while alone, and then the door opened and the captain of the guards appeared with an order for his arrest. He was taken immediately to Vincennes, while the King explained to Gaston the reasons for this action. Puylaurens, he said, had sent twenty-two couriers to Brussels since he had left there; the information they had carried was that the King was disgusted with Richelieu, that Puylaurens himself would soon be his successor, and that if Gaston did not get the satisfaction he demanded it would be easy for him to flee to Italy.

Gaston, who had learned to dissemble, took the arrest of Puylaurens quietly, and his very docility was disquieting. It was thought that he was in communication with his Lorraine relations, and extra precautions were taken to prevent his escaping yet again to Spain, or to some other European country. Fond of boating, Monsieur undertook an extended excursion on the Loire, and Richelieu, agitated lest he might slip out of the estuary and sail for England with Chavigny, who was accompanying him, ordered six warships to guard the area. Gaston, however, turned back before reaching the sea and went to Richelieu to inspect the great château which the Cardinal was building there, and was given one of the new garden statues as a souvenir. After some months he heard that Puylaurens had died of some strange malady at Vincennes at the age of twenty-eight. Since the Duke's trial was still pending, and the investigation was dropped we have little knowledge of the evidence against him.

A commission composed of the bishops of Montpellier, Nîmes, Sées, Chartres and St Malo had been set up to examine the question whether marriages of the princes of the blood in succession to the throne, in order to be valid, required the King's consent; and conversely, whether they were invalid if contracted against his will. It was a novel question, and the proceedings should not be judged according to the assumptions common to a later age. At this time the relationship between Church and state was fluid; in Catholic countries it was true that the state could not accept as valid a marriage not contracted according to canon law; but was it not also true that canon law had to accommodate the law of the state? The point was a nice one and of its nature controversial. The texts yielded little guidance, and the bishops could discover only three historical precedents, the earliest being the case of Baudouin, Grand Forester of Flanders, who had abducted Judith, daughter of the Emperor of Charles the Bald, and widow of King Ethelwulf of England. They thereupon enlisted the aid of the Sorbonne and the theologians of the religious orders. It took the bishop of Montpellier two hours to read the report of the commission, which was rich in citation of authority, and which reached the conclusion that in France the requirement of royal consent for the validity of a royal marriage was a matter of the 'fundamental law of the realm'. The report was adopted by the Assembly of the Clergy of France on 10 July 1635, which bridged the logical gap between civil law and canon law, between state and Church, by postulating that the custom of France had been 'affirmed by legitimate prescription and authorized by the Church'. In other words, the necessity for the royal consent was a prescriptive gloss on the canon law in France.

It was not an altogether unreasonable conclusion for the Assembly to reach, but since it raised implications for the whole issue of Church – state relationships, which at the time was highly provocative, there was no possibility that the Pope would agree to it. Under canon law Gaston had a right of appeal to Rome, and to prevent him from exercising it his disavowal of the marriage became a necessity. Pressure was therefore put upon him to sign a document attesting its invalidity. The document, which he signed in Richelieu's own cabinet at Rueil, recited the opinions of the great numbers of doctors and religious which had been given to the commission and the findings of the Assembly, and concluded with the words: 'We have believed ourself to be in conscience bound to acquiesce, recognizing as null the marriage made between us and the princess Marguerite of Lorraine, and declare, as we now do, that we shall never in the future hold the said Dame Marguerite for our wife.'[4] Marguerite, as one would expect from a girl who had crossed the French lines disguised as a cavalier, was of sterner character. She exercised her rights to appeal to the Pope, and Rome was now canonically seised of the affair.

The facts laid before the Pope were that the marriage had been celebrated in a chapel of the priory of St Romain at Nancy by a Benedictine (whom Richelieu arrested as soon as Nancy was captured), in the presence of four witnesses. François, Marguerite's brother, who happened also to be her diocesan bishop, had dispensed her from banns and had authorized the celebrant to replace the parish priest. Although there was an element of sleight of hand in all this, the formal requirements of canon law had been met. The issue for the Pope, then, was simply this: does the sacrament of marriage depend upon the mutual consent of the parties alone, or may the state require the additional consent of an outsider to the contract? If it may do this it would follow that the state might usurp the Church's claims to universal jurisdiction in the spiritual sphere by adding to the conditions under which the sacrament, ordained by Christ, might be administered.

To deal with the marriage question and other issues with Rome, Richelieu needed an ambassador at the Holy See who would be a little more cognizant of theology than the Comte de Noailles, who had represented France during the previous few years. He decided to send his brother Alphonse. The Cardinal of

Lyons had found himself overwhelmed with unexpected honours, becoming in 1632 Grand Aumônier of France with jurisdiction over court ecclesiastics and all the hospitals in the kingdom. His appointment to Rome was not at all pleasing to him, and caused him great anxiety. He found that keeping up appearances in Rome was quite beyond his means, and his allowances from France were ever in arrears. It cost him 3,000 crowns on his arrival in October 1634 to buy the audience coach of the Maréchal de Créqui. The Duke of Parma rented him the Farnese Palace as an embassy, and Alphonse proceeded to stock it with one hundred and fifty puncheons of the best French wine, which earned him the reputation of having the best cellar in Rome. A great deal of money was spent on illuminating the palace for a grand reception to Cardinal Antonio Barberini; altogether there were in Rome thirty-two cardinals to be entertained, and it was some little time before Alphonse discovered that their pages by tradition swooped off with the sweets, glassware, linen, and even the silver, all of which had to be guarded vigilantly. The embassy fed and housed fifty persons and fifteen horses, and it was an embittered ambassador who wrote to Père Joseph saying that he had been so simple-minded when accepting the appointment as to be content with promises of money, but that now everyone laughed at his credulity. He suspected, he said, that Bullion had become so used to dealing with persons of bad faith that he had come to suspect everyone, even those who should be above suspicion of trying to extort money out of him on pretext. He was not the last ambassador to make this complaint of his treasury. In fact his financial situation worsened, for as France entered the war the supply of coin dried up, and the revenues from his ecclesiastical properties could not be raised.

As a diplomat Alphonse began badly. When Prince Filippo Colonna, the Prefect of Rome, whose daughter was married to a nephew of the Pope, made his official call he was received, not with the ceremonial due to an ambassador, but simply as a private person. Colonna was outraged, turned his back and walked out of the Farnese Palace. In a city where questions of etiquette provoked serious conflicts, resulting even on occasion in the shedding of blood, this was a grave affront. Alphonse, though he affected an air of disdainful indifference, reported to Chavigny that the rapiers of the French were vibrating in their scabbards, but that he had 'prevented our Frenchmen to be French'. And he added slyly,' It is necessary to go abroad to realize the mettle of the French.' Needless to say there was constant strife with the Spanish faction, which made an issue out of Alphonse's refusal to address the Cardinal of Savoy as 'Highness'. To effect an accommodation, Cardinal Franceso Barberini gave a reception at carnival time in honour of the Cardinals of both Lyons and Savoy, which lasted for two days. The Spaniards also waxed indignant that Alphonse should be permitted to reside away from his diocese of Lyons. Urban had just won his battle to have Borgia exiled to his see of Seville, and he could hardly make an exception in the case of a Richelieu. Armand de Richelieu overcame the difficulty by making his brother resign his bishopric. Alphonse obeyed reluctantly, complaining with much exaggeration that he would now have nowhere where he could permit his hairs to whiten in tranquillity. A final issue with the Spaniards was the fate of d'Elbène, who, after the Montmorency rebellion, had had to flee from his see of Albi, and was a refugee in his native Florence. He appeared in Rome and demanded restitution. Despite the support of the Spanish cardinals, however, the consistory rejected his claims.

With Urban VIII Alphonse was quickly on good terms. The Pope recognized his honesty and intellectual ability, and was prepared to overlook his diplomatic maladroitness. A major difficulty in Franco-papal relations was the poor system of communications. In the reign of Henri IV there had been a regular courier service between Paris and the embassy every three weeks; now it operated only six times a year. In the result both Alphonse and the Pope were badly informed over developments in the matter of Gaston's marriage process. It should have been Alphonse's task to present to the Pope the documents drawn up by the commission, but Richelieu found the situation too delicate to leave in the hands of his brother, who was out of touch with the question, and decided instead to send Fenouillet, the bishop of

Montpellier, to Rome in his capacity of chairman of the commission, to argue the case in person. Alphonse warned him of the
futility and danger of this course of action, since the Pope had
demonstrated his opposition to the whole procedure. In January
1636 Montpellier arrived in Rome. He was nervous about his
task and sought Alphonse's aid in presenting his arguments. The
latter did not hide his apprehensions, and for months Montpellier
vacillated. Eventually, he fell ill of one of the innumerable fevers
that gripped Rome in the summer, and on this excuse Alphonse
persuaded him to return to Paris, leaving his documents with him.
These the ambassador retained, and he was later to be criticized by
Richelieu for his failure to hand them to the Pope. The latter,
meanwhile, summoned the Sacred College in secret conclave to
discuss the marriage affair, and on 3 July 1636 two papal briefs
were issued, one to the King, the other to Gaston, in effect reserving the whole question for papal decision.

When the papal nuncio arrived to communicate this news to
Richelieu he found the Cardinal in a good humour, which did
not, however, endure for long. A look of severity came over
Richelieu's face, and the nuncio attributed this to pique that his
will had not prevailed. Much more than pique, however, was
involved, for Richelieu had a clearer vision than anyone else of
the magnitude of the issues raised. In short, the marriage affair
embodied the fundamentals of the debate between ultramontanism and gallicanism which had convulsed France for two
generations – a debate which Richelieu had been struggling for
years to suppress.

The gallicans were the party, mainly jurists not clerics, which
argued for the divine origin of the state and for the exclusion of
papal jurisdiction from at least temporal affairs, but also, among
the extremists, from the sphere of Church government in France
as well. Their maxim was that 'the King holds his crown and his
sword of God; he depends on God alone'. The opposing view,
propagated by the Jesuit philosophers of the period, Suarez,
Mariana and Bellarmine, that the King derives his sovereignty
mediately from God through the people, and not from Him
directly, was anathema to them because it carried the implication

of subordinacy of the monarchy to the papacy. As one writer put it a few years after these events, 'There is still another Power which some attribute to Popes over the temporal affairs of Christian princes which I combat with all my strength because I am a good Frenchman.'[5]

The ecclesiastical pressures upon Henri IV to take measures against the Huguenots transformed gallicanism from a religious issue into an issue of practical politics, and one result of it was the refusal of the Parlement of Paris to register the decrees of the Council of Trent on the ground that they conflicted with gallican freedoms. The assassination of Henri IV was attributed by the gallicans to the subversive doctrine that the subject may disobey the King; and after this event the Parlement of Paris banned Mariana's writings. Two years later a theologian named Edmund Richer produced a book which was to play an important role in the propagation of gallicanism. He was less concerned than his predecessors with the problem of the relationship of Church and state, and more occupied with that of the government of the Church itself. In essence, he argued for an aristocratic government of the Church by councils and bishops, and virtually repudiated the supremacy of the Pope. At the time he went too far and was deposed from his position as a syndic of the Faculty of Theology at Paris, and refused a canonry at Notre Dame, which was his right. He lived on in Paris for the next twenty years, the archpriest of a gallican cult which attracted an increased following as the political issues in France and in Europe crystallized and hardened.

Between 1624 and 1630 the situation became explosive, and politically highly dangerous. Just before Richelieu came to power an Italian Jesuit named Santarelli published a book bearing the imprimatur of the general of the Order, in which he took an extreme position with respect to papal authority. The Pope, he said, in the struggle against heresy was competent to depose kings; this was bad enough, but he went further and added that this power might also be exercised when kings offended against the law of the state, and even when they might be incompetent. The work was brought clandestinely into France and provoked the Parlement of Paris to launch a campaign against the Jesuits.

339

The Sorbonne censured it as scandalous and pernicious, and Richelieu, who thought its maxims likely to 'ruin the whole Church of God', had it burned on 13 April 1626 by the common executioner. The Jesuit provincial and three heads of Jesuit houses were then asked to make a declaration that it was true Catholic doctrine that the king derived his realm from God alone, and that the Pope could not for any reason discharge his subjects from their duty of loyalty. They qualified this statement slightly before agreeing to it, and the Parlement took this to be recalcitrance and wanted to close all Jesuit colleges, and even expel the Order altogether from France. To Richelieu this was carrying matters much too far, and he intervened, managing the Parlement to the point where it accepted the Fathers' disavowal of Santarelli's doctrine.

The question flared up again in 1629 when the gallicans and ultramontantists in the Sorbonne split violently on the question of the oath to be taken by bachelors of theology receiving their degrees. Should the oath include respect for the Holy See? This time Spada, the papal nuncio, asked Richelieu to intervene. The moment was inopportune, for he had just returned to Paris from the siege of La Rochelle and was on the point of departing for Italy to support the Duc de Nevers. The uproar in the Sorbonne thus continued for the whole year pending Richelieu's return. He decided that the root cause of the evil was the prevalence of Richerism in the University, and that the best way of suppressing this would be to get Richer himself to retract his opinions. The ex-professor was sought out and summoned before the Cardinal on 7 December 1629. Richelieu, who had no small opinion of his own theological ability, set out quietly to convince Richer that his doctrines were erroneous. He was charming and gentle, for he knew that if any element of pressure were involved in Richer's retraction, the Richerists would claim it had been forced, and the last situation would be worse than the first. In addition, he was not the man to force religious convictions on people, for he believed in the power of reason to retrieve men from error; and as he said himself on this occasion, it was important that one should renounce with the heart and not merely with words. The Cardinal laid before Richer a declaration which he wanted him to sign. In this Richer would recognize the Holy See as 'mother and mistress of all churches and infallible seat of truth',[6] and would retract such of his writings as were incompatible with this proposition. Richer demurred, and there followed a long discussion between the two men on the question whether infallibility is a property of the Pope acting alone, or whether it resides in the whole Church to the exclusion of the Pope or in conjunction with him. In the end Richer signed, and Richelieu took the credit, writing with satisfaction in his *Mémoires* that he had won the heretic over by force of argument. Richer, however, put it about that he had been overawed by the Cardinal and deluded into making the retraction.

Urban VIII was delighted when the news reached him of the way in which Richelieu had handled the extreme gallican party, and he indicated his satisfaction by making Alphonse de Richelieu a cardinal. Gallicanism, however, was far from crushed, and a new idea was afoot, that of creating apostolic delegates in France to judge all appeals to the Holy See; in other words, to locate the ultimate ecclesiastical authority in the Church in France. Now that the question of Monsieur's marriage had been removed to Rome the whole controversy was likely to revive in a new and more violent form. The ultramontanists were leagued with the anti-war party; the gallicans claimed to be the patriots. It would be impossible to keep the doctrinal issue from spilling over into a political crisis of a particularly dangerous character at a moment when France, plagued internally by peasant unrest and aristocratic conspiracy, was defending herself against the Habsburg onslaught. To yield in the matter of the marriage was now impossible, for the Church in France had declared it to be null. It could not be validated, therefore, in gallican eyes, save by remarriage, and the last thing Richelieu wanted was to have one of the terrible Lorraine family seated in the midst of the French royal family and creating further dissension.

It was therefore as a statesman rather more than as a man of the Church that Richelieu looked at the problem; and since he saw the problem as a political one he proposed to handle it by every manner of political obstruction, striving always to keep controversy suppressed and both factions satisfied. He himself, in his attitude towards the Holy See, was entirely orthodox, but in the administration of the Church, as distinct from its doctrine, he had to yield to some extent to gallicanism. He expressed himself on the subject in two propositions, one in his state papers, the other in his *Maximes*. The first was that 'while religiously obeying the Pope in spiritual matters, one can justly oppose him in his temporal designs';[7] and the second was that 'one would have to be a very bad theologian not to know that the King receives his crown and his temporal power from God alone.'[8] Except, therefore, in the matter of doctrine, he supported the independence of the state as against Rome, and tended to assimilate the government of the Church in France to that of the state. But in the marriage affair it was doctrine, not government, that was involved, and Richelieu could not deny the competence of the Holy See in the matter without demolishing the boundary between religious and political gallicanism which he had so carefully established in his own mind, and which he hoped to establish also as the keystone of Church-state relations. His zeal for Catholicism in all of Europe cannot be questioned; but what he regarded as Catholic cosmopolitanism had to yield to the primordial right of national self-defence.

In all of this Richelieu showed himself to be the intellectual and not the humanist, a theologian more concerned with justice than with charity, a canon lawyer by inclination more than a spiritual director. Père Joseph, for all his devious political manoeuvres, was the opposite, and the difference between the two men became clear on the issue of Gaston's marriage. The Capuchin, with his passionate love for souls, was affected by the moral wrong done to Marguerite, and for this reason he threw his weight on the side of the ultramontanists and in favour, if not of the initial validity of the marriage, at least of the moral duty of everyone involved to rectify the matter by bringing Gaston and Marguerite together in a new union. To this end he set himself to work on the King's conscience, and in the long run he was to prove himself more subtle than the Cardinal.

The Cardinal very often disagreed with Père Joseph, but never ceased to be under the Capuchin's spiritual influence. As his own

The face of the lawyer.
Pierre Séguier. By
Henri Testelin.
Chancellor of France,
he wielded the sword
of justice remorselessly
but with scrupulous
regard for the law.

The face of a Queen.
Anne of Austria.
Anonymous.
Portrayed with her
sons Louis and
Philippe at the time of
Richelieu's death, this
is the matronly figure
of the Habsburg
woman whose loyalties
to Spain made her the
victim of every palace
intrigue.

The face of the aristocrat. Henri, Marquis de Cinq Mars. By Mathieu Le Nain. The wilful youth who instigated the last revolt against the failing Richelieu and died arrogantly beneath the axe.

The face of resignation. A drawing of Richelieu in his last days by C. Mellan. The eyes seek no longer for human recalcitrance but anticipate the justice and mercy of God.

health gradually deteriorated Richelieu began to regard Père Joseph as his successor, and it therefore became important to secure for him a scarlet hat. The first rumours of this intention reached Rome at the end of 1632 through the nuncio Bichi. It was a most unfortunate moment to raise the question; Gustavus Adolphus had just been killed, and Richelieu, in face of the violent protests of the Pope, was negotiating with Oxenstierna; the Pope had just refused the hat to the abbot of Kremsmünster, Père Joseph's rival at Regensburg, despite the pressures of the Emperor, and it would be impossible now to give it to Père Joseph without the gravest offence to the Habsburgs. To the latter Père Joseph was a devil, a liar, betrayer of Christ, the worst of all possible schemers. There was also the consideration that ecclesiastical preferment was incompatible with the Capuchin way of life. The papal objection, however, appeared to Richelieu to take on a political character when Urban, exasperated beyond measure by the abuse of Borgia and his following, and no less by Richelieu's recalcitrance in the matter of Pinerolo, snapped at the Maréchal de Créqui, when he formally raised the question of Père Joseph's promotion, 'That is my Pinerolo!'[9] Richelieu therefore became somewhat standoffish towards the Pope. The matter was made worse when the hat which François of Lorraine had to yield up after his marriage was not bestowed on Père Joseph, and Richelieu, taking no account of the impossible situation in which the Pope found himself, regarded this as a deliberate slight.

Richelieu at this time was finding his ecclesiastical problems complicated by a new movement in the French Church, that of jansenism. Jansenius was a Belgian who, after his graduation from Louvain, had arrived at the Sorbonne in 1605 and remained there for five years. He was now bishop of Ypres. At Louvain he had a fellow student, a French cleric, Duvergier de Hauranne, later abbot of St Cyran, whom, however, he did not meet until he became a colleague of his at the Sorbonne. When Richelieu became bishop of Luçon Duvergier was the vicar-general of Richelieu's friend, La Rochepousay, bishop of Poitiers, and the two met frequently to discuss theological questions. La Rochepousay fell under Duvergier's influence, as did several others of

343

Richelieu's acquaintances, and Richelieu himself had considerable respect for Duvergier's literary ability. After the assassination of Henri IV a public controversy developed concerning the duty of the subject to sacrifice his life to save that of the King. Duvergier intervened with a book which established this obligation as one of morality, and Richelieu perceived in him one sympathetic to the idea of a centralized monarchy. During Condé's rebellion in 1614 Duvergier again appeared in print. La Rochepousay had closed the gates of Poitiers on Condé's forces, donned sword and armour and prepared to do battle. The duty of a bishop to refrain from warlike acts also became a controversial issue, and Duvergier defended his bishop, an act which again merited Richelieu's approval. It was largely through the efforts of La Rochepousay and Duvergier that Richelieu was elected to the States General, and in a sense, therefore, he owed his career to them. He sought to reward Duvergier ten years later by having him nominated chaplain to Queen Henriette Marie of England, and lost interest in him when Duvergier declined.

In these early days of their acquaintance the doctrine that was to receive the name jansenism had not been formulated. It was, in fact, hammered out over the years in correspondence between Duvergier and Jansenius, and as it took shape it embodied a series of ideas which were destined to distort the scheme of redemption: Man is sunk in an abyss of sin; it is necessary to awaken in his soul the fear of God's justice and of hellfire; he should be made aware of the quite gratuitous outpouring of God's grace, which he has failed to merit, and which alone can redeem him. Good works, it followed, are insufficient and are to be depreciated, while the sacraments, individual cognizance of God and personal experience of grace are to be emphasized. At the social level the result was puritanism (Philippe de Champaigne took to portraiture to avoid painting nudes); at the political level, since Jansenius argued for an aristocratic government of the Church as a necessary channel of divine grace, the doctrine linked up with theological gallicanism.

For a long tim Richelieu failed to detect the tendencies in Duvergier's writings, finding him, indeed, an ally on many points. Later, he was alarmed at the things that were coming from

344

Duvergier's mouth and pen, such as that Luther had erred not in fundamentals but in form; that St Thomas Aquinas had ravaged theology; and, in a conversation with St Vincent de Paul, who was in some senses a disciple, and who described Duvergier as one of the best men he ever saw, that God had made it clear to him that there was no longer a Church; the Church of old that was like a great clear flowing river was now slime. Duvergier's personal spiritual fervour was gaining him great influence over many Catholic zealots in high places, Bérulle, the Prince de Condé, the *procureur-général* Molé, the advocate-general Bignon, and many less elevated people such as the mother of Ste Jeanne de Chantal. The dangers in Duvergier's doctrine were revealed when he published a book under the pseudonym *Aurelius*, which provoked widespread controversy because of its extreme gallican tenets of Church government. The Sorbonne became involved, and fearing another upheaval there Richelieu intervened, and by order of the council referred the book for examination to a special commission.

Jansenius was violently anti-French and had written an extremely intemperate, indeed a vile, pamphlet directed against French policies; yet Duvergier was his close collaborator; Duvergier himself was opposed to the annulment of Monsieur's marriage. Despite, therefore, the gallican strain in his doctrine, Duvergier politically stood with the anti-war faction. Discussing the problem, Richelieu said: 'One would have been able quite successfully to remedy the evils and disorders of the time if one had locked up Luther and Calvin when they began to dogmatize.'[10] There were, in his opinion, compelling motives to do the same with Duvergier before Church and state alike should suffer from his views and his activities.

It so happened that an Oratorian priest, Père Seguenot, published an edition of St Augustine's *Treatise on Virginity* the notes to which indicated the influence of Duvergier and the new jansenism. Père Joseph went through these and prepared a catalogue of errors which he handed to Richelieu. The orthodox doctrine on grace distinguishes between actual grace and sanctifying grace. Actual grace is grace gratuitously given by God, whether the recipient is in a state of mortal sin or not. Sanctifying grace is grace earned by the recipient through good works and reception of the sacraments, but only when the recipient is not in a state of mortal sin; and it is a measure of the soul's sanctification. Seguenot's notes overlooked the meritorious character of grace and tumbled down Luther's precipice in saying that all grace justifies or condemns the object thereof, that good works are not productive of grace, and, much worse, that all the actions of Christ, even the most indifferent, are predestined. Because forced poverty is the result of divine will it is more a source of grace than voluntary poverty which is not, and on this basis Seguenot condemned monastic vows as a mere expedient of human frailty. At this point the scepticism about man's moral goodness which permeated jansenism became quite clear. This was really too much, and Richelieu summoned the superior of the Oratorians, Père de Condren. The latter disclosed that Duvergier was the inspiration of Seguenot's book. That same day Seguenot was put in the Bastille and Duvergier in Vincennes, from which neither was to emerge while the Cardinal lived.

At the bottom of all this controversy lay an issue on which Richelieu, as a theologian, had already taken a stand. The issue was this: when a penitent goes to confession, must he repent out of love of God? Or is fear of hell sufficient for effective absolution and the reception of grace? The jansenists, in Richelieu's view, would frighten away from confession those who found themselves unable to approach without emotions of regret and horror of sin, and would find that their only penitents would be those already advanced in sanctity. Puritanism in practice would thus be assimilated to predestination. As an intellectual, Richelieu placed the emphasis on an intention to avoid sin in the future, and on acknowledgement of a deliberate violation of God's commandments, and he minimized the importance of emotional experience. The issue was not only one for theological debate, but also one for state supervision. France was imperilled by the ferment of ideas no less than by the passions of unrestrained men; religious and political issues were inextricably interwoven, and France was a theocratic society whether Richelieu wished it that way or not. He himself in his writings never mentions the dangers to the Church without mentioning those to the state, and this drift towards intellectual as well as political absolutism, based on a pessimism about human liberty which he shared with all contemporary intellectuals, was to lead France in the reign of Louis XIV into an extremely gallican position.

The declension from libertinism to anarchy can be rapid, as it was a century before Richelieu, and as it threatens to be once again now that the Counter-Reformation has been finally extinguished in a mood of unhappy protest. After periods of radical and protracted change, when it has become obvious that modification is not necessarily panacea and that diversity often breeds only insecurity, there develops an instinct for authority and for the refuge that total submission affords. Such was the age of Richelieu, when the moral and also the cultural and social values of Catholicism were being rigidified, and when dogmatically and liturgically the Church was being cemented in a mould which was not to be fractured for three centuries. At least in the French context, Richelieu was the architect of a system of religious discipline and deference to orthodoxy which tended to brand as insubordination any criticism or the utterance of any alternative to the official point of view. Truth in the Age of Reason was delineated down to the finest details; and if this inhibited the development of doctrine to take account of the altered human needs and emotions of more recent times, or led on occasions to episcopal tyranny of minds and souls, it had the merits of exhibiting the deposit of faith with clarity, of framing the rules for temporal and eternal happiness with certainty, of inspiring by the majestic panorama of tradition and of gratifying by a triumphal representation of divine mystery.

Richelieu's eagerness to implement the decrees of Trent was due not only to his personal submission to the majesty of the Church, but to his conviction that unorthodox practices confuse the mind, corrode the structure of belief, and by generating disquiet lead to human restlessness.

20

The Most Pernicious Man
1636-7

Du Bec, the governor of the frontier fortress of La Capelle, displayed little fortitude when, at the end of July 1636, the Spanish army of the Netherlands finally began its long-expected invasion of France under Prince Thomas of Savoy. At the first sight of its hedgehogs of pikes moving along the road beneath the red ragged diagonal crosses of Burgundy, and of its enormous cannon lurching behind teams of oxen, La Capelle capitulated. Du Bec fled and his whereabouts was unknown, but in his absence he was condemned to be dismembered by horses on the Place de Grève for high treason. The sentence was in fact carried out in effigy, the Paris mob being regaled with the spectacle of four horses straining to pull apart a life-size doll. Le Catelet, only forty leagues from Paris, also surrendered at the first summons, and its commander, St Léger, likewise disappeared. At the court there was consternation, and a decree was issued calling to the colours all the nobility and their levies who were not already on the regimental rolls; and as the armourers were profiteering out of the unexpected demand for their wares, price-control was imposed on weapons, helmets and breastplates. La Force was in Paris, and at the Hôtel de Ville he himself ran the recruiting depot. At the beginning of August the Spaniards crossed the Somme with twenty-five thousand troops, and found themselves

348

opposed by Soissons with only ten thousand men who had no more than half a dozen bullets apiece. Richelieu's nephew, Brézé's son, was dispatched with orders to destroy all the bridges by which the Spaniards could cross the Oise. At five in the afternoon of 5 August the deputies of the federation of craft guilds appeared at the Louvre, and on their knees offered their goods and their lives to the King to help chase the enemy from the realm. Crowds on the quay outside shouted '*vive le roi!*'

Paris, under threat of attack, was suddenly taken by war fever. The Parlement voted financial aid with unprecedented haste, though it was stubborn about supervision of expenditure; the guilds, the University and all manner of institutions opened their treasuries and poured the contents into the Louvre. The communes busied themselves conscripting all able-bodied men and forbade merchants to employ them. The Cardinal's enemies called a truce in their struggle with him, and the peasants of Guyenne, who were in open revolt against his fiscal policies, volunteered to lay down their arms so as to release troops for the defence of the capital. Richelieu sent orders to Soissons to hold the line of the Oise: if he failed to do so he was to retire on Paris, keeping himself between the city and the invaders. The panic intensified when news arrived that the town of Corbie had also surrendered after a defence of merely eight days; Corbie was just east of Amiens, and only eighty miles from Paris. As the Cardinal surveyed the city he was in despair. He himself had destroyed the walls to make the gardens of the Palais Cardinal, and the bastions that protected the gardens of the Tuileries and the new suburbs of St Honoré and Montmartre were inadequate, or were screened by new housing that no one had bothered to prevent. Placards appeared on walls denouncing him for this folly. He made no secret of his despair to Père Joseph, but the Capuchin, whose faith in God was unshakable, rebuked him with the thought that it is only in time of peril, when strong resolution and extreme confidence in divine providence are necessary, that men are tried. That night the two men came closer to each other than ever before, the grizzled old friar assuming the role of spiritual adviser to the shrunken prelate who from that moment was to be less concerned with the things of this world and more with those of the next. Corbie, in fact, meant the Cardinal's conversion.

Now came the stream of refugees. Through the southern gates of Paris poured the population, not stopping to watch the governor of Corbie, who had fled to England, dismembered in effigy like his fellow-officer du Bec. There was no army available to bring to Soissons' aid, save new levies, for La Valette was holding Gallas in Alsace, and the Prince de Condé had just been forced by Charles of Lorraine to raise the siege of Dôle in Franche-Comté. Thomas of Savoy, however, failed to exploit the drama of his invasion of France. A cautious general, he was afraid to advance further until he had taken all the French positions in his rear or on his flanks, and, while he dallied, La Force assembled thirty thousand men, most of them untrained and ill-equipped, but still formidable in numbers. Gaston d'Orléans emerged from his retreat on the Loire, having raised eight hundred of the local gentry and four thousand troops from the towns in his government, and marched with supplies of food and powder to join the new army of national liberation. He was promptly appointed its commander-in-chief, with Soissons as general and La Force and Châtillon, who had taken over Brézé's command when the latter fell ill, as corps commanders. Monsieur wrote to Soissons: 'Dear cousin, my appointment which the King has been pleased to make has given me great pleasure, and I hope to serve him as nobly as you have done.'

On 15 September Gaston reached Roye in Picardy, where there was an advanced Spanish position, and after two days' bombardment the place capitulated with the honours of war. Monsieur was in high spirits, aud when Thomas of Savoy sent an officer under flag of truce to suggest to him that he should defect and join his wife Marguerite, who had been brought as bait up to the Spanish lines at Cambrai, he just grinned and said, 'Tell the Duc de Mars that if he wants to come and play piquet at Péronne he will find me there in good company.' Although the King was displeased that Gaston had failed to make prisoners of the defenders of Roye, the court applauded the vigour and gallantry with which he cleared the area of the Somme, and the poet François l'Hermite wrote some verses in which Gaston was described as 'the young and glorious Achilles' dumbfounding a new Hector. Unfortunately for the hero's reputation his army gradually succumbed in the autumn rains to the white mud of Picardy, and, stung by the King's reproaches to do something, Monsieur decided to invest Corbie, which the Spaniards had heavily garrisoned. Scarcely had he opened the siege-lines when Louis appeared in person, and Richelieu, who had advanced to Amiens with the King, sent him written instructions to do nothing without the King's orders.

It was the third time that Gaston had in effect been superseded by his brother, and for the third time Gaston demonstrated his disgust in the customary manner; he threw up his command in the face of the enemy and withdrew. He even tried to take his eight hundred gentry with him, but Richelieu intervened to prevent this. Gaston's misery was not relieved when Richelieu himself took the surrender of Corbie on 14 November, the King having withdrawn because of an epidemic in the army, and signalized his triumph by executing two collaborators in the market square. Gaston's own military success had, in fact, reinforced the Cardinal's position, and vexation increased his hatred of him. In the *Gazette* he read the report of Maréchal de Châtillon that, but for the Cardinal's determination and the King's solid judgement and firmness, Corbie could not have been taken at that season.

The Cardinal's determination may have been, though Gaston was not to know it, due in part to his new piety and to Père Joseph's mysticism, which was now bordering on religious hysteria. One of the Capuchin's Calvarian nuns was experiencing divine revelations, and Père Joseph was so overcome that he failed to question the worldly character of the knowledge vouchsafed to her. She reported that a voice had told her that Corbie and La Capelle would both surrender, and Père Joseph wrote this revelation enthusiastically to Richelieu. When the first part of the prediction was verified by events it was expected that the second would shortly follow. But the nun now heard a voice saying, 'I did not mention La Capelle.' This was baffling until news arrived of a victory of Condé in Franche-Comté. That, decided Richelieu, was the predicted event, and the nun had been mistaken about La Capelle. God, he decided, had granted two miracles, and was on the side of France after all.

The Cardinal's preoccupation with heavenly intelligence caused him for once in his career to neglect his sources of earthly information. Unknown to him a group of officers had plotted to murder him in his lodgings in Amiens, and had tried to enlist the support of Gaston and Soissons. How far these two royal personages listened to the plotters is unclear, but most likely they declined to be involved and told the conspirators to be more cautious. At all events, nothing occurred except that Monsieur and his cousin acquired guilty consciences. The day after he received the news of the victory of Corbie, Gaston, swallowing his vexation, travelled from Blois to Paris, to congratulate the King, and there to his surprise he found Soissons, who had been summoned to the court. The two put their heads together. Such a summons in the past had often been the prelude to arrest. Had the Cardinal, who had a reputation for being omniscient, learned of the plotting in Amiens? The fact that the cousins might be innocent was no safeguard, for innocent men had suffered before from Richelieu's suspicions. Soissons decided not to wait to find out; next day he fled towards the eastern frontier, while Gaston returned to Blois. Their sudden disappearance caused the wildest rumours to circulate around Paris, and Richelieu's suspicions were thoroughly aroused when the King received a curiously defensive letter from his brother.

There was never a moment when the realm was not disturbed by some internal upheaval. This time Soissons entered into communication with the Duc de Bouillon, son of the old Huguenot champion, and now in his middle thirties. Soissons made for Bouillon's seat at Sedan, and in the winter of 1637 one of his following braved the ice, snow and ambushes of the Cardinal to bring a message to Gaston at Blois. Bouillon offered Monsieur shelter behind his walls at Sedan and Soissons begged him to accept. All help was promised to get him over the Marne and the Aisne. It quickly transpired, however, that the bridges over the Seine were well guarded, and several of Gaston's gentlemen were captured there, so that his communications with Sedan were broken. The King in his anger was for taking stern measures against Gaston, but Richelieu counselled patience and accommodation with both Monsieur and Soissons, for fear the former might flee again into Spanish hands. It was decided that Louis himself should proceed to Blois and effect yet another reconciliation. Accompanied by an escort of his guards the King left Fontainebleau in the depths of winter, and at Orléans he was presented with a list of Gaston's terms. This began with demands for money to pay his debts and to complete the new wing at the château of Blois, and it continued with a request for amnesties and various immunities. Louis agreed to most of the points.

This time, however, he went further and suggested that he might consent to Gaston's remarriage with Marguerite of Lorraine.[1] It is tempting to see in this sudden gesture of magnanimity a cunning attempt to forestall a papal decision validating the previous marriage, and thereby to avoid loss of face. In fact, however, there was nothing devious about the King's decision. He took it himself over Richelieu's head, and apparently because the question was weighing heavily on his conscience. Père Joseph was exultant, but the Cardinal was far from pleased. Although he was in no position to dictate to the King, who was won over by persuasion only, he managed to forestall Marguerite's return to Gaston for another five years on a variety of political excuses, and only after the Cardinal's death were arrangements completed to bring her from Belgium. The King died before her arrival, and it was in the first year of the reign of Louis xiv that Gaston and Marguerite went through the form of marriage for the third time, she in her bewilderment shedding tears at the thought that for a whole decade she might have been in a state of mortal sin.

It now became a question of enticing Soissons back from Sedan, but when he made his demands known – and they were no more outrageous than those of his cousin Gaston – Louis declared he was 'impertinent'. Again Richelieu intervened to soothe the King, and he wrote to Soissons that, even though his conditions could not be granted, he was to be assured of the King's goodwill.

Soissons, however, was not to be tempted, and opened up negotiations with Marie de Médicis with a view to obtaining Spanish
money to maintain himself. News reached Richelieu that he
had raised over a thousand soldiers who passed their time at
Sedan in wild debauches. He was abetted in this by Gaston, who,
despite his new declarations of loyalty, was still writing to him
advising him to stay where he was and 'take your time to harm
M. le Cardinal'. To the King Richelieu reported that Soissons had
said that no peace would be made between France and Spain
except through the rebels, to which Louis replied that he did not
believe peace would be made during his lifetime. Soissons' words
were no bluff. From intercepted letters it became clear that
a treaty had been signed between Marie de Médicis and the
Cardinal-Infante, according to which Spain would not make
peace or even a truce with France without obtaining satisfaction
for both herself and Soissons, and the removal of Richelieu by one
means or another. Spain would also compensate Bouillon and
Soissons for the loss of their revenues derived from lands in France
and would garrison Sedan. Soissons, so the Cardinal-Infant
reported to Philip IV, would raise rebellion in France and link up
with the dissident peasants of Guyenne, who should be given full
support from Madrid.

The defection of Soissons, which implied also that of Bouillon,
was received by the Cardinal-Infante with delight, not only
because it had disruptive potentialities in France, but because it
gave the Spanish army access to the agricultural production of
France. Although Luxembourg had been ruined by the war, the
valley of the Upper Meuse had not, and its flour and wine were
still flowing downstream to Sedan. With Sedan in Spanish hands
it would follow that Champagne would be supporting the Spanish
war-effort; and if France tried to stop the traffic, Soissons' troops
could be used to requisition foodstuffs within France and bring
them inside the walls of the city. Louis' disposition was to regard
this as nothing but talk, but eventually Richelieu persuaded him
that the situation was dangerous, and that Soissons should be
bought off. Soissons thereupon learned to his surprise that in
terms of a money grant Louis was outbidding the Cardinal-Infante.

He accepted the offer, and by the end of July 1637 he had signed an accommodation with the King. Soissons, so everyone thought, was securely netted, and the gates of Sedan were shut on the Spaniards.

The recapture of Corbie was regarded by everyone as a great victory. In fact its significance was greatly exaggerated, for the Spaniards were still on the soil of France; and though Gallas had been driven into Franche-Comté this territory also was still in Spanish hands at the end of 1636. The Marqués de Valparaiso, governor of Spanish Navarre, tried to come over the Pass of Roncevalles, and, being checked, crossed the Bidassoa and occupied the Pyrenean foothills. In the Mediterranean things were not going well. The archbishop of Bordeaux, Henri d'Escoubleau de Sourdis, was appointed admiral-in-chief of the Levant, and, collecting some thirty-nine ships and eight smaller boats from the Atlantic ports, he sailed for the Mediterranean in June 1636 to launch a combined operation with the army of Maréchal de Vitry, the murderer of Ancre, against the Spaniards on the Iles de Lérins. On 18 August, having been joined by two galleys, the fleet arrived at Cannes, and Sourdis climbed the hills behind the town to study the Spanish dispositions on the islands. A naval attack seemed impossible, and a blockade was therefore necessary. The Spaniards, however, had an enormous fleet of galleys sheltering at Monte Carlo, and whenever the French ships were driven offshore by the wind they would emerge, row to the islands and revictual them. Sourdis decided that as a preliminary measure he should take Monaco.

Sourdis' proposal was that Vitry attack Monaco from Nice and the Comte d'Harcourt, who commanded the troops in Sourdis' fleet, should attack from Menton. The latter, however, detested the odious and brutal Vitry and would cooperate only if Vitry were placed under his command. Vitry in his turn refused to leave Provence, of which he was governor. A conference was held on the flagship, at which a dinner of thirty courses was served, but the reconciliation was temporary. Sourdis became ever more frustrated. Whenever the wind dropped the Spanish galleys emerged and hovered about the anchored French ships, threatening attack; and whenever it rose they disappeared into shallow water or into Monte Carlo harbour. For want of something better to do Sourdis made a demonstration off Genoa in the hope of forcing the Republic to permit passage of French troops to help the beleaguered Duke of Parma, but, with eleven galleys in their docks, the Genoese were unimpressed. Sourdis then returned to Cannes, and on 21 November another council of war was held, at which a quarrel developed between d'Harcourt and Vitry, which ended with Vitry slapping with his cane the breviary which Sourdis was carrying, and indicating that he regarded him as a clerical hypocrite.

Richelieu was never more angry. To Vitry he wrote that it was scarcely credible that a man of his profession could have acted in this manner;[2] and when it became evident that the Spaniards were not to be expelled quickly the King wrote to Sourdis that there was no possible excuse for his failure. Sourdis was also blamed for failing to succour Parma, who made his peace with Spain early in the new year of 1637. Although on this occasion the archbishop was supported against Vitry, it was not forgotten in Paris that only two years previously in Bordeaux he had attracted the blows of the old Duc d'Épernon, and it had been said that it was his design to fight with everyone so as to fill France with the excommunicated.

Goaded into doing something, Sourdis on 24 March 1637 took the risk of opposing ships to shore batteries, and began a day-long bombardment. One fort fell into French hands, but Ste Marguerite held out. Sourdis was in despair as another month passed without developments. Eventually in May a mutiny among his Neapolitan soldiers caused Don Miguel Perez de Goya, the Spanish commander, to surrender with the honours of war, and he marched out his six hundred men with drums beating and colours flying for transportation to Spain. The same tactics were now employed against St Honorat, and the ships' cannon gradually reduced the bastions to ruins and forced the garrison to take refuge in a tower on the middle of the island. Most of the troops were Neapolitan, and again there was a mutiny. When his garrison ran out of their positions shouting 'pace, pace', the governor, Don Juan de Tamayo, yielded.

Meanwhile the Pope's peace offensive had not slackened. More scandalized than ever by the spectacle of the Eldest Daughter of the Church and the Arm of the Church locked in mortal combat while the Protestants seemed to be watching from the sideline, he worked energetically for a peace conference to be held at Cologne. Although Richelieu preferred to work silently and underground for peace, he agreed in principle to participate. Brézé was nominated as the French plenipotentiary, but he fell ill, and Richelieu decided to nominate Alphonse de Richelieu in his place, and to replace Alphonse in Rome by someone who would bully the Pope in the matter of Gaston's marriage instead of ineffectually cajoling him. The Maréchal d'Estrées (Coeuvres) was appointed ambassador to the Holy See, but the Pope told Alphonse that he would refuse to accept him, on the ground that he had fought the papal troops in the Valtelline. Alphonse, taking a leaf out of his brother's political book, arranged for the embassy courier carrying the papal letter to Paris to stop *en route*, feigning illness. A French agent in the town where he would halt would send a new courier, but the papal letter would be 'accidentally' omitted from the dispatches. In this way Alphonse hoped to bring d'Estrées innocently to Rome: 'When he is here,' he said, 'God will provide.' He also wrote to Paris saying that he hoped that d'Estrées would bring his wife. 'This sort of beast is necessary in an ambassador's house,' he said, 'because they wheedle secrets out of people.' God, in fact, did not provide. D'Estrées, when he arrived in Rome was not received by Urban VIII, and being a violent man he proposed to imitate Borgia's conduct and force his way into the Quirinale. Alphonse sought to restrain him, working through the Barberini cardinals to have him recognized. These plans were upset by d'Estrées himself, who behaved brutally, fighting with the Barberini, threatening to bring the Duke of Parma's cavalry into the papal states, and writing rude letters to other ambassadors.

It was in this deplorable atmosphere that Alphonse had his two-hour farewell audience with Urban VIII. The latter said he did not want him to leave, and Alphonse had to plead the necessities of the Cologne peace mission in order to secure the Pope's release. From Rome Alphonse travelled to Venice, intending to avoid the enemy front by crossing through Switzerland to France. However, he changed his mind and secured passes to cross the Milanais, arriving in Lyons to find that he had been superseded in the mission to Cologne by a professional diplomat, St Charmont. He thereupon proceeded to Paris to take up his office of Grand Aumônier. He had been replaced because Richelieu had become sceptical of the possibility of a successful meeting where all the cross-currents of European politics would be exposed.

In fact the Pope's project was doomed when the Emperor called the imperial diet to a meeting in Regensburg. In Richelieu's eyes Ferdinand's decision was a deliberate attempt to forestall a general settlement by having all negotiations conducted within the framework of the imperial constitution. To Mazarin, as the Pope's peace emissary in Paris, he explained that 'it is evident that the diet of Ratisbon has been convoked by the House of Austria for only two reasons – one to elect the King of Hungary King of the Romans, the other to get a league of all Germany against France and her allies'.[3] On 22 December 1636 the election of Ferdinand's son was effected. Richelieu, who had studied the Golden Bull which regulated the imperial elections, affected to discover four defects in the proceedings which would render them null and void: first, the Electors had been inveigled into attending the diet on the pretext that it was to discuss peace, and had been given no notice of the election; second, the Bull required elections to take place at Frankfurt; third, the Elector of Bavaria had usurped the Palatinate vote; and fourth, the Elector of Trier was a prisoner of the Spaniards. With scandalized air Richelieu paraded these arguments before the papal nuncio.

Once more a legal issue added an element of rigidity to an already intractable diplomatic situation, and assisted in defeating the papal peace aims. When Ferdinand II died less than two months after the election, Louis XIII refused to recognize Ferdinand III as more than King of Hungary, and therefore to sit down at any conference table with his representatives. The papal legate, Cardinal Ginetti, who had arrived in Cologne in October to prepare for the peace conference, found that the Spaniards interposed as many difficulties as the French. The new Emperor, too, was aloof; the Protestants, he told the papal nuncio, were nothing but traitors and he would neither recognize them at a conference table nor accept their full powers. In this argument the radically different conceptions entertained by the Habsburgs and the French of the constitution of the Holy Roman Empire became evident: to Ferdinand the Empire was an entity owing allegiance to himself as its sovereign; to Richelieu, it was a 'mixed monarchy which elects its chief, but in which the members make foreign alliances' – an international organization rather than a state.

The status of Lorraine, as a territory of the Holy Roman Empire, was naturally affected by these incompatible views on the imperial system. In the negotiations with the nuncio concerning the projected Cologne conference Richelieu argued that according to the law of succession in Lorraine neither Charles nor his brother François was eligible, and that the Emperor could not remedy this defect in their pretensions. This implied a refusal by France to restore the Duchy. To his credit, however, Richelieu relaxed his position late in 1636 in order to get the Cologne conference started. He was prepared, he said, to agree to the restitution of Lorraine, but naturally on condition that the Emperor agreed to a similar restitution of the lands of the Protestant princes. This Ferdinand rejected outright, and on this point the papal effort failed. No French envoy in fact appeared in Cologne, and the two imperial plenipotentiaries and the grand chancellor of Milan sat there in growing impatience. At last Ginetti left for Rome where he laid on Richelieu the entire blame for the failure of the project.

Richelieu's private peace overtures failed also. These had begun in November 1635 when Père Joseph suggested that Mazarin be sent to Madrid to negotiate. Mazarin was at that moment having a fit of pique about the Capuchin and conceived the idea that Père Joseph was jealous of his influence with Richelieu and wanted him out of the way. Accordingly he made all manner of difficulties about going, and wrote secretly to Cardinal Antonio Barberini asking him to use his influence with the Pope to quash the notion. In the end he stayed in Paris. Richelieu then used the opportunity of an exchange of prisoners-of-war to begin overtures with Olivares. A Spaniard, the Conde de Salazar, had been interned in France at the outbreak of war and was to be icnluded in the exchange. He was asked to let Olivares know that Richelieu was not opposed to peace. News of his mission got abroad in Holland to disquiet the Dutch, and Richelieu had to write to Charnacé to say it was all an invention of the busy-bodies in Paris. Nothing came of the Salazar mission, and in January 1637 a second attempt was made. This time Anne of Austria sent to Spain a priest, Bachelier, whose cloth enabled him to travel across the line of war, to obtain a relic of St Isidore of Seville. The official reason given out for this mission was that the Queen, who had been married for twenty years without children, was seeking the blessing of God on Louis' intermittent and reluc-tant efforts to perform his marital obligations. St Isidore was well known to Richelieu as a political theorist and theologian, but hitherto had no reputation in the matrimonial field. This defici-ency he was quickly to redeem, for, within a matter of months after Bachelier's return from Madrid with the relic, Anne of Austria announced that she was pregnant.

The relic and St Isidore's goodwill were, unhappily, all that Bachelier was able to bring back to Paris. When Olivares at the meeting of the Council of State on 28 March 1637 discussed Bachelier's peace mission, which was the real purpose of his expedition, he said 'we should be rather suspicious. We cannot thus negotiate without guarantees.'[4] He than went on to say that nothing should be done which might discourage Gaston d'Orléans who should be assured of Spanish help and prompted once more to overthrow his brother. Olivares' reply to Bachelier was thus noncommittal. About this time, however, Chavigny received a latter from a Frenchman named Baron de Pujol, who was in the service of a Savoyard in Madrid. Pujol reported that Olivares was out for glory for himself but was not unwilling to treat. At first Richelieu was suspicious and held aloof, but let Chavigny continue his correspondence with Pujol. Gradually it becamc clear that Pujol had Olivares' ear, and after the failure of Bachelier's mission Richelieu began to use his services to attempt to negotiate with Spain.

Pujol's negotiations were interrupted for a time by Richelieu's discovery that Anne of Austria was in close and constant correspondence with the Marqués de Mirabel, the former Spanish ambassador in Paris. This woman, who is little heard of after her dramatic entrance into history as the object of Buckingham's indiscretion, suddenly ceased to be anonymous and overlooked. Her correspondence was the height of folly, for Richelieu's men tapped everyone's mail, and hers was carefully opened, copied, closed again and delivered without her suspicions being aroused. Her attempts at cloak-and-dagger intrigue were ludicrously amateur. She would retire to the convent of Val-de-Grâce on religious pretexts. On the terrace of the garden stood a casket, and one of the nuns was wont to bring this into the Queen's cabinet when she was alone there with the abbess, Louise de Milley, who came from Franche-Comté, and was thus a Spanish subject. One of her ladies-in-waiting, who was a spy of the Cardinal, could not fail to find the regularity of this performance significant. All this Richelieu reported to the King. The chancellor, Pierre Séguier, and the archbishop of Paris were instructed to go to the convent and take an inventory of the Queen's possessions there and interrogate the abbess. The latter denied ever having seen the Queen write or receive a letter, and nothing incriminating was found. She was, however, deposed that night by the archbishop and locked up in another convent, while the Queen's portemanteau, Pierre de La Porte, who admits in his *Mémoires* to having coded the Queen's letters and decoded the Spanish replies, was put in the Bastille and his papers searched. Again nothing serious was found.

Séguier was now instructed to interrogate the Queen herself. He produced a copy of a letter from Mirabel, which she did not deny, but which she claimed to be innocent of political content. The Court became agitated at the way the Cardinal continued to persecute her, and in the end the King's confessor, Père Caussin, intervened to stop the interrogation. Richelieu persisted, arguing that it was necessary to know the whole story. He was vindicated by events, for, confronting her in person, he disclosed letters of hers to Mirabel and to the spider in every web of intrigue, Mme de Chevreuse, which were highly political in content and would be traitorous if written by anyone else; whereupon she succumbed. On 17 August 1637 she signed a confession, promising to live with the King in complete loyalty to his person and his state. The latter signed a pardon written out by the Cardinal, and forbade her henceforth to correspond with Mme de Chevreuse, or to enter any convent building. Mme de Chevreuse, seeing the net falling around the Queen's associates, fled from Couzières to the Spanish frontier, where Philip IV arranged for one of his own carriages to be waiting to take her to Madrid. From there she travelled to London to become the focus of a little huddle of political and military refugees.

That the Queen had been in touch with her brother the Cardinal-Infante through her correspondents was clear, and there was even talk of Louis rejecting her. It was decided to save the faces of both Anne and her brother Philip IV by blaming Mirabel for his impertinence in writing to her. This interpretation pleased Madrid and, after the initial indignation had worn off, disposed Philip IV to look more kindly on Richelieu's overtures for peace. Some months after the affair of the Val-de-Grâce a draft armistice agreement was sent by Richelieu to Pujol to place before Olivares. The latter wanted to send one Don Miguel de Salamanca to Brussels to take up his functions as secretary of state of the Spanish Netherlands, and Pujol arranged with Richelieu for him to pass through France and continue the discussions in Paris *en route*. Don Miguel, who spoke excellent French, arrived with great mystery dressed as a Frenchman, and was put in touch with Chavigny. He insisted, however, on seeing Richelieu, and after much hesitancy was taken to him in the greatest secrecy at Compiègne, where they met in a church. It is not completely clear what passed between the two men, but Don Miguel reported to Olivares that nothing was likely to be achieved. Olivares, discussing the report at the meeting of the Council of State on 18 June 1638, said of Richelieu that 'he is, without doubt, the most pernicious man there is or ever has been; the worst Frenchmen are angels alongside him!'[5]

21

The Firmament of Truth
1638

The Cardinal, suffering miseries from piles, had a new problem to
occupy his worried mind: the King had fallen in love. The girl
was the sixteen-year-old Louise de la Fayette, one of the Queen's
ladies-in-waiting, and sister of an ancestor of the hero of the
American revolution. Richelieu had favoured this interest of the
King's which promised to be entirely innocent, and this was
connived at by Louise's uncle, the bishop of Limoges. She was
docile, sang to the King and played games with him, accommodating herself to his every mood, and she was politically
neutral, whereas Mlle de Hautefort, another of the Queen's
ladies for whom Louis had been pining, was pro-Spanish. But
Louise conceived for the Cardinal a dislike shared by much of the
court, and he became anxious lest she might be used as a tool by
his enemies. It was therefore with satisfaction that he heard from
Père Carré, the superior of the Dominican Noviciate of St
Thomas d'Aquin, that Louise had expressed the desire to enter the
convent. The poor girl's vocation now became a political issue,
for the pro-Spanish faction, led by the *gouvernante* of the ladies-
in-waiting, constituted a cabal to combat Père Carré in order to
keep Louise in her position of influence; and the Cardinal, finding
that virtue and self-interest happily coincided, threw his weight on
the side of the will of God.

When Père Caussin was appointed the royal confessor in March 1637 on Richelieu's own recommendation, the Cardinal referred to the King's attachment to Louise. 'I don't suspect anything wrong in it,' the Cardinal had said, 'but such affection between people of different sexes is always dangerous.'[1] He advised Caussin not to break the affair immediately, but to watch it. On his first day in his new office the confessor was approached by Louise and asked for an interview. He began to wonder if her anxiety to take the veil was not due to a desire to escape from a compromising situation, and he counselled patience and reflection. In this he gratified the King but not the Cardinal, who made his displeasure clear to Caussin. He told the Jesuit, in fact, that as the King's confessor he was in no position to meddle in the affair.

Louise de la Fayette entered the convent of the Visitation on 19 May 1637, and the King was inconsolable. Standing by his carriage in the courtyard of the château of St Germain, he caught one last glimpse of her at a window, while she groaned, 'Alas, I shall never see him again!' She was wrong: the King appeared at the convent. The mother superior, overwhelmed by the circumstances, suggested that, if he wished to exercise the royal prerogative, he might enter the clausura. This he indignantly rejected, saying he would sooner lose an arm than do such a thing. He was then conducted to a grille where for three hours he talked with the postulant. That night Richelieu received a letter from Caussin telling him what had occurred, and, anxious to know what conversation had occupied these three hours, he summoned the Jesuit to him. 'I am really astonished,' Richelieu told Caussin when he arrived, 'that the King should keep me in the dark about this; after all, I have no anxiety about the affair.'[2] In some way he seemed to blame the Jesuit for what had occurred, and became excited. Far from being the cold-blooded and calculating tyrant of tradition he was in fact a man who easily fell into fits of nervous irritability whenever he thought someone was deceiving him, and all too often he lost his sense of perspective. 'You are not wicked,' he finished by telling Caussin, 'but I must teach you about the malice of the world.' Caussin came away from the interview perplexed by the grave view of the matter which Richelieu had taken, while the Cardinal, even when he had calmed his nerves, continued to doubt the confessor's sense of prudence.

The visits continued, and Richelieu became ever more persistent that Caussin disclose what was going on. The Cardinal's brother, Alphonse, was dragged into the affair in his capacity of Grand Aumônier of France, and, saintly and unworldly though he was, expressed himself of the opinion that Caussin was unreliable, naïve and understood nothing of politics. He compared him, in fact, with the angel of the Apocalypse, one foot on earth the other in heaven. It gradually became clear that Caussin was doing more than merely tolerating the visits; he was actively conniving at them. It also became clear that through the grille Louise was not averse to being spiteful about the Cardinal, though she stopped this when Louis indicated his displeasure and instead gave nunly advice about his duty to his wife. He was not disposed those days to sport in the shade with his Amaryllis, as he had once nicknamed the Queen, and to whom he had dedicated his beautiful chanson, *Tu crois ô beau soleil*. Who knows if, perhaps, the girl was the voice of St Isidore? For, while the King was listening to her advice, a storm arose which made it impossible for him to return to Versailles, where he was lodged, and determined him to take shelter in the Louvre. There nothing was prepared for him, and on the suggestion of the captain of the guards he asked the Queen, who was in residence in the palace, if he could sup with her. Anne's dining hours were Spanish, his were French, but on this occasion she conceded to him and they dined at his convenience. The storm continued and he was forced to share her bed. The result was the birth of Louis XIV, ten months and two days later, on 5 September 1638. In a quite unexpected way, Richelieu's peace mission to Olivares had earned for France a grandeur that not even he could ever have dreamed of.

This providential intervention, however, did not save Père Caussin, in whom Richelieu had by now lost all confidence. The confessor committed one indiscretion after another, finally deciding that his office required him to denounce the war as immoral. On 8 December 1638 the King was about to go to confession when the Jesuit began to lecture him, deploring the

French alliance with the Protestants, and the scandals of Germany, where six thousand Catholic churches were in ruins. 'You,' he said, 'brought the Swedes into Germany, and you will answer to God for all the burnings, violations and other disorders which they will commit. It is not enough to live well in the state in which you are, all the good you do is useless. Now you want to bring the Turk down on Christendom!' 'That is false,' said the King, 'I have never thought of it!' 'It is true!' cried Caussin, who then went on to describe the evils of France, the mounting taxes, and the quartering of the armies on the people. The Cardinal was not the only one hated in France; the King was also losing the loyalty of his subjects.[3] From this point he went on to say that the King should pay back her dowry to Marie de Médicis, picturing her, with poetic licence, dying of hunger in Flanders. After this tirade the King went to confession to Caussin and then to communion. At the altar rails the Jesuit delivered another harangue, reminding Louis of what he had earlier said, and the King left the chapel 'sombre and thoughtful'.[4]

The crisis of the King's conscience was also a crisis for France. Next morning Louis told Père Caussin that he had seriously reflected upon what he had said; that night he was to dine with Richelieu at Rueil, and he wanted the confessor to go there also and repeat what he had said. Caussin, full of apostolic fervour, presented himself to the Cardinal shortly before dinner, and was coldly received. 'I perceive,' said Richelieu, 'that clouds are assembling in your heart to make a storm against me.'[5] The noise of the King's carriage entering the *cour d'honneur* was heard, and Richelieu asked Caussin to wait in another room. When the King appeared his eyes ran around the salon seeking his confessor. 'He has gone,' Richelieu said. The King thereupon told the Cardinal all that had occurred, and the latter, summoning every ounce of intellectual energy he possessed, proceeded to counter Caussin's argument.

There was no one in France better equipped to put the case for the just war than Richelieu, for he had read the philosophers and theologians and had struggled long with his own conscience. With theological and canonical arguments he rebuilt Louis' broken morale. What, he concluded, would the King do as a matter of fact when Savoy was in Spanish hands, and France reduced, by a dishonourable and precipitate peace, to suffer under the yoke of the House of Austria? Louis sought to apologize for Caussin, whose intentions, he said, had been good, but Richelieu, playing his trump card of threatened resignation, told him he must choose between the Jesuit and himself. In the next room Père Caussin waited, and eventually returned to St Germain not having seen the King. The following morning he blundered, not without obstacles, into the royal presence. 'I did not see you at Rueil,' began the King. 'I was there, Sire, and waited a long time to be called, firmly decided to say everything. I persist in my views. I have only said what the law of the gospel and the whole school of the fathers teach.'[6] Chavigny and Sublet de Noyers intervened before the King could lose his temper, and took Père Caussin out. At their advice he retired to the Jesuit house in Paris. Next day his papers were seized and he was exiled by *lettre de cachet* to Rennes.

The Caussin affair is likely to be misunderstood if one accepts the view that Richelieu was entirely the politician. In fact it was at this moment that his thoughts were turning increasingly to the problem of saving his soul. He was, he knew, nearing his end, and it was time to examine closely his spiritual condition. As usual when he needed to clarify his mind he took his pen and began to write, probably sitting propped up in bed in the small hours of the morning, pale, his sunken cheeks shadowed by the light of a candle, fondling one of his fourteen cats. Affairs distracted him from formulating his thoughts, and the task took over two years, but the result was an important contribution to spiritual literature, his *Treatise on Christian Perfection*, the manuscript of which was found among his papers after his death and published in 1646 by Mme de Combalet. He said in the preface that it was a work intended for himself as well as for others, and it is clearly the result of a personal struggle to identify the path of grace. It is tightly dogmatic, indicative of complete intellectual conviction, and aims at delineating the various degrees of the spiritual life from prayer to ecstasy. Its theme is that 'he always acts well who always prays', and prayer is not the privilege of the priest but is available to everyone, even those most occupied with human affairs. To progress in the spiritual life, he said, 'it is sufficient to set oneself in the divine presence at different times of the day.' Indeed, 'it is better to work continually for God by a general designation renewed at different hours of the day, than to live in continual reflection.'[7] Again, 'one moment of elevation of the soul and heart, in the troubles which it is necessary to suffer in bounty to the world, can be more efficacious and more agreeable to God than whole days passed in idle solitude'.[8] This was the apologia of a man of God who had devoted less of his time to his Creator than to his King.

The path to perfection, he wrote, is that of good conduct, sincere faith, surveillance of the passions, and sane reason. Neither tolerance nor severity should be exaggerated. 'The life of a Christian must therefore be a perpetual combat, a continual action far removed from idleness, which is the real source of vice – a solicitude which is never interrupted and which unceasingly works to affirm in him the empire of reason.' And, dealing jansenism a mortal blow, he added: 'There are many souls who cannot love God unless they are affected by a sensible passion, and unless their affection has its roots in the senses. But they deceive themselves: the seat of love is in the will. Those who love God are those who will what He wills.' God is continually knocking on the doors of our souls so that they should be opened; confession gives access to the frequent reception of the sacraments, and therefore 'it is necessary to confess frequently, even if one is guilty of only venial sins'. And, he wrote a chapter on the utility of frequent communion.

It was this man, genuinely seeking the path of perfection amid the preoccupations of politics and war, who at this point was being represented to a worried Pope as a potential schismatic, if not heretic, by a hostile nuncio. Far in advance of his time, Richelieu believed that it was desirable and possible to reunite the Catholics and the Protestants; and rationalist as he was, he believed that a dialogue between the two Churches would lead to the recognition by the Protestants of their errors. At this time his relations with the Jesuits had become close, and some of them were active supporters of his ideas of religious toleration. The Roman curia, however, was by no means ready to make even minor concessions to heresy, and was deeply suspicious of Richelieu's continued leniency towards the Protestant cult in La Rochelle, which it attributed to his consideration for his Protestant allies. It was reported that in order to achieve political unity in France he would be prepared to drop certain doctrines which had not been dogmatically proclaimed, and that he was even ready to compromise on the dogma of purgatory.

That this was a malicious distortion of Richelieu's policy is clear from a work which he was currently writing on the best manner of converting 'those who are separated from the Church'. This was never finished, but the manuscript was published in 1651 and had a considerable effect on the Huguenot problem. The authoritarian in politics could naturally brook no particularism in religion, which he regarded as 'absurd'. There can be only one belief, only one visible Church; there can be no faith without preachers, but preaching presupposes recognized authority and qualified ministers, and thus a hierarchic Church, 'the column and the firmament of Truth'. The true Church had been visible for sixteen centuries; if the Reform had lived hidden and ignored, it had not been visible; if it were new, then it had fractured the unity of faith. On this dilemma he rested his argument. Luther, he pointed out, preached the need for reception of the blood as well as the body of Christ; Calvin preached the opposite. But the Calvinists pretend to be the same body as the Lutherans; how can they be thus divided on a point on which they both base salvation?

The grandeur of France to Richelieu was the grandeur of Catholicism, for was not France the realm of the Most Christian King, the France of the crusades, of the Mother of God? In his new fervour he suddenly conceived the idea of crystallizing this unity of monarchy and faith by making a formal dedication of France to the Blessed Virgin, placing the country under her protection in this hour of trial and suffering. The King, himself passing through a similar phase of spiritual awakening, received the idea with enthusiasm, and at the end of 1637 the proclamation was made. The act of consecration began with an echo of the theory of divine right in calling upon 'God, who raises kings to the throne of their grandeur'. It then goes on:

We consecrate to her [the Virgin] particularly our person, our state, our crown and our subjects, beseeching her to inspire in us such saintly conduct, and to defend this realm against the efforts of all its enemies with such care that, whether it suffers the scourge of war or enjoys the sweetness of peace, which we ask of God with all our heart, it will not depart from the ways of grace, which lead to those of glory.[9]

In a sense this gesture was one of thanksgiving and relief, for by the end of 1637 the Spanish invasion of France had been repulsed. There was no real fighting, merely a series of elaborate movements and sieges. In the early summer Landrécies fell, to be followed in September by La Capelle. The latter's Spanish governor, when he arrived at Valenciennes, was court-martialled and beheaded on the orders of the Cardinal-Infante. On the eastern frontier, however, there was a stalemate, while from the Grisons there was nothing but bad news. The Spaniards had completely won over these tiresome mountaineers, who at Innsbruck had signed a treaty with the Emperor by which they gained troops and cannon to drive Rohan out of his fortified position near Chur. Surrounded by imperialists and Grison mutineers, Rohan on 26 March 1637 capitulated and abandoned to the Grisons the Valtelline and the counties of Chiavenna and Bormio.

Neither Rohan's subordinates in the Valtelline itself nor the government in Paris would believe the news; surely it was some stratagem on Rohan's part? All Rohan's orders to the French in the Valtelline were disobeyed, but when it became clear that they were cut off by Gallas who was at Lindau, by Spaniards on the road over the St Gotthard, and by imperialists in the Tyrol, evacuation became necessary. It now became a question of saving the army from capture or destruction, and Richelieu was forced to accept Rohan's engagement. The Cardinal's acquiescence did not prevent him from being highly critical of Rohan's failure; and Rohan, believing that the Bastille awaited him if he returned to

Paris, made for Geneva, where he became ill, or said he did. His suspicions were well founded, for Richelieu in fact had issued orders for his seizure. After pondering whether or not he should return to Venice, of whose forces he was still nominally commander-in-chief, he decided to join his friend Bernard of Saxe-Weimar, then in winter quarters on the Upper Rhine, and there he betook himself on his last journey. On 28 February 1638 he was mortally wounded at Rheinfeld in Alsace, and died in the abbey of Königsfelden, whither he was taken. His body was transported to Geneva, the Calvinist Rome, with great pomp, and he lies splendidly entombed there in the cathedral of St Pierre.

Meanwhile, the exactions in the south of France, plus the diminishing volume of money with which to meet them, had led to a revolt in Guyenne. Eight thousand peasants, taking the name Croquants, and led by a local nobleman, the Sieur de La Mothe-La Forêt, went on the rampage and were finally besieged in Bergerac. It was necessary to suppress this movement before the Spaniards, lodged by now on the French side of the Pyrenees, made common cause. The Duc de La Valette, brother of the Cardinal of that name, was therefore dispatched with an army to deal with this 'rabble' as Richelieu called them; and the rebels, terrified by the ruthless way in which his soldiers, contrary to orders, had dealt with the district, burning, raping, garrotting and torturing their parents, wives and sisters, offered to surrender if they would be pardoned. La Mothe-La Forêt emerged from the walls to the royalist entrenchments and conferred with La Valette's lieutenant. He told him he had been dragged into the business only because the communes of Périgord had threatened to burn his wife and children in his own house if he would not be their chief. He was told to return and disarm his following if he expected the King's mercy. When he attempted to do so a local doctor led a mutiny, and with five thousand of the rebels retired into the citadel of Bergerac. La Mothe-La Forêt then stormed them with the remainder of his force, killed the doctor himself, and turned Bergerac over to La Valette. The five thousand Spaniards in Guyenne had not budged, but neither did La Valette exhibit any intention of expelling them. Prodded by Richelieu to do so, for some three months he kept replying that he had insufficient forces. Condé was therefore given command in the area, and by the end of the year he had cleared the Spaniards out of the south of France.

While France was thus preoccupied with the expulsion of the invaders, the Swedes were finding themselves enmeshed in a profitless war in north Germany. Saxony had turned against them, Brandenburg was a competitor in the struggle to seize Pomerania when the Duke should die, and Oxenstierna felt his grasp on the Duchy slipping. He was thus in a mood to negotiate with France, which he imagined by now to be so humbled that Richelieu would have to modify the terms which the Swedish government had found so impossible; on the contrary Richelieu thought Sweden to be so weakened that it would be forced to swallow them. There took place in Hamburg a diplomatic duel between adversaries worthy of each other, Salvius the Vice-Chancellor of Sweden, and the Comte d'Avaux the French plenipotentiary, whom Pufendorf, the jurist who recorded the event, described as being a man who, when you thought you had caught him, was found to have slipped through your hands. The fencing went on for weeks, and in the end d'Avaux won. On 5 March 1638 a treaty was signed, and immediately ratified by the Swedish government. Sweden undertook to continue the war against Ferdinand III and France to pay her 400,000 thalers a year. France guaranteed no support for Sweden's claims to Pomerania, and Sweden none for France's claims to Lorraine. From Richelieu's point of view the importance of the engagement was that a renewed Swedish offensive in the areas of Saxony, Silesia and Bohemia, where he had hoped to confine Gustavus Adolphus, would draw imperial armies away from the French frontier, and leave France to deal with Spain alone.

Holland, also, was becoming a more active diversionary, retaking Breda late in 1637. Charnacé fell during the assault. When the news reached Madrid the decaying Olivares fell into another of his fits of depression. Nothing in the world, he said, could now console him. 'Richelieu is the leader of the persecution;

he is responsible for all the ills from which Christendom suffers. Everything he does is manifest trumpery! It needs miracles to alter the present situation.'[10] On 17 December 1637 a new treaty was signed between the Dutch and French by which an annual subsidy of 1,200,000 *livres* was to be paid by France, and by which the Dutch promised to attack either Dunkirk or Antwerp in return for a French undertaking to besiege Thionville, Namur or Mons.

Richelieu committed France to payment of these enormous sums of money without really considering the country's ability to pay them. As a result the subsidies were always in arrears, and the allies came to trust France's undertakings less and less. Grotius, in particular, was proving a nuisance at the head of a coterie of foreign agents who kept pressing for payment. In 1638 the year's subsidy to Bernard of Saxe-Weimar was due in February; by April Bullion had been able to raise only a quarter of it. 'We are now,' he groaned, 'at the bottom of the pit, and I fear that our foreign war is degenerating into civil war.'[11] In addition, although the total of French forces amounted on paper to 123,000, it was never possible, because of the cumbersome feudal structure, to place at the disposal of the allies the numbers of troops promised.

Bernard's needs, in Richelieu's eyes, were the greatest, for unless he could be kept in the field in Alsace and the Black Forest France would be exposed to invasion again by the imperial armies. To this end Feuquières, who had become friendly with him, was sent to Bernard with promises of aid which, in fact, did not materialize. At the end of January 1638 Bernard began a winter campaign, fell on the imperial cantonments in Alsace and added three thousand imperial prisoners to his army. Towns as far apart as Hünigen and Freiburg fell to him, and he now commanded the communications to Breisach, the most formidable fortress on the upper Rhine. He did this without French money or French lives, but that did not prevent the French from rejoicing in what they treated as a French victory. The French army in Franche-Comté, which was supposed to link up with Bernard, would have deserted *en masse* if required to march in the winter, and even in the spring it had to be bribed with abundance of supplies and its destination had to be concealed from it. While the eighty-year-old La Force, overcoming what Richelieu described as the 'irremediable evil' of age, took Le Catelet, Bernard began the siege of Breisach, which, if taken, would block the Rhine communications between Italy and Flanders.

Urban VIII was now over seventy and, weary of the struggle to reunite Catholicism, had lapsed into inactivity. There were now a dozen vacancies in the Sacred College which he made no attempt to fill, and in Paris this was attributed to a malevolence which determined the Pope never to admit Père Joseph. In October Richelieu wrote to d'Estrées telling him not to press the nomination of Père Joseph further. Instead, having begun to think of Mazarin as his successor, he nominated the wily Sicilian. Unknown to Richelieu, Urban VIII, faced with this choice, resolved privately to promote Père Joseph. On 13 December 1638 Père Joseph fell violently sick while giving spiritual instructions in the early morning to his Calvarian nuns. That night he made a general confession, and his mind turned again to his youthful dreams of preaching the last crusade. Speaking of this to the mother superior he said that he had always had an inner command to do all he could to withdraw Jesus from captivity. Next day he was able to say mass, and, after he had said his office, had the history of the conquest of the Holy Places by Godefroy de Bouillon read to him before receiving extreme unction.

As the news circulated that Père Joseph was mortally ill a strange collection of figures out of his past life appeared to take their farewells, among them the nuncio Bichi and Gaston d'Orléans. On 15 December Richelieu was giving a theatre party. Père Joseph had been brought to Rueil and was in bed upstairs. Jokingly the Cardinal said he should come to the comedy, it would do him good. 'I am going to have some comedy with my breviary,' replied the Capuchin.[12] As the play was being performed a message was passed in to Richelieu, who immediately rose, and, his face grave, rustled out of the theatre, a slight ageing figure in watered scarlet. Père Joseph had had a stroke and was dying. He lasted for another three days, more or less in a coma. On 16 December the King wrote to the Pope informing him of the news and formally withdrawing Père Joseph's candidature for the hat. Père Joseph died on Saturday 18 December, and on that day Urban VIII, as yet unaware of events in Paris, appointed him to the Sacred College. The King's comment when he heard of the death was, 'I have lost today the most faithful of my servants, and M. le Cardinal his confidant and support.'[13] The Cardinal now looked into a black future without this support, which was as necessary to the well-being of his soul as to the success of his policies.

Père Joseph was laid in his grave by royal order before the high altar of the Capuchin church in the Faubourg St Honoré in the presence of one hundred and sixty members of his Order, and at the requiem mass were Richelieu, the nuncio, and a great assembly of prelates and nobility. At the funeral oration two days later some five hundred carriages were counted. On that same day a courier arrived in Paris from Bernard of Saxe-Weimar. Breisach had fallen. The conjunction of Père Joseph's death and the capture of the fortress did not escape the attention of an age reared on classical drama, and the legend grew up that Richelieu, leaning over the ear of the unconscious Père Joseph, had sought to rally him with the words 'Breisach is ours!'

22

The Diabolical Menace

1638-40

As Richelieu knelt beside Père Joseph's tomb he must have reflected how a whole generation was passing, and how, with its passing, his own strategic and political edifice was crumbling. There are no constant presumptions in history; trivial events can upset great calculations and effect vast changes; and of all trivial events death is the most frequent and most significant. Bernard of Saxe-Weimar was to die within the next few months; thereby was removed one whose ambitions to be sovereign of Alsace were irritating and inconvenient, but whose military genius had made him indispensable. On 21 September 1637 Charles de Gonzague, the Duke of Mantua, had died, and on 7 October he had been followed to the grave by Victor Amadeus of Savoy.

In Mantua there was now an infant ruler, and the regent was Charles's daughter-in-law, Maria, brought up in imperial circles and pro-Spanish by inclination. She immediately began negotiations for peace with the Spanish governor of the Milanais, the Marqués de Legañez, and on 25 March 1638 signed a treaty by which she agreed to deliver Montferrat, including Casale, to Spain. The unfortunate governor of Casale, Montiglio, was in an impossible position, for in the fortress was a French garrison. Upon receiving his instructions from Maria to open his gates to the Spaniards he decided that he had no alternative but to obey.

He was, however, arrested by the Cardinal de La Valette, whom Richelieu had dispatched to take command in Italy, and court-martialled. The commissioners in charge of his trial promised him his life if he would confess all, and this he did. When the papers of the proceedings reached Paris Richelieu had a fit of scruples. Was he bound to honour the promise? He consulted Père Joseph and his confessor, whose advice remains a secret. Suffice it to say that Montiglio was shortly afterwards beheaded.

Casale was cut off from the advanced French base at Pinerolo by the whole breadth of Savoy, and for the moment the attitude of that country was obscure. Again there was an infant heir, but this time the regent, Christine, was the sister of Louis XIII and was pro-French. However, two of Victor Amadeus' brothers, the Cardinal of Savoy and Prince Thomas of Savoy, were pro-Spanish, the one being in league with the Spanish faction in the Sacred College, the other being the Spanish general on the Belgian frontier. They could legitimately claim a say in the tutorship of their nephew, and hence in the government of his duchy. It was expected that they would return to Turin, where a large element in the population would welcome them; and a Thomas in charge at home would be more useful to Olivares than a Thomas besieging towns in Picardy. For the moment, however, this was not the most serious danger, for Christine, jealous of her power, was no less anxious than Richelieu to shut the door in the face of the two brothers. The real danger was that, to placate the faction which might support them, she would withdraw Savoy into neutrality as soon as the treaty of alliance expired in July 1638. France was unpopular, the war was burdensome and without result, and the populace restless.

The neutrality of Savoy would be a serious blow to Richelieu's strategic conceptions. The passage of the armies of the Cardinal-Infante from the Milanais to the Rhine and Flanders had left the Milanais devoid of troops, and the Spanish government had had the greatest difficulty in making up the deficiency. Indeed, had France not been so preoccupied on her own borders, the overthrow of Spanish power in Italy might have been accomplished. Richelieu's primary objective was still the taking of Milan, which would have the effect either of withdrawing the Spanish armies from Belgium in order to recover it or of cutting the lifeline between them and Spain. In either event, the pressure on France would be greatly relieved. To make a demonstration of French power and intent, Cardinal de La Valette appeared in Turin in May and was grandly received by Christine. She, however, was willing to renew the French alliance only on condition that it was specified to be a defensive alliance against the enemies of the King, and not an offensive alliance against Spain. While she was debating this with La Valette a Spanish army invaded Montferrat, and, overcome with fright at the news of the devastation it was causing, she yielded and signed a treaty of alliance against Philip IV on 3 June 1638, and placed the Savoyard army under French command. Suddenly, while the Spaniards were yet advancing, having taken Vercelli from the French, the whole thing was undone by the death of the young Duke of Savoy, which automatically terminated the regency of his mother. The new duke was the five-year-old brother, Charles Emmanuel II, and it was now necessary to summon the States General to appoint a new regent, and, since Savoy was an imperial fief, refer the matter to the Emperor.

Since the two brothers could not now be kept out of the question, Richelieu decided that the only thing to do was to cultivate them. Next in line of succession was the Cardinal of Savoy, and Mazarin, then in Rome, was to be used to open negotiations with him first. Like François of Lorraine, the Cardinal was not in holy orders, and he was to be enticed with the prospect of a marriage to Condé's daughter and the grant of estates in France, where he would be treated as a prince of the blood. The Cardinal, however, slipped out of Rome in the habit of a knight of Malta, and joined the Spaniards in Montferrat. There was now nothing to do but support Christine in what promised to become a civil war in Savoy, and to persuade her to seize her brother-in-law should he set foot in the Duchy.

Events moved quickly. The Emperor quashed the will of Victor Amadeus, invalidated the regency of Christine and deprived her of the tutelage of the Duke; Spain dispatched Prince Thomas of

Savoy to execute the imperial decree, and he appeared in Milan to concert plans with Legañez. Richelieu's instructions to La Valette were that in any crisis he should seize the young Charles Emmanuel and his capital and hold them, and try also to capture Thomas should he seek to exercise any authority in Savoy. In addition Louis wrote to his sister in his usual blunt fashion that, should she let Thomas into her estates, he would have no confidence in her, and she need not expect any testimony of his affection. As Thomas advanced at the head of a Spanish army, the governors of the Piedmont towns opened their gates to him one by one. Christine called to La Valette for succour, but at the same time she sent Charles Emmanuel over the Alps to Savoy where he would be out of French as well as Spanish hands. Outnumbered, La Valette failed to save Turin, and he was forced to agree to a truce while Christine and her garrison retired into the citadel.

Legañez was a man of a different character from Gonzalo de Cordoba or Feria. Recalling his meeting with Richelieu when he and Spinola had visited La Rochelle, he told La Valette that there was no one in the world of Richelieu's merit, and that Olivares wanted to have a picture of the Cardinal in his room. We do not know Richelieu's reaction to this interesting essay in Castilian courtesy. When informed of it, he was on his way with the King to meet Christine at Grenoble, in the hope of persuading her to hand Charles Emmanuel over to France. Christine left Turin during the truce, and her discussions with her brother and the Cardinal were stormy. She said she would not deliver any of her towns into French hands, she would hold out against the Spaniards behind the alpine barrier, and she would not have Savoy reduced to the condition of Lorraine. After scenes of emotion she left for Chambéry and her son without satisfying Richelieu in any respect. Bad news continued to arrive: Nice, held by the brother of St Francis de Sales, was taken by the Cardinal of Savoy, and Richelieu said he was 'pierced to the heart'; La Valette died of pneumonia at the age of forty-seven; and his successor, the Comte d'Harcourt, was forced to retreat from Turin when the truce expired.

Olivares was once more on the wings of optimism, exclaiming

with typical but unjustified hyperbole, 'Successes such as God has worked by the hand of Your Majesty in Italy have never seen their equal in the world, not alone in one year, but in many!'[1] Now, he decided, was the time to reopen negotiations for peace. It was difficult to find anyone who spoke French sufficiently well to go to Paris. Eventually the bishop-designate of s'Hertogen-bosch was sent, but he met with little response. 'One would have to be blind,' said Richelieu, 'not to see the diabolical menace of the Spaniards. They negotiate only to avoid the bad reputation which they have acquired in Christendom when one knows their evil designs.'[2] Borgia, now a member of the Spanish Council of State, capped this on 6 August 1640 when he argued that 'there is nothing else to do than carefully prepare the campaign for this year and pursue the war next year.'[3]

Harcourt, a Lorrainer, was a flamboyant character, and he wore an enormous pearl attached to one ear. In the spring he was back in the field and laid siege to Turin. There were French in the citadel; Thomas lay between them and the walls with six thousand troops and several thousand armed citizens. Outside the walls were the French siege lines, and outside them again lay the army of Legañez, twenty thousand strong. Legañez told Thomas to invite the ladies of Turin to open their windows so they could see the great pearl when Harcourt was brought in as a prisoner. Instead, the ladies witnessed the evacuation of Thomas' forces, for Harcourt's cavalry general, Bouillon's brother, the young Turenne, drove Legañez off, and Thomas was forced to capitulate in September 1640.

Nothing in Piedmont could be done, it seemed, without Mazarin, who had appeared on the scene, cheeks more puffy than ever. His is perhaps the most astonishing career of the seventeenth century. Papal peace-envoy to Paris in the years before the formal outbreak of war, he had then become the vice-legate in Avignon, and later an active French agent in Rome. His ability was remarkable, and Richelieu had come to esteem him highly. Following Père Joseph's death the Cardinal decided to groom Mazarin as his successor, and in 1639 he persuaded him to vacate the papal service, come to Paris and become a naturalized Frenchman. In

December 1641 Urban VIII's reluctance to promote him to the Sacred College was to be overcome, and he was to receive the hat a few months before Richelieu's death. Now, in 1640, he was sent to Turin to employ his skill in negotiating its surrender to the French, and this he managed cleverly. As Thomas rode out of the city on the route to Ivrea he passed Harcourt, and, without stopping or uttering a word, perfunctorily saluted him and went his way, taking with him the keys of the Holy Shroud. These he returned a little later to Christine when she was in possession once more of the capital.

This defeat disposed Thomas to listen more attentively to Richelieu's overtures. His wife, Soissons' sister, and his children were, however, in Madrid and were in a sense hostages, and he was unwilling to commit himself until they had been withdrawn from Spanish hands. Also, Thomas and his brother the Cardinal were, like Rosencrantz and Guildenstern, inseparable; peace would have to be made with both at the same time, or with neither. In fact long tedious negotiations went on with them all during 1641, while towns were besieged and sieges raised, and there was no apparent end to the affair. Not until 1642 was a treaty signed between Christine, the two princes and France by which the Duchy was reunited and the towns held by either the French or the Spaniards were returned to it. And by that time the strategic concept had so far altered that the use of Savoy as a base for the seizure of Milan was no longer in contemplation.

This was due to a shift in emphasis to the western Mediterranean where invasion of Spain seemed to be rendered possible by revolution in Catalonia. The Spaniards had entered France at both ends of the Pyrenees. Their advance into Guyenne had faltered and been driven back, and their attack from Roussillon on the Mediterranean coast fared no better. In August 1637 they appeared in strength before Leucate, the outpost on the French frontier between Narbonne and Perpignan. The governor, Sieur de Barry, was secretly approached by a Spanish agent who sought to suborn him with a large bribe. Barry gave him an indignant answer and held out against a rain of bombs, some as much as a foot in diameter. Richelieu grew more and more choleric as he repeatedly ordered Sourdis to use his galleys to relieve Leucate, and was repeatedly informed that in the opinion of the pilots there was not a port on the Languedoc coast where the galleys could shelter against the levant, which at that season would blow regularly. The navy having proved useless, it was decided to employ the army. The governor of Languedoc, Schomberg, now the Duc d'Halluin, advanced from Béziers on the Spanish lines around Leucate. A night attack was decided on, when the moon, rising late, would illuminate the battle after darkness had covered the surprise. The commander of the attack fell with a bullet wound and eight blows of pike and sword, but the infantry cleared a passage through the Spanish defences for the cavalry, who, in the light of the rising moon, fought a desperate battle at close quarters with the Spanish horse for five hours. By dawn the Spanish army was in retreat, leaving much of its artillery behind. Philip IV ordered an investigation of this 'disgraceful, disastrous and unauthorized action, if only because history will condemn the engagement, and with reason'.[4]

There were three routes by which the war could now be carried into Spain – by sea, at the Atlantic end of the Pyrenees, or into Roussillon. All three were attempted. In the summer of 1638 Condé, with the Duc de La Valette under his command, laid siege to Fuentarabia, the frontier fortress near San Sebastian, and the gateway to Navarre. The affair proceeded slowly, and only at the end of August had the walls been sufficiently breached to make an assault possible. Sourdis had crossed from the Mediterranean after his ineffective efforts to relieve Leucate, and had taken command of a new fleet which had been gathered in the Atlantic ports, amounting to over fifty vessels. With these he supported the operations against Fuentarabia, preventing the Spaniards from victualling the fortress by sea. The indiscipline of the nobility, about which Richelieu never ceased to complain, condemned this project to frustration as it had so many others. The Duc de La Valette, whose father, the Duc d'Épernon, had hit Sourdis with his stick, refused to sit at the council table with the archbishop; and because his troops were then relieved by Sourdis, he refused to participate in the assault. By night the French army had been scattered, and Condé himself was in a boat making for Bayonne. Richelieu's wrath is understandable when he read Condé's despatches, and orders went out for La Valette's arrest. The Duke, however, anticipating the Cardinal's vengeance, boarded a Scottish wine-boat at Bordeaux and fled to England, where he joined the growing collection of disgruntled refugees.

It was now necessary to await the next summer before trying anything further against Spain. This time it was decided that Sourdis should descend upon the Spanish coast in a series of combined operations. He spread his sails, and with forty ships appeared off Corunna in May 1639, and was much encouraged when the thirty-five Spanish vessels moored in the harbour made no attempt to engage him, relying upon the shore batteries to defend the coast. In June he was driven by a storm back into Bordeaux. Richelieu became sceptical about the utility of such expeditions, which could inflict little damage on Spain but in which the risk to the French fleet and troops was considerable. None the less, he gave Sourdis permission to descend on Corunna a second time. It so happened that Sourdis' sailing coincided with the passage from Spain to the Channel of the ill-fated fleet of Don Antonio de Oquendo, which van Tromp was to destroy off the English coast in October; but all that Sourdis saw of it was the eight-hundred-ton galleon *Almiral de Galice* aground on a sandbank at Laredo. Sourdis' men had a splendid time landing at Laredo, demolishing its fortifications, and thoroughly looting the galleon, whose guns they carried away. That was the end of the maritime enterprise for the year.

The castle of Salses lies twelve miles north of Perpignan. Built in 1504 by Ferdinand of Aragon to protect the frontier of Roussillon, it had not been modernized, but its walls are twenty-six feet and its parapets sixteen feet thick. The moat is bricked and the counterscarp formidable. Its main strength, however, lies in its low elevation in flat countryside, out of range of any eminence on which cannon could be sited. To this fortress Condé laid siege in June 1639. The walls proved impervious to artillery so it became necessary to mine. A Major Tréville, who was said never to be so gay as when in peril, made his will and went to confession, then donning his armour talked to everyone as if it was his last day. The mine exploded, a breach was made in the walls, and Tréville walked through it, sword in one hand, cane in the other, followed by the assault party. From the donjon burst a clatter of musketry, and Tréville who had just raised his right arm to flourish his sword received a bullet in the cuirass beneath it. He uttered one word, '*donnez!*', and fell dead. The storming party went over his body, and a few minutes later a white flag was seen hanging from the donjon. Condé was delighted with himself, and asked Richelieu's permission to celebrate his success by coming on leave to Paris. He was told to stay where he was until he saw his troops properly quartered for the winter. Before he had time to make any arrangements whatever the Spaniards were back. Old Spinola's son, the Marqués de Spinola, came over the Pyrenees and laid siege to Salses in his turn with seventeen regiments of Irish, Walloons and Italians. All of Condé's efforts to drive him off failed, and the siege went on. In Leucate the son of Barry, the governor, was in a mentally deranged condition, due, it was believed, to a wound received during the siege of that fortress in 1637. Instructed to revictual the garrison of Salses by barge, he turned the supplies over to Spinola. Barry was ordered to hand over his command, but he replied with dignity that his family had guarded Leucate for sixty-four years in the service of France without reproach, and he would sooner run his sword through his son's body than quit the service of the King. A month later he appeared in Spinola's camp and took an oath of fidelity to Philip iv.

Condé was dismayed. He wrote to Chavigny:

I have been in every peril, I have exposed my person to everything; my troops, the best in France, have served well, the regiment of my son is in Salses; I have created two armies to aid it. Oh! Although this has not succeeded, shall I merit disgrace or praise? Oblige me by telling this to M. le Cardinal.[5]

In fact Condé had occupied thirty thousand Spanish troops who, as he said, should have been in Italy, and this thought was some compensation when on 6 January 1640 Salses capitulated, and the situation was as it had been a year previously, with the Spanish frontier unviolated. It was crushing news to Richelieu and his master, but, had they known it, the Spanish preoccupation with Salses had won for France new and formidable allies in the people of Catalonia, who now rose behind Spinola's back in widespread and violent revolt.

Olivares had for fifteen years been sowing dragons' teeth in Catalonia and now that these had been watered by the blood of one quarter of the nobility of the principality, dead on the ramparts of Salses or in the camps around it, the harvest was ripe. In 1635 and 1636 the plate fleets had come safely to haven and financial collapse was staved off, but in 1637 Madrid had failed to raise its budgeted thirteen million ducats and the vast army of which Olivares had dreamed was unrealized. By 1639 the proposed raising was reduced to a mere seven million ducats, but even this the bankers could meet only with the greatest difficulty. The financial pressure on Barcelona was tightened, and the appointment of Spinola to command on the Roussillon front inspired trepidation among the Catalans, for 'they say he comes with great powers, and that he is a terribly cruel man. This cannot be a good thing for us Catalans – it is bad enough his being Genoese.'[6] Most of the ten thousand troops who died of disease in the siege lines at Salses were Catalan and resentment of the war intensified. In 1640 Olivares was more desperate for money than ever, for he had to re-establish communications with Flanders, broken on land by the loss of Breisach and at sea by the defeat in the Downs, and one further turn of the financial screw became necessary. Catalonia should not be permitted to shelter behind 'vague and airy points, such as all privileges must be on occasions like the present'.[7] Anyway the Catalans were 'a weak lot'. 'This is no time to pray,' he said, 'but to command and be obeyed. Let it be known that the safety of the people and the army should be preferred to all laws and privileges.'

To keep Spinola supplied, the government in Madrid embarked on a thorough policy of requisition in Catalonia, and as the winter descended it was decided that his army should be billeted in the principality, and at the principality's expense. The Catalans, who cherished their laws and privileges above the safety of the Castilians or that of the Habsburg forces, protested violently, and they were supported by the viceroy, the Conde de Santa Coloma, who pointed out that even in the Milanais the Crown paid for rations, and that Catalonia was quite incapable of meeting this burden. When the *tercios* marched to the towns and villages in which they were to be billeted they were ambushed by countless thousands of armed peasants who hounded them in some cases almost into the sea. Disobedience, followed by repression, became widespread. At Rio de Arenas the troops burned the hosts in a church while revenging themselves for the indignities to which they had been subjected by the populace, and were excommunicated by the bishop of Gerona, who thereby transformed political and economic resentment into a holy war. Spontaneously throughout the province vast masses of people stirred in a great upheaval.

Cardinal Borgia was now the president of the Council of Aragon, and his reaction to the course of events was typical. 'Bridle that province!' he advised Olivares.[8] The latter, now thoroughly dismayed, wavered between leniency and ruthlessness and this equivocation was further stimulus to the rebels. What was he to do? he pleaded. Only withdrawal of the troops would quieten the disturbed populace, but withdrawal would leave the frontier undefended against France. On 22 May armed peasants entered Barcelona and soon constituted an army marching beneath the banner of the cross, and crying, 'Viva the Church, viva the King. Death to bad government!' The next day was the feast of Corpus Christi, the occasion of a great religious procession through the Ramblas. Among the robed figures were mountaineers carrying scythes over their shoulders who, as tradition prescribed, had come to Barcelona to hire themselves out for the harvesting; and by evening the army of sedition was vastly swollen. One of these mountaineers became involved in a brawl, and this precipitated dramatic revolution. The houses of government officials were burned, and their occupants murdered, mobs swayed back and forth through the streets. A Genoese galley had arrived in the harbour, and Santa Coloma went to the dockyard intending to board it. There he hesitated, fearing that with his departure all law and order would evacuate the city, and while he hesitated the mob broke into the dockyard. The three bishops and the nobles who were with the Viceroy scattered, the galleys put to sea, and Santa Coloma set off on foot along the rocky seashore towards Montjuich. A fat man, sweating in the afternoon sun, he was over-taken, fell on to the rocks and was pierced as he lay by six dagger blows. On the same day Richelieu's nephew, the young Marquis de Brézé, with twenty-one sail, encountered off Cadiz the gal-leons coming home from New Spain, and two of them, one the flagship carrying the admiral, went to the bottom.

Olivares was once more plunged in depression, saying he wanted to die because his heart was beyond consolation.[9] When a representative of Barcelona sought an interview with him he told him three times to 'go away'. He did not know, he said, if he was eating or sleeping, he was so out of his mind.[10] He blamed Richelieu for the uprising, but in fact the Cardinal had nothing to do with it. Like Olivares he had to fight his war while looking over his shoulder at the unruly situation at home; his Catalonia was Languedoc, and it was not his policy to provide that province with a model of successful disobedience. The revolt in Catalonia probably took him by surprise, and he entered into communica-tion with its leaders only when they made overtures to him. No one knows when exactly this was, and the only significant con-temporary testimony is that of a judge of the Catalan Audiencia who wrote:

The moment when the Diputats began to treat with the French is much debated. Some say it was years before. This view is held by those who claim to have secret information on the evils of the age, and they fail to realize that a corporation is incapable of secretly planning a rebellion years in advance. My own view is that the Diputats grew afraid when they saw the viceroy dead, and tried to find out what sort of help they could expect from France if His Majesty should attempt to punish the province, and the first person to enter France was Francesc Vilaplana, the cousin of the Diputat Eclesiastic, Claris.[11]

Claris was a canon of the cathedral chapter of Urgell who had led ecclesiastical resistance to his royalist bishop, whom he believed to be prepared to sacrifice the interests of Catalonia to his own favour with Madrid. An agitator who projected his personal resentments as a gesture of patriotism, Claris became the focus of a group of clerics and border gentry, motivated by private discontents and disappointments, personal ambition and genuine belief in Catalonia's separate destiny. These approached Richelieu, and offered to make common cause with the French and to introduce them into the principality. In December 1640 their delegates were received by Richelieu with every mark of favour, and given the status of ambassadors of the Republic of Catalonia. He agreed to give them lieutenants-general of infantry, artillery and engineers, and troops, arms and munitions as required, speaking to them, so an eyewitness reported, in 'very pure Castilian'. Then they dined with the King, were received by the Queen, who exhibited no pleasure at the experience, and paid their respects to the future Louis XIV, already at the age of two sitting with conscious dignity on a high stool. French troops, supported by Richelieu's creation the French navy, carried the war as far south as Tarragona, and Brézé became commander-in-chief of a combined Franco-Catalan army.

Although the Catalan revolt placed in France's hands a military advantage which Richelieu would have been foolish to spurn, he was not easy in his mind about the implications of a Franco-Catalan alliance. France had no ambitions south of the Pyrenees, but an offer of suzerainty from the Catalan rebels involved an Iberian commitment the end of which was difficult to foresee. He thought in terms of a Catalan declaration of independence, which would have the effect of creating a new small state around which France and Spain could again regain equilibrium, and he sought to impose this notion on the Catalan delegates. Philip IV's general, the Marqués de los Veléz, burning with indignation, was invading Catalonia, and Tarragona surrendered to him. When the news reached Barcelona the mob turned savage, and the Diputats of Catalonia urgently appealed to Richelieu to save them from the twin disasters of Castilian vengeance and popular fury. Richelieu's agent, Bernard Duplessis Besançon, entered Barcelona for secret discussion with Claris and told him that unless Catalonia declared its independence he would negotiate no further. On 16 January

1641 Claris declared a republic, which lasted only a week. The governing class of the principality might bitterly oppose Castile, and even betray Spain to the French, but it was not anti-monarchical and had no desire to sever the royal connection. The attempted independence led only to the disintegration of the Catalan governmental system and a lapse into anarchy. France had no alternative but to take the principality under its control and fight Madrid on Spanish soil. The result was disastrous, for as the years wore on the French were substituted for the Castilians in the minds of the Catalans, and sowed in turn their own dragons' teeth. All this Richelieu foresaw, as Bernard Duplessis Besançon recorded:

> Cardinal Richelieu, who foresaw the difficulties that acceptance [of the Catalan offer to place themselves under French suzerainty] might one day place in the way of peace, hesitated for long to recommend it to His Majesty. He often explained that it would have been of greater advantage to France if this province had been set up as a republic under French protection, both because it would probably have made greater efforts to preserve its liberty, and because it would in this way have saved France part of the expenditure that it was afterwards called upon to make. But in the end, seeing that Catalonia was not capable of this form of government, and that otherwise it might rapidly return to subjection to Spain ... His Excellency was of the opinion that it was necessary to accept.[12]

It was the moment for peace. 'God wants us to make peace,' Olivares told Philip IV, 'for He is depriving us visibly and absolutely of all the means of war.'[13] His terms to Richelieu had previously been that the Dutch restore Brazil, which they had conquered from the Portuguese, and Breda; that Spain should retain one fortress in Piedmont or Montferrat, preferably Casale; and that Charles of Lorraine be included in the negotiations. In his desperation he was now prepared to abandon Charles and to insist only on the retention of the Spanish conquests in Italy during a period of truce, and on the restoration of Brazil. These were entirely reasonable terms, especially the demand concerning Brazil, loss of which had bred serious Portuguese resentment of Castilian rule, but Richelieu was snared in a dilemma of his own contrivance. He had undertaken not to make peace without

Holland's consent, but the Dutch had no inclination for peace now that the war was producing substantial dividends for them. They had just defeated a last attempt of the Spanish navy to reconquer Brazil, and were enjoying the material advantages of having captured the principal source of Europe's sugar supply. Richelieu was engaged in overtures which were to result in the holding of a peace conference in Münster after his death, but in 1641, with Spain obviously in serious trouble, he had no incentive to put pressure on Holland. In this fidelity to an ally he erred. At Münster the Dutch were to make peace with Spain and to release Spain's flagging energies to carry on the struggle with France for another eleven years. Catalonia became a well swallowing up French blood and money and the Catalans proved the least grateful of partisans.

The Catalan revolt, and the evidence of French support given it, inspired the Portuguese to attempt the restoration of their monarchy, suppressed in 1581 by Philip II. Here Richelieu was not innocent. In 1638 he had sent a certain Sieur de St Pé on an English ship to Lisbon to meet a Portuguese captain named d'Azevedo. He was to ascertain if the Portuguese were willing to revolt, in which case the French fleet would take over all the forts in the Tagus estuary as far as the tower of Belem, and put them in Portuguese hands. The Portuguese were to be assured of France's complete disinterest in the matter. Should they want French or Dutch military aid, St Pé was to report on the guarantees they could offer for the security of an army deposited on Portuguese soil. St Pé's report is unavailable, and it remains unclear to what extent the Portuguese uprising was fostered by Richelieu's agents. At the end of 1640 the palace at Lisbon was stormed by a crowd crying, 'Freedom. Viva don Juan IV, King of Portugal'. The Spanish governor, Marguerite of Savoy, Dowager Duchess of Mantua, was forced at sword-point to order the governor of the fortress of Lisbon, which dominates the city and harbour, to hand it over to the rebels. For a time Olivares kept the news of this disaster from his royal master, and then tried to misrepresent to him its extent and significance. Prices rose in Spain in this same year by eighty per cent, and when Olivares intervened to halt this he brought them back to par, but only at vast cost to industry and trade. Spain began to collapse, bringing Olivares down in the general ruin.

The war was also carried into the Spanish Netherlands. In 1639 Hesdin was captured, and in 1640 it was the turn of Arras. This city had a garrison of only fifteen hundred foot and four hundred horse, commanded by an Irish officer, Owen Roe O'Neill, who was learning the trade that he was in the next few years to practise so ably against the Parliamentary generals in Ireland; but the Spaniards sang a song to the effect that when the French took Arras, the mice would eat the cats. In June 1640 Maréchal de La Meilleraye, nephew of old Amador de La Porte, and Richelieu's first cousin, with sixteen regiments and siege artillery, appeared before the city and began the bombardment. Richelieu, though from afar, kept a tight control on the tactical situation, advising what routes to take to pass supplies and munitions to the besieging army so as to avoid the Spanish cavalry which was seeking to intercept them. Within two months Arras was in French hands, the garrison withdrawing to Douai with the honours of war, taking with them four cannon and a mortar. Richelieu was insistent that the loyalty of the inhabitants be won by exact but mild treatment. With the fall of Arras the province of Artois was reunited to the French Crown.

23

The Bishops are for the Pope
1639-41

The war was clearly moving in France's favour by 1641. But it had already lasted six years, and Richelieu could not but reflect sadly on the cost to France in lives and wealth. At the very beginning of the war he had said 'I confess my ignorance in the matter of finance'[1]; and as he sat at his desk puzzling over sheets of figures which made no sense and seemed to bear no relationship to reality he was driven to despair. The only really comprehensive statement of the finances of the realm at this time was made by a researcher in the eighteenth century. One or two modern essays have produced quite different sets of figures; and Richelieu in his *Testament politique* gives yet another set.

The only thing they disclose in common is that the war galloped away with the national income: the audited accounts for 1626 show the total expenditure of the royal treasury, which did not include the total governmental expenditure by any means, as around forty-four million *livres*. By 1640 this had reached about one hundred and sixteen million *livres* of which a little over one-third was derived from receipts of income, the balance being made up from the sale of lands, timber and offices, and from various governmental enterprises. Another estimate is that in 1639 total expenditure amounted to about one hundred and seventy-two millions, the budget showing a half per cent surplus balance, resulting, no doubt, from loans. Richelieu says himself that in 1636 the receipts were about fifty millions and the total income of the government around eighty millions. If the two sets of figures are in any way accurate, which is doubtful, it means that in the first four years of the war expenditure was more than twice the income.

Of course income had to be raised proportionately to increased expenditure; but whenever new taxes were imposed this was used as an excuse to put up prices, and Richelieu struggled against this inexorable tendency in vain, threatening publicly to burn the merchandise of those who added the tax to their prices, but finding the problem beyond his capacities. Often he said that the reduction of taxes was necessary to stimulate the people to work and to make them prosperous, and that it was a matter for regret that, instead of enriching the people who constituted the nation, taxes seemed only to impoverish them. Baffled, he referred to this as a paradox, but added sadly, 'It is impossible to examine the proposition thoroughly without realizing the justice and truth of it.'[2] He indicated that he recognized the mechanism of economics even if he failed to understand it:

It is clear that, if the income is increased by this means [taxation], the expenditure is also increased since one has to buy at a higher cost that which previously was bought more cheaply. If meat becomes dearer, if the price of cloth and everything else increases, the soldier will find it more difficult to feed and maintain himself, and so it will be necessary to increase his pay, and the wages of the craftsmen will be higher than previously.[3]

Then, remembering the impoverished state of the class from which he sprang, he added: 'The poor gentleman, whose wealth consists only in land, will not increase his revenue by such taxation, the fruits of the soil remain always at the same price.' The war was accelerating the social revolution which was to make the squirearchy dependent upon crown offices and employment in the army.

Drowned in a morass of figures, Richelieu penned a reflection of despair in the preface to the balance sheet of 1640. Often, he wrote, he was in tears, and he was extremely sad in his heart that so many extraordinary charges had had to be imposed on the people because of the war, and against his inclination.[4] To raise money new offices were being created and sold, but, as Bullion reported to the bewildered council, this only had the effect of draining away money that could be taxed. If any more pressure were imposed on the tax-collectors, he said, they would all be bankrupted. In seven months expenditure had exceeded the total income for the year by four million *livres*.

In 1639 there was another upheaval of the peasantry, this time in Normandy. The tax-collectors there, frustrated at the widespread incidence of non-payment, devised the expedient of making the parishes corporately liable for the evasion of the *taille* by any residents. The peasants who had already paid naturally refused to pay for their neighbours, and some were gaoled. At Avranches and Coutances assemblies of the people elected chiefs and formed themselves into regiments, defying the authorities at the same moment as they appealed to the King and the Parlement of Rouen. The records of the tax-collectors were seized and burned or scattered, and the commissary-general of the *gabelle* for the province was besieged in his house. Richelieu was perplexed: 'I know not what the remedy is,' he said; 'it being impossible to find the troops which are asked for if one does not want to drop all the affairs of the King and abandon France to the foreigner.'[5] There were by now about five thousand men well-armed in eight or ten regiments, and known as *nu-pieds*, and a movement of protest had degenerated into one of violence, with the rich being murdered in their homes, families ruined, and properties burned, as the peasants vented their rage on everything. Some royal cavalry and two infantry regiments were assembled and disarmed the people of Caen. At Avranches they found the rebels barricaded and defiant. There was a fierce contest for two hours before the barricades were broken and the peasants driven into the estuary, where they were sabred wholesale by the cavalry or drowned in their flight.

The officialdom of the province, if it had not actively supported the uprising, was at least sympathetic towards it. The chancellor

Séguier wrote a memorandum to Richelieu, proposing that the Parlement of Rouen should be made to pay for the damage and to reimburse the royal treasury for the loss of revenues. The privileges of Normandy should be cancelled, and the province reunited administratively to the Crown; the town hall of Rouen should be razed and in its place a pyramid erected on which would be engraven the decree of the council terminating Normandy's separate existence. Humour not being the Cardinal's strong point, he took this last suggestion seriously, replying ponderously that the memorandum seemed good, 'with the exception of the razing of the town hall of Rouen'.[6] In January 1640 Séguier arrived in Rouen and proceeded to execute the policy he had proposed. 'Always remember,' Richelieu instructed him, 'that we cannot make too great an example on this occasion.'[7] Severe measures were taken against the tax-collectors who had abused their authority, but this did not solve the underlying problem of too little money for too great commitments, and the troubles continued for the remainder of the war, though not in such a dramatic form.

The extent of Richelieu's financial dilemma can now be appreciated with the revelation of the contents of Séguier's papers, which have lain in Leningrad, and which detail the classes and personalities involved in the Normandy uprising. The additional taxes which were imposed year by year were slight in themselves, but it is clear that the peasantry was so near subsistence level that even the slightest increase threatened starvation. The insurgents had nothing more to lose, and they were supported by the gentry, or at least not opposed by them, because the last *sol* extracted from an artisan meant a *sol* less for rent or dues to the seigneur. Neither were they opposed by the middle classes of the towns, themselves the victims of fiscal pressure, who failed to employ their defence organizations against them until the revolutionary movement became indiscriminately anti-social. It took this turn because it was felt that the additional taxation, ostensibly for war, was being milked by the tax-collectors or going to support Richelieu's centralizing policies, while, in a kind of double taxation, the tax-payers still had to support the army through

billeting, requisitions and all manner of supplementary impositions. The evil was compounded as more and more of the middle-
class tax-paying community escaped the liability to taxation by
ennoblement, office and privilege, so concentrating taxation on
the classes least able to bear it. In this there was a vicious circle:
less privilege would mean more revenue; but it also threatened an
alliance of classes against the state.

In fact there was no solution to the financial crisis short of peace
and the revival of production and trade. The import of gold and
silver into Spain from America declined in the decade 1631–40 to
sixty per cent in actual weight of what it had been in the previous
decade, while the ratio of silver to gold increased from 21 : 38 to
13 : 12. Since gold was used mainly for large international transactions and the coins of higher denomination, there was not only
less specie available to keep trade moving, but much less silver in
Europe for mint purposes. The resulting shortages of cash were
embarrassing every government at a time of inflation and vast
war expenditure. This tended to inhibit military activity on all
fronts, and the loss of the Grisons was due as much to an inability
to raise coin to pay subsidies as to anything else.

The war had interrupted trade and the established channels for
the circulation of money became blocked. This made the raising
of additional war levies difficult, and increasingly Richelieu had
to go to a diminishing and highly competitive international loan
market. Richelieu's agent here was a Spanish Jew located in
Amsterdam, named Lopez; but as the loans he raised sometimes
carried huge interest rates it became difficult to budget for their
amortization. The Cardinal had an almost medieval suspicion of
financial practices, and the tax-collectors he described as men who
would thieve with impunity, and were a menace to the state. But,
he sighed, they were absolutely necessary: 'Gold and silver are the
tyrants of the world, and, although their substance and their
Empire are in itself unjust, they are sometimes so much required
that it is necessary to suffer their domination.'[8] When the machinery for servicing loans broke down, poor Lopez found himself
short of cash, and wrote to Richelieu asking for some repayment
so that he could buy up Rubens' furnishings, which were being

auctioned in Haarlem in 1640. Everyone was so short of money, he said, that the tapestries were expected to go at bargain prices. 'After having served and done everything asked of me,' he complained, 'I now have no money to get myself out of this country.'⁹

The financial crisis also brought on another gallican controversy. In order to ascertain the resources of France it was decided to require every public institution to make an inventory of its property and income, on pain of forfeiture. When it became clear that the intention behind this was the taxing of the Church there was an uproar. Bullion, arguing the case for the treasury, said that 'the King, as sovereign over all his subjects, has the right to make all the orders of the kingdom contribute to the costs of war.'¹⁰ And Richelieu, reflecting that up to this point the clergy had escaped all exactions, added that the war had been sustained for five years without affecting the pockets of the officials or the funds of the clergy. It had been the tradition for the Church to contribute exceptional payments voluntarily in time of war, which it did to the point of ruination during the Hundred Years War; and as usual Richelieu took his stand on history, seeking justification in research into the relationship of ecclesiastical lands to the crown domain in the feudal edifice. He stimulated two brothers, Pierre and Jacques Dupuy, to write a book on the historical origins of the liberties of the Church in France, but they went too far, conceding some of the major points of ecclesiastical gallicanism, and thus turned a financial dispute into a theological one. At the end of 1640 eighteen bishops met in the house of Cardinal de La Rochefoucauld and denounced the book as 'the work of the devil'.

To indicate his disapproval of the tenor of the Dupuy book Richelieu accepted the dedication of a reply to it written by Petro de Marca, who argued for the supremacy of the Pope over a council of the Church. The liberties of the Gallican Church, Marca contended, had two foundations, first the recognition of the primary and sovereign authority of the Holy See to make general laws and to judge without appeal, and secondly, the sovereign authority of kings who know no superior in temporal affairs. Rome, however, found passages in it to which objection was taken, and the book was put on the Index by the Holy Office. In 1646 Marca recanted. Since Richelieu was identified with the book it was assumed that he was equally in error. Accusations were made against him in an anonymous publication, written by a professor at the Sorbonne, that he was preparing a schism, and the charge caused the wildest excitement. While Richelieu had the book burned and a search made for its author, writers appeared to defend his religious orthodoxy and the excellent example he had given as a priest. Again the enthusiasts went too far. A Jesuit named Rabardau not only justified the annulment of Gaston's marriage and the taxation of the clergy but argued that France could be turned into a patriarchate without the Pope's consent. The book was also put on the Index.

It is regrettable that Rome should have attempted at this point to separate Richelieu from the French hierarchy, for its own position was not above criticism. Urban VIII was old and there were intemperate men surrounding the papal throne. A series of little things, misrepresented to Richelieu, engendered coldness in him towards the Holy See, and caused him to complain that the Pope thought only of offending France. First of all, the Pope would neither say a requiem mass for Cardinal de La Valette nor allow the Holy Office, of which La Valette had been a member, to celebrate one at Santa Maria della Minerva. The Pope's reasons were sound enough, it being provocative to the Spanish faction to pay particular attention to the soul of a prelate who had been an enemy general at the date of his death; and also unusual to have public mourning for a cardinal who did not die in Rome. But the matter was dealt with in Rome in such a way that it appeared to be a rebuff to France.

There was constant turmoil in Rome with the quarrelling and lobbying of the French and Spanish embassies. Four Turkish slaves belonging to the Spanish embassy took refuge in the French church of the Trinità dei Monti and claimed asylum there. Three hundred papal soldiers dragged them out and placed them in the College of Catachumens. Then a grave breach of diplomatic privilege occurred which heightened the tension because the

Pope's nephew, Cardinal Francisco Barberini, was involved. A Roman servant of an equerry of the French ambassador opened a gaming den, and was arrested by the pontifical police, tried and sentenced to the galleys. Three of the French ambassador's servants arranged his escape from his escort. The equerry was then ambushed from behind a hedge and shot. His head was cut off and exhibited on the public scaffold in Rome, with a notice attached saying, 'Behold the head of the equerry of the French ambassador!' It was removed two hours later and thrown into the pit with the skulls of common malefactors. The report that reached Paris from d'Estrées, who, as might have been expected, made the most of an occasion for hostilities, was that Cardinal Barberini was rumoured to have paid the assassins. Louis XIII thereupon instructed d'Estrées to appear no longer at a papal audience, nor any assembly of the Barberini.

It was in the midst of this series of crises that the nuncio in Paris was replaced by a new nuncio, Ranuccio Scotti, whom Louis XIII described as committing 'all the extravagances that one expects from a fool'. He certainly acted like one, adding to this disadvantage the fact that his reputation was pro-Spanish. He was coming on a new peace mission from Urban, but peace with Spain was to figure much less in his negotiations than the problem of reparation for the affronts which Louis had experienced at the hands of the Holy See, or thought he had. Scotti took up his residence in the Hôtel de Cluny, and both he and Chavigny became embroiled in problems of protocol. The nuncio made his official call on Chavigny, but refused to offer his hand to him because he was not a prince. Chavigny, a conceited and easily offended man, failed to return the call until it became necessary to demand apologies from the Pope in the matter of the murdered equerry. He thereupon let Scotti know that he would call upon him if Scotti would extend his hand, as his predecessors had been accustomed to do. This Scotti would not agree to, but he would meet Chavigny unofficially at the convent of the Cordeliers.

Chavigny was late for the appointment, which probably did nothing to soothe the nuncio. When he arrived he said he had three matters to raise, the refusal of a requiem for La Valette, the affair of the Trinità dei Monti, and the murder of a French diplomatic official. While Spain had behaved outrageously towards the Holy See, he said, France had never done anything disrespectful; but see how badly France was treated by the Pope! Scotti said that the Pope had never been anything but neutral between France and Spain, and he proceeded to explain the Holy See's position in respect of the three matters raised. The allegation that Barberini was involved in the murder he described as pure calumny, and he indicated his surprise that Richelieu should accept d'Estrées' word against that of the Church. The Pope, he said, was a sovereign, and he would not let Rome become a battleground between Spaniards and French. This was reasonable enough, but Scotti could not resist the temptation to say triumphantly that most of the bishops were on the Pope's side. Chavigny accused him of trying to excite trouble, and then said he had a document to communicate from the King to the nuncio, in which the former demanded reparation for the breach of the law of nations concerning diplomatic privilege. Scotti replied that the King had an ambassador in Rome; let him deliver it. Chavigny recognized this to be a gauche attempt to force d'Estrées to have an audience with the Pope, and thus to compromise the very issue raised in the document. 'What, Monsieur,' he cried, 'you will not take this letter?' Scotti refused. Chavigny then tried to read the document to him, but was interrupted by the nuncio, who, taking offence at an allusion to himself in the paper, said it was clear that France had no wish to make peace, and had just 'amused' the legate at Cologne three years previously, having never had any intention of attending the peace conference there.

After this meeting the *chef-de-protocol* and bailiff of the council appeared at the Hôtel de Cluny to hand the document to the nuncio officially. He was told that Scotti was with the Cardinal de La Rochefoucauld at the abbey of Ste Geneviève. They would wait for him. At five in the evening he returned. The document, magnificent with great seals, was extended to him. He refused to accept it. 'Then,' said the *chef-de-protocol*. 'I am instructed by the King to read it to you.' Scotti turned and walked into the next room, closing the door in his face. No one else would take the document, and when the *chef-de-protocol* left it on a table someone threw it at him. The *chef-de-protocol* refused to pick it up and returned to his carriage. He had just entered it when a servant burst through the courtyard gate, which is still the entrance to the Musée de Cluny, threw the document through the carriage window and slammed the gate. A few days later the bishops were ordered by royal decree to have no communication with Scotti, and a guard was placed outside the Hôtel de Cluny to stop anyone entering or leaving it after dark.[11]

Richelieu was only on the periphery of this diplomatic squabble, and the letter which he wrote to the Cardinal Secretary of State, Bagno, complaining of Scotti's behaviour was mildly phrased and of great dignity. He said he knew Scotti to be a good and zealous prelate, but that he understood France so badly, and conformed so little to the excellent instructions which Bagno had given to him, that his mission would be more prejudicial than useful.[12] But, from the explanation given to the bishops why they should hold themselves aloof from Scotti, it appeared that what had mortally offended Richelieu was the assertion that the bishops were 'for the Pope and against the King'.

The resistance of the bishops to the government's attempts to tax Church revenues made Richelieu's position on the gallican issue appear to the Pope, contemporaries and historians as more revolutionary than in fact it was. In February 1641 an extraordinary assembly of the clergy met in Paris to discuss a royal edict levying an amount of seven million *livres* on the Church. Consideration of this was adjourned to Mantes, and Richelieu sought to ensure the election to the new assembly of persons who would be 'peaceable and easy to govern'.[13] There was, in fact, a grave conflict of opinion at Mantes, and in the outcome Richelieu had to express himself satisfied with two-thirds of the amount, and then only after banning two archbishops and four bishops from the debates. The Pope intervened with a bull against those who interfered with the rights of the Church, and when Scotti's successor, Grimaldi, handed this to Richelieu the latter said it was a matter for the Parlement. That gallican body forbade its publication in France under pain of high treason. The old and failing Richelieu seemed to the worried Urban VIII to be a very different person from the young Richelieu who at the States General had championed the ultramontanist cause and had sought the implementation of the decrees of Trent.

24

To be Young and Wholly Wise

1641

'It is impossible to be young and wholly wise,' Richelieu wrote to the King on 11 December 1639.[1] He was replying to Louis' morose complaints to him about the royal favourite, the nineteen-year-old Henri d'Effiat, Marquis de Cinq Mars. It was an apologetic remark intended to allay the royal jealousy of a gilded youth who was very much the Cardinal's protégé; but in a sense it was prophetic of the tragic events which were to poison Richelieu's last days, distract him from a task yet far from ended, and threaten to plunge France back into the abyss from which he had so painfully and for a whole lifetime struggled to withdraw her. Antoine, the Marquis d'Effiat, had been Richelieu's friend and confidant since the days when he had so capably negotiated with Buckingham and had won his marshal's baton in the battle at Avigliana; and Richelieu had been saddened by his sudden death in 1632 from some strange fever. He left a wife of stern virtue and six children, the second son Henri being then twelve years old, and the heir to an Effiat seigneury called after its medieval château Cinq Mars. The widowed Marquise lived in the handsome new château of Chilly; Richelieu was a frequent visitor, and like all the world he was enchanted by the languid Henri with his fascinating mixture of vivacity and sadness, serenity and caprice. His interest in the family was consecrated by the marriage of Henri's sister Marie to his own cousin Maréchal de La Meilleraye, nephew of Amador de La Porte. Richelieu believed in furthering the interests of his enormous tribe of relations and of their relations, even if in an imperious fashion, and he arranged a minor place at court for Cinq Mars and then steadily secured his advancement. Extravagant in his devotion to his toilet, Henri seemed to Richelieu just the person to take over the office of Grand Master of the Wardrobe, which La Force's son wished to sell; and thereby Henri came into intimate contact with the King.

There is no doubt that Richelieu aimed to use Cinq Mars in his own struggle to retain his hold on Louis. He remembered that it was he himself who had introduced Saint-Simon, then aged nineteen, to the King, and that Saint-Simon had repaid him admirably on the Day of Dupes. Saint-Simon's favour had declined, and once Louise de La Fayette had taken her final vows, Marie de Hautefort was restored to her influential position – and with her return, the anti-cardinalist and pro-Spanish pressures around the court had intensified. Louis, by now chronically ill from tuberculosis, plagued by an uneasy conscience, and dismayed by the misery of his country, was shaken in his resolve to continue the war; and after the Caussin affair Richelieu had good reason to fear that he would weaken at the very moment when the war was turning in France's favour, and when France could contemplate sitting down at a peace conference with strengthened hand. In fact, negotiations were in train which were to result in an agreement in 1641 between Spain, Austria and France to commence talks at Münster and Osnabrück – an agreement which was to lead seven years later to the Peace of Westphalia. It seemed essential to have someone with the King's ear who could oust the defeatist influence and strengthen Louis' will.

The lonely King was under irresistible compulsion to give himself completely to some other human being, though his intense piety and dense personality inhibited any tendency towards overt expression. 'Oh God forbid', he once exclaimed, 'that adultery should ever enter my house! The more I am King and in a position to make myself hear, the more I must think that God forbids me, for He has made me King only to obey Him, so as to give an example to my subjects and make all those whom He has made subject to me obey Him.'[2] None the less, as he wistfully admitted, he was a man, and subject to the senses. The gay, handsome Cinq Mars released in him the tensions that his character, health and environment all helped to forge, and by the end of 1638 he was completely absorbed in his affection for him. Cinq Mars' exploitation of his position astounded everyone. When the court was with the army at Mézières Cinq Mars dared to reply in kind to the raillery of the Duc de Nemours over the dinner-table. As a simple gentleman it was not for him to back-chat with a prince, and the Duke, angered by his riposte, intensified the attack, Cinq Mars returning the abuse, until Nemours threw a cherry-stone at his nose. Cinq Mars threw it back, and hit Nemours in the eye, and quickly the two men were at each other's throats. It was an unheard-of event, and what made it even more astonishing was that the King, when told of it, supported Cinq Mars. No one could recollect when a King of France had previously addressed a subject as 'dear friend'.

The weakness of Cinq Mars' character, however, promised disaster for his relationships with the King. Louis, who retired and rose early, expected the young man to follow his own habits, but Cinq Mars had no intention of being anyone's slave. Totally undisciplined, a libertine, spiteful, wasteful and pugnacious, he wandered about Paris all night, trailing his rapier, debauching with his boisterous adolescent companions, philandering and quarrelling. He took up with a young married woman of fabulous beauty, Marion de Lorme, carried her off from under her virtuous husband's nose and exhibited her in the salons. There is some evidence that Richelieu summoned her to his château and met her privately; probably he intended to talk her out of a relationship which was stirring the troubled soul of the King, but he only succeeded in giving the malicious Cardinal de Retz the opportunity of suggesting that he was sharing her favours with Cinq Mars. The Marquise d'Effiat was as scandalized as the King at the misconduct of her son, and she even came to the point of a rupture with him and of legal proceedings for 'seduction' against Marion.

The young man's extravagance knew no limit. He possessed

fifty-two suits of clothing of rich material, and when he bought an absurdly expensive carriage the smouldering Louis refused to inspect it, growling that he disapproved of waste of money. At the same time the King was incapable of resisting this new Buckingham, and was resolved to elevate him still further to the office of Grand Écuyer. This was held by the ageing Duc de Bellegarde, the one-time favourite of Henri III and the lover of Gabrielle d'Estrées. For years Bellegarde had resisted selling his appointment to Brézé; and even now, in face of what was virtually a demand from the King, he hesitated and bargained hard before yielding. On 15 November 1639 Cinq Mars assumed his new office. As Chavigny wrote to Mazarin, it was not a bad beginning for a boy of nineteen, but 'never has the King had such a violent passion for anyone'.[3]

Richelieu's aim to have Cinq Mars in a position of influence had been realized, but the influence that was wielded was not his. Cinq Mars' associates determined his ideas for him, and for the most part they were ideas hostile to the Cardinal. François-Auguste de Thou, lawyer, and son of a parliamentary family, was several years older than Henri, clever, experienced and travelled. He was also ambitious and he excited Cinq Mars' wilfulness in the expectation of rising in his wake to power and influence. Louis d'Astarac, Marquis de Fontrailles, was a different character, a born intriguer and a man who bitterly resented his own ugliness of feature. On one occasion Richelieu had referred to him in his presence as a 'monster'. It was one of those sharp remarks which the Cardinal, whose wit was of an ironic kind, could not resist uttering; he had later apologized, but Fontrailles had joined the large band of the unforgiving who had been driven to murderous intent by Richelieu's scorching tongue. Cinq Mars felt the lash himself, for the Cardinal intervened to remonstrate with him about his mode of life, only to meet the resentment of an arrogant youth. A period of coldness set in between the Cardinal and the Grand Écuyer, and when La Meilleraye was sent to try to talk Cinq Mars into behaving reasonably he too was driven to exasperation and broke off the discussion. From that moment there was an open breach between Richelieu and the favourite.

The hostilities became a matter of public comment at the time of the siege of Arras in 1640. As Richelieu knew from captured Spanish dispatches, a convoy of six or seven thousand carts bringing the ammunition which the French mortars at Arras gobbled up, was to be intercepted by enemy cavalry, and he himself had made elaborate plans for its protection. Anxious to distinguish himself, Cinq Mars asked the King for the command of the convoy, and Louis, without telling the Cardinal, acceded. When the latter was informed he was, naturally, angry, not only at matters being taken out of his hands, but principally at this whimsical appointment which, owing to Cinq Mars' character and inexperience, could hazard the whole operation. He went to the King and pointed this out, with his usual tact and loquacity, but one sullen look from Louis silenced him, and there was nothing for him to do but withdraw defeated. Louis was making more frequent demonstrations these days that he was prepared in the interests of France to allow Richelieu to dictate to the nation, but that he was determined that he should not dictate to him in matters which he regarded as personal.

Richelieu then applied pressure directly to Cinq Mars, and the youth was persuaded to give up his claims to the convoy, and take instead the command of 1,400 young noble volunteers, called the 'Immortals'. This, the Cardinal suggested, was a post worthy of the heroes of antiquity, and far more honourable than mere convoy-escorting. Cinq Mars made the exchange enthusiastically, his mind clouded with visions of glory in the breaches of Arras. Among the volunteers were three princes of the blood, the Duc d'Enghien, Condé's son, and the Ducs de Mercoeur and Beaufort, the sons of Vendôme; they refused to take orders from Cinq Mars, who quarrelled with them constantly. On the way to the front with the King Cinq Mars also stirred Louis' wrath, and the two of them drew up a pathetic little contract in writing by which they agreed to have Richelieu arbitrate their petty squabbles. When Cinq Mars' volunteers reached Arras the Spaniards were in possession of certain of the French siege-works, and it was his task to eject them. Cinq Mars' horse was shot from under him. When he rose pale-faced, his undisciplined subordinates broadcast that he preferred to be at a ball than at a fight. Stung by this allegation, Cinq Mars ran to join an infantry unit which was on the point of assaulting an outwork, but Maréchal de Châtillon ordered him back to the firing line. The official despatches which appeared in the *Gazette* were doctored by Richelieu, Cinq Mars was maliciously told, so that his disgrace would not become public knowledge. Worse, the *Mercure* attributed the command of the volunteers to d'Enghien and failed to mention the Grand Écuyer. Resentment of the Cardinal thus became for Cinq Mars a means of restoring his self-respect.

As the King's health worsened, so did his jealousy increase, and storms at the palace became ever more frequent. Their origins were trivial, their emotional cost high. One day Louis took Cinq Mars to inspect the two-year-old Dauphin. When Cinq Mars tried to pick him up the future Louis XIV began to cry. His father became purple with rage, and stormed off to Anne of Austria choking with passion. 'My son cannot stand the sight of me,' he roared, 'a strange education he is getting, but I shall put it in order.' The Queen wrote to Richelieu in alarm, and the King wrote also, saying with unconscious prophecy 'my son is obstinate'.[4] Every few days Richelieu received some complaint of Cinq Mars' behaviour and impertinence to the King, which threw the monarch into fits of moodiness. Even when Cinq Mars disappeared for days at a time and sulked after one of his rows with Louis, Richelieu had no peace, for he would be deluged with letters from the King complaining at the way he was being treated.

The Cardinal might have groaned the more at this unnecessary and frivolous intrusion on his time but for the fact that he was even then negotiating what, to any member of the French lower nobility into which he had been born, was the next best thing to attaining the beatific vision – the contracting of an alliance with the royal family. The House of Richelieu was about to arrive. In early 1641 the final arrangements were made for the marriage of Claire-Clémence de Maillé, daughter of Maréchal de Brézé and the Cardinal's sister Nicole, to the heir to the House of Condé, and son of First Prince of the Blood, the young Duc d'Enghien. It must surely have been one of the pleasures reserved for Richelieu when he gained access to universal knowledge in the next world that his nephew-in-law, the Great Condé, was, in a military sense, to carry his own work to fruition.

The marriage proposal originated with Condé, not with Richelieu. The avaricious First Prince was mesmerized by the great fortune which the Cardinal had accumulated, by the vast Palais Cardinal then nearing completion, and by the paintings and sculptures that were filling it, and hoped d'Enghien would become the heir to it all. The seventeen-year old d'Enghien was not in the slightest degree interested in the pouting, baby-faced girl of twelve, and had to be ordered by his father to pay his court to her. When it came to settling the marriage contract Condé was disappointed, for though Richelieu provided the impoverished Maréchal de Brézé with 300,000 *livres* with which to furnish the bride with a dowry – provision being made that it might be used to pay off ancient debts of the Condé family – he announced that she would be excluded from his will. Condé secretly prepared a document of protest by which he hoped to upset the will after the Cardinal's death, and, optimistic that he would deceive Richelieu in the end, he exhibited extraordinary enthusiasm for the match. D'Enghien was forced by him to say that he had never been so gay as at this matrimonial prospect, but in fact he exhibited no indication of anything but disgust.

On 14 January 1641 the Cardinal gave a theatrical and a ball in the Palais Cardinal, attended by the King and Queen. He himself collaborated in writing a play, *Mirame* – a satire of a pronounced political flavour on the peoples of Europe – and, it was said, led the applause when it was produced. At the curtain-fall an ingenious gilded bridge suddenly unfolded itself in front of the royal box, so that the Queen might walk down to the floor to open the ball. Condé kept exclaiming as he watched the pathetic Claire-Clémence, 'Oh, she is so pretty'. Her ill-luck did not desert her. While dancing a courante she tripped and fell while the whole company, including the bridegroom, laughed cruelly. The ball went on until dawn and a ballet was performed comprising thirty-six entries divided into five acts. The Cardinal also

arranged a re-enactment in the Place Royale of the famous
carousel of 1612, and to add poetry to the occasion Bassompierre,
who had organized that event, was distracted by the noise of it
as he sat in his cell in the nearby Bastille.

The King was an eager supporter of the marriage, exerting
himself even beyond the usual to provide game for the banquet. 'We shall do all we can,' he informed Richelieu, 'to kill
young wild boars, which is rather difficult at this time of the
year.'[5] Never, it was reported, had Richelieu been seen in better
humour, and he celebrated his triumph by arranging in the new
theatre he had just built a ballet on the prosperity of the arms of
France, which displayed the crossing of the snow-clad Alps, the
relief of Casale and the taking of Arras. To add just the right
degree of piquancy to the occasion, four enemy generals who
were prisoners-of-war in Vincennes, and who had participated in
these campaigns, were invited to the performance so that they too
might celebrate the grandeur of France; they were Pedro de
León, Jean de Werth and the two Enkendorfs. At about this time
Richelieu's niece, Mme de Combalet, married the Duc d'Aiguillon, one of the members of the House of Lorraine, and his cousin,
the widow of Puylaurens, married the Comte d'Harcourt, also a
member of that House.

The rest of the royal family was not at all inclined to share
Richelieu's joys with him. The Duc de Vendôme had been out of
sight and out of mind since those far-off days when he instigated
the Chalais conspiracy. Now suddenly he was again the centre of
attention. Two wretched old hermits were arrested in some trifling
criminal matter, and one of them purported to confess that Vendôme had instigated him to murder the Cardinal. This immediately gained for them the unaccustomed dignity of being transferred from the gaol to the Bastille, and an interrogation by the
chancellor, Séguier, himself. Vendôme offered to come to Louis
and prove his innocence, but at the gates of Paris, reflecting on the
fate of so many others who had earned the Cardinal's suspicions,
he turned his horse and took the road to Cherbourg, whence he
went to England.

This in Louis' eyes was sufficient to establish his guilt, and a court of twenty-four judges was constituted, presided over by the King in person, to try Vendôme in his absence. Vendôme, ever stupid, had written a letter to Anne of Austria which, of course, had been intercepted, and in which he had said that he would have murdered the Cardinal in thought but never in deed. This was probably the truth, but to Louis thoughts could be crimes as well as sins, and the letter, produced in court, was, he said, sufficient proof. Richelieu now intervened, and the event which follows demonstrates once again the fallacy of the tradition of the Cardinal's domination of the King, to whose will Richelieu had often to yield, and whom he had to manage with the utmost care and tact. A letter was received by Séguier during the proceedings. In it the Cardinal asked the King to pardon Vendôme and drop the matter. The King said that, because it was so difficult to find ministers as loyal and able as Richelieu, he would reserve the question to himself, suspend judgement and pardon Vendôme only if the latter's conduct merited it. Séguier intervened and pointed out in front of the whole court that the Cardinal was asking, with insistence, for a pardon for Vendôme. Louis remained stubborn, and then told Séguier to read Richelieu's letter aloud to the court, for he would not.[6] In the end not even Louis could find sufficient in the preposterous evidence of the hermits to proceed with the matter.

With Soissons the case was different. Since his apparent submission he had remained close to Bouillon, and there was suspicion that he was in communication with Marie de Médicis, and the coterie of noble refugees in England, including Marie de Chevreuse, Benjamin de Soubise and the Duc de La Valette. A letter from La Valette to his father, the Duc d'Épernon, was intercepted, and it confirmed the existence of a widespread conspiracy. The bearer of the letter, upon interrogation, implicated Soissons, who, he said, was to enter Champagne while the Huguenots would rise in Guyenne and Soubise would attack the French coast. When this was reported to Soissons he sent Campion, one of his following, to the King to protest that this was a lie. Campion was brought to Richelieu who said he wished he could believe Soissons, but that Bouillon was even then at Montmédy

conferring with the Duc de Guise and Don Miguel de Salamanca. Richelieu decided to appear to be duped, and, exercising
the maximum vigilance, catch the plotters off guard. By April
1641 he thought he had collected sufficient evidence to take
action. Soissons was deprived of his governorship of Champagne, the properties of Bouillon in France were seized, and
all trade with Sedan was forbidden. The Duc d'Épernon was told
to break all communication with his son La Valette.

The extent to which Soissons was implicated in a plot by
Bouillon to bring the Spaniards into France is obscure from the
evidence, but it is clear that, after these measures, Bouillon persuaded Soissons that hesitation was the road to disaster; Soissons
should opt either for an accommodation with the King or for
revolt. In either event he could count on Bouillon's support, but
if he chose revolt he could not trust Spanish promises. The
interests of himself and Soissons, he said, were the opposite of
those of Spain; they wanted the overthrow of Richelieu and
peace; Spain wanted the destruction of France. Soissons' hatred of
Richelieu was such that he cast prudence aside, and, dragging
Bouillon with him, and joined later by Guise, the Baron du Bec
and other refugees, signed an agreement which was sent to the
Cardinal-Infante for him to sign also. At the same time Soissons
sent messages to d'Épernon, asking him to rise, negotiated through
the mediation of Fontrailles with Cinq Mars, asking for his
intervention with the King, and, of course, communicated with
the target of all would-be conspirators, Gaston d'Orléans. The
agent who carried the message to Monsieur was, it seems, a
double spy, and he disclosed all to the Cardinal. Gaston, perhaps
warned, gave no indication that this time he would be drawn
into rebellion, and kept the King informed. Richelieu was satisfied with his behaviour.

Soissons, at the head of a Spanish force, encountered Châtillon
at La Marfée on the Meuse on 6 July 1641 and repulsed him. But in
the moment of victory he raised the visor of his helm and received
a ball between the eyes. How this happened became a matter of
controversy between the cardinalists and the anti-cardinalists. The
former said that Soissons had the habit of pushing up his visor

with the muzzle of his pistol, and on this occasion had accidentally shot himself; the latter claimed that Soissons had been assassinated on Richelieu's orders. Bouillon hastened to seek an accommodation with the King, made his submission on his knees, and afterwards had dinner with the Cardinal. Later he found himself in Cinq Mars' room, where the young man disclosed his ferocious hatred for Richelieu, and his 'deepest despair' at the news of Soissons' death. The King, he said, was persecuted by Richelieu, was overjoyed at the reconciliation with Bouillon, and hoped that Bouillon would help him get rid of the Cardinal. Bouillon expressed astonishment at this revelation, and said he could scarcely believe it. Cinq Mars then said that the King could not find a better man for his government than Bouillon. The latter, however, would not be drawn, and he and all his following received their pardons, save Bec and Guise, who were decapitated in effigy.

Bouillon went home and the affair seemed to be over. Cinq Mars, his resentment nourished by all the recalcitrants at the court, kept sounding people out. When Gaston d'Orléans appeared at Amiens, where the King was lodged during the campaign of 1641, he was approached by the youthful serpent. Gaston, as usual, was peeved. He felt that he was not particularly welcome in the royal camp, and he complained bitterly that, although the 'merest captains' had access to the council of war, he was excluded. Cinq Mars portrayed to him a felicitous picture of a France without the Cardinal; at Gaston's merest nod, Cinq Mars said, cavaliers would rise to make the dream a reality. Gaston, however, like Bouillon, had lost his enthusiasm for conspiracy, and he made it clear that Cinq Mars' approach was ill-received.

It is likely that Cinq Mars would have been frustrated in his attempts to organize an anti-Richelieu conspiracy but for the fact that a woman had entered the picture in the person of Marie de Gonzague, the daughter of Nevers. When her father inherited the Duchy of Mantua she had been kidnapped by Marie de Médicis and locked in Vincennes, and her marriage to the Duc d'Orléans forbidden. Nothing would convince her that Richelieu was not the architect of her frustration, though in fact it had only one cause, the traditional hatred of the Medicis for the Gonzagas. When in 1637 her father died she inherited his French properties, including the Duchy of Nevers, and thereupon became a sovereign princess. Now nearing thirty years of age, unmarried, a glowing and important figure about the French court, she became the object of Cinq Mars' idolatry. A feverish love-affair developed, which caused Cinq Mars the more violent transports of emotion in that Marie refused to compromise her chastity.

Married to a sovereign, Cinq Mars could look forward to a future of immense power, and de Thou and Fontrailles steadily pushed him along the path of indiscretion. He decided he would ask Louis to make him a duke and a peer so that the difference in rank between himself and Marie would not appear too scandalous. Richelieu was shocked. Knowing the hatred that Marie bore him he watched events with growing alarm. He decided that on this occasion he should overwhelm the weak Cinq Mars by presenting the issue to him quite bluntly. 'I do not know,' he said, 'how you can pretend to such an alliance, you must remember that you are nothing but a simple gentleman.' But, protested Cinq Mars, his mother approved of his marriage proposal. 'If what you say is true,' replied Richelieu, 'your mother is a fool; and if the Princess Marie contemplates this marriage she is more of a fool than your mother!'[7] Assuming the role of martyrs, Henri and Marie worked like fiends together to bring Richelieu down.

Marie de Gonzague's cousin, Charles of Lorraine, provided a suitable epilogue to the Soissons plot. This intemperate man had abandoned his wife Nicole, who was virtually a prisoner in Paris, and to the great scandal of all Catholic Europe had committed a bigamous marriage with his mistress Beatrix Cosenza, Princesse de Cantecroix, whom he dragged around with his army like a camp-follower. After failing to raise the siege of Arras in 1640 he had a difference with the Spaniards, and opened negotiations with Richelieu for a peace settlement. A secret agent sent by him to Paris pictured the Duchy of Lorraine depopulated and in ruins, and said it would take a century to restore it. Charles would like to dedicate himself to this task. As Richelieu commented to Louis, Charles changed his thoughts and words every day;[8] but, when in February 1641 Charles announced that he was coming to Paris himself to negotiate, it was decided to receive him. At first he could not get beyond Chavigny, who treated him according to precise instructions from Richelieu like any other suppliant. Later he managed to see Richelieu, who, savouring the occasion, repeated in his honour the ballet on France's military prosperity; and in the end he was received by the King.

It was decided to restore him in the Duchies of Lorraine and Bar, provided he would do homage to Louis for the latter, and leave France in possession of Clermont and Nancy, which would be held until the end of the war. All was agreed to, and the restored Duke swore the necessary oaths. It is astonishing that Richelieu, merely to suborn one of the best imperial generals, should have hazarded as much as he did in letting Charles back into his territory. Before departing for Lorraine, Charles called on Nicole, who had to be implicated in the legal acts of restoration, and she with tears asked him 'Am I really not your wife?' Coldly he addressed her as 'cousin'. His bewildered – or perhaps, who knows, sarcastic – subjects greeted him with shouts of 'God save the Duke, his two wives, and his daughter!'[9] Hardly had he arrived in Nancy when Charles began to conspire with Guise, and then unexpectedly on 28 July 1641 he fled to Flanders and rejoined the Spaniards. Louis declared war on him and reoccupied Lorraine, while the Lorraine army retired up the Saar to rejoin its exiled leader, who now resumed his career as an imperial general.

25

He is Cardinal and Priest

1642

Pursuing chimeras of vengeance, and exasperating the King by reason of his caprices, the petulant Cinq Mars ran his fatal course. There were regular explosions between the ulcerated monarch and the cruelly selfish favourite, followed by equally regular reconciliations. Cinq Mars' entourage was grander than the Queen's; he compensated for his ideal love for the Princesse de Nevers by continuing to indulge his profane love for Marion de Lorme; time and again Richelieu was drawn by the King into the tiresome affairs of his erstwhile protégé. To get rid of him, Richelieu offered to appoint him governor of Touraine, but Cinq Mars' ambitions were not so easily satisfied; pushed by Marie de Gonzague, he asked for a seat on the royal council. He was in touch with Bouillon, who in the meantime had been made commander-in-chief of the army in Piedmont opposing Thomas of Savoy, and he saw Gaston again late in 1641, telling him that the coolness between himself and the King was only a feint to deceive Richelieu, whose downfall Louis himself was planning. It needed only a suggestion for the King to throw himself into the arms of the peace party and sacrifice his minister; if he could be sure of Gaston's backing, Cinq Mars would make the suggestion. Apparently he secured Monsieur's undertaking, or thought he had, because he reported as much to Bouillon. When the King, in a quite unaccustomed way, unburdened his mind to Monsieur on the subject of France's miseries, the latter was convinced that Cinq Mars was not deceiving him. Nervously, Gaston lent his authority to yet another, but this time the last, conspiracy against Richelieu.

The intermediary who linked Gaston and Cinq Mars together in clandestine designs was Fontrailles, and he was the central figure at meetings by candlelight in the Hôtel de Venise. Bouillon reported that he could not hold Sedan alone against the King's armies, and that as a condition of his participation in any rebellion he would require that Sedan be sufficiently garrisoned by the Spaniards. It was decided, therefore, to ask the King of Spain for military and financial assistance. To this end a draft treaty was drawn up which would be signed by Gaston, as the King's brother, and by Philip IV. It was quite the most treacherous and scandalous of all the similar documents to which Gaston had appended his name, for it guaranteed internal support for an invading Spanish army, which should hand over to the French rebels all French towns which it might capture. A curious clause was inserted in which Monsieur declared that he intended nothing against the King's will, and it may be that this was devised as an escape clause, should Louis, in fact, not move against Richelieu. Probably Anne of Austria was shown this document before it was taken by Fontrailles to Madrid to be delivered to Olivares.

On the face of it the treaty did not disclose the intention to murder Richelieu; it merely stated that the object of the alliance was to 'ruin M le Cardinal'. There is no reason to believe that either Monsieur or the Queen was a party to an assassination plot, for they were really only dupes in the affair, but there is reason to believe that the real plotters, Cinq Mars, Fontrailles and their clique of court officers, and perhaps even Bouillon, envisaged Richelieu's elimination by death. Just when the conspiracy was maturing, Cinq Mars was thrown into despair by the nomadic Louis, who, tired as he said of sitting with his arms crossed in St Germain, and craving excitement, announced his intention of going to the south to conduct the siege of Perpignan in person. Richelieu, knowing his own days were numbered, was no doubt impatient at this decision once more to drag the government around France: he agreed to undertake the fatigues of the journey with the remark that it did not really matter where he died. Cinq Mars made a scene, trying to dissuade Louis from leaving; for, if the conspirators were to be separated, and Richelieu withdrawn from his usual routine, it would be all the more difficult to effect the coup. The King was adamant, and in February 1642 the movement began.

Richelieu knew something, but not all, about the conspiracy. His nephew, Brézé, told him of a disquieting conversation he had overheard between Cinq Mars and the King, referring to Richelieu. He knew of the liaison between Cinq Mars and Gaston. In an indiscreet moment he asked the King to send Cinq Mars to Touraine or elsewhere, and was disquieted at the cold response. The court and the army were divided between 'cardinalists' and 'royalists', the latter pretending to protect the King against Richelieu's dictatorship. All the way to Lyons Cinq Mars denounced to Louis the evils of this eternal war without military decision. His co-conspirators were for overwhelming Richelieu in the King's presence and leaving him dead at Louis' feet, but Cinq Mars would not agree to this without the King's previous assent. Hints to this effect produced only the cold observation that 'he is cardinal and priest; I should be excommunicated'. To which Tréville, the commander of the Musketeers, is said to have exclaimed that Rome would be only too glad to absolve the King. When the court arrived at Lyons there was news of a French victory over the imperial army at Kempen on the upper Rhine, a victory which caused Bouillon to write to Gaston that the imperialist cause was now in such a plight that it would be foolish to count on the Spaniards to support a rising in France. Captured Austrian colours were paraded and a *Te Deum* was sung in the cathedral by Richelieu's brother. Richelieu was closely accompanied by the captain of his guards, even into the King's presence, where they embarrassed Louis and Cinq Mars by surprising them in close conversation.

At Valence, on the way down the Rhône, the King presented the hat to Mazarin, who had rejoined the court after his diplomatic essays in Savoy, and the new cardinal's humility was favourably commented upon. From there until Narbonne Richelieu kept his distance from the court, travelling, in fact, two days behind. Louis went on to the siege lines at Perpignan, where the squabbles between him and Cinq Mars were renewed. 'There is not a man so ruined by vice, or so lacking in desire to please,' cried Louis; 'he is the most ungrateful man in the world. Several times he has made me wait for hours in my coach while he was on his debauches. A kingdom would not cover his expenses. Even now he has up to three hundred pairs of boots!'[1] But still he did nothing to break an association that became ever more trying.

While the court was proceeding slowly into Languedoc, Fontrailles was carrying the secret treaty to Madrid, closely followed by one of Richelieu's secret police. Because the Spanish frontier was guarded it was necessary for him to take an obscure route. He thereupon ascended the valley of the Aspe, took a local guide, crossed near the Somport, and reached Huesca. A letter from Gaston gained him immediate access to Olivares on his arrival in Madrid. A conspirator even among his friends, Fontrailles hedged at disclosing the parties to the plot until Philip IV would sign the treaty. This method of negotiating irritated Olivares, and evoked from him the plaintive comment, 'We have been deceived too often to engage ourselves to anything without proper guarantees.' When Fontrailles remained devious Olivares told him to return to France; whereupon Fontrailles was forced to disclose the extent of the conspiracy. For four days Olivares quibbled over the terms of the treaty, leading Fontrailles to exclaim that it was not surprising that the Spaniards did so badly when they occupied themselves to such an extent with trifles; if Olivares wanted to save Perpignan, and indeed Catalonia, he had better stop amusing himself. On 13 March 1642 Fontrailles was brought before a jaded Philip IV and the treaty was signed.

Carrying an original signed copy Fontrailles mounted his horse to return to France, and, crossing the Pyrenees by the same route, he made his way to Narbonne to report to Cinq Mars. Meanwhile the papal nuncio at Madrid had informed Richelieu that 'a certain Frenchman had been seen for two or three days in the ante-chamber of the Count-Duke and he had had had a long conference with the minister'. From Narbonne Fontrailles rode to Toulouse to meet de Thou, who had vainly tried to implicate the Ducs de Mercoeur and Beaufort. De Thou went to Paris to obtain from Anne of Austria blank signed letters which could be drafted as orders to various officers in the realm, and on 20 May Fontrailles arrived at Chambord to report to Gaston. He found Monsieur in a high state of nerves, his person neglected and his beard whitening, and he did nothing to calm him when he told him that, from what he had heard in Narbonne of the stormy scenes between the King and Cinq Mars, the latter's downfall was imminent. Having delivered this discouraging news he fled a little later to England, saving his head and writing his part of the story for the benefit of history. Gaston's experience in conspiracy over the previous fifteen years should have warned him against readily believing that the King would dismiss the Cardinal, and that it merely required organized persuasion to bring him to this decision. On this occasion, however, his naïvety may be pardonable, for the rumour was widespread that the King was tired of Richelieu, and even the nuncio had reported as much to Rome.

Meanwhile, in Narbonne Richelieu became ill with some dreadful eruption on his arm, and took to his bed. Lying there he dictated a letter to Chavigny, who was to tell Louis that if the Cardinal should die he would know then what he had lost; but that if he should die through the King's fault the latter's credit would be quite gone. Then he set about making his will, which was seventeen pages long, and which, owing to his illness, he was unable to sign. His cash should go to his niece Marie-Madeleine and, after payment of his debts, to Sublet de Noyers. The Palais Cardinal should go to the King, together with one and a half million *livres*; the Sorbonne, the rebuilding of which had been largely at his charge, benefited enormously. The Duchy of Fronsac should go to the Brézé family, and the Duchy of Richelieu to the Pontcourlay family. The arriviste in him repudiated his own ancestry: the heirs of these families were forbidden to marry persons who were not 'strictly noble'. And he ended:

After having lived a life of languishing health, and having served the State with some success in difficult times and thorny affairs; and having experienced on various occasions good and bad fortune, rendering to His Majesty the services which his goodness and particularly my position as his subject required of me, I have never failed in the obedience or the respect which I owed to the Queen Mother, in spite of all the calumnies with which some have tried to blacken my reputation in this respect.[2]

The Roman baths at Arles were not far away, and he decided to go there to take the waters. *En route* he received a reply from Louis: 'I love you more than ever; we have been together too long to be separated.'[3] This was reassuring; but at Arles news was awaiting Richelieu which did more than the waters could have done to stimulate his flagging health and spirits: the agreement between the Spaniards and the conspirators had been discovered. How a copy of it came into Richelieu's hands is a mystery. One theory is that Pujol, the secret intermediary of the Cardinal in Madrid, had wheedled it out of Don Andres de Rozas, the secretary of Philip IV, or out of Carnero, the secretary of the Council of State, with both of whom he was intimate. It is possible that this was so, for Olivares had been specially attentive to Pujol these last few months, retaining him in Madrid when he wished to retire to France, in the desperate hope of bringing Richelieu to a peace conference in Narbonne or anywhere else in the world. Recently, however, a new theory has been advanced, that Anne of Austria disclosed the plot. Certainly the Queen's actions were curious. Richelieu received the copy of the agreement about 11 June 1642. On 30 April, however, Anne, with something serious on her mind, had written to Richelieu that, if she were forced to separate from her children at their tender age, she did not think she would have the strength to stand it. Richelieu had failed to reply, and had thereupon been pestered with letters from the Queen pleading desperately for his intervention to ward off the King's wrath.

It seems reasonable that the Queen, conscience-stricken and worried about her position with respect to the children, had sought to warn Richelieu of his danger by oblique hints, and that this was the source of the information which he had passed cautiously on to the King – not daring to confront Louis as of old because he was uncertain how far the whispering campaign against him had been successful. Once Richelieu was on the track of something it was more than likely that he would ferret out everything, and it is possible that a little mild blackmail had been applied to the Queen by her own Master of the Household, who was a cardinalist, and that she, in the end, had produced a copy of the agreement and a list of the traitors. It was all over Paris that the plot had been discovered, for Marie de Gonzague had written as much to Cinq Mars who had shown the letter to Fontrailles: the latter had advised Cinq Mars to fly to Sedan.

Richelieu wasted not a moment. The day he received the evidence he dispatched Chavigny to Narbonne, where Louis had taken up residence in the great donjon in the centre of the town. The King was still sleeping when Chavigny clattered in early in the morning; and, after some time conferring with his colleagues, Chavigny presented him with the facts. Orders went out immediately for the arrest of Bouillon, who was then negotiating with Thomas of Savoy at Casale, and the same evening the King signed the order for Cinq Mars' arrest. The latter must have been warned, for he attempted to flee, but, finding all the gates of the town locked, had perforce to hide himself in a house, from which he was dragged next morning. Louis continued to have doubts, saying that surely someone must have put Cinq Mars' name on the list in error, but, when reassured that there was sufficient evidence against the young man, fell into a 'profound reverie'.

The Comte du Plessis-Praslin and the *maréchal-de-camp*, M. de Castelnau, took the road together to Casale. When they arrived and Bouillon was informed that Plessis-Praslin wanted to see him, he asked if Castelnau was also there; and, being told that he was, sensed their mission. Having tried vainly to slide down the sloping sides of the walls of the fortress, he hid among bales of hay in a loft of one of the houses in the town, and was in due course discovered and brought to Lyons. Gaston, already on the point of making yet another of his dashes over the Spanish frontier of Belgium, was tricked by a letter from the King referring to the 'extraordinary insolence' of Cinq Mars, but giving no hint of suspicion of himself. Gaston had reached Moulins when the news of Cinq Mars' arrest reached him and he was in two minds about his future movements. He decided to write a letter, half in indignation at the plot, half in amity towards the Cardinal, and see what happened.

As yet he did not know that the text of the treaty, and his own commitment, were in Richelieu's hands, and the Abbé de la Rivière whom he sent to deliver his letter was dumbfounded when Louis showed it to him. Rivière, having essayed some excuses for his master, promptly returned to Gaston with the news that all was discovered. Richelieu, knowing his Gaston only too well, decided by gentle treatment to lure him into denouncing his fellow conspirators. After some weeks of frantic wanderings among the hills and forests of Auvergne to avoid the royal troops, whom he wrongly suspected of trying to surround him, Monsieur did what the Cardinal expected of him, and on 7 July 1642 wrote to the King disclosing what he knew of the conspiracy. He petulantly blamed Cinq Mars for duping him, but acknowledged his own primary responsibility for the treaty with Olivares; he denied that Cinq Mars had discussed with him the assassination of Richelieu.

In Paris there was consternation. D'Enghien reported Cinq Mars' arrest to Marie de Gonzague, who, having burned her own papers, begged Richelieu's niece, the Duchesse d'Aiguillon, to recover from the Cardinal's files all correspondence which had been seized and in which she figured. In this she was successful, and everything incriminating was destroyed. Cinq Mars, who was held at Montpellier, and de Thou, who was locked in the château of Tarascon where the Cardinal was running the affairs of France from his bed, denied everything, and Richelieu decided to bring them face to face with Gaston and Bouillon. This suggestion embarrassed Monsieur, and caused him to take the course of action which Richelieu was trying to avoid: he fled.

This time, however, he made for his sister Christine, and appeared in the Savoy town of Annecy, where he lodged in the castle overlooking the lake. There he heard of the death of Marie de Médicis, who, having exhausted the patience of the Spaniards and failed to find asylum with her daughter in England, had drifted to the court of the Elector of Cologne. Gaston, already in a mood of despair, was utterly distraught at the thought that he had not seen his mother since his dramatic gallop from Brussels five years previously, and would now never bid her farewell; and he was to be seen praying with unwonted piety at the tomb of St Francis de Sales in the church at the foot of the castle rock. Since his testimony was needed against Cinq Mars he was coaxed back to France in August. He added nothing to his previous disclosures, save the sour comment that if he were as repentant of his sins as he was of his fault respecting the King, God would pardon him with more heart than the King had done. He had in the meanwhile burned the original of the treaty with Spain, and at Villefranche on 29 August he certified to the accuracy of a copy. He also consummated his life of betrayals by signing a declaration that two of the persons mentioned but unnamed in the treaty were Cinq Mars and Bouillon. This was sufficient evidence to condemn them both.

Before the news of Marie de Médicis' death reached the King, but when it was known she was ill, Richelieu drafted a stilted letter which Louis sent her, saying he was unhappy to hear of her indisposition and that he prayed for her recovery. When he heard she was dead, Richelieu's comment was 'I pray God with all my heart that He has given eternal rest to the Queen's soul. I am happy to have seen, by letters, that she had had great repentance of her sins, and that she pardoned generously those whom she held to be her enemies.'[4] Since he knew he was shortly to join her, these were words of sincerity. Although he did not leave his bed, he was as busy as ever, working from seven in the morning, giving audiences, dictating, hearing mass, and even fruitlessly interrogating de Thou himself at his bedside. When Perpignan fell, after young Brézé had destroyed the fleet of Ciudad-Real and the last hopes of its relief, and the King withdrew from the south, there was no point in Richelieu's waiting longer at Tarascon; and in the middle of August he decided to go up the Rhône to Valence, taking de Thou with him, and having Cinq Mars brought afterwards from Montpellier.

The procession of boats that slowly passed the Pont d'Avignon made a magnificent spectacle. A frigate went ahead, sounding the passage, followed by a boat full of musketeers. The Cardinal lay invalided in the cabin of his barge, which was decorated with crimson leaves on a field of gold, and his bed was hung with purple taffeta. Guards stood fore and aft in scarlet livery. In a small boat just behind came de Thou, watched also by the Cardinal's guards. Other boats contained bevies of bishops, priests and cavaliers, and chests of plate and clothes, while on both banks marched a scattered string of pikemen, their black morions and half armour over their scarlet jerkins making them look like ladybirds. At night his bed was lifted off the barge, and he was carried on a litter into the lodging prepared for him sometimes through a window, even through a hole made in the wall. Watching the burning southern sun of August bleaching the pale walls of the papal palace at Avignon, Richelieu's mind undoubtedly went back to those days when he had taken his exercise on the banks of the Rhône. It was, in terms of eternity, but yesterday.

Cinq Mars reached Lyons under escort on 3 March, de Thou, who had been sent on from Valence by carriage, on 4 March, and Richelieu the next day. There he had news from Sedan. Eleanor de Berg, Bouillon's wife, had locked the gates of Sedan and threatened to hand the city over to the Spaniards if Bouillon were not released. The first thing to do, therefore, was to settle affairs with Bouillon. The Duke played into Richelieu's hands nicely. Incriminating the conspirators in his confession, he claimed that his part in the plot was conditional on the death of the King. This was sufficient excuse to grant him his life in return for the surrender of Sedan and his political extinction. Mazarin, who arranged this with Bouillon, merited Richelieu's praise. 'He has negotiated so adroitly', he said, 'that M de Bouillon has said enough to make our proof complete!' He was so much in terror of execution that he would surrender three Sedans if he could save his life.[5] Armed with a letter from Bouillon to his wife, Mazarin travelled to Sedan and secured the surrender of the fortress. The principality of Sedan was extinguished by formal legal acts, and Bouillon was allowed to retire to Rome, where a little later he abjured Calvinism, became a Catholic, and was given command of the papal army. As for Gaston, the document he signed, by which he earned yet another royal pardon, provided that he should henceforth live as a private person without a governorship, guards, or any part in public affairs. It was a crushed and docile Monsieur who crept back home and retired from conspiracy until the next reign.

The trial of Cinq Mars and de Thou, which began in the first week of September, was, according to the custom of the time, an inquisition rather than a hearing. The miserable Bouillon was brought face to face with the two accused, and made to repeat his confession in front of them. De Thou, who was a lawyer, argued that nothing that Bouillon said could be construed as proof of his complicity, and every action of his was consistent with his innocence. One of the judges demeaned himself, possibly with Séguier's knowledge, though this is not clear, by going to Cinq Mars' cell and falsely telling the accused that de Thou had incriminated him as well as himself. Stung at the thought of his friend's act of betrayal, Cinq Mars thereupon signed a confession implicating de Thou.

Before the court Cinq Mars defended himself by pleading the King's will for whatever he had done, but a letter was produced which must surely be unique in the annals of the law; Louis himself, the fountain of justice, became a witness in the trial, writing that Cinq Mars was an 'impostor and calumniator'. On the morning of 12 September Richelieu left Lyons for Lentilly, where he awaited the verdict. It was brought to him that afternoon in a letter from Séguier, who, as chancellor, had presided in court. Cinq Mars was condemned for high treason, not for having plotted against Richelieu, but for having been a party to the agreement with Spain; and de Thou was condemned as an accessory, after having pleaded in vain that the law required corroboration of Cinq Mars' testimony against him – a point on which he was supported by the *procureur-général* in a sharp debate in open court with Séguier.

'De Thou!' exclaimed Richelieu when the verdict was read to him, 'Monsieur le chancelier has relieved me of a great burden!'

Then he added, recollecting that the public executioner had broken a limb, 'but they have no executioner.' They assured him that there would be no difficulty in finding one. And he went on his way to Roanne, writing a note to Chavigny in which he said 'these three words will let you know that Perpignan is in the hands of the King and that M. le Grand (Écuyer) and M. de Thou are in the next world, where I pray God they might be happy.'[6] He remained obsessed by the affair, referring to Cinq Mars as this 'devil from hell', and, forgetting his friendship with Cinq Mars' father, went so far as to rusticate Cinq Mars' innocent mother in Touraine, and to order the destruction of the château of Cinq Mars. He also asked the names of the two judges who had voted against de Thou's death sentence.

The execution of Cinq Mars gave the young man his final opportunity to flaunt himself in the public eye. As he climbed the scaffold in the Place des Terreaux at Lyons one of the archers of the provost guard took off the condemned man's hat, for it was forbidden to wear one. Cinq Mars snatched it back, then putting it on his head made two or three turns around the scaffold, hands on his hips, returning the stares of the crowd. Then he saluted them and tossed them his big floppy and feathered hat with great drama, before testing the block and fitting his neck in it. Then he got up and strutted about a little longer, holding the crucifix without taking off his gloves. He refused to have his eyes bandaged.

De Thou, who was much more subdued, asked the priest if he could be given time to pray. Cinq Mars turned to him saying, 'Haven't you prayed to God?' The executioner, who had never performed his function previously, made a butchery of it and roused the wrath of the crowd, which broke the barriers and swarmed over the scaffold dipping their handkerchiefs in the warm blood that flowed through the cracks in the flooring. There is some reason to believe that they assassinated the maladroit headsman. When these stories were reported to Richelieu he was genuinely scandalized, and he wrote to Chavigny from Roanne:

It is said that he [Cinq Mars] often said that he would show more resolution about dying than M. de Montmorency and M. de Saint

Preuil: but in my opinion the others died in a more Christian fashion. Not that I do not believe he died well; his confessor, who has come here on his behalf to tell me many things, indicates himself to be satisfied. His confessor has been charged by him to ask my pardon, and I have undertaken to ask the King's on his behalf.[7]

Richelieu's role in the trial of the two young men has been the subject of general criticism by historians, including even Père Griffet in the eighteenth century. Modern writers have accused him of pursuing personal vengeance for the anxieties he had suffered, and his words and actions have been interpreted as indications of base vindictiveness. The explanation is superficial; deplorable though Richelieu's attitude was, his motives must be judged by the standards of the time, and those standards are clearly enunciated in the court's judgement, which so echoes Richelieu's own sentiments in the *Testament Politique* that he might well have written it:

A crime of high-treason can be justly punished, even when it is established only by strong and pressing conjecture. This is said particularly because many classical doctors and jurisconsults of great reputation openly teach it, and because the reason behind the opinion is that states, whose preservation must be extremely dear, would often suffer considerable harm and perhaps their entire ruin, if, in the matter of crimes which tend to their overthrow, proofs were required which are as clear as those required in ordinary cases.[8]

To make yet another demonstration was as important to the security of France, in Richelieu's opinion, as to get the peace conference in Westphalia started; Richelieu was implacable, but always for a higher motive than revenge; and the security of a democratic society is a precondition for the luxury of the rights of man.

There remained the problem of dealing with the King, whose conduct during the previous two years had contributed decisively to the tragedy, and had constituted a disastrous departure from the standards required of the Anointed. Now at the end of his career Richelieu was horrified to discover that his own work in reconstructing France could so easily be jeopardized by 'the sentiments of individuals' which kings should eschew. His lifetime had been too short to establish institutions which would be resistant to human passions, and his personal dictatorship was a necessary expedient during a transitional phase of reorganization. But it was a system dependent upon the king's acting always in a role that the people could recognize as prescribed by God. For a Richelieu there was only one substitute – a Louis XIV.

At Nemours the Cardinal's taffeta bed was put in a carriage, and he travelled by road to Fontainebleau, where he arrived a month later. He was carried, a very sick man, into the Hôtel d'Albret. The King arrived and surprised him sitting for a moment in a chair. Supported on the arms of Chavigny and Noyers the frail man rose with difficulty. They embraced, there was a long silence, and then the King ordered everyone out. For three hours he and the Cardinal were alone together. It was the first heart-to-heart talk they had had for many months, for the Cinq Mars affair had interrupted their communications. In October Richelieu was well enough to return to Paris and take up residence in the Palais Cardinal. There he drafted a memorandum to the King, recalling the Cinq Mars story in all its miserable details, and outlining the consequences to himself and good government. He reminded the King that on several occasions he had tendered his resignation, and that this had been refused. He would tender it again unless the King agreed with five propositions, which he then proceeded to outline. These would engage the King not to let favourites meddle in politics, to close his ear to vicious talk about his ministers, to ascertain the truth of charges against them before acting, to punish those who were found guilty of calumny, and to keep the secrets of council meetings. Then, not sparing the royal feelings in the slightest, he reminded Louis of the way he himself had been treated after the death of Ancre, 'banished, not only from the King and the Queen his mother, but from the Kingdom on suspicions which had no foundation other than a false appearance'.[9] The document was sent to the King but no acknowledgement was received, and so, on 5 November 1642, Richelieu offered his resignation. The King was at St Germain, and Chavigny, who was with him, reinforced the Cardinal's arguments. Louis seemed to take it all in good part, but, without indicating what was in his mind, went off hunting. He returned late at night and went to bed. Next morning Chavigny was at the royal levee, and he waited anxiously for some indication of the King's will. Louis remained silent.

Chavigny, like Richelieu, was agitated that the King continued to keep about himself Cinq Mars' friends, many of whom, they suspected, were in the murder plot, although this could not be proved. Whenever Chavigny sought to press the King on this point he found him irritated, and, fearing an attack on the Cardinal's life, he advised Richelieu to have his guards constantly at his side. His disquiet increased when Louis treated as insolent Chavigny's suggestion that Richelieu's guards should enter St Germain with him. Still without indicating what were his thoughts, Louis went off hunting for the next few days.

On 13 November Richelieu wrote a third letter, this time asking for a frank reply, and especially for the King to state on what conditions he would agree to peace; not his own conduct but the injustice of the Spaniards was preventing it, for he had religiously followed the King's intentions. Five days passed and then on 20 November the King wrote his reply: He had nothing to say to his cousin the Cardinal de Richelieu, except what he knew only too well, and he referred to the little credit he had given to Cinq Mars' insinuations against the Cardinal, adding that there was no question of his wishing Richelieu to retire, but that, on the contrary, the minister should act with more liberty and power than ever. 'I promise him, moreover, that I shall keep inviolate any secret which he wants me to keep.'[10] He then went over the diplomatic situation, explaining why he would never compromise over Lorraine, Arras, Hesdin, Bapaume, Perpignan, Breisach, or Pinerolo, or fail to support his young nephew Charles Emmanuel II of Savoy. A week later Cinq Mars' associates were banished from the court. It was Richelieu's last victory, for on 28 November he was taken with fever and complained of a serious pain in the side.

The Cardinal Never Dies
1642

Winter had closed in over Paris and the candles burned at four in the afternoon in the Palais Cardinal. The relatives had arrived, Maréchal de Brézé, the Comte d'Harcourt, and the Duchesse d'Aiguillon, and had taken up residence there. The Cardinal was being bled, with intermittent improvement, but the fever grew worse, and he was choking and spitting blood. The doctors diagnosed pleurisy. On 2 December 1642 the King arrived from St Germain and entered the sick room at two o'clock in the afternoon with his captain of the guard.

Sire [murmured Richelieu] behold the last farewell. In taking leave of Your Majesty I have the consolation of leaving your Kingdom in the highest degree of glory and of reputation which it has ever had, and all your enemies beaten and humiliated. The only recompense of my trouble and services which I dare to demand of Your Majesty is that he will continue to honour with his protection and goodwill my nephews and my relations. I shall give them my blessing only provided they do not depart from the fidelity and obedience which they owe you, and which they have vowed for ever.[1]

The words might have come straight out of one of his own plays; on his deathbed the concept of the grandeur of France preoccupied him as much as it ever had, and the notion of the

King's 'reputation', summarizing as it did a whole moral and political philosophy, was paramount in his thoughts.

He then went on to advise the King to appoint Mazarin as his successor, and to keep the other ministers in office so that there would be no breach of continuity. Louis, who behaved tenderly, gave his promise, and then fed the Cardinal two egg yolks with his own hand. Having taken his farewell, he delayed to inspect the works of art with which Richelieu the connoisseur had furnished the palace, and then retired across to the Louvre, because, he said, he did not want to go back to St Germain until he knew the outcome of the illness. The family entered, Harcourt with tears in his eyes to match his great pearl. Richelieu asked the doctors how long they thought he would live, telling them not to be frightened to confess to him, for they were speaking to a man perfectly resigned to the will of God for life and death. They replied that they did not know.

That night the fever grew worse, he was bled twice, and was told that he probably had only twenty-four hours to live. The bishop of Chartres was brought in to hear his general confession, and he told his servants to awaken him at midnight so that he could hear mass and receive communion. At one in the morning the parish priest of St Eustache brought him the viaticum, and Richelieu was heard saying aloud, 'My Master, my Judge who will shortly judge me: I pray Him with all my heart to condemn me if I have ever had any intention other than the good of religion and the state.'[2] It was his apologia for his whole life. Several contemporary accounts record that he said that he had never had any enemies except those of the state. Whether he said this or not is immaterial; he certainly believed it.

At three in the morning he received extreme unction from the same priest. He recited the Our Father and the Credo 'with great contrition and tenderness of heart', kissing the crucifix which he held in his hands. The room was now full of bishops and clergy, and the priest asked him to give his blessing to those present. 'Alas,' he replied, 'I am not worthy to give it, but, since you ask me, I shall receive it from you to give it to them.'[3] In the afternoon the King came again and stayed until five o'clock.

Richelieu expressed the hope that he would be able to suffer until the end the pain which God had sent. As to his officers who were weeping, he muttered whether 'they thought he was immortal'.[4] The doctors gave him pills, and the night of 3 December passed quietly. Next morning the Abbé de la Rivière arrived on behalf of Gaston d'Orléans, and was received; to complete the drama of Richelieu's career, there was a death-bed reconciliation with Monsieur. At midday he called the Duchesse d'Aiguillon to his bedside and said that he had esteemed her above all other persons, and that for this reason he wished her to retire so that she would not see him expire. Marie-Madeleine, in tears, said that a religious had had a vision to the effect that the Cardinal would not die of this illness. And the Cardinal, perhaps casting his mind back to the misdirections of Père Joseph's nun, and regaining his theological sanity, replied: 'Niece, there are no truths but those in the Gospel; one should believe in them alone.'

Mme d'Aiguillon retired and a discalced Carmelite, Père Léon, came and gave the Cardinal a new absolution, while the bishop of Chartres began to read the prayers for the dying. As he murmured the text, Richelieu, who was pale and still, eyes fixed on the ceiling, gave two sighs, and when a candle flame was placed near his lips it did not flicker. An epoch had come to an end; the Cardinal was dead.

He died with the same serene indifference to his own faults as he had exhibited towards the human misery of those he had sacrificed to the Moloch of the state; and there were those who were awed and horrified by it. It was left for God to review the balance sheet: a fatal designation of the nation as a paramount moral end, and the justification of means by reference to it, would be weighed against the cleansing of the Church, the assertion of its moral authority and the preservation of its doctrine; avarice would be weighed against a magnificent charity and unremitting support of works of mercy; vanity against unexampled courage, dedication and self-sacrifice; misuse of others in the implacable pursuit of power against a scrupulous use of this power for the good of the body politic; subordination of Catholic unity to national unity against zeal for the reunification of Christ's separated brethren; detachment from the priestly life against a profound faith, a touching devotion to the Blessed Virgin and a sense of dependence upon providence.

His responsibility for the unparalleled miseries of war was enormous, but he had assumed it in the absolute conviction that he was right. On this as on other matters contemporaries did not judge with divine mercy, and their own passions obscured the record; the historians have judged more by reference to the long-term consequences of his actions in the evolution of Europe than by reference to the intentions of the man, and their prejudices have compounded controversy. If Louis de Marillac were among those who greeted Armand-Jean du Plessis de Richelieu at the threshhold of eternity he would have done so with forgiveness. It is not given to history to be charitable, but it is given to it to be understanding.

Long live the Cardinal! The door opened and Cardinal Mazarin entered, symbol of continuity, or perhaps of transition, and with him were Séguier, Chavigny, Noyers, bishops and officials. Chavigny and Noyers then left and walked over to the Louvre to bring the news to the King. Louis instructed them to convey his sympathies to the relations, and a few hours later informed Mazarin that he wanted him to undertake the affairs of the state with the same care as the late Cardinal had given them. Mazarin's mind no doubt went back to the extraordinary career which he had begun before the walls of Casale thirteen years previously; he wished to decline the appointment. Louis pressed him, and eventually he accepted. To forestall any attempt by Gaston to reassert his claims to have a say in the government at this opportune moment, he sent a messenger to the President of the Parlement of Paris asking that body to confirm the royal declaration that Monsieur, on account of his faults, was declared incapable of any administration. The three Chambers of the Parlement were summoned, and the legal formalities were rushed through. It was rumoured that Gaston had again left France, but in fact he was sitting at home, very subdued.

For four days Richelieu's body lay in state while all Paris defiled before it. He lay in his scarlet with the cardinal's hat and its

434

four rows of tassels, and at his feet was a ducal coronet and mantle. On a table stood a silver crucifix flashing in the moving light of candles. In robes of mourning sat the captain of the Cardinal's guards. Members of religious orders recited the psalms. After dark on 13 December 1642 the body was carried on a wagon, surrounded by the Cardinal's pages and accompanied by carriages carrying the mourners, and taken into the church of the Sorbonne which Richelieu had begun to build, and which was still un-finished. The bishop of Orléans in full pontificals received it at the door, and the parish priest of St Eustache began to speak in Latin. Such was the heat from the candles and the crowd of people that he fainted and had to be carried behind the choir to be resusci-tated. The candles were extinguished one by one and Richelieu was left in silence in the atmosphere of scholarship he so loved.

Richelieu's death, like his life, was theatre, and his contem-poraries expected an epilogue. Their disappointment was ex-pressed by Goulas, one of Gaston's companions:

Those who came forward with the notion of helping their relations and friends persecuted under the previous government, or to profit from the death of His Eminence were extremely discontented, and the same ministers remaining and acting according to the same maxims it seemed that Cardinal Richelieu had not died at all.

It remained for history to construct the epilogue, which was, in fact, as dramatic as the Cardinal might have wished. Two months after Richelieu's funeral, and when Bassompierre, Vitry and the other denizens of the Bastille were breathing the air of liberty again, and Olivares was disgraced, Louis XIII began a rapid decline. It was decided to proceed with the official baptism of the five-year-old Dauphin. After the ceremony the King asked him, 'And what is your name now?' The reply was immediate and direct: 'I am Louis Quatorze!' 'Not yet,' said the King, 'but soon.' By April he was bedridden, reading Kempis' *Meditation on Death*, and as the tuberculosis devoured him he had a vision of d'Enghien, whom he had appointed to command on the northern front: 'Oh,' he murmured, 'I did well to entrust my army to him!' On 19 May

1643 while they were burying the King in St Denis the twenty-one-year-old d'Enghien, who had never before seen a pitched battle, destroyed the Spanish army of the Netherlands at Rocroy: it was a victory as great as that at Nördlingen, the first time that Spanish *tercios* had been beaten in the field. And, when it was over, the eighty-three-year-old Fuentes, with his long white beard, was dead in the litter from which he had wielded his marshal's baton. It was the same Fuentes who, by building his fort in the Valtelline exactly forty years previously, had instituted the chain of events which had led him to this fate, Richelieu to the judgement of God, and France to her grandeur.

Four years later Corneille articulated the epilogue in a eulogy to the founder of the French Academy – the Corneille who, according to the most malicious of the false legends about Richelieu, had earned the Cardinal's jealousy because *Le Cid* was a better play than *Mirame:*

Even if I knew nothing else about you except that you are the choice of that great genius, who has performed nothing but miracles, the late M. le Cardinal de Richelieu, I should be utterly devoid of common sense if I did not have for you an extraordinary esteem and veneration, and if I could not perceive that, with the same hand with which this great man sapped the foundations of the Spanish monarchy, he deigned to lay those of your establishment, and to confide to your care the purity of a language which he wished to be understood and to predominate throughout the whole of Europe.

Notes

(Names in capitals are abbreviations of works appearing in the Bibliography)

Chapter 1

1 *T.P.*, p. 222.
2 H. and LA F., vol. 1, p. 348.
3 *Mémoires*, vol. 1, p. 555.
4 *T.P.*, p. 93.
5 The story is told by Abbé de Pure, *Vita Eminentissimi cardinalis Arm. Plessei Richeliei*, 1656, and may have been told to him by Alphonse de Richelieu. For the Rome visit see AUBERY, bk. 1, ch. 2, p. 14.

Chapter 2

1 AVENEL, vol. 1, pp. 23–8.
2 *Traité qui contient la méthode la plus facile ... pour convertir ceux qui sont séparés de l'Eglise*. Edition of 1663, p. 2.
3 Bremond (cited below, p. 478), vol. 1, p. 95.
4 ibid., vol. 2, p. 168.
5 AVENEL, vol. 1, p. 59.

Chapter 3

1 The text is given in full in H. and LA F., vol. 2, p. 27.
2 *Harangue prononcée en la salle du Petit Bourbon, le XXIII février 1615, à la closture des Estats tenus à Paris, par réverend père en Dieu,*

messire Armand-Jean du Plessis de Richelieu, évesque de Lusson, p. 14. The *Mercure français*, 1616, vol. 3, p. 404, and AVENEL, vol. 1, no. CXXIII give only extracts. A modified version is in the Petitot edition of *Mémoires*, vol. 11, p. 201.

3   *Harangue prononcée devant le roy et la royne, en la salle de Bourbon, à la présentation du cayer du tiers-estat, par Messire Robert Miron, le lundy 23 fevrier 1615*, p. 21.

4   *Lettere diplomatiche di Giulio Bentivoglio*, 1852, vol. 1, p. 97.

5   Archives of Simancas, A 74, fol. 36/122, letter of 28 November 1616.

6   Correspondence of the Venetian Ambassadors, vol. 1770, fol. 226, cited by H. and LA F., vol. 2, p. 154.

7   AVENEL, vol, 1. p. 381.

8   *T.P.*, p. 347.

Chapter 4

1   H. and LA F., vol. 2, p. 105.

2   ibid., p. 193.

3   AVENEL, vol. 1, p. 537.

4   *Mémoires*, vol. 1, p. 159.

5   ibid., p. 161.

6   H. and LA F., vol. 2, p. 218.

7   *Espitre au Roy*, p. 3.

8   pp. 253–4.

9   H. and LA F., vol. 2, p. 262.

10 AVENEL, vol. 1, p. 587.

11 *Mémoires*, vol. 1, p. 205.

12 H. and LA F., vol. 2, p. 328.

13 ibid., p. 338.

14 *Harangue à la Royne mère du Roy contre les plaintes de messires les princes . . . à chasteau d'Angers le 3 juillet 1620.*

Chapter 5

1   *T.P.*, p. 94.

2   H. and LA F., vol. 2, p. 425.

3   *Avis adressé au roy après la révolte de Soubise.* Pub. in *Les sentiments illustres de quelques grands hommes d'Estat et de très prudents ministres*, 1686.

4   *T.P.*, p. 379.

5 AVENEL, vol. 1, p. 698.
6 ibid., p. xcix.
7 ibid., p. 747.
8 ibid., p. 752.
9 H. and LA F., vol. 2, p. 551.
10 AVENEL, vol. 2, p. 6.
11 *Mémoires*, vol. 1, pp. 290–300.
12 ibid., p. 303.

Chapter 6

1 *Relazione di R. Zeno Ambasciatore Ordinario alle Corte di Roma 1621–1623*, 1856, p. 173.
2 FAGNIEZ, vol. 1, p. 196.
3 F. von Hurter, *Geschichte Kaiser Ferdinand II*, 1860, vol. 9, p. 385.
4 FAGNIEZ, vol. 1, p. 228.
5 AVENEL, vol. 3, p. 208.
6 ibid., vol. 2, p. 120.
7 ELLIOTT, p. 200.
8 ibid., p. 198.
9 AVENEL, vol. 2, p. 77.
10 ibid., p. 85.
11 ibid., p. 189.

Chapter 7

1 Francisco de Jesús, *Narrative of the Spanish Marriage Treaty*, trans. by S. R. Gardiner, 1869, p. 205.
2 In which Walter Montagu acted, Hardwicke, *State Papers*, vol. 1, p. 465.
3 Cabala, *Sive Scrinia Sacra, Mysteries of State and Government*, 1691, p. 290.
4 H. and LA F., vol. 3, p. 32.
5 MOTTEVILLE, p. 20.
6 S. R. Gardiner, *History of England (1603–42)*, 1893, vol. 6, p. 35.

Chapter 8

1 *Mémoires*, vol. 9, pp. 33, 36.
2 BATIFFOL, Chevreuse, p. 5.
3 ibid., p. 19.

4 BATIFFOL, Chevreuse, p. 21.
5 ibid., p. 32.
6 ibid., p. 72.
7 ibid., *passim*.
8 H. and LA F., vol. 4, p. 323.
9 *T.P.*, p. 288.
10 ibid., p. 292.
11 ibid., p. 297.
12 JOURDAN, vol. 16, p. 529.
13 E. Glasson, *Le Parlement de Paris*, 1901, vol. 1, p. 123.
14 *Treize livres des Parlemens de France*, p. 707.
15 ibid., p. 704.
16 *T.P.*, p. 93.
17 *Oeuvres: Traité des seigneuries*, p. 8.
18 *De la souveraineté du roy*, p. 1.
19 *T.P.*, p. 330.
20 loc. cit., p. 71.
21 *T.P.*, p. 325.
22 ibid., p. 296.

Chapter 9

1 p. 153.
2 AVENEL, vol. 2, p. 159. For the *règlement* of the clergy see ibid., p. 168.
3 p. 151.
4 PASTOR, p. 433.
5 H. and LA F., vol. 2, p. 522.
6 Caillet, *De l'administration en France sous le ministère du cardinal de Richelieu*. Paris. 1857, p.257.
7 *T.P.*, p. 388.
8 *Mercure français*, vol. 12, p. 759. For an excerpt of Richelieu's instructions to Marillac see AVENEL, vol. 2, p. 291.
9 ibid., p. 297. That Richelieu disclosed the following grievances against Spain to the Notables is clear from *A.E. mém. doc.*, vol. 59, fol. 94.
10 AVENEL, vol. 2, p. 290.
11 *T.P.*, p. 408.
12 AVENEL, vol. 2, p. 290.
13 *T.P.*, p. 423.

14 H. and La F., vol. 4, p. 558.
15 Jourdan, vol. 16.

Chapter 10

1 *Calendar of State Papers, Domestic Series*, 1627–8, p. 159.
2 Vaux de Foletier, *Le siège de La Rochelle*. Paris, 1931, p. 88.
3 *Mémoires de Beaulieu-Persac*, Paris, 1913, p. 174.
4 H. and La F., vol. 3, p. 121.
5 *Mémoires de Beaulieu-Persac*, p. 183.
6 Alvarez, *Don Gonzalo Fernández de Cordóba y la guerra de sucesión de Mantua y del Monferrato, 1627–9*. Madrid, 1955, p.22.
7 *Calendar of State Papers, Venetian*, 1626–8, p. 543.
8 P. Mervault, Rochelais, *Journal des choses les plus mémorables qui se sont passées au dernier siège de La Rochelle*, p. 336.
9 Avenel, vol. 3, p. 120.
10 H. and La F., vol. 3, p. 160.
11 Vaux de Foletier, *op. cit.*, p. 246.
12 Bassompierre, p. 410.
13 ibid., p. 412.
14 *Mercure français*, vol. 14, p. 713.
15 ibid., p. 721. On 12 April 1635 La Porte wrote that Richelieu had long intended gently to replace Protestants by Catholics in the government of La Rochelle, but that this had not been successfully carried out. Mousnier, vol. 1, p. 229.
16 Fontenay-Mareuil, p. 174.

Chapter 11

1 Khevenhüller, *Annales Ferdinandei; oder wahrhafte Beschreibung Kayser's Ferdinandi*, Leipzig, 1721–6, vol. 11, p. 36.
2 Avenel, vol. 2, p. 619.
3 ibid., vol. 3, p. 76.
4 ibid., p. 82.
5 ibid., p. 73.
6 ibid., p. 82.
7 Alvarez, *op cit.*, p. 33.
8 Avenel, vol. 3, p. 150.
9 ibid., p. 181.
10 H. and La F., vol. 3, p. 203.

11 Avenel, vol. 3, p. 73.
12 ibid., p. 223.
13 ibid., p. 237.
14 *Mémoires de Sieur de Pontis*, vol. 1, p. 512.
15 Bassompierre, vol. 4, p. 10.
16 Alvarez, *op. cit.*, p. 56.

Chapter 12

1 *Mémoires du Duc de La Force*, vol. 3, p. 315.
2 *Mémoires de M. de Puységur*, vol. 1, p. 84.
3 *Friedensakten* 9a I, fol. 31.
4 *A.E. corr. pol.*, *Allemagne*, 7, fol. 22.
5 Khevenhüller, *op. cit.*, vol. 11, p. 1233.
6 *Friedensakten* 9a I, fol. 23. Brûlart's instructions, and those of Père Joseph, are published in full in Albrecht I, p. 423, and paraphrased in Fagniez, vol. I, p. 448. The original draft is in *A.E. corr. pol.*, *Allemagne*, 7, fol. 40. How far removed Richelieu was from the tenor of the Regensburg talks is clear from his letter to Père Joseph in Avenel, vol. 3, p. 893, and his despatch to Brûlart of 5 September 1630 in ibid., p. 896.
7 Published in full in Keller, *Die Friedensverhandlung zwischen Frankreich und dem Kaiser auf dem Regensburger Kurfürstentag, 1630*. Bonn, 1902, p. 20, but in French, whereas the copy in the Vienna archives is in Latin!
8 The minutes of the Regensburg negotiations, published in Albrecht I, p. 574, shows that the powers were handed over on 14 September 1630.
9 *Mémoires de M. de Puységur*, vol. 1, p. 93.
10 Avenel, vol. 2, p. 962.
11 ibid., p. 958.
12 *T.P.*, p. 115.
13 ibid., p. 355.
14 Klopp, *Der dreissigjährige Krieg bis zum Tode Gustav Adolfs*. 1932, vol. 3, pt. 2, p. 313.
15 ibid., p. 229.
16 ibid., p. 315. The full text is in *Friedensakten*, 9a I, letter of 24 August 1631 and reply of the Electors of 30 September 1631. Execution of the treaty was a stated object of the draft Habsburg League of 1632, so described in *A.E. corr. pol.*, *Allemagne*, 8, fol.

228. Its validity was asserted in a letter of the Emperor to Louis XIII of 5 February 1632, ibid., fol. 221.

Chapter 13

1 *Mémoires de M. de Chizay*, p. 177. LE VASSOR, vol. 3, p. 381.
2 *Mémoires*, vol. 6, p. 86.
3 Discovered by Hanotaux and published in H. and LA F., vol. 3, p. 294.
4 BASSOMPIERRE, vol. 4, p. 121.
5 Batiffol, *Richelieu et le roy Louis XIII*, p. 306.
6 GRIFFET, vol. 2, p. 84.
7 ibid., p. 114.
8 Richelieu, *Journal*, p. 76.
9 AVENEL, vol. 4, p. 53.
10 ibid., p. 230.
11 *Journal*.
12 *T.P.*, p. 343.
13 Henrard, *Sept ans de l'histoire de Belgique 1631–8. Marie de Médicis dans les Pays-Bas*. Brussels, 1876, p. 70.
14 Vaissière, *L'affaire du maréchal de Marillac*. Paris, 1924, p. 158.
15 ibid., p. 215.
16 AVENEL, vol. 4, p. 269.
17 LONCHAY, nos. 1783, 1804, 1820.
18 GRIFFET, vol. 2, p. 359.

Chapter 14

1 ROBERTS, vol. 2, p. 403.
2 LEMAN, p. 31.
3 For the propositions made at this meeting see AVENEL, vol. 4, p. 239.
4 AVENEL, vol. 4, p. 251.
5 Weibull in *Revue historique*, 1934, p. 227.

Chapter 15

1 ROBERTS, vol. 2, p. 699.
2 LEMAN, *Urbain VIII*, p. 57.
3 ibid., p. 134.
4 AVENEL, vol. 4, p. 283.

5 LEMAN, *Urbain VIII*, bk. II, ch. I.
6 ibid.
7 AVENEL, vol. 4, p. 415.
8 FAGNIEZ, vol. 2, p. 108.
9 *Avertissement a tous les Estats de l'Europe*, pub. in the Appendix to ALBERTINI, p. 1940.
10 LONCHAY, nos. 1693, 1752, 1831.
11 ibid., nos. 2055, 2073.

Chapter 16

1 *Le conseiller d'Estat*, p. 322.
2 *Discours* III, p. 24.
3 C. Hersent, *De la souveraineté du Roy à Metz*, 1632, p. 224.
4 *Mémoires*, vol. 1, p. 24.
5 AVENEL, vol. 3, p. 181.
6 ibid., vol. 4, p. 424.
7 ibid., p. 490.
8 *Mémoires*, vol. 10, p. 159.
9 AVENEL, vol. 6, p. 877.
10 *La recherche des droicts*, p. 9.
11 LEMAN, *Urbain VIII*, p. 283.
12 ibid., p. 287.
13 ibid., p. 328.

Chapter 17

1 FAGNIEZ, vol. 2, p. 193.
2 Grotius, *Epistolae quotquot reperiri potuerunt*. Amsterdam, 1687, p. 135.
3 ibid., p. 139.
4 AVENEL, vol. 4, p. 720.
5 ibid., p. 660.
6 GRIFFET, vol. 2, p. 569.
7 AVENEL, p. 735.
8 ibid., p. 765.
9 ibid., p. 761.
10 LEMAN, *Urbain VIII*, p. 483.
11 ELLIOTT, p. 306.
12 LEMAN, *Urbain VIII*, p. 496.
13 *Mémoires*, vol. 7, p. 53.

14 *T.P.*, p. 144.
15 *Mémoires*, vol. 9, p. 126.
16 *Maximes*, p. 784.
17 ibid., p. 785.
18 *De la souveraineté du roy*, p. 193.
19 H. and LA F., vol. 4, p. 23.

Chapter 18

1 *Memorandum of 1635*, pub. in H. and LA F., vol. 4, p. 410.
2 H. and LA F., vol. 4, p. 157.
3 First pub. in H. and LA F., vol. 4, p. 161.
4 BATIFFOL, *Chevreuse*, p. 131.
5 AUBERY, vol. 3, p. 413.
6 AVENEL, vol. 4, pp. 431–41, 456–9.
7 *Harangue du Cardinal de Richelieu au Parlement en 1634*. Ms. de la Bib. Mazarine, no. 1360.
8 H. and LA F., vol. 4, p. 171.
9 *Mémoires*, vol. 6, p. 321.
10 Ranum, *Richelieu and the Councillors of Louis XIII*. Oxford, 1963, p. 77.
11 AVENEL, vol. 5, p. 763.
12 Ranum, *op. cit.*, appendix B.
13 AVENEL, vol. 5, p. 647.

Chapter 19

1 LEMAN, *Urbain VIII*, p. 262.
2 ibid., p. 471.
3 H. and LA F., vol. 5, p. 56.
4 GRIFFET, vol. 2, p. 654.
5 J. de Silhon, *De la certitude des connoissances humaines* (1661), *Dedication*.
6 FAGNIEZ, vol. 2, p. 14.
7 AVENEL, vol. 2, p. 202.
8 *Maximes*, p. 812. In his *T.P.*, p. 202, he wrote that 'princes are obliged to recognize the authority of the Church and to submit to its holy decrees to render entire obedience thereto in what affects the spiritual power', and that 'it is their duty to preserve the honour of the Popes as successors of St Peter and vicars of Jesus

Christ'. But he added that it was by no means easy to distinguish the political and spiritual spheres.

9 FAGNIEZ, vol. 2, p. 248.
10 ibid., p. 73.

Chapter 20

1 AVENEL, vol. 5, p. 748.
2 ibid., p. 709.
3 ibid., p. 603.
4 LEMAN, *Richelieu et Olivares*, p. 40.
5 ibid., p. 73.

Chapter 21

1 GRIFFET, vol. 3, p. 8.
2 Rochemonteix, *Nicolas Caussin, confesseur de Louis XIII et le cardinal de Richelieu*. Paris, 1911, p. 145.
3 AVENEL, vol. 5, p. 812.
4 GRIFFET, vol. 3, p. 109.
5 Rochemonteix, *op. cit.*, p. 254.
6 ibid., p. 258.
7 p. 38.
8 p. 276.
9 AVENEL, vol. 5, p. 908.
10 LEMAN, *Richelieu et Olivares*, p. 85.
11 AVENEL, vol. 6, p. 608.
12 FAGNIEZ, vol. 2, p. 411.
13 H. and LA F., vol. 5, p. 342.

Chapter 22

1 MARAÑON, p. 85.
2 *A.E. corr. pol., Espagne*, vol. 20, fol. 56.
3 LEMAN, *Richelieu et Olivares*, p. 152.
4 ELLIOTT, p. 326.
5 AVENEL, vol. 6, p. 629.
6 ELLIOTT, p. 369.
7 ibid., p. 403.
8 ibid., p. 433.
9 MARAÑON, p. 87.

10 ELLIOTT, p. 452.
11 ibid., p. 469.
12 ibid., p. 533.
13 ibid., p. 402.

Chapter 23

1 Hauser, *La pensée et l'action économique du cardinal de Richelieu*, Paris, 1944, p. 171.
2 *T.P.*, p. 432.
3 ibid.
4 Caillet, *op. cit.*, p. 420. See the letter to Richelieu from Laon of 4 February 1637 in MOUSNIER, p. 404, and the papers of Séguier in Porchnev, showing the impossibility of raising more money.
5 AVENEL, vol. 6, p. 500.
6 H. and LA F., vol. 6, p. 35.
7 GRIFFET, vol. 3, p. 255.
8 *T.P.*, p. 428.
9 H. and LA F., vol. 4, p. 360.
10 ibid., vol. 6, p. 203.
11 GRIFFET, vol. 3, pp. 241–6.
12 AVENEL, vol. 6, p. 645.
13 ibid., p. 742.

Chapter 24

1 ibid., p. 642.
2 Erlanger, *Cinq Mars. La passion et la fatalité.* Paris, 1964, p. 43.
3 AVENEL, vol. 6, p. 645.
4 ibid., p. 728.
5 BEAUCHAMP, p. 402.
6 GRIFFET, vol. 3, p. 317.
7 Erlanger, *op. cit.*, p. 119.
8 AVENEL, vol. 6, p. 747.
9 GRIFFET, vol. 3, p. 319.

Chapter 25

1 Tallement des Réaux, *Historiettes*, vol. 1, p. 450.
2 *Testament de son Eminence le cardinal Duc du Richelieu du 23 Mai 1642*, DUMONT, vol. 6, p. 248.

3 AVENEL, vol. 6, p. 926.
4 AVENEL, vol. 1, p. 44.
5 ibid., p. 128.
6 ibid., p. 123.
7 ibid., p. 134.
8 GRIFFET, vol. 3, p. 541.
9 AVENEL, vol. 7, p. 163.
10 ibid., p. 177.

Chapter 26

1 GRIFFET, vol. 3, p. 575.
2 Lalanne, 'Un récit inédit de la mort du Cardinal de Richelieu', in
  Revue historique, 1894, p. 305.
3 AUBERY, vol. I, p. 570.
4 Letter first pub. in H. and LA F., vol. 6, p. 431.

Bibliography

Archives, Documents and Principal Works

PARIS: *Archives du Ministère des Affaires Etrangères.* Diplomatic correspondence is collected in bound volumes comprehended in *État numérique des fonds de la correspondance politique de l'origine à 1871.* Covering the Richelieu period are the following: Germany, 6–17, Supp. 1–2; Salm, 54; Bouillon, 15; England, 26–49; Spanish Netherlands, 6–14; Austria, 11–16; Bavaria, 1; Cologne, 1; Spain, 12–21, Supp. 3–4; Grisons, 3–9; Netherlands, 9–23, Supp. 1; Mainz, 1; Milanais, 1–3; Lorraine, 7–33, Supp. 7, 8; Rome, 27–80; Sweden, 1–5, Supp. 1 bis.

 Abbrev.: *A.E. corr. pol.*

 Internal affairs, mostly but not all in Avenel, are in *État numérique des fonds mém. et doc. France.*

 Abbrev.: *A.E. mém. doc.*

VIENNA: *Haus, Hof und Staatsarchiv, Friedensakten (Reichskanzlei).*

 Abbrev.: *Friedensakten.*

ALBRECHT, D. *Die Politik Maximilians I von Bayern und seine Verbündeten, 1618: Briefe und Akten zur Geschichte des 30 jährigen Krieges,* 2nd pt, vol. 5. (1629–30), Vienna-Munich, 1964. Contains numerous documents, including, as well as Bavarian, many French and imperial. Abbrev.: ALBRECHT I.

Die auswärtige Politik Maximilians von Bayern, 1618–1635, 1st pt, Göttingen, 1962.

Abbrev.: ALBRECHT II.

GOETZ, W. *Die Politik Maximilians I von Bayern und seine Verbündeten, 1618–1651: Briefe und Akten zur Geschichte des 30 jährigen Krieges*, Munich, 2nd pt, vol. 3, (1626–7); vol. 4, (1928–9), 1948.

Abbrev.: GOETZ.

LONCHAY, H., CUVELIER, J. and LEFEVRE, J. *Correspondance de la Cour d'Espagne sur les affaires des Pays-Bas au XVIIe siècle. II. Précis de la correspondance de Philippe IV avec l'Infante Isabelle, 1621–33.* Brussels, 1927.

Abbrev.: LONCHAY.

JOURDAN, DECRUSY and ISAMBERT. *Recueil général des anciennes lois françaises depuis l'an 420 jusqu'à la révolution de 1789.* Paris, 1821–33. Vols. 15 and 16 cover 1610–43.

Abbrev.: JOURDAN.

AVENEL, D. L. M. *Lettres, instructions diplomatiques et papiers d'État du cardinal de Richelieu.* Paris, 1853–77. 8 vols. Contains the most important, but by no means all, of Richelieu's correspondence.

Abbrev.: AVENEL.

RICHELIEU, Card. de. *Mémoires.* Extracts were first published in 1650. The complete text was published by M. Petitot in *Collection des mémoires rélatifs à l'histoire de France*, vols. 21–30, Paris, 1823, and covers from 1610 to 1638. The *Société de l'Histoire de France* published the text from original MS. in 10 vols. edited by Baron de Courcel, L. Delavaud and G. Lacour-Gayet etc., Paris, 1908–31. The same period is covered in a 4-vol. folio edition. Paris (Javal), 1961.

The authenticity of the *Mémoires* is controversial, but while it is conceded that Richelieu may have left their preparation in part to secretaries, their principal authorship is now generally conceded. On the question – See *Rapports et notices sur l'édition des Mémoires du cardinal de Richelieu préparée pour la Société de l'Histoire de France.* Paris, 1922.

Abbrev.: *Mémoires.*

Testament Politique d'Armand du Plessis, Cardinal duc de Richelieu. Amsterdam, 1688. The standard edition is the *Édition critique publiée avec une introduction et des notes par Louis André et une préface de Léon Noël.* Paris, 1947.

A. Aubery attacked the authenticity of the *Testament* in his *Histoire du cardinal de Mazarin*, vol. II., in 1688, and Voltaire, of course, had to add his measure of scepticism. He provoked a controversy which has not yet ended, the history of which is detailed by André. Much of the debate centres on points of literary criticism on which it would be presumptuous for an alien to express an opinion. On balance, however, there is enough internal evidence in the substance of the work to lead to conviction as to its authenticity.

Seventeen MS copies exist, differing in detail.

Abbrev.: *T.P.*

Journal de M. le cardinal duc de Richelieu qu'il a faict durant le grand orage de la cour, en l'année 1630 et 1631. 1648. Republished in 1838 in the *Archives curieuses de l'histoire de France*, 2nd series, vol. 5.

Abbrev.: *Journal.*

Lettres du cardinal duc de Richelieu, où l'on voit la fine politique et le secret de ses plus grandes négotiations. Paris, 1695.

Correspondance inédite du duc de Rohan, du cardinal de Richelieu et de Louis de Mont Calm au sujet de la paix d'Alais, 1629. Paris, 1862.

Quelques lettres inédites du cardinal de Richelieu, 1635–1642, par E. Barry. Toulouse, 1847.

Abbrev.: *Lettres.*

Extraits des oeuvres du cardinal de Richelieu, pub. avec une introduction et notes de Roger Gaucheron et une notice de Jacques Bainville. Paris, 1929.

Maximes d'État et fragments politiques, pub. par Georges Hanotaux dans les documents inédits sur l'histoire de France, série 2. Mélanges historiques, vol. 3. Paris, 1880. Edited by J. and R. Wittlmann. Paris, 1944.

Abbrev.: *Maximes.*

Instructions que je me suis données pour me conduire à la cour. Written before 1610. *Pub. par A. Baschet.* Paris, 1880. Probably written by J. B. Matthieu.

Les principaux poincts de la foy de l'Église catholique défendus contre l'escrit adressé au Roy par les quatre ministres de Charenton. 1618. Went through six editions in the seventeenth century, and a folio edition in 1642. Repub. Paris, 1842. Translated into English, 1635.

Instruction du chrestien. Poitiers 1621. Went through twelve editions in the seventeenth century. Translated into Arabic, 1640, and Italian, 1656.

Traitté de la perfection du chrestien. Paris, 1646. Went through nine editions.

Traitté qui contient la méthode la plus facile et la plus asseurée pour convertir ceux qui se sont séparéz de l'Eglise. Paris, 1651. Went through four editions.

FAGNIEZ, G. *Le Père Joseph et Richelieu.* Paris, 1894. 2 vols. A narrative of Père Joseph's diplomatic papers, based on Lepré-Balin's MS in the British Museum and *Supplément* in the Bibliothèque Nationale, the work is of first importance on the diplomatic and ecclesiastical aspects of Richelieu's career up to 1638. Aldous Huxley in his *Grey Eminence,* London 1942, discredits Fagniez in a fictional bibliographical note. Fagniez gives full citations to Lepré-Balin's MS.

 Abbrev.: FAGNIEZ.

LEMAN, A. *Urbain VIII et la rivalité de la France et de la maison d' Autriche de 1631 à 1635.* Lille, Paris, 1920. Based on diplomatic documents in the archives in Paris, Rome, Simancas and Vienna, this work is fundamental.

 Abbrev.: LEMAN, *Urbain VIII.*

 Richelieu et Olivares. Leur négotiations secrètes de 1636 à 1642 pour le rétablissement de la paix. Lille, 1938. Continues the previous volume.

 Abbrev.: LEMAN, *Richelieu et Olivares.*

 Recueil des instructions générales aux nonces ordinaires de France, de 1624 à 1634. Paris, 1620.

 Abbrev.: LEMAN, *Instructions.*

LONCHAY, H. *La rivalité de la France et de l'Espagne aux Pays-Bas 1635– 1700. Étude d'histoire diplomatique et militaire.* Brussels, 1896.

PASTOR, L. Freiherr, von. *The History of the Popes from the Close of the Middle Ages.* Vol. 28. Translated by Dom Ernest Graf, O.S.B. London, 1938. Too critical of Richelieu; accepts the interpretation of events by papal agents, and while detailing the hostility of Spain and Austria to Urban VIII does less than justice to the French position. Exaggerates Richelieu's gallicanism.

 Abbrev.: PASTOR.

DUMONT, J., Baron de CAKELS-CROON. *Corps Universel Diplomatique du droit des gens contenant un Recueil des Traitez d'Alliance, de Paix, de Trève etc.* Amsterdam, 1726–31.

 Abbrev.: DUMONT.

MOUSNIER, R. *Lettres et mémoires adressés au chancellier Séguier (1633– 1649).* Paris, 1964.

 Abbrev. MOUSNIER.

Biographies of Richelieu

(a) *Principal biographies and studies (chronological order)*

VIALART, C., Bishop of Avranches. *Histoire du ministère d'Armand-Jean du Plessis, cardinal duc de Richelieu, sous le règne de Louis le Juste, XIIIe de nom.* Paris, 1649.

AUBERY, A. *Histoire du cardinal duc de Richelieu.* Paris, 1660. Uncritical of Richelieu; based on materials provided by the Duchesse d'Aiguillon.

    Abbrev.: AUBERY.

    Mémoires pour l'histoire du cardinal duc de Richelieu. Paris, 1660. 2 vols. Collection of 500 letters.

AVENEL, G. Vicomte d'. *Richelieu et la monarchie absolue.* Paris, 1884–90. 4 vols.

HANOTAUX, G. and LA FORCE, Duc de. *Histoire du cardinal de Richelieu.* Paris, 1893–1947. 6 vols. The leading work on Richelieu. The volumes by Hanotaux are superior to those by La Force in style, subject-matter and reliability. The work is unbalanced, diplomatic affairs receiving inadequate treatment.

    Abbrev.: H. and LA F.

BURCKHARDT, C. J. *Richelieu.* Vol. 1, *Der Aufstieg der Macht.* Munich. English and US abridged edition, *Richelieu, His Rise to Power.* Oxford, New York, 1940. Vols. 2 and 3 were published after completion of this manuscript. 1965–66.

(b) *Secondary biographies (alphabetical order)*

ANDREAS, W. *Richelieu.* Göttingen, 1958; Stuttgart-Berlin, 1922.

BAILLY, A. *Richelieu.* Paris, 1934. (*The Cardinal Dictator*, 1936; *Der Kardinal als Diktator*, 1937).

BAINVILLE, J. *Richelieu, 1585–1642.* Paris, 1935.

BARTZ, K. *Der grosse Kardinal, Herzog Armand von Richelieu, Principal Minister von Frankreich.* Berlin, 1935.

BATIFFOL, L. *Richelieu et le roi Louis XIII. Les véritables rapports du souverain et de son ministre.* Paris, 1934.

    Autour de Richelieu. Paris, 1938.

BELLOC, H. *Richelieu 1585–1642.* London and Philadelphia, 1930. Trans. by Théo Varlet, Paris, 1933.

BURNAND, R. *Richelieu.* Paris, 1937.

CAPEFIGUE, J.-B. H. R. *Le cardinal de Richelieu.* Paris, 1865.

CARRÉ, H. *La jeunesse et la marche au pouvoir de Richelieu.* Paris, 1944.

CHASSÉ, C. *Résumé de la conférence faite par M. Ch. Chassé le 16 février 1963. A la poursuite de la tête et du petit doigt du cardinal.* Paris, 1963.

CORNE, H. *Le cardinal de Richelieu.* Paris, 1855.

CRAPELET, C. *Le cardinal de Richelieu.* Paris, 1839.

DESPREZ, A. *Richelieu et Mazarin. Leurs deux politiques.* Paris, 1883. *Richelieu et son oeuvre.* Paris, 1883.

DUSSIEUX, L. *Le cardinal de Richelieu. Étude biographique.* Paris, 1886.

FEDERN, K. *Richelieu.* Vienna, Leipzig, 1926. English translation, 1928.

FIDAO-JUSTINIANI, J. E. *Richelieu, Précepteur de la nation française.* Paris, 1936.

FONT-RÉAULX, H. de. *Le cardinal de Richelieu et Louis XIII.* Paris, 1887.

FUNCK-BRENTANO, F. *Richelieu.* Paris, 1938.

GRISELLE, E. *Louis XIII et Richelieu. Lettres et pièces diplomatiques.* Paris, 1911.

HANOTAUX, G. and LA FORCE, Duc de. *Richelieu.* Paris, 1943.

HARTMANN, R. *Richelieu, Eine psychologische Studie.* Berlin, 1940.

LE CLERC, J. *La vie du cardinal, duc de Richelieu.* Cologne, 1695, Amsterdam, 1753.

LODGE, R. *Richelieu.* London, 1896.

MARTIN, B. L. H. *Trois grands ministres. Sully, Richelieu, Colbert.* Paris, 1898.

MARTINEAU, A. *Richelieu.* Poitiers, Paris, 1866.

MOMMSEN,W. 'Richelieu als Staatsmann', in *Historische Zeitschrift,* 1923.

PERKINS, J. B. *Richelieu and the Growth of French Power.* New York, 1900.

RAUMER, K. von. 'Richelieu', in *Historische Zeitschrift,* 1937.

RICCIARDI, Marchese P. *Vita di Armando, cardinale, duca di Richelieu.* Vienna, 1699.

SAINT-AULAIRE, A. F. L. Comte de. *Richelieu.* Paris, 1932.

TOPIN, M. *Louis XIII et Richelieu.* Paris, 1876.

VALLEREY, G. *Richelieu.* Paris, 1933.

WEDGWOOD, C. V. *Richelieu and the French Monarchy.* London, 1954.

General Works on the Period

AYMÈS, N. *Trente années du grand siècle. La France de Louis XIII.* Paris, 1909.

BALAS, L. *Scènes et tableaux du règne de Louis XIII.* Corbeil, 1935.

BAZIN, A. *Histoire de France sous Louis XIII.* Paris, 1838. 4 vols.

BATIFFOL, L. *Au temps de Louis XIII.* Paris, 1904.

BEAUCHAMP, F. S. J. R., Comte de. *Louis XIII d'après sa correspondance avec le cardinal de Richelieu.* Paris, 1902.

Abbrev.: BEAUCHAMP.

BERNARD, C. *Histoire de roy Louis XIII.*

Abbrev.: BERNARD.

BOURGEOIS, E. and ANDRÉ, L. *Les sources de l'histoire de France. XVIIe siècle (1610–1715).* Paris, 1901–35. 8 vols. A full bibliography.

BRANDI, K. *Deutsche Reformation und Gegenreformation.* Leipzig, 1927–30.

CAPEFIGUE, J. B. *Richelieu, Mazarin, la Fronde et le règne de Louis XIV.* Paris, 1835–6. 8 vols.

CHUDOBA, B. *Spain and the Empire 1519–1643.* Chicago, 1952.

DUPLEIX, S. *Histoire de Louis le Juste, treizième de nom, Roy de France et de Navarre.* Paris, 1635. Important because the text is alleged to have been approved by Richelieu before publication. But adds little to other accounts. Went through several editions.

ELLIOTT, J. H. *The Revolt of the Catalans. A Study in the Decline of Spain (1598–1640).* Cambridge, 1963.

Abbrev.: ELLIOTT.

ERLANGER, P. *Louis XIII.* 10th ed. Paris, 1946.

FRIEDRICH, K. *The Age of the Baroque, 1610–1660.* New York, 1952.

GRAMOND, G. B. de. *Historiarum Galliae ab excessu Henrici IV libri XVIII.* Toulouse, 1643.

GRIFFET, Père., S. J. *Histoire du règne de Louis XIII.* Paris, 1758, 3 vols. A work of importance as the author had access to material which has disappeared. But constructed on the 'filing card' system, and the *oratio directa* used by it is not in character.

Abbrev.: GRIFFET.

GRISELLE, E., Chanoine. *Louis XIII et Richelieu. Lettres et pièces diplomatiques.* Paris, 1911.

HONELL, J. *Lystra Ludovici, or the Life of the late victorious King of France, Lewis the XIII and of his Cardinal de Richelieu.* London, 1646.

JESSEN, H. *Der dreissigjährige Krieg in Augenzeugenberichten.* Düsseldorf, 1963.

LA GAILLE, G. *Lettres inédites de Louis XIII à Richelieu.* Paris, 1901.

LE COINTE, J. *Histoire du règne de Louis XIII.* Paris, 1716–7. 5 vols.

LE VASSOR, M. *Histoire du règne de Louis XIII roy de France et de Navarre.* Amsterdam, 1700–11. 10 vols.

Abbrev.: LE VASSOR.

LEATHES, S. In the *Cambridge Modern History*, vol. 4. Cambridge, 1906.

LOUGH, J. *An Introduction to Seventeenth Century France.* London, 1954.

PAGÈS, G. *La Guerre de trente ans, 1618–1648.* Paris, 1939.

PRÉCLIN, E. and TAPIÉ, V. L. *Le XVIIe siècle. Monarchies centralisées, 1610–1715.* Paris, 1949. (Clio, vol. 7, pt. 1.)

RANKE, L. von. *Französische Geschichte vornehmlich im sechszehnten und siebzehnten Jahrhundert.* Stuttgart-Tübingen, 1852, 4 vols. *Histoire de France, principalement pendant les XVIe et XVIIe siècles. Traduction de J.-J. Porchar.* Paris, 1854–89. 6 vols. *Civil Wars and Monarchy in France in the Sixteenth and Seventeenth Centuries: a History of France principally during that period.* Translated by M. A. Garvey. London, 1852. 2 vols. Of capital importance in the nineteenth century, but now dated. Drew extensively on Venetian documents.

RENAUDIN, P. *Résurrection de la France, 1589–1640.* Paris, 1941.

ROCA, E. *Le grand siècle intime. Le règne de Richelieu (1617–1642) d'après des documents originaux.* Paris, 1906.

ROMAIN, C. *Louis XIII, un grand roi méconnu, 1601–1643.* Paris, 1934.

SIRI, V. *Mémoires secrets tirés des archives des souverains de l'Europe depuis le règne de Henri IV. Ouvrage traduit de l'italien par J. B. Requier.* Amsterdam, 1665–1674.

    Memorie recondite dal'anno 1601 sino 1640. Ronco, 1776.

    Abbrev.: SIRI.

    Anecdotes du ministère du cardinal de Richelieu et du règne de Louis XIII. Amsterdam, 1717.

    Anecdotes du Ministère du comte-duc d'Olivarès. Paris, 1722.

TAPIE, V. L. *La France de Louis XIII et de Richelieu.* Paris, 1952.

    Abbrev.: TAPIÉ.

TODIÈRE, L. *Louis XIII et Richelieu.* Paris, 1864.

TOPIN, M. *Louis XIII et Richelieu.* Paris, 1870.

VAUCHER, P. *Étude sur la France de Henri IV et Louis XIII.* Paris, 1961.

VAUNOIS, L. *Vie de Louis XIII.* Paris, 1936.

WEDGEWOOD, C. V. *The Thirty Years War.* London, 1938.

Memoirs

BASSOMPIERRE, F. de, Marquis d'Harouel. *Mémoires du maréchal de Bassompierre, contenant l'histoire de sa vie et de ce qui est fait de plus remarquable à la Cour de France.* Cologne, 1665. Edited for the Société de l'Histoire de France by the Marquis de Chantérac. Paris, 1870–7. 4 vols.

    Abbrev.: BASSOMPIERRE.

FONTENAY-MAREUIL, F. du VAL, Marquis de. *Mémoires*. Pub. by Michaud and Poujoulat, 2nd series, vol 5. Paris, 1837.
    Abbrev.: FONTENAY-MAREUIL.

GASTON, DUC d'ORLÉANS. *Mémoires de ce qui s'est passé de plus considérable en France depuis l'an 1608 jusqu'en 1636*. Pub. by Michaud and Poujoulat, 2nd series, vol 9. Paris, 1838.
    Abbrev.: GASTON.

GOULAS, N. *Mémoires*. Pub. by C. Constant. vol. 1, 1627–1643. Paris, 1879–82.
    Abbrev.: GOULAS.

LA FORCE, J. NOMPAR de CAUMONT, Duc de. *Mémoires authentiques de Jacques Nompar de Caumont, Duc de la Force, Maréchal de France, et de ses deux fils, les Marquis de Montpouillan et de Castelnau, depuis la Saint-Barthélemy jusqu'à la Fronde, pour faire suite à toutes les collections de Mémoires sur l'histoire de France*. Pub. by the Marquis de la Grange. 1843.
    Abbrev.: LA FORCE.

LA PORTE, P. de. *Mémoires contenant plusieurs particularités des règnes de Louis XIII et de Louis XIV*. Pub. by Michaud and Poujoulat, 3rd series, vol. 8. Paris, 1839.
    Abbrev.: LA PORTE.

MONTGLAS, P. de CLERMONT, Marquis de. *Mémoires contenant l'histoire de la guerre entre la France et la Maison d'Autriche durant l'administration du cardinal de Richelieu et du cardinal Mazarin depuis la déclaration de la guerre en 1635*. Pub. by Michaud and Poujoulat, 3rd series, vol. 5. Paris, 1838.
    Abbrev.: MONTGLAS.

MOTTEVILLE, F. BERTAUT, Dame LANGLOIS de. *Mémoires pour servir à l'histoire d'Anne d'Autriche depuis 1613 jusqu'en 1666*. Amsterdam, 1723. Pub. by Michaud and Poujoulat, 2nd series, vol. 10. Paris, 1838. Repub. Paris, 1925.
    Abbrev.: MOTTEVILLE.

LA VALETTE, L. de NOGARET, Cardinal de. *Mémoires*. Paris, 1771.
    Abbrev.: LA VALETTE.

ROHAN, H. Duc de. *Mémoires du duc de Rohan sur les choses qui se sont passés en France depuis la mort de Henri le Grand jusqu'à la paix faite avec les réformés au mois de juin 1629*. Amsterdam, 1656.
    Abbrev.: ROHAN.

Other Biographies

BATIFFOL, L. *Marie de Médicis*. Paris, 1905. *La Duchesse de Chevreuse. Une vie d'aventures et d'intrigues sous Louis XIII*. Paris, London, 1913.
 Abbrev.: BATIFFOL, Chevreuse.

BAUDON, E. *Charles de Gonzague*. Paris, 1947.
 Abbrev.: BAUDON.

BONNEAU-AVENANT, A. *La duchesse d'Aiguillon, nièce du cardinal de Richelieu. Sa vie et ses oeuvres charitables*, Paris, 1879.

BOUDON, P. M. *Le maréchal de Bassompierre, 1579–1646*. Paris, 1925.

BUCHANAN, M. *Anne of Austria, the Infanta Queen*. London, 1937.

CAPEFIGUE, J. B. *Marie de Médicis*. Paris, 1861.

COCHOIS, P. *Bérulle et l'école française*. Paris, undated.

DEDOUVRES, L., Chanoine. *Politique et apôtre. Le Père Joseph de Paris. Capucin. L'Eminence Grise*. Paris, 1932.

DELOCHE, M. *Un frère de Richelieu inconnu, chartreux, primat des Gaules, cardinal, ambassadeur. Documents inédits*. Paris, 1935.
 Abbrev.: DELOCHE.

DETHAN, G. *Gaston d'Orléans, conspirateur et prince charmant*. Paris, 1959.
 Abbrev.: DETHAN.

HERBILLON, C. *Anne d'Autriche, reine, mère, régente*. Paris, 1939.

HOUSSAYE, M. *Le Cardinal de Bérulle et le Cardinal de Richelieu, 1625–29*. Paris, 1875.

KERVILER, R. *Le Chancellier Pierre Séguier*. Paris, 1874.

LA VARENDE, J. de. *Anne d'Autriche, femme de Louis XIII, 1601–1666*. Paris, 1938.

MARAÑON, G. *El Conde-Duque de Olivares. La pasión de mandar*. Madrid, 1936.
 Abbrev.: MARAÑON.

PARDOE, J. *Life of Marie de Médicis, Queen of France*. London, 1852.

PFISTER, K. *Kurfürst Maximilian I von Bayern und seine Jahrhunderte*. Munich, 1949.

ROBERTS, M. *Gustavus Adolphus: A History of Sweden, 1611–1632*. London 1953–8. 2 vols.
 Abbrev.: ROBERTS.

STURMBERGER, H. *Kaiser Ferdinand II und das Problem des Absolutismus*. Munich, 1957.

THIROUX d'ARCONVILLE, M. G. C. *Vie de Marie de Médicis, princesse de Toscane, reine de France et de Navarre.* Paris, 1774.

Special Studies and Sources

CHAPTER 1

H. and LA F., vol. 1, book 3, chaps. 1–3; DELOCHE, chap. 1.

CERF, L. 'La maison natale de Richelieu', in *Revue politique et littéraire,* 1934.

DELOCHE, M. *Les Richelieu. Le père du cardinal, François du Plessis de Richelieu, grand prévôt de France. Documents inédits.* Paris, 1923.

'La maison natale du cardinal de Richelieu', in *Bulletin de la Société des Antiquaires de l'Ouest,* 1931.

DUCHESNE, A. *Histoire généalogique de la maison du Plessis de Richelieu, justifiée par titres, histoires et autres bonnes preuves.* 1631.

CHAPTER 2

T. P., chap. 2; *Mémoires,* books 1–4; AVENEL, vol. 1, pp. 11–64 esp. docs. nos. 9–12, 18, 50, 53, 54. H. and LA F., vol. 1, book 1, chaps., 4–5; book 2, chap. 4; vol. 4, book 1, chap. 1; FAGNIEZ, vol. 1, chap. 1. The sermons are in the Bib. Nat., *cabinet des manuscrits, fonds français,* nos. 22661 and 25666. Other works, see Richelieu above.

LACROIX, L. *Richelieu à Luçon, sa jeunesse, son épiscopat. Nouv. éd.* Paris, 1958.

LATREILLE, A., DELARUELLE, E., and PALANQUE, J. R. *Histoire du catholicisme en France.* Vol. 2: *sous les rois très chrétiens.* Paris, 1960, chap. 2.

CHAPTER 3

Mémoires, books 5–8; *T.P.* chap. 5; AVENEL, vol. 1, pp. 121–485, esp. docs. nos. 105, 123, 143, 156, 160, 214, 224, 256, 264, 389. H. and LA F., vol. 3, book 1; LE VASSOR, vol. 1; GRIFFET, vol. 1; FONTENAY-MAREUIL; FAGNIEZ, vol. 1; LACROIX (cited in references to chap. 2). DUMONT, vol. 5, p. 789.

BATIFFOL, L. 'Le coup d'Etat du 24 avril 1617', in *Revue historique,* 1907–8.

DELAMARE, *Le Maréchal d'Ancre.* Paris, 1961.

FRANKLIN, A. *La Cour de France et l'assassinat du maréchal d'Ancre.* Paris, 1913.

CHAPTER 4

Mémoires, books 9–12; AVENEL, vol. I, pp. 485–690, esp. docs. nos. 473, 474, 560; H. and LA F., vol. 2, book 2; PASTOR, chap. 2; FAGNIEZ, vol. I.

PAVIÉ, E. 'La guerre entre Louis XIII et Marie de Médicis, 1619–1620,' in *Révue Anjou*, 1888.

POEYDAVANT, *Histoire des troubles survenus en Béarn dans le XVIe siècle et la moitié du XVIIe siècle*. Paris, 1819–21. 3 vols.

ZELLER, B., *Le Connétable de Luynes. Montauban et la Valtelline d'après les archives d'Italie*. Paris 1879. (Chap. VII. Treaty of Madrid.)
 Louis XIII, Marie de Médicis, Richelieu Ministre. Étude nouvelle d'après les documents florentins et vénitiens. Paris, 1899. (Chap. VII, IX, Italy 1616.)

Déclaration des églises réformées de France et souveraineté de Béarn de l'injuste persecution qui leur est faite par les ennemis de l'Estat et de leur religion. La Rochelle, 1621.

Histoire véritable du siège de Montauban, commencé à la fin du mois d'octobre en la mesme année. Paris, 1622.

Lettre de M. le Duc de Bouillon, maréchal de France, envoyée à sa Majesté le vingt-deuxième de juin, 1621.

Articles de reconciliation entre Louis XIII Roi de France et Marie de Médicis sa mère conclus à Angoulême le 30 avril 1619. DUMONT, vol. 5, p. 332.

Articles accordez par Louis XIII Roi de France à Marie de Médicis sa mère faits au Ponts de Sé, 10 août 1620. DUMONT, vol. 5, p. 370.

CHAPTER 5

Mémoires, books 12–15; AVENEL, vol. I, pp. 703–786; H. and LA F., vol. 2, book 3; FAGNIEZ, vol. I; LA FORCE.

LA FORCE, Duc de. *Le Maréchal de la Force 1558–1652*. Paris, 1950–2. 2 vols. (up to 1621 only).

LEONARD, E. G. *Le protestant français*. Paris, 1953.

PONTCHARTRAIN, P. Phélypeaux, Seigneur de. *Mémoires concernant les affaires de France sous la régence de Marie de Médicis, contenant un détail exact des intrigues de la cour, des désordres et guerres dans la Royaume et de tout ce qui s'y est passé de plus remarquable depuis 1610 jusqu'en 1620*. Pub. by Pétitot, Michaud et Poujoulat.

ZELLER, B., *Études critiques sur le règne de Louis XIII. Richelieu et les ministres de Louis XIII de 1621 à 1624, la cour, le gouvernement, la diplomatie*. Paris, 1880.

Articles accordez par le roy aux subdéléguez de la religion prétendue réformée, le tout en faveur du sieur de la Force, ses enfans, autres seigneurs et gens de guerre qui le l'ont assisté. Paris, 1622.

Articles de la paix générale accordée par le roy à ses subjects de la religion prétendue réformée. Paris, 1622.

Déclaration du roy sur la paix qu'il a donnée à ses subjects de la religion prétendue réformée, confirmant les précédents edicts de pacification. Paris, 1622.

Ordonnance du roy pour la paix. Paris, 1622.

Réduction de la ville de Montpellier à obeyssance du roy. Paris, 1633.

Mémoire touchant la composition des finances, A. E. mém. doc. 779, fol. 96; *Projet pour l'establissement du conseil,* ibid., 780, fol. 112; *Revue historique,* vol. 107, pp. 311 et seq.

CHAPTER 6

Mémoires, books 15, 16, 17; AVENEL, vol. 2, pp. 51–151, esp. docs. 21, 22, 28, 29, 31, 58, 62; vol. 3, p. 208; *A.E. corr. pol.,* Grisons 3–5; Rome 30–39; FAGNIEZ, vol. 1; SIRI, vol. 5; PASTOR, chap. 2; RANKE, *Französische Geschichte,* vol. 2; DETHAN, chap. 4; ELLIOTT, pp. 204–62.

Anonymous. *Catholique d'Estat.* Paris, 1625.

BAZZONI, A. 'Il cardinale F. Barberini, legato in Francia ed in Ispagna 1625–26', in *Archivio di storico italiano,* 1893.

GIRARD, A. 'La saisie des biens des français en Espagne en 1625', in *Revue d'histoire économique et sociale,* vol. 19 (1931), p. 297.

GÜNTHER, H. *Die Habsburg Liga, 1625–1635. Briefe und Akten aus dem General-Archiv zu Simancas.* Chap. 1.

MORTINELLI, U. *La guerra per la Valtellina nel secolo XVII.* Varese, 1935.

NABHOLZ, H. 'Die öffentliche Meinung in Frankreich und die Veltlinerfrage zur Zeit Richelieus', in *Jahrbuch für schweizerische Geschichte,* 1901.

TAPIÉ, V. L. *La politique étrangère de la France et le début de la guerre de trente ans, 1616–21.* Paris, 1934.

Traité entre Louis XIII Roi de France et Philip IV Roi d'Espagne au sujet de la Valteline, avec la déclaration dudit Roi d'Espagne faite à Monsieur de Bassompierre, Ambassadeur de France, pour la restitution de la Valteline. Madrid, 25 avril 1621. DUMONT, vol. 5, p. 395.

Trois traitez ou accords passez à Milan le 22 janvier 1622 entre les Députez du Roi d'Espagne et de la Maison d'Autriche et les Députez des deux Ligues Grises. DUMONT, vol. 5, p. 406.

Lettre des Grisons aux ambassadeurs de France résidans en Suisse sur le sujet du traité fait par lesdits Grisons à Milan au mois de janvier l'an 1622, ladite lettre datée du 3 mars de la même année 1622. DUMONT, vol. 5, p. 408.

Traité entre Louis XIII Roi de France, la République de Venise et le Duc de Savoye pour la restitution de la Valteline. Fait à Paris le 7 février 1623. DUMONT, vol. 5, p. 417.

Scrittura overo convenzione per la quale il Re Cattolico si contenta por dar sodisfattione à tutto il mondo, a particolarmente à tutta l'Italia, giudicando haver sodisfatto al suo zelo della causa Cattolica di consequare à Sua Santità e alla Sede Apostolica i Forti della Valtellina in desposito, sino alla conclusione finale del negotio principale con la corona di Francia. Fatto à li 14 febraio 1623. DUMONT, vol. 5, p. 417.

Traité entre la France et l'Espagne pour l'accomodement des affaires des Grisons et Valteline. Fait à Monçon le 5 mars 1626.

Discours sur le sujet de la paix, A.E. mém. doc. 252, fol. 127; *Revue historique,* vol. 107, pp. 314 *et seq.*

CHAPTER 7

Mémoires, books 25–27; H. and LA F., vol. 3, book 1; *A.E. mém. doc.* 246; *A.E. corr. pol., Angleterre,* 27–42; *Hollande,* 10, 11; AVENEL, vol. 2, pp. 3–315, esp. docs. nos. 15, 19–22, 28–31, 36, 38, 42, 51–56, 59, 98, 118; vol. 7, pp. 534–556, esp. docs. nos. 104, 114; FONTENAY-MAREUIL; LA PORTE; MOTTEVILLE; *Mercure françois,* 1625; BATIFFOL, Chevreuse, chap. 3; BAUDON, chap. 14; BASSOMPIERRE.

CAMMELL, C. R. *The Great Duke of Buckingham.* London, 1939.

ERLANGER, P. *George Villiers, Duke of Buckingham.* Translated by Lionel Smith-Gordon. London, 1953.

GIBB, M. A. *Buckingham (1592–1628).* London, 1935.

GRISELLE, E. 'Le prince de Galles et l'alliance anglaise au temps de Henri IV et de Louis XIII', in *Revue de l'histoire diplomatique,* 1914.

Estat des villes de Montpellier, Nismes, Uzais, Orange et Privas au mois d'aoust. Paris, 1662.

Confirmation par le Roi Louis XIII Roi de France du Traité de Commerce entre la France et l'Angleterre fait à Paris le 24 février 1600. A Fontainebleau le 14 avril 1923. DUMONT, vol. 5, p. 430.

Diverses pièces concernant le Mariage de Charles Prince de Galles, Fils de Jacques I Roi d'Angleterre avec Marie Infante d'Espagne Fille de Philippe III negocié au mois d'avril et suivans l'année 1623. DUMONT, vol. 5, p. 431.

Déclaration des Ambassadeurs de Jacques I d'Angleterre sur la signature des Articles du Mariage de Charles Prince de Galles avec Madame Henriette Marie, Soeur de Louis XIII Roi de France. A Paris le 20 novembre 1624. DUMONT, vol. 5, p. 468.

Traité entre Louis XIII Roi de France et les Provinces-Unies des Pays-Bas, pour envoyer vingt Vaisseaux de Guerre contre Gênes. A le Haye le 24 décembre 1624 et ratifié par ledit Roi le 25 février 1625. DUMONT, vol. 5, p. 469. *Traité supplémentaire au sujet des vingt Vaisseaux que lesdites Provinces se sont obligées de mettre en Mer par le Traité précédent. Fait à la Haye le 12 avril 1625.* P. 47.

Contrat de Mariage entre Charles I Roi d'Angleterre et Madame Henriette-Marie, Soeur de Louis XIII Roi de France. Fait à Paris le 8 mai 1625. DUMONT, vol. 5, p. 476.

Déclaration du Roi de France Louis XIII portant interdiction du Commerce avec l'Angleterre, donnée à Paris le 8 mai 1627. DUMONT, vol. 5, p. 506.

CHAPTER 8

Mémoires, book 27; T.P. pt. 1, chaps. 5, 6, 8, pt. 2, chaps. 1–8; *Maximes;* H. and LA F., vol. 3, book 1, chap. 2; *A.E. mém. doc.* Vendôme process 781–4, 793, 795; Chalais trial 781–7; AVENEL, vol. 2, esp. docs. nos. 68–71, 77, 82, 86, 91, 92, 106; MOTTEVILLE; FONTENAY-MAREUIL; GASTON; LA PORTE; BASSOMPIERRE; *Pièces du procès de Henri de Tallerand, comte de Chalais, décapité en 1626.* London, 1781, in LABORDE, *Recueil de pièces intéressantes pour servir à l'histoire des règnes de Louis XIII et de Louis XIV;* BATIFFOL, Chevreuse, chap. 4; DETHAN, chap. 5; JOURDAN, vol. 16, p. 529.

ALBERTINI, R. von. 'Die französische Monarchie des Ancien Régime im Urteil der venezianischen Relationen', in *Archiv Kulturgeschichte*, 1951.

   Das politische Denken in Frankreich zur Zeit Richelieus. Marburg, 1951.

   Abbrev.: ALBERTINI.

AVENEL, G. Vicomte d'. *Étude d'histoire sociale. La noblesse française sous Richelieu.* Paris, 1901.

Bañares y Magàn, J. *Cisneros y Richelieu. Ensayo de un paralelo entre ambos cardenales y su tiempo.* Pontevedra. 1911.

Bignon, J. *De l'excellence des roys et du royaume de France.* Paris, 1610.

Cardin le Bret, Sieur de Vély. *De la souveraineté du roy.* Paris, 1632.

Colomby, F. de. *De l'autorité des roys.* Paris, 1631.

Cousin, V. *Madame de Chevreuse.*

Kerviler, R. de. *La presse politique sous Richelieu et l'académicien Jean de Sirmond, 1589–1641.* Paris, 1876.

La Roche-Flavin, B. de. *Treze livres des parlemens de France.* Bordeaux, 1617.

Loyseau, C. *Traité des seigneuries,* 1608. Pub. in *Oeuvres,* 1666.

Mousnier, R. 'Recherches sur la création des intendants des provinces, 1634–1648', in *Forschungen zu Staat und Verfassung. Festgabe für Hartung.* Berlin, 1958.

Stankiewicz, W. J. *Politics and Religion in Seventeenth Century France.* Berkeley and Los Angeles, 1960. chap. 3.

Copie d'une requeste envoyée à Messieurs du Parlement, par Gaston Duc d'Orléans. 1631 (Brit. Mus. 8050 bbb. 19).

Sur les affaires présentes, A.E. mém. doc., 252, fol. 127; *Mémoire ancient et très considérable sur les necessités urgentes des affaires du Roy.* ibid., 783, fol. 6–8.

Avis, ibid., 787, fol. 23; *Revue historique,* vol. 107, pp. 316 *et seq.*; vol. 108, 77 *et seq.*

CHAPTER 9

T.P., Pt. 1, chap. 1; pt. 2, chap. 9; Avenel, vol. 2, pp. 159–315, esp. docs. nos. 68–71, 77, 82, 86, 91, 126, 135; vol. 3, pp. 3–178, esp. docs. nos. 98, 103, 104; vol. 4, doc. no. 93; Fagniez, vol. 2, chap. 10; H. and La F., vol. 4, book 1, chap. 1; Albertini and Cardin le Bret; for both see references to chap. 8; Pastor, chap. 4; Deloche, chaps. 2, 4. The Code Michaud is in Jourdan, vol. 15, pp. 223–344; its title is *Ordonnance du Roi sur les plaintes et doléances faites par les députés des Etats de son Royaume, convoqués et assemblés à la ville de Paris l'an 1614 et 1615 et sur les avis donnés à S.M. par les Assemblées de Paris l'an 1614 et 1615 et sur les avis donnés à sa Majesté par les Assemblées des Notables tenues à Rouen en l'an 1617 et à Paris l'an 1626.* The Assembly of Notables docs. are in *A.E. mém. doc.* 779–81, 783–7; Avenel, vol. 2, pp. 207–21, 297–304; vol. 3, pp. 499, 500.

BATIFFOL. L. 'La fortune du cardinal de Richelieu', in *Revue des deux mondes*, June 1935.

BOITEUX, L. A. *Richelieu, grand maître de la navigation et du commerce de France*. Paris, 1955.

BONAFFÉ, E. *Recherches sur les collections des Richelieu*. Paris, 1883.

CAILLET, J. *De l'administration en France sous le ministère du cardinal de Richelieu*. Paris, 1857.

DELOCHE, M. *La maison du cardinal de Richelieu. Document inédit*. Paris, 1912.

   Le cardinal de Richelieu et les femmes. Paris, 1931.

DENIS, Dom P., O.S.B. *Le cardinal de Richelieu et la réforme des monastères benedictins*. Paris, 1913. Though uncritical of Richelieu this work deserves more attention than it has received, since it is based on Benedictine documents.

DOLLOT, R. *Richelieu, grand maître de la navigation et du commerce de France*. Paris, 1956.

DOUBLET, E. *Le cardinal de Richelieu et les colonies*. Bordeaux, 1926.

ESMONIN, E. *Études sur la France des XVIIᵉ et XVIIIᵉ siècles*. Paris, 1964.

FAGNIEZ, G. 'L'opinion et la presse sous Louis XIII', in *Revue des questions historiques*, 1890.

   'Fancan et Richelieu', in *Revue historique*, 1911.

GELEY, L. *Fancan et la politique de Richelieu de 1617 à 1627*. Paris, 1884.

HAUSER, H. *Recherches et documents sur l'histoire des prix en France de 1500 à 1800*. Paris, 1936.

   La pensée et l'action économique du cardinal de Richelieu. Paris, 1944.

HOUSSAYE, M. *Le cardinal de Bérulle et le cardinal de Richelieu, 1625–29*. Paris, 1875.

LA BRUYÈRE, R. *La marine de Richelieu*. Paris, 1958.

LACOURT-GAYET, G. *La marine militaire de la France sous les règnes de Louis XIII et Louis XIV*. Vol. 1, 1624–1661. Paris, 1911.

LA ROCHE-FLAVIN, B. *Treze livres des Parlemens de France*. Bordeaux, 1617.

LATREILLE, A., DELARUELLE, E. and PALANQUE, J. R. *Histoire du catholicisme en France*. Vol. 2: *sous les rois très chrétiens*. Paris, 1960. chap. 2.

LE NOBLE, P. *Les amours d'Anne d'Autriche, épouse de Louis XIII avec M. le cardinal de Richelieu, le véritable père de Louis XIV, roi de France*. London, 1738.

LOISEL, A. *Institutes coustumières ou manuel de plusieurs et diverses règles, sentences et proverbes tant anciens que modernes du droict coustumier et plus ordinaire de la France.* Paris, 1607.

LOYSEAU, C. *Traité des seigneuries.* Paris, 1608. Pub. in *Oeuvres,* 1666.

MASSON, P. *Histoire du commerce dans le Levant au XVIIe siècle.* Paris, 1896.

MECKLENBURG, G. Herzog zu, Graf von Carlow. *Richelieu als merkantilistischer Wirtschaftspolitiker und der Begriff des Staatsmerkantilismus.* Jena, 1929.

MONTCHRESTIEN, A. de. *Traicté de l'Oeconomie politique.* 1615. Pub. by Funck-Brentano. Paris, 1889.

MOUSNIER, R. *La venalité des offices sous Henri IV et Louis XIII.* Rouen, 1945.

PAHL, H. *Die Kolonialpolitik Richelieus und ihre Beziehungen zu seiner Gesamtpolitik.* Heidelberg, 1932.

PALM. F. C. *The Economic Policies of Richelieu.* Urbana, Ill., 1920.

PERRAUD, A. Cardinal. *Le cardinal de Richelieu, évêque, théologien et protecteur des lettres.* Paris, 1882.

PETIT, J. *L'Assemblée des Notables de 1626–7.* Paris, 1936.

PRUNEL, L., Mgr. *La renaissance catholique en France au XVIIe siècle.* Paris, 1921.

   Les premiers séminaires en France au XVIIe siècle. Paris, 1909.

RÉMOND, N. *Sommaire traité de revenue.* Paris, 1622.

RUDLOFF, M. P. 'A. de Montchrétien et les problèmes du développement économique', in *Revue d'histoire économique et sociale,* 1960.

SILHON, J. de. *Le ministre d'Etat avec le véritable usage de la politique moderne.* Paris, 1631.

TOURNYOL du CLOS, J. *Richelieu et le clergé de France.* Paris, 1912.

TRAMONT, J. *Manuel d'histoire maritime de la France, des origines à 1713.* Paris, 1716.

WIENS, E. *Fancan und die französische Politik 1624–27.* Heidelberg. 1908.

WILLAERT, L., S.J. *Histoire de l'église depuis les origines jusqu'à nos jours,* vol. 18, chap. 4.

Status et reglemens pour l'ordre de Cluny faits par Mgr. l'éminentissime Cardinal duc de Richelieu. Paris, 1633.

CHAPTER 10

Mémoires, books 18, 19, 20; *A.E. corr. pol., Espagne,* 15; *Lorraine,* 8; *Rome,* 41, 42; *Pays-Bas espagnols,* 7; AVENEL, vol. 2, pp. 335–778; esp. docs. nos. 26, 31, 98; vol. 3, pp. 3–120; H. and LA F., vol. 3, book 2; PASTOR, chap. 2; CAMMELL, ERLANGER and GIBB (cited in references to chap. 7); LA PORTE; ROHAN; FONTENAY-MAREUIL; BATIFFOL, Chevreuse, chap. 5; LONCHAY, esp. docs. nos. 994, 1080, 1253; GRIFFET, vol. 1; Calendar of State Papers, Domestic Series 1627-28. *Tricentenaire du siège de La Rochelle*. La Rochelle, 1928.

BAUDIER, M. *Histoire du Mareschal de Toiras*. Paris, 1666. 2 vols.

BLANCHON. *Jean Guiton et le siège de La Rochelle*. La Rochelle, 1911.

FRAINEAU, L. *La dernière guerre de La Rochelle. 1627-1628*. Deux-Sèvres, 1916.

GACHARD, L. P. *Histoire politique et diplomatique de Pierre Paul Rubens*. Brussels, 1877.

HAUSSONVILLE, J. O. B. Comte d'. *Histoire de la réunion de Lorraine à la France*. Paris, 1854-9.

RODOCANACHI, E. *Les derniers temps du siège de La Rochelle. Relation du nonce apostolique*. Paris, 1899.

ROOSES, M. *Codex Diplomaticus Rubenianus*. Antwerp, 1887-1909. 6 vols.

RUBENS, P. P. *The Letters of Peter Paul Rubens*. Cambridge, Massachusetts, 1955.

VAUX de FOLETIER, F. de. *Le siège de La Rochelle*. Paris, 1931.

VILLEMAIN, P. *Journal des assiégés de La Rochelle. 1627-28*. Paris, 1958.

ZELLER, G. *La réunion de Metz à la France*. Paris, 1926. 2 vols.

Traité entre Charles I Roi de la Grande Bretagne et le Maire, les Echevins, Pairs, Bourgeois et Habitans de la Ville de La Rochelle. Fait par leurs Deputez le 28 janvier, 1628. DUMONT, vol. 5, p. 528.

CHAPTER 11

Mémoires, books 20, 21; *A.E. corr. pol., Angleterre*, 42, 43; *Espagne*, 15; *Rome*, 42; *Sardaigne*, 9-14; AVENEL, vol. 3, pp. 179-502, esp. docs. nos. 105, 121, 122, 124; H. and LA F., vol. 3, book 3, chap. 1; LA FORCE; LONCHAY, esp. docs. nos. 1377, 1418; GRIFFET, vol. 2; PASTOR, chaps. 4, 6; FAGNIEZ, vol. 1; BAUDIER, d'HAUSSONVILLE (cited in references to chap. 10).

ALVAREZ, M. F. *Don Gonzalo Fernández de Cordóba y la guerra de sucesión de Mantua y del Monferrato, 1627-9*. Madrid, 1955.

QUAZZA, R. *La guerra per la successione di Mantova e del Monferrato*. Mantua, 1926. 2 vols.

AUBREY, A. *Histoire du cardinal de Mazarin*, Paris, 1688.

BAILLY, A. *Mazarin*. Paris, 1935.

GARDE, H. de la. *Le duc de Rohan et les Protestants sous Louis XIII.* Paris, 1884.

HASSAL, A. *Mazarin.* London, 1896.

KHEVENHÜLLER, F. C., Graf von. *Annales Ferdinandei, oder wahrhafte Beschreibung Käyser's Ferdinandi.* Leipzig, 1721–6. vols. 10, 11.

SCHNEIDER, B. *Der Mantuanische Erbfolgestreit.* Marburg, 1905.

Traité de Paix entre Monsieur le Cardinal de Richelieu au nom de Louis XIII Roi de France et Mr. le Prince de Piémont au nom de Charles Emmanuel I Duc de Savoie. Fait à Suze, le 11 mars 1624. DUMONT, vol. 5, p. 571.

Projet d'une Ligue entre le Pape Urbain VIII, Louis XIII Roi de France, Charles Emmanuel I Duc de Savoye, la République de Venise et le Duc de Mantoue. Fait le 11 mars 1629. Ratifié par ledit Duc de Savoye le 20 mars 1629. DUMONT, vol. 5, p. 572.

Traité de Conféderation et d'Alliance pour six ans entre le Pape Urbain VIII, Louis XIII Roi de France, le République de Venise, et le Duc de Mantoue, pour la défense de leurs Etats, contre la Maison d'Autriche. Fait à Venise le 8 avril 1629. Le Pape ne signa pas ce Traité. DUMONT, vol. 5, p. 580.

Traité de Paix et Conféderation entre Louis XIII Roi de France et Charles I Roi d'Angleterre, fait à Suze le 24 avril 1629. DUMONT, vol. 5, p. 580.

Traité fait entre le Cardinal de Richelieu au nom de Louis XIII Roi de France avec Charles Emmanuel I Duc de Savoie, pour le partage des Terres de Montferrat, avec le Duc de Mantoue. Fait à Bassolin le 10 mai 1629. DUMONT, vol. 5, p. 583.

Mémoire sur les Affaires d'Allemagne, A.E. corr. pol., Allemagne, 6, fol. 279. Reprinted in *Revue Historique*, vol. 107, p. 75. *Mémoire touchant Bavière et le Liège.* A.E. corr. pol., Bavière. Supp., fol. 29, ibid., p. 310.

CHAPTER 12

Mémoires, book 21; *T.P.*, pt. 2, chaps. 4, 7; AVENEL, vol. 3, pp. 530–966, esp. docs. nos. 312, 513–9; vol. 4, doc. no. 40, *A.E. corr. pol., Allemagne*, 7; esp. fol. 40–5, 174, 485–7, 505, 557–61. *Sardaigne*, 11–14; *Autriche*, 15; *Bavière*, 1; *Espagne*, 16; *Hollande*, 12; *Rome*, 43; *Friedensakten*, 9a I, esp. fol. 23–31, 78–88; PASTOR, chap. 4; FAGNIEZ, vol. 1; ALBRECHT, I, esp. no. 170. GOETZ; KHEVENHÜLLER (cited in references to chap. 11); GÜNTHER (cited in references to chap. 6), chap 2.

ANDREAS, W. *Geist-und staatliche historische Porträts*. Munich, 1922, pp. 45 *et seq.*

BAUR, J. *Philipp von Sötern, geistlicher Kurfürst zu Trier und seine Politik während des dreissigjährigen Krieges.* Speyer, 1897, vol. 1. pt. 2, chap. 1.

BÜHRING, J. *Venedig, Gustav Adolf und Rohan.* Halle, 1885, chaps. 5–9.

HEYNE, O. *Der Kurfürstentag zu Regensburg von 1630.* Berlin, Jena, 1866.

KELLER, R. *Die Friedensverhandlung zwischen Frankreich und dem Kaiser auf dem Regensburger Kurfürstentag, 1630.* Bonn, 1902.

KLOPP, O. *Der dreissigjährige Krieg bis zum Tode Gustav Adolfs.* 1932. book 5, chap. 2.

O'CONNELL, D. P. 'A Cause Célèbre in the History of Treaty Making. The Refusal to Ratify the Peace Treaty of Regensburg in 1630', in *The British Yearbook of International Law*, 1967.

RICHELIEU, A. J. *Relation fidelle de ce qui s'est passé en Italie en l'année 1630, entre les armes de la France, et celles de l'Empereur d'Espagne et du Duc de Savoye, jointes ensemble.* Paris, 1631. (Attributed to Richelieu.)

Édit et Déclaration de l'Empéreur Ferdinand II touchant les Edits et Traictez de Pacification pour la Religion et la Restitution des Biens Ecclésiastiques. À Vienne le 6 mars 1629. DUMONT, vol. 5, p. 564.

Traité et renouvellement d'Alliance entre Louis XIII Roi de France et les États Généraux des Provinces-Unies des Pais-Bas, fait à la Haye le 17 juin 1630 ledit Roi fournira aus dites États en don sept ans durant un million de livres chaque année. DUMONT, vol. 5, p. 605.

Articles de Trêve général entre les Généraux de l'Empéreur, de la France, d'Espagne et de Savoie, sur les instances de Mr. de Mazarini, Ministre du Pape, jusqu'au quinzième octobre. Fait au Camp de Rivalta le 4 septembre 1630. DUMONT, vol. 5, p. 614.

Traité de Paix entre l'Empereur Ferdinand II et Louis XIII Roi de France touchant le différend par la succession des Duchez de Mantoue et du Montferrat. Fait à Ratisbonne le 13 octobre 1630. Avec diverses pièces servant d'éclaircissements à ce Traité, ou expliquant les suites qu'il euct. DUMONT, vol. 5, p. 615.

Primo Trattato di Cherasco trà la S. Cesarea Maesta dell Imperatore Ferdinando II et la Maesta Christianissima del Rè di Francia Luigi XIII per l'esecutione e stabilmento della Pace in Italia et sopra le differenze del Duca di Savoia con il Duca di Mantova. Li 18 giugno 1631. DUMONT, vol. 6, p. 9.

Secondo Trattato di Cherasco per l'esecutione di quello delli 6 di Aprile; fatta trà li Signori Ambasciadori e Plenipotentiarii di S. M. Cesarea e di

S. M. Christianissima li 19 di giugno 1631. DUMONT, vol. 6, p. 14.

CHAPTER 13

Mémoires, book 22; *T.P.* chap. 5; *Journal;* AVENEL, vol. 4, pp. 3–395, esp. docs. nos. 31, 32, 62, 119, 136, 210; vol. 4, pp. 237–418, esp. docs. nos. 119, 136, 210; H. and LA F., vol. 3, book 3, chap. 2; *A.E. mém. doc.* 252, 802–5, 1485. (Montmorency's trial); 794, 795 (negotiations with Gaston); 798–802 (Marillac's trial); DETHAN, chaps. 6–9; FONTENAY-MAREUIL; BASSOMPIERRE; MOTTEVILLE; GASTON; MONTGLAS; LONCHAY, esp. docs. nos. 1783, 1804, 1820.

ANON. *Relation véritable de ce qui ce s'est passé au jugement du procès du Maréchal de Marillac . . . et de ses dernières paroles et actions, devant et sur le point de sa mort.*

BRIENNE, H. A. de. LOMÉNIE, Comte de. *Mémoires contenant les évènements les plus remarquables du règne de Louis XIII et de celui de Louis XIV jusqu'à la mort du cardinal Mazarin.* Pub. by Michaud and Poujoulat, 3rd series, vol. 3.

ARNAULT de la MÉNARDIÈRE, C. *Essai sur Michel de Marillac, garde des sceaux sous Louis XIII.* Poitiers, 1856.

BATIFFOL, L. *La Journée des Dupes.* Paris, 1925.

CAILLEMER, E. *Étude sur Michel de Marillac.* Paris, 1862.

CHARVÉRIAT, E. 'Louis XIII et Richelieu. La méthode de Richelieu, ses sourcis, sa puissance, 1629–30', in *Revue Lyonnais,* 1891.

DUCROS, S. *Histoire de la vie d'Henri de Montmorency.* Paris, 1643.

EVERAT, E. *Michel de Marillac, sa vie, ses oeuvres.* Paris, 1894.

FORSYTH, E. *La tragédie française de Jodelle à Corneille (1553–1640): le thème de la vengeance.* Paris, 1962.

GUYNEMER, M. 'L'isolement de Marie de Médicis au château de Compiègne, son évasion, d'après de manuscrits inédits', in *Bulletin de la Société de Compiègne,* 1911.

HAY du CHASTELET, P. *Les entretiens des Champs-Elizées. 1631.* Pub. in *Recueil de diverses pièces pour servir à l'histoire.* Paris, 1640.

   Observations sur la vie et la condemnation du Mareschal de Marillac. Paris, 1633.

HOUSSAYE, M. Père. *Le cardinal de Bérulle et le cardinal de Richelieu 1625–1629.* Paris, 1875.

LANCASTER, H. C. *A History of French Dramatic Literature in the Seventeenth Century,* pt. 1. vol. 2. Baltimore, Paris, 1929, p. 522

discusses the suggestion that Corneille's *Clitandre* was inspired by the Marillac affair.

MARILLAC, L. Maréchal de. *Requêtes présentées à MM. les commissaires de la chambre souveraine ... contenant les causes de récusation ... tant contre ladite chambre que contre M. le Garde des sceaux et autres juges d'icelle.* 1632.

MARILLAC, P. de. 'Les Marillac et Richelieu. La Journée des Dupes', in *Revue des questions historiques*, 1923.

MONGRÉDIEN, G. *La Journée des Dupes.* Paris, 1961.

   Le bourreau du cardinal de Richelieu, Isaac de Laffemas. Paris, 1929.

PAGÈS, G. 'Autour du "Grande Orage". Richelieu et Marillac: deux politiques', in *Revue historique*, 1937.

QUAZA, M. CAPITELLI. *Marie de Gonzague et Gaston d'Orléans. Une épisode de politique secrète au temps de Louis XIII.* Mantua, 1925.

SAINT SIMON, Duc de. 'Fragment historique' published in the *Revue des Deux Mondes*, 15 Nov. 1834, reproduced in MONGRÉDIEN (*Supra*), p. 201.

VAISSIÈRE, P. de. *L'affaire du maréchal de Marillac.* Paris, 1924.

Articles de paix que Louis XIII Roi de France accorde à Gaston Jean Baptiste de France Duc d'Orléans son Frère. Faits à Béziers le 29 sept. 1632. DUMONT, vol. 6, p. 42.

Lettre escrite au Roy par la Reyne Mère de sa Majesté, 1631 (Brit. Mus. 831.b.21); *Lettre de la Reyne Mère du Roy à Messieurs du Parlement de Paris, 1632* (ibid.); *Offres de la Reine Mère au Roy sur sa Resolution, 1631* (asking Parlement to decide between her and Richelieu). (Brit Mus. 8050. bbb. 19.)

CHAPTER 14

Mémoires, book 22; A.E. corr. pol., *Allemagne*, 7, 8; *Pays-Bas espagnols*, 9; *Bavière*, 1; *Cologne*, 1; *Espagne*, 16; *Grisons*, 7, 8; *Hollande*, 12; *Mayence*, 1; *Rome*, 44, 45; *Suède*, 1, 2, Supp. 1 bis; AVENEL, vol. 4, pp. 237–418, esp. docs. nos. 119, 128; *Friedensakten*, 9a I, docs. 24 Aug. 1631, 4 Sept. 1631; FAGNIEZ, vol. 1, chap. 9; DETHAN, chap. 9; PASTOR, chap. 4; LEMAN, *Urbain VIII*, chaps. 1, 2; D'HAUSSONVILLE (cited in references to chap. 10); BÜHRING (cited in references to chap. 13), chaps. 10, 12; KLOPP (cited in references to chap. 13), vol. 3, pt. 2; BAUR (cited in references to chap. 12); vol. 1, book 2, chap. 2; PFISTER; ROHAN; ROBERTS, vol. 2 (standard work); Vatican Library. Barberini Library, Latin, 6968, 6974.

ALBRECHT, D. *Richelieu, Gustav Adolf und das Reich.* Munich, Vienna, 1959.

BATIFFOL, L. 'Richelieu et la question d'Alsace', in *Revue historique,* 1921.

BAUSTAEDT, B. *Richelieu und Deutschland. Von der Schlacht bei Breitenfeld bis zum Tode Bernhards von Weimar.* Berlin, 1936.

EHSES, S. 'Papst Urban VIII und Gustav Adolf', in *Historisches Jahrbuch,* 1895.

GREGOROVIUS, F. *Urban VIII im Widerspruche zu Spanien und dem Kaiser.* Stuttgart, 1879.

HARTUNG, F. *Deutsche Geschichte im Zeitalter der Reformation, der Gegenreformation und des 30 jährigen Krieges.* Berlin, 1951.

LEMAN, A., Chanoine. *Recueil des instructions générales aux nonces ordinaires de France, de 1624 à 1634.* Paris, 1920.

MOMMSEN, W. *Richelieu, Elsass und Lothringen, ein Beitrag zur elsass-lothringischen Frage.* Berlin, 1922.

PAVIÉ, E. 'Missions diplomatiques du baron Hercule de Charnacé en Allemagne 1629-32', in *Mém. Soc. Angers,* 1910.

PUFENDORF, S., Freiherr, von. *Commentariorum de rebus Sueciis. Lib.* 2, 3. Ultrajecti, 1686.

ROBINET de CLÉRY, G. A. *Première occupation de la Lorraine par les Français, 1632-41.* Nancy, 1900.

VERAGUTH, D. *Herzog Rohan und seine Mission in Graubünden und Veltlin.* Biel, 1892.

WADDINGTON, A. *La république des Provinces-Unies, la France et les Pays-Bas espagnoles de 1630 à 1650.* Paris, 1895-7. 2 vols.

WEIBULL, L. 'Gustave Adolphe et Richelieu', in *Revue historique,* 1934.

Traité de Trève pour six années entre Sigismund III Roi de Pologne, et Gustave Adolphe, Roi de Suède. Fait au camp d'Altenmarck le 25 septembre, 1629. DUMONT, vol. 5, p. 594.

Traité de Conféderation et d'Alliance entre Gustave Adolphe Roi de Suède et Bogislaus Duc de Stettin de Pomeranie etc. Fait à Stettin le 10/20 juillet 1630. DUMONT, vol. 5, p. 606.

Manifeste de Gustave Adolphe Roi de Suède par lequel il déclare ses raisons qui l'ont obligé à prendre les Armes, et à entrer en Allemagne, publié au mois de juillet ou au mois d'août de l'année 1630. DUMONT, vol. 5, p. 608.

Lettre de Gustave II Roi de Suède à Louis XIII Roi de France pour lui demander du secours. Ecrite à Stralsund le 17 septembre 1630. DUMONT, vol. 5, p. 615.

Foedus inter Ludovicum XIII Regem Galliae et Gustavum Adolphum Regum Sueciae ad communes Amicos oppressos, et inprimis Status et Principes Germaniae adjurandum omniaque in eundum Statum quo ante Bellum erant, restituendum. Actum in stativis Bernwaldi 13 Januarius 1631. DUMONT, vol. 6, p. 1.

Traité de Conféderation, d'Alliance et de Ligue défensive pour huit ans, entre Louis XIII Roi de France et Maximilian Elector de Bavière, signé à Fontainebleau le 30 mai 1631. DUMONT, vol. 6, p. 14.

Traité entre Louis XIII Roi de France et Victor Aimé Duc de Savoye pour un libre passage en Italie. Fait à Millefleur le 19 octobre, 1631. DUMONT, vol. 6, p. 20.

Déclaration de Philippe Christophe le Électeur de Trèves, par laquelle il se met lui et ses Etats sous la protection de Louis XIII Roi de France. Donné à Coblens le 21 décembre 1631. DUMONT, vol. 6, p. 24.

Traite de Neutralité entre Gustave Adolphe, Roi de Suède et les Etats Catholiques d'Allemagne. Fait à Mayence le 29 janvier 1632. DUMONT, vol. 6, p. 29.

Traité entre Louis XIII Roi de France et Philippe Christophe le Electeur de Trèves, par lequel Sa Majesté s'oblige de l'assister contre tous ceux qui le voudront opprimer, et de faire sortir les Suédois de ses Etats. Fait à Ehrenbreitstein le 9 avril 1632. DUMONT, vol. 6, p. 35.

Traité secret, fait et conclu entre Louis XIII Roi de France et Victor Aimé Duc de Savoye par lequel un autre Traité fait et signé le même jour entre les mêmes pour la Cession et Transport à sa Majesté de la Ville et Château de Pignerol est déclaré null, et celui du dernier mai 1631 confirmé et corroboré. A Turin le 5 juillet 1632. DUMONT, vol. 6, p. 40.

CHAPTER 15

Mémoires, books 23–5; AVENEL, pp. 419–647, esp. docs. nos. 226, 268; A.E. corr. pol., *Allemagne*, 8, 9, 10; *Pays-Bas espagnols*, 9–11; *Autriche*, 15, *Bavière*, 1; *Cologne*, 1; *Espagne*, 17; *Hollande*, 14, 15, 16; supp. 1; *Lorraine*, docs. on the occupation of, 9, 10, 11, *procès verbaux* on the seizure of Bar (copies), 12; occupying administration, 13, 14, 15; inventory of the treasury of Charles IV, 16, docs. concerning Metz, 17, 19 (history of French rights from 762 to 1630); supp. 5 (docs. concerning Verdun); *Rome*, 45–8; *Suède*, 2, 3; DETHAN, chap. 10; H. and LA F., vol. 5, book I; FAGNIEZ, vol. 2, chap. 12; LEMAN, *Urbain VIII*, book 1, chaps. 2–5; PASTOR, chap. 4; BÜHRING, KLOPP, BAUR, GÜNTHER, chaps. 3–5 (all cited in references to chap. 12); BAUSTAEDT, chap. 2; ALBRECHT;

CLÉRY; EHSES; GREGOROVIUS; HARTUNG; MOMMSEN; ROBERTS; WADDINGTON and WEIBULL (all cited in references to chap. 14); LONCHAY, esp. docs. nos. 1752, 1766, 1783, 1804, 1820, 1823, 1831, 1839, 1840, 1846, 1861, 1889, 1895, 1954, 2009, 2055, 2073, 2156, 2164, 2171; D'HAUSSONVILLE(cited in references to chap. 10), vol. 1.

HAMILTON, E. J. *American Treasure and the Price Revolution in Spain.* Cambridge, Mass., 1934.

'The Decline of Spain', in *Economic History Review,* 1938.

HENRARD, P. J. *Sept ans de l'histoire de Belgique 1631-1638. Marie de Médicis dans les Pays-Bas.* Brussels, 1876.

MORIZET, G. 'La princesse Marguerite de Lorraine de 1633 à 1643', in *Annales de l'Est,* 1899.

Foedus inter Ferdinandum II Imperatorem Romanorum et Philippum IV Regem Hispaniarum contra Regum Sueciae Gustavum Adolphum et ejus adhaerentes ad annos sex initium. Vienne die 14 Februarii 1632. DUMONT, vol. 6, p. 30.

Traité de Paix entre Louis XIII Roi de France et Charles III Duc de Lorraine par lequel la place de Marsal demeure entre les mains du Roi pour trois ans. Fait à Vic le 6 Janvier 1632. DUMONT, vol. 6, p. 28.

Traité entre Louis XIII Roi de France et Charles III Duc de Lorraine, par lequel les villes, châteaux et citadelles de Stenai et Jametz demeurent en depôt entre les mains de Sa Majesté pour quatre ans, et le Comté de Clermont en Argonne en pleine propriété et Souveraineté. Fait à Liverdun le 26 juin 1632. DUMONT, vol. 6, p. 39.

Traité entre Louis XIII Roi de France et Charles III Duc de Lorraine, fait au Camp devant Nanci le 6 septembre 1633. Et les Articles ajoutez audit Traité à Charmes le 20 septembre 1633. DUMONT, vol. 6, p. 54.

GIACHETTI, C. *La tragica aventura dei Concini. La fine del Maresciallo d'Ancre 1600-1617.* Milan, 1939.

Défense de la confession des églises reformées de France, contre les accusations du sieur Arnould Jesuite, deduites en un sermon faict en la présence du Roy. Charenton, 1617.

Treaties of Fonteney le Comte, 20 January 1616, and *Loudun,* May 1616, are in DUMONT, vol. 5, pp. 278, 282.

Articles presentés à Louis XIII de la part des princes etc. retirez de la cour depuis la détention de la personne du Prince de Condé avec les résponses du Roi sur ce sujet. 30 Septembre 1616.

Cession et Transport des Duchez de Lorraine et de Bar au Cardinal de Lorraine par son Frère le Duc de Lorraine. A Mirecourt le 19 janvier 1634. DUMONT, vol. 6, p. 56.

Traité entre le Marquis d'Ayetone au nom de Philippe IV Roi des Espagnes et Gaston Jean Baptiste Duc d'Orléans par lequel ce Prince s'engage dans le parti et les Intérêts de la Maison d'Autriche contre ceux du Roi son Frère. A Bruxelles le 12 May 1634. DUMONT, vol. 6, p. 73.

CHAPTER 16

Mémoires, books 25, 26; *A.E. corr. pol.*, Allemagne, 10, 11; Autriche, 15; Bavière, 1; Cologne, 1; Hollande, 15, 16; Rome, 46, 48; GRIFFET, vol. 2; H. and LA F., vol. 5, book 2; FAGNIEZ, vol. 2, chap. 12; LEMAN, *Urbain VIII*, books, 2, 3; PASTOR, chap. 5; BAUSTAEDT, chap. 2; GÜNTHER, chap. 5 (both cited in references to chap. 12); MOMMSEN, WADDINGTON (both cited in references to chap. 14).

ALBERTINI, R. von. *Das politische Denken in Frankreich zur Zeit Richelieus.* Marburg, 1951.

BÉTHUNE, P. de. *Le conseiller d'Estat ou recueil des plus générales considerations servant au maniment des affaires publiques.* Paris, 1633.

FEUQUIÈRES, M. de PAS, Marquis de. *Lettres et négotiations du Mis. de Feuquières, ambassadeur extraordinaire du roi en Allemagne en 1633 et 1634.* Amsterdam, 1753. 3 vols.

KAEBER, E. *Die Idee des europäischen Gleichgewichts in der publizistischen Literatur vom 16. bis zur Mitte des 18. Jahrhunderts.* Berlin, 1907.

PANGE, J. Comte de. *Charnacé et l'alliance franco-hollandaise, 1633–37.* Paris, 1905.

SUAREZ, L. *Notas a la política antespañola de Richelieu.* Simancas, 1950.

VIGIER, O. 'La politique extérieure du cardinal de Richelieu. Projets d'alliance avec l'Angleterre', in *Revue des questions historiques*, 1889.

Traité entre Louis XIII Roi de France et Christine Reine de Suède, fait à Heilbronn le 9 avril 1633. DUMONT, vol. 6, p. 48.

Traité d'Alliance entre la Couronne de Suède, d'une part, et les États Evangéliques des quatres Cercles du Rhyn Electoral, de Franconie, de Suabe, et du Haut Rhyn, d'autre part. DUMONT, vol. 6, p. 51.

Confoederatio inter Ludovicum XIII Galliae Regum et Christianam Reginam Sueciae, pro se et Principibus Germaniae confoederatis, ad stabiliendam Pacem in Romano Imperio, et conservandam Principibus Germaniae Libertatem. Francofurti ad Moenum die 15 Septembris 1633. DUMONT, vol. 6, p. 56.

Traité entre Louis XIII Roi de France et les États Généraux des Provinces-Unies des Païs-Bas, pour sept années. Fait à la Haye le 15 avril, 1634. DUMONT, vol. 6, p. 68.

Traité entre Louis XIII Roi de France, le Chancellier Oxenstiern pour

Christine, Reine de Suède, et les États Évangéliques des Cercles et Provinces Electorales du Rhin, Franconie et Suabe, pour le depôt de la Forteresse de Philipsbourg. Fait à Francfort le 20 septembre 1634. Dumont, vol. 6, p. 78.

Traité entre Louis XIII Roi de France et Christine Reine de Suède pour les places d'Alsace. Fait le 9 octobre 1634. Dumont, vol. 6, p. 78.

Traité de Confédération entre Louis XIII Roi de France et le Duc de Württemberg et autres Princes d'Allemagne. Fait à Paris le 1 novembre 1634. Dumont, vol. 6, p. 78. Oxenstierna had full power from the Swedish Regency, and art. 1 of the Treaty described him as '*intervenant en ce Traité au nom et avec Plein-Pouvoir de ladite Couronne*'. What delegation of this power Löffler had from Oxenstierna is unknown.

CHAPTER 17

T.P., book 2, chap. 9; *A.E. corr. pol.*, *Allemagne*, 11, 12; *Pays-Bas espagnols*, 10, 11; H. and LA F., vol. 4, books 1–3; Avenel, vol. 4, esp. doc. nos. 163, 762; Leman, *Urbain VIII*, book 3; Fagniez, vol. 2, chap. 12.

Binville, de. *Les véritez françoises opposées aux calomnies espagnolles.* Paris, 1635.

Fagniez, G. 'L'opinion et la presse sous Louis XIII', in *Revue des questions historiques*, 1890.

Knight, W. S. M. *The Life and Works of Hugo Grotius.* Grotius Society Pub. No. 4 (1925).

Laderchi, L. *La campagna del duca di Rohan in Valtellina nell' anno 1635.* Rome, 1888.

Mallet. *Comtes rendus de l'administration des finances du royaume de France.* Paris, 1789.

Marsy, A. C. A., Comte de. *Oxenstierna et Richelieu à Compiègne, Traité de 1635.* Paris, 1878.

Montbas, H. de. 'Richelieu et l'opposition pendant la guerre de trente ans (1635–38)'. *Extrait de la correspondance historique et archéologique.* Paris, 1913.

Nys, E. *Les théories politiques et le droit internationale en France jusqu'au XVIIIᵉ siècle.* Brussels, Paris, 1891.

O'Connell, D. R. 'Rationalism and Voluntarism in the Fathers of International Law', in *Studies in the History of the Law of Nations, the Indian Year Book of International Affairs*, 1964.

Traité de Confédération et d'Alliance entre Louis XIII Roi de France et de

Navarre, et les Etats Généraux des Provinces-Unies des Pays-Bas, contre l'Empéreur Ferdinand Second Archiduc d'Autriche, Philippe IV Roi d'Espagne et ses Adhérans. A Paris le huitième jour de Février, mil six cens trente-cinq. DUMONT, vol. 6, p. 80.

Éclaircissement et Amplification des précedens Traités entre Louis XIII Roi de France et Christine Reine de Suède. Fait à Compiègne le 28 Avril 1635. DUMONT, vol. 6, p. 88.

Lettre de Louis XIII Roi de France écrite à Monsieur le Duc de Montbazon, Pair et Grand Veneur de France, Gouverneur et Lieutenant-Général pour le Roi de Paris et l'Ile de France; contenans les justes causes que Sa Majesté a eues de déclarer la Guerre au Roi d'Espagne; qui peut passer pour un Manifeste et une Déclaration de Guerre. Écrite à Monceaux le 9 Juin 1635. DUMONT, vol. 6, p. 106.

Traité de Confédération et d'Alliance entre Louis XIII Roi de France et Christine Reine de Suède contre l'Empéreur Ferdinand II. Fait à Wismar le 20 Mars 1636. DUMONT, vol. 6, p. 123.

Traité de Confédération et d'Alliance entre Louis XIII Roi de France et les Etats Généraux des Provinces-Unies des Païs-Bas. Fait à la Haye le 16 Avril 1636. DUMONT, vol. 6, p. 124.

CHAPTER 18

A.E. corr. pol., *Allemagne,* 11, 12; *Pays-Bas espagnols,* 10, 11; *Grisons,* 8, 9; H. and LA F. vol. 5, book 2; AVENEL, vol. 5, docs. nos. 190, 211, 425; LA FORCE; GRIFFET, vol. 2; BAUSTAEDT, book 2; GÜNTHER (cited in references to chap. 12), chap. 5; MOMMSEN; PUFENDORF (cited in references to chap. 14); ALBERTINI (cited in references to chap. 16).

ANDRÉ, L. *Michel Le Tellier et l'organisation de l'armée monarchique.* Paris, 1906.

BOUVIER, J. *Finances et financiers de l'ancien régime.* Paris, 1964.

CHARMEIL, J. P. *Les trésoriers de France.* Paris, 1964.

LADERCHI, L. *La campagna del duca di Rohan in Valtellina nell'anno 1635.* Rome, 1888.

MALLET. *Comtes rendus de l'administration des finances du royaume de France.* Paris, 1789.

MARSY, A. C. A., Comte de. *Oxenstierna et Richelieu à Compiègne, Traité de 1635.* Paris, 1878.

MOUSNIER, R. 'Le conseil du roi de la mort de Henri IV au gouvernement personnel de Louis XIV', in *Études d'histoire moderne et contemporaine,* 1947.

'Les règlements du conseil du roi sous Louis XIII', in *Annuaire-Bulletin de la Société de l'Histoire de France*, 1946–7.

PAGÈS, G. 'Le conseil du roi sous Louis XIII', in *Revue d'histoire moderne*, 1937.

'Études sur l'histoire administrative et sociale de l'ancien régime', in *Société d'histoire moderne*, 1938.

RANUM, O. A. *Richelieu and the Councillors of Louis XIII. A Study of the Secretaries of State and Superintendents of Finance in the Ministry of Richelieu, 1635–1642.* Oxford, 1963.

SCHMIDT, C. 'Le role et les attributions d'un intendant des finances aux armées. Sublet de Noyers de 1632–1636', in *Revue d'histoire moderne et contemporaine*, 1901.

VINCART, J. A. *Les relations militaires des années 1634 et 1635, rédigées par Jean Antoine Vincart, secrétaire des avis secrets de guerre aux Pays-Bas.* Brussels, 1958.

Traité de Confédération entre Louis XIII Roi de France et Victor Amadeus Duc de Savoye pour la conquête du Duché de Milan, à Rivolles le 11 Juillet 1635. DUMONT, vol. 6, p. 109.

Traité entre Louis XIII Roi de France et Bernard Duc de Weimar comme Général en Chef des Forces des Princes et Etats Confédérés d'Allemagne, pour la levée et l'entretien d'une Armée de 18,000 Hommes, moyennant un subside de quatre millions par an, que le Roi promet de lui payer. A St Germain en Laye le 27 Octobre 1635. DUMONT, vol. 6, p. 118.

CHAPTER 19

Mémoires, books 21, 26, 27; *T.P.* chap. 2; AVENEL, vol. 7, p. 720; Gaston's marriage process is in *A.E. mém. doc.* 807, 810–2, and correspondence with the Holy See in *A.E. corr. pol.*, Rome, 56–9; Vatican archives, *Nunciatura di Francia*, 82, 83; the Puylaurens process is in *A.E. mém. doc.* 813, 816; H. and LA F., book 5, chap. 1; PASTOR, chap. 6; FAGNIEZ, vol. 2, chap. 10; DETHAN, pt. 1, chap. 10, pt. 2, chaps. 2, 3, 6; DELOCHE, chaps. 4, 5; BAUR (cited in references to chap. 12); ALBERTINI (cited in references to chap. 16).

ABERCROMBIE, N. *The Origins of Jansenism.* Oxford, 1936.

ADAM, A. *Sur le problème religieux dans la première moitié du XVIIe siècle.* Oxford, 1959.

AMOUDRU, B. *Le sens religieux du grand siècle.* Paris, 1946, chaps. 1, 2.

AVENEL, Vicomte G. d'. *Prêtres, soldats et juges sous Richelieu.* Paris, 1907.

BREMOND, H., Abbé. *Histoire littéraire du sentiment religieux en France depuis la fin des guerres de religion jusqu'a nos jours.* Paris, 1927, vol. 3.

BUSSON, H. *La religion des classiques.* Paris, 1948, chap. 1.

DEGERT, A., Abbé. 'Le mariage de Gaston d'Orléans et de Marguerite de Lorraine', in *Revue historique*, 1923.

GAZIER, A. *Histoire générale du mouvement janseniste, depuis les origines jusqu'à nos jours.* Paris, 1922. 2 vols.

GELLOT, H. 'Le mouvement spirituel du Grand Siècle', in *Revue des sciences religieuses*, 1922.

HANOTAUX, G. 'Théorie de gallicanisme', in *Sur les chemins de l'histoire*. Paris, 1924, vol. 1.

LAPORTE, J. *La doctrine du Port Royal*, vol. 1. *Saint-Cyran*. Paris, 1922.

MARTIN, V. Mgr. *Le gallicanisme politique et le clergé de France.* Paris, 1929.

  Le gallicanisme et la réforme catholique. Essai historique sur l'introduction en France des décrets du Concile de Trente (1563–1615). Paris, 1919.

ORCIBAL, J. *Les origines du jansenisme*, vol. 2: *Jean Duvergier de Hauranne Abbé de Saint Cyran et son temps, 1581–1638.* Louvain-Paris, 1947, chaps. 10, 11. Of capital importance, with original documents.

PERRAUD, A., Cardinal. *Le cardinal de Richelieu, évêque, théologien et protecteur des lettres.* Paris, 1882.

PITHOU, P. *Les libertez de l'Eglise gallicane.* Paris, 1594.

POURRAT, P. Abbé. *La spiritualité chrétienne*, vol. 3, Paris, 1927.

PRÉCLIN, E. 'Edmund Richer', in *Revue d'histoire moderne*, 1930.

PRÉCLIN, E. and JARRY, E. *Les luttes politiques et doctrinales aux XVIIe et XVIIIe siècles.* Paris, 1935.

RICHELIEU, Alphonse L. de. 'Six Lettres écrites au roi Louis XIII et à ses ministres pendant son ambassade extraordinaire à la Cour de Rome en 1635 et 1636', in *Conservateur*, May, 1757.

Articles de l'Accomodement fait entre Louis XIII Roi de France et Gaston Jean Baptiste Duc d'Orléans son Frère unique; par lequel ce Prince renonce à tous les engagements qu'il avoit pris contre son service. A Escouän le 1 Octobre 1634. DUMONT, vol. 6, p. 73.

CHAPTER 20

Mémoires, books 27–9; *A.E. corr. pol., Allemagne,* 13–15; *Pays-Bas espagnols,* 11–14; *Espagne* (Correspondence with Pujol), 19, 20; *Grisons,* 9; *Hollande,* 19–22; *Rome,* 57–68; AVENEL, vol. 5, esp.

doc. no. 105; vol. 6, pp. 3–263; H. and LA F., vol. 5, book 2, chap. 2; FAGNIEZ, vol. 2, chap. 13; GRIFFET, vol. 3; BAUSTAEDT (cited in references to chap. 14); LA FORCE; DETHAN, chap. 7; PUFENDORF (cited in references to chap. 17).

GROTIUS, H. *Epistolae ad Christinam Sueciae reginam, A. Oxenstiernam.* Marburg, 1759.

NOAILLES, A. M. R. A., Vicomte de. *Episodes de la guerre de trente ans; I. Le cardinal de la Valette; II. Bernard de Saxe-Weimar 1604 à 1638 et la réunion de l'Alsace à la France.* Paris, 1908.

Ordres, instructions et lettres de Louis XIII et de Richelieu à M. de Sourdis concernant les opérations des flottes françaises de 1636 à 1642 accompagnés d'un texte historique. Paris, 1839.

Traité fait au nom du Roi de France Louis XIII avec les Grisons par le Duc de Rohan, Général de l'Armée de Sa Majesté, pour la sortie de ses Troupes dudit Païs, du 26 mars 1637. DUMONT, vol. 6, p. 146.

Convention faite entre Louis XIII Roi de France et le Duc de Weimar. A Paris le 17 Avril 1637. DUMONT, vol. 6, p. 147.

Traité d'Alliance et de Secours entre Louis XIII Roi de France et les États des Provinces-Unies des Païs-Bas, avec assistance ausdits États de douze cens mille Livres pour un an. Fait à Paris le 17 Décembre, 1637. DUMONT, vol. 6, p. 150.

Traité nouveau de Confédération entre Louis XIII Roi de France et Christine Reine de Suède. Fait à Hambourg le 5 Mars 1638. DUMONT, vol. 6, p. 161.

CHAPTER 21

Mémoires, books 27–9; H. and LA F., vol. 5, book 3; FAGNIEZ, vol, 2., chap. 13; GRIFFET, vol. 3; DELOCHE, chap. 5; MARAÑON, p. 85; LEMAN, *Richelieu et Olivares,* chaps. 1–3; PASTOR, chap. 6; MOTTEVILLE; LA PORTE; PUFENDORF (cited in references to chap. 14).

BONDOIS, P. M. *L'affaire du Val-de-Grâce (Août 1637). Les documents de la cassette de Richelieu.* Paris, 1922.

FREER, M. W. *Anne of Austria, Queen of France, Mother of Louis XIV.* London, 1912.

ROCHEMONTEIX, Père C. de, S.J. *Nicolas Caussin, confesseur de Louis XIII et le cardinal de Richelieu.* Paris, 1911.

    Abbrev.: ROCHEMONTEIX.

TONGAS, G. *Les relations de la France avec l'empire ottoman et l'ambassade à Constantinople de Ph. de Harlay, Comte de Césy 1619–1640, d'après des documents inédits.* Toulouse, 1642.

VAUTHIER, G. *Anne d'Autriche et le Val-de-Grâce*. Paris, 1916.

CHAPTER 22

AVENEL, vol. 6, pp. 265–664, esp. docs. nos. 226, 284, 293, 315; vol. 7, pp. 806–86; GRIFFET, vol. 3; H. and LA F., vol. 5, book 4; GASTON; *A.E. corr. pol.*, *Allemagne*, 15, 16; *Pays-Bas espagnols*, 14, 15 (supp.); *Espagne*, 19–21 (*affaires de Catalogne*); *Hollande*, 21; *Rome*, 63–75; LEMAN, *Richelieu et Olivares; ELLIOTT.*

BLET, P., S.J. 'Richelieu et les débuts de Mazarin', in *Revue d'histoire moderne et contemporaine*, 1959.

DETHAN, G. 'Mazarin avant le ministère', in *Revue historique*, 1962.

MELO, F. M. de. *Guerra de Cataluña*. Madrid, 1912.

MUN, G. Comte de. *Richelieu et la maison de Savoie; l'ambassade de Particelli d'Hémery en Piémont*. Paris, 1907.

RÉVALY, I. S. *Le cardinal de Richelieu et la restauration de Portugal*. Lisbon, 1950.

RODRIGUES CAVALHEIRO, A. *Richelieu e o Duque de Bragança*. Lisbon, 1942.

SANABRE, J. *La acción de Francia en Cataluña en la pugna por la hegemonia de Europa, 1640–1659*. Barcelona, 1956.

VASSAL-REIG, C. *La guerre en Roussillon sous Louis XIII, 1635–39*. Paris, 1934.

    Richelieu et la Catalogne. Paris, 1935.

    La prise de Perpignan, 1641–42. Paris, 1939.

Traité de Ligue offensive et défensive entre Louis XIII Roi de France et Madame la Régente de Savoy contre l'Espagne. Fait à Turin le 3 juin, 1638. DUMONT, vol. 6, p. 162.

Traité de Louis XIII Roi de France avec le Prince Thomas de Savoye pour la restitution des Places fortes du Piédmont, tenuës par Sa Majesté et le Roi d'Espagne à Turin le 2 Décembre 1640. DUMONT, vol. 6, p. 195.

Traité de Confédération et d'Alliance du Roi de France Louis XIII. Avec la Principauté de Catalogne et les Comtés de Roussillon et Cerdagne contre le Roi d'Espagne. Fait à Barcelone le 16 Décembre 1640. DUMONT, vol. 6, p. 196.

Déclaration des Trois Etats des Royaumes de Portugal, touchant la Proclamation et le rétablissement du Roi Don Jean IV et le Serment que les mêmes Etats lui ont prêté. Faite le 28 janvier 1641. DUMONT, vol. 6, p. 202.

Traité de Confédération et Alliance entre Louis XIII Roi de France et Jean IV Roi de Portugal, à Paris le 1 Juin 1641. DUMONT, vol. 6, p. 214.

Traité entre Louis XIII Roi de France le Cardinal de Savoye et son Frère le Prince Thomas. A Turin le 14 Juin 1642. DUMONT, vol. 6, p. 253.

Traité entre Madame Chrestienne de France Duchesse de Savoye et les Princes de Savoye, accordez par l'extremise du Sieur d'Angoulême, Ambassadeur de Louis XIII Roi de France à Turin le 14 Juin 1642. DUMONT, vol. 6, p. 254.

CHAPTER 23

GRIFFET, vol. 3; H. and LA F., vol. 6, book 4; LEMAN, *Richelieu et Olivares*; ALBERTINI (cited in references to chap. 16); PASTOR, chap. 6; d'AVENEL, *Prêtres* etc. (cited in references to chap. 19).

BLET, P., S.J. 'Richelieu et les débuts de Mazarin', in *Revue d'histoire moderne et contemporaine*, 1959.

BOISSONADE, R. 'L'administration royale et les soulèvements populaires en Angoumois en Saintongue et en Poitou pendant le ministère de Richelieu', in *Mémoires de la Société des Antiquaires de l'Ouest*, 1902.

DUPUY, P. and J. *Preuves des Libertez de l'Eglise gallicane.* Paris, 1639.

MARCA, P. de. *De concordia sacerdotii et imperii seu de libertatibus ecclesiae gallicanae.* Paris, 1641.

MONTCHAL, C. de, Archbishop of Toulouse. *Mémoires, contenant des particularitez de la vie et du ministère du cardinal de Richelieu.* Rotterdam, 1718, vol. 2.

MOUSNIER, R. 'Recherches sur les soulèvements populaires en France avant la Fronde', in *Revue d'histoire moderne et contemporaine*, 1958.

PORCHNEV, B. *Les soulèvements populaires en France de 1623 à 1648.* Paris, 1963. Translated from the Russian, this work, based on Séguier's papers which are in Leningrad and had not previously been used, has created great interest among French historians. There is also a German translation. For *Nu-Pieds* pp. 303–391.

TOURNYOL DU CLOS, J. *Richelieu et le clergé de France.* Paris, 1914.

VILLA REAL, F. de. *El politico cristianissimo, o discursos politicos sobre algunas acciones de la vida des señor Cardenal duque de Richelieu.* Madrid, 1647.

L'état général des finances de France dressé par le commandement de M. le cardinal de Richelieu en l'année 1639. Bibliothèque de l'Université, MS 7.

CHAPTER 24

AVENEL, vol. 6, pp. 641–957, esp. doc. no. 315; vol. 7, pp. 3–173, esp.

docs. nos. 45–7, 100; H. and LA F., vol. 6, book 4; GRIFFET, vol. 3; DETHAN, chap. 9; BEAUCHAMP.

AVENEL, D. L. M. *La dernière épisode de la vie du cardinal de Richelieu, Louis XIII, Cinq Mars, Aug. de Thou, etc.* Paris, 1868.

BASSERIE, J. P. *La conjuration de Cinq Mars.* Paris, 1896.

ERLANGER, P. *Cinq Mars. La passion et la fatalité.* Paris, 1964.

GODLEY, Hon. E. *The Great Condé. A Life of Louis II de Bourbon, Prince of Condé.* London, 1915.

HAUCOUR, L. d'. *La conjuration de Cinq Mars.* Paris, 1902.

LANCASTER, H. C. *French Dramatic Literature in the Seventeenth Century.* Paris, Baltimore, London, 1932. Vol. II, pp. 375 *et seq.* Contains full critique of Richelieu's *Mirame.*

RICHELIEU, A. J. *Mirame.* Pub. in *Recueil des meilleurs pièces dramatiques faites en France depuis Rotrou jusqu'à nos jours, ou Théâtre français. Tragédies,* vol. 4, Lyons, 1780. The play is the result of cooperation between Richelieu and Desmaretz.

VAISSIÈRE, P. de. *La conjuration de Cinq Mars.* Paris, 1920.

Arrêt du Parlement de Paris contre les Princes unis retirés à Sedan, savoir les Ducs de Guise et de Bouillon, le Comte Soissons et autres, par lequel ils sont déclarez criminels de lèze Majesté. Fait en Parlement le 5 Juillet 1641. DUMONT, vol. 6, p. 218.

Conditions auxquelles le Roi de France Louis XIII veut bien pardonner au Duc de Bouillon, sa Rebellion. Du 3 Août 1641. DUMONT, vol. 6, p. 219.

Traité Préliminaire entre Ferdinand III Empéreur et Philippe IV Roi d'Espagne, d'une part, et Louis XIII, Roi de France, pour l'Assemblée de Munster et d'Osnabruck. Fait à Hambourg le 25 Déc. 1641. Ratifié le 21 Mai 1643. DUMONT, vol. 6, p. 231.

CHAPTER 25

AVENEL, vol. 7; H. and LA F., vol. 6, book 4; GRIFFET, vol. 3; DETHAN, chap. 9; AVENEL, BASSERIE, ERLANGER, HAUCOUR, VAISSIÈRE (all cited in chap. 24).

Traité entre Philippe IV Roi d'Espagne et Gaston de France, Duc d'Orléans fait à Madrid le 13 Mars 1642, et Ratifié par le Duc d'Orléans le 29 Août de ladite année. DUMONT, vol. 6, p. 244. The document described as a ratification is not; it is the certification which was used as Gaston's evidence at the trial of Cinq Mars.

Lettres de Grace et d'Abolition accordées par Louis XIII Roi de France à Frédéric Maurice, Duc de Bouillon prisonnier à Pierre-encise, en vue et à cause de la Cession de la ville et Souveraineté de Sedan par lui offerte à Sa Majesté. Avec la Promesse du Cardinal Mazarin faite audit Duc au Nom du Cardinal de Richelieu pour sa liberté, dès que Sedan sera remis au Roi. A Lyon le 15 Septembre 1642. DUMONT, vol. 6, p. 269.

Vérification et enregistrement au Parlement de Paris des Lettres de Grace accordées au Duc de Bouillon, moyennant la Cession de sa ville et Principauté de Sedan. Fait le 5 Décembre 1642. DUMONT, vol. 6, p. 270.

CHAPTER 26

H. and LA F., vol. 6, book 6; GOULAS; GODLEY (cited in references to chap. 24).

BATIFFOL, L. *Richelieu et Corneille. La légende de la persécution de l'auteur du Cid.* Paris, 1936.

LALANNE, L. 'Un récit inédit de la mort du Cardinal de Richelieu', in *Revue historique,* 1894.

Index